Universities as if
Students Mattered

Universities as if Students Mattered

Social Science on the Creative Edge

John Scanzoni

BOWLING GREEN STATE UNIVERSITY LIBRARIES DISCARDED

ROWMAN & LITTLEFIELD PUBLISHERS, INC.
Lanham • Boulder • New York • Toronto • Oxford

ROWMAN & LITTLEFIELD PUBLISHERS, INC.

Published in the United States of America
by Rowman & Littlefield Publishers, Inc.
A wholly owned subsidiary of The Rowman & Littlefield Publishing Group, Inc.
4501 Forbes Boulevard, Suite 200, Lanham, Maryland 20706
www.rowmanlittlefield.com

PO Box 317
Oxford
OX2 9RU, UK

Copyright © 2005 by Rowman & Littlefield Publishers, Inc.

All rights reserved. No part of this publication may be reproduced,
stored in a retrieval system, or transmitted in any form or by any
means, electronic, mechanical, photocopying, recording, or otherwise,
without the prior permission of the publisher.

British Library Cataloguing in Publication Information Available

Library of Congress Cataloging-in-Publication Data

Scanzoni, John H., 1935-
  Universities as if students mattered : social science on the creative edge / John
Scanzoni.
    p. cm.
  Includes bibliographical references and index.
  ISBN 0-7425-4566-0 (cloth : alk. paper) — ISBN 0-7425-4567-9 (pbk. : alk. paper)
  1. Education, Higher—Aims and objectives—United States.   2. Social sciences—
Study and teaching (Higher)—United States.   3. Action research in education—United
States.   I. Title.

  LA227.4.S32 2005
  378'.001—dc22   2004029354

Printed in the United States of America

♾™ The paper used in this publication meets the minimum requirements of American
National Standard for Information Sciences—Permanence of Paper for Printed Library
Materials, ANSI/NISO Z39.48-1992.

Contents

Preface

Most colleges and universities are responding to the challenges and opportunities presented by a changing world. They are evolving to serve a new age. But most are evolving within the traditional paradigm. . . . Is such glacial change responsive enough to allow the university to control its own destiny? Or will a tidal wave of societal changes sweep over the academy, transforming the university in unforeseen and unacceptable ways?[1]

—*Former university president*

Given what we know and likely future social, technological, and economic realities, if we were creating a college or university today, what would it look like?[2]

—*The Project for the Future of Higher Education*

Most of our efforts to improve higher education depend on the assumption that students really want to learn and simply need new and improved techniques to help them do so. But many students are disillusioned by and uninterested in academics. They are on our campuses because they think they need a degree to get a good job, because their parents expect them to go to college, or because they don't know what else to do. Asking professors to find more effective ways to educate those students is like asking chefs to find ways to entice customers who aren't hungry to eat.[3]

—*University professor*

For almost two decades the American people have been aware of and dismayed by the gap in the nation's colleges and universities, the gap between grand, traditional, and almost unexamined professions of high principle, lofty mission, and splendid purpose—and institutional behavior that is often venal, self-serving, and shoddy.[4]

—Former university president and past commissioner of baseball

I believe that professors would be much happier if they did not have to stand in front of a room year after year teaching the same things over and over again. All they do, for the most part, is lecture from the same pile of notes every year. . . . I spent my time volunteering at Evanston hospital. . . . Quite honestly, I have learned more from my year of working at the hospital than from my two and a half years of classes at Northwestern. Northwestern has not provided, nor has it facilitated my experiences.[5]

—University student

It is ironic indeed that [universities] that have played such a profound role in developing the digital technology now reshaping our world are the most resistant to reshaping their activities to enable its effective use. . . . As with most monopoly organizations, today's university is provider-centered, functioning primarily to serve the needs and desires of the faculty rather than the students whom they teach or the broader society that supports them.[6]

—Three professors, including a former university president

Even if the overall conclusion is that there is less immediate threat [to colleges and universities] than we might have imagined from . . . new technologies, that threat is potentially more insidious because when it becomes obvious the game may already be over.[7]

—University professor

Higher education [is being] taken away from the educators—by removing money, imposing controls, capping tuition, enforcing affirmative action for conservatives, stigmatizing research on partisan grounds, privatizing student loans—and handing it over to a small group of ideologues who will tell colleges and universities what to do and back up their commands by swinging the two big sticks of financial deprivation and inflamed public opinion.[8]

—University dean

How far the American academic profession has fallen over the past quarter century! From its once pristine high estate of the 1950s and 1960s, it has descended (plummeted) to barely a notch above lawyers in the minds of government policy leaders, the press, and the general public.[9]

—University professor

I teach at Duke University, probably one of the best private institutions of higher education in the U.S. . . . . But getting a good education is only optional here, as it is at most institutions, and many Duke students only go through the motions academically. . . . It principally provides social and economic credentials for its students. . . . Many of our students remain intellectually disengaged. The hardest thing for students at Duke—and at most elite institutions—is getting in. Once admitted, a smart student can coast, drink far too much beer, and still maintain a B+ average.[10]

—University professor

The BA signifies that the candidate can tolerate boredom and knows how to follow rules, probably the most important lesson in postsecondary education.[11]

—University professor

If someone had predicted 50 years ago that, in 1999, the primary and secondary schools would be a mess, and urban public schools an absolute disaster, most Americans would have called that person an alarmist. Today, when anyone dares to suggest that U.S. higher education has serious problems, most listeners give the same response. We have the greatest colleges and universities in the world. But if current trends continue, we will soon face a day of reckoning.[12]

—Past chair of a state board of higher education
and former university trustee

Higher-Education leaders, like most Americans, believe that we have the best postsecondary-education in the world. Yet a dangerous gap is growing between what the public needs from higher education and how colleges and universities are serving those needs. That gap has received little attention . . . because [they] lack clear measurements for their performance and . . . they are generally satisfied with the status quo. But if the gap is not closed, it will increasingly impede higher education's ability to serve the public and ultimately threaten colleges' ability to thrive and grow.[13]

—Leaders of the Futures Project on Higher Education

Every year, colleges turn out thousands of defective products—dropouts and undereducated graduates—without consequence. . . . [But] higher education must change greatly if it is to continue to avoid media scrutiny and, ultimately, public resistance. Only then will it rise from being one of America's most overrated products to the invaluable service it markets itself to be.[14]

—Career counselor and education and
admissions consultant to college presidents

These few selected comments are but a tiny sprinkling of all the numerous things that have been said recently about U.S. higher education. The remarks range from the severely caustic to sounding almost like Pollyanna—the blindly optimistic heroine of Eleanor Porter's early—twentieth-century novel by that same name.[15] Many observers point the reproachful finger of blame—either at students who are allegedly indifferent and disengaged, or at professors who are supposedly self-absorbed, politically radical, and otherworldly, or at politicians who are said to be perversely biased against higher education, or at taxpayers who are allegedly unappreciative of the many benefits of university research. When it's time to find a scapegoat for what's wrong with higher education, the target is typically one or more of those highly visible groups.

This book, however, points the finger of blame at no one. It accuses no particular set of persons of being responsible for whatever (if anything) ails higher education, that is, post-K–12. Instead, as a card-carrying social scientist, I'm persuaded by the logic of the first comment cited above. The Achilles' heel afflicting at least some floors on the ivory tower is that we've not yet come to grips with the fact that certain profound changes have been occurring, and will continue to occur, in the larger society around us. The greatest peril in our failure to discern the times, and then to seize the day, is that we shall ultimately lose control of our own destiny—an outcome that is neither in our own best interest nor in the best interest of students or the larger society.

Nonetheless, getting control of the university's future is like trying to rein in a team of runaway horses, each one hell-bent on going its own way. If there ever was, there's surely now no such thing as the *uni*versity in the sense of being some type of unified and coherent whole. It's rather a *multi*versity, made up of many disparate parts, each one with its own individual interests and objectives.[16] Furthermore, these discrete parts possess varying degrees of influence, wealth, status, and prestige. But whether we call it a university or a multiversity, getting any sort of grip on its twenty-first-century future will be a long and arduous task. We must, however, begin somewhere, sometime. Our own self-interest compels us to make such a move—no matter how tentative or hesitant. *And I propose that the social sciences take the first step.*[17] Allow us to be the model—the guinea pig, that is, the experimental subject, for the kind of preemptive innovation necessary to stave off any imposed transformations of the university that could turn out to be "unforeseen and unacceptable."

I readily admit that I have a selfish motive in proposing the social sciences as a test case for innovation. We are at significantly greater risk for a "hostile takeover" than, say, the sciences. (At the same time, we're less vulnerable than, for instance, the humanities.[18]) Indeed, the sciences are in hardly any danger at all because, by and large, they're fortunate enough to be able to command their own destiny.[19] They occupy the spacious, luxurious, and richly appointed penthouse suite of the ivory tower. The rest of us are crowded together onto the lower floors with lesser status, prestige, and money. Accordingly, I suggest that we in the social sciences reduce our vulnerability, and take charge of our future, by engaging public officials, citizens, and students in exploring innovations that meet three essential criteria.

- *Authenticity*. First, the innovations must be authentic—they must ring true to the essence of what social science is. We can in no way make some sort of Faustian bargain in which we exchange our soul for a "mess of pottage."
- *Usefulness*. Second, the innovations must be something that society wants and needs—the changes must, in short, be socially useful and helpful. Any proposed modifications for the better cannot merely be one more example of window-dressing aimed at impressing the public that leaves things essentially as they were before.[20]
- *Prototype*. Finally, the innovations should be a trial product aimed at getting the attention of other parts of the university. Each of the other segments (e.g., sciences, humanities, and so on) could critique the changes and perhaps decide such modifications don't fit what they're all about. Consequently, they might devise an entirely different approach to innovation. Or, they might possibly conclude that, in their domain of learning, new ways of doing things are not even called for.

A LEARNING PARADIGM—*MAKING THE STUDENT EXPERIENCE MATTER*

I propose two closely allied innovations for the social sciences that would meet all three bedrock criteria. The first calls on us to change significantly the ways we do our undergraduate education. It asks us to shift from what's been described as a "teaching" or "instructional" paradigm to what's known as a "learning" paradigm.[21] It has also been identified as "inquiry-based" learning,[22] while others call it "discovery-based" learning.[23] Discovery-based learning can be seen as a bridge between the first and the second proposed innovations.

ACTION RESEARCH—*MAKING SOCIAL SCIENCE MATTER*

The second innovation aims at serving society by addressing urgent social issues or problems. And, in the interest of self-interest, such an innovation might go a long way toward erasing the stigma that social science doesn't much matter to anyone—aside, of course, from its practitioners. Once upon a time it did matter to others, and it's high time that it mattered once again.[24] In order to achieve such an ambitious renewal, I suggest that some of us (by no means everyone) within the social sciences significantly change the ways we do our service to society—and our research at the same time. We might do so by engaging in what's been described as "action research."[25]

Action research aims to accomplish what Joseph Spengler called the two principal and linked features of scientific research in general—to gain understanding, and to do so by disturbing and/or redirecting the particular slice of the real world that one happens to be studying.[26] Importantly, we would do action research in concert with undergraduates. And, at the same time, graduate students and postdocs (and sometimes citizens) would also be directly involved. Any type of research is, by its very nature, *learning* based on some sort of active inquiry, exploration, or investigation. Hence, by connecting undergraduates to action research we are, at one fell swoop, involving them in discovery-based learning.

In sum, the innovations I'm proposing would seek to accomplish several crucial objectives simultaneously.

- First, the changes would coach college students to become active, that is, self-directed, learners. Furthermore, the vital element of their obligation to serve society is integral to their active learning.
- Next, alongside college students, the innovations would focus the attention, energy, and considerable talents of professors, graduate students, and postdocs alike on some potential ways and means of addressing urgent social issues. Students and professionals alike would be striving to plumb the spirit behind Horace Mann's entreaty "Be ashamed to die until you have won some victory for humanity."[27]
- Finally, the innovations, because they pivot around action research, would contribute to a more thorough and comprehensive understanding of the social world.

WHY I WROTE THIS BOOK

I started my own university career during the mid-1960s in the sociology department at Indiana University–Bloomington. Although I (mistakenly) believed I was entering a vocation in which teaching would be pivotal, I was in reality becoming a professor at an institution that was on the cusp of its entry into the top tier of America's public research universities. My undergraduate days had been spent at a liberal arts college whose faculty mission was to teach students how to think rigorously and to reason in a compelling fashion, and thereby to resolve problems. My years in graduate school were preoccupied with social science research—what it is and how to do it. No one spoke much about undergraduate teaching, and I ignored it until my final year when, alongside writing my dissertation, I was assigned to teach an introductory sociology class. The hitch was that although I'd been a research assistant I'd never even been a teaching assistant, much less a teacher. But as the semester began, the editor of the student newspaper published an essay called "College Is for Thinking." Everything he wrote jelled with my image of undergraduate teaching, and so I organized my class the only way I knew how, namely, the way I'd experienced it in college.

When I landed at Indiana, I was naïvely oblivious to its goal of becoming a world-class research university. Although my identity was that of "teacher" more or less in the John Dewey tradition, I'd also found research and writing to be irresistibly seductive. Nonetheless, I still felt that my primary mission was to cultivate analytic thinking and problem solving among my students. That task was formidable because I was assigned three different classes of some seventy students each. Still, I sought to keep the nurturing of their "human capital skills" (though no one called it that) my paramount goal—an objective requiring many exhausting hours of intensive labor. In addition, I wanted to emulate my college professors by getting involved in the lives of my students. Hence, I was invited regularly to their dorms for lunch and dinner and spent many hours in my office acting as a sounding board for their existential crises.

At the start of my second semester, our chair took me to lunch for a "Dear John" homily. He averred that my activities both in and out of the classroom were quite admirable. However, he firmly but tactfully warned that I would never get tenure if I continued along that route.[28] Those student-centered pursuits were robbing me, he stated, of the time and creative energies necessary to do the grantsmanship and publication that would make my national reputation, and thus enhance the department's and the university's stature. His meaning got through at once, and I quickly switched my primary identity to "researcher." Teacher drifted quietly into a distant second place.

Furthermore, my colleagues helped me become a very different kind of teacher from anything I'd ever imagined. I learned from them how to fulfill the "Teaching Paradigm." They jokingly called it the "ingestion and regurgitation" style of teaching—*you tell students, they tell you what you said.* They showed me how to be a competent sage-on-the-stage, that is, a guru who transmits information in ways that students would find both interesting and enjoyable. My colleagues also advised me that in the interests of conserving my limited time, I should start using multiple-guess test questions. I was told that such items quickly and efficiently found out how much information students had memorized by having them repeat it back to me. The quaint notion that students should be evaluated by how incisively they critiqued their reading materials, and also by the cogency of the alternative arguments they developed to address those materials, was lost in the shuffle. And, needless to say, the time spent with students outside of class was curtailed to virtually nothing.

The guilt I felt about dumping my original teaching/service mission was assuaged via pity parties over drinks with colleagues who felt equally compromised. Although we frequently lamented the deplorable state of teaching, we consoled ourselves by saying there was nothing to be done. We were, after all, (said a colleague and friend who later left IU to become a high-ranking administrator at another university) in the "ed biz." We were forced to process as many "widgets" as efficiently as possible in order to have the time and creative energies required to pursue our overriding objective of achieving international stature for ourselves, and thus for IU. As one wag put it, "Stack 'Em Deep and Teach 'Em Cheap" is our modus operandi. And, observed another, "This would be a great place if it weren't for the students."

Throughout the following years during which I successfully pursued a professional reputation based on research and scholarship, and thus closed my eyes to my original teaching/learning mission, I would from time to time recollect it briefly, and then just as quickly forget it. I cannot honestly report that I now regret the fact that for so many years I relegated that mission to the furthest recesses of my mind. What's done is done.

More recently, however, I've discovered that I've been unable and also unwilling to dismiss that original mission from my mind. Nor, at the same time, have I been able to ignore (as I did for many years) the "historic mission of the social sciences to enable mankind to take possession of society."[29] That mission was, in fact, one big reason why I got into social science in the first place! Because I feel keenly the importance of renewing both vocations, I'm trying to regenerate my commitment to each of them.

Among the several reasons for my recent efforts at renewal was and is the presence in my life of what later chapters call a "coach." I could see plainly that in her duties as a professor in the University of Florida School of Design, Construction and Planning, Mary Joyce (Jo) Hasell was carrying out John Dewey's simple yet profound notion that *learning happens as you are doing and as you think about what you are doing.* Her admirable style notwithstanding, I sought to dissuade her from her coaching efforts because that strategy might impede her progress toward tenure. Although I myself had earlier changed course markedly in reaction to just that same reasoning, she did not!

She was instead able to fuse the making of knowledge (scholarship) with the coaching of players (students) in the process of learning by doing and in thinking about what they're doing. Her coaching was thus a nagging reminder of my own past ideals and, at the same time, a goad toward finding out if I might somehow revive my original objectives.

Despite the fact that it's been extremely gratifying, my efforts at renewal have turned out to be much more of a struggle than I'd ever anticipated. Though it's not been possible to experiment with a full-blown model of discovery-based learning, I've tried to edge in that direction for several years.

- Accordingly, this book is dedicated on the one hand to those professors, grad students, and postdocs who sense that the prevailing ways of doing your job may not be the only or best ways to do it. Some of you, like me, have been struggling for a while to try to find new ways to do it. Other colleagues are joining the struggle for the first time. Welcome!
- This book is simultaneously dedicated to those students (and soon-to-be-students and their parents) who need no one to tell them that college is, in all too many cases, a whole lot less meaningful than it ought to be. Despite the fact that it's a necessary prelude to their degree, students are keenly aware that all too often college is, aside from the sports, activities, and partying, rather disappointing. Nonetheless, what's not apparent to them and their parents is how college might become a whole lot more substantial. You too are invited to join the struggle to try to find out how!

NOTES

1. Duderstadt 1999:38.
2. Project for the Future of Higher Education (home page), Antioch University (www.pfhe.org), italics in original.
3. Cabin 2003.
4. Giamatti 1988:190, as cited by Anderson 1996:24.
5. David Geller, as cited in Schank and Cleary 1995:74–75.
6. Duderstadt et al. 2002:18, 125.
7. Collis 2002:200.
8. Fish 2003:C2.
9. Finkelstein 2001:323, italics in original.
10. Rojstaczer 2001:B5.
11. Aronowitz 2000:127.
12. Carlin 1999:A76.
13. Newman et al. 2004:B6.
14. Nemko 2003.

15. For highly unflattering critiques of professors, see Anderson 1996; Huber 1992; Sykes 1988.

16. Kerr 1963; Bok 1982:63–64.

17. Huber and Morreale 2002.

18. Berube and Nelson 1995; Showalter 2003; Lanham 1993.

19. Ikenberry 1999.

20. See Cuban (1999) for a discussion of "reform without change" within twentieth-century universities.

21. Barr and Tagg 1995; De Corte 1996; Schank and Cleary 1995.

22. Boyer Commission 1998.

23. See, e.g., www.colby.edu/admissions/academics/research and www.Williams.edu/home/about_fastfacts.php.

24. Flyvbjerg 2001

25. Brydon-Miller et al. 2003; Whyte 1982, 1991a; Schon 1983; Levin and Greenwood 2001.

26. Spengler 1969; Schank and Cleary 1995.

27. Antioch University home page, www.antioch.edu.

28. Tenure = lifetime job security, a matter discussed further in chapter 7.

29. Gouldner and Miller 1965:vii.

Acknowledgments

Needless to say, I treasure deeply the numerous candid discussions I've had in recent years with undergraduates who reflected with me on their experiences while enduring the anomalous ways in which our classes were set up and carried out. My conversations with both undergraduates and interested grad students were of inestimable benefit to me. During our informal sessions, the undergrads (often several at a time) were not above being brutally frank in pointing out serious flaws and weaknesses. At the same time, they were quite generous in identifying potential strengths. If allowed to select one comment from among the scores that were voiced, it would be from the senior who, in the flow of a lengthy conversation reflecting back on the previous semester, suddenly blurted out, *"In this class, you've got to teach yourself!"* Whether he fully recognized it or not, I was gratified to see he'd gotten at least a preliminary feel of the fundamental distinction between a teaching paradigm and a learning paradigm. I was equally thankful to note that he was quite pleased with himself over what he'd accomplished. Following the many failures he'd endured in our class, alongside the fewer successes he'd enjoyed, he felt especially proud that he was finally on the road to becoming a self-directed learner.

I'm also deeply indebted to colleagues (especially Bill Marsiglio, Leonard Beeghley, Charles Gattone) and graduate students (especially Alex Goldman and Amanda Moras) for their infinite patience with my recent experiments to reinvent my undergraduate teaching/learning and also for their forthright criticisms of the ways in which I've struggled to do it.

Needless to say, while writing this book I've been "standing on the shoulders of giants." Numerous people have, for many decades, been thinking and writing about how to do post-K–12 better, and they've had considerable influence on my own thinking.[1] Naming some inevitably omits others, for which I apologize. With that limitation clearly understood, the singular giant and patron saint from the past must, of course, be John Dewey. More contemporary giants include the late Ernest W. Boyer.

Many thanks are due, moreover, to Alan McClare, executive editor at Rowman & Littlefield. His faith in, and patient encouragement of, the manuscript was, in my experience, unmatched. And, thanks, too, to my older son, Steve, who ever since his adolescent years has been a relentless and unforgiving critic of what chapter 1 calls "the peculiar spin of basic social science." Although I stoutly resisted his skepticism by defending the spin, I must now do something that horrifies every parent—recant and admit with chagrin that one's child (in my case, Steve) was right after all. Thanks also to my younger son, Dave, who, along with Steve, was a friendly but blunt critic of this entire project from its inception. Dave also supplied a great deal of highly useful editing of the next-to-final version of the manuscript.

And, most of all, beyond her stellar personal example of being a coach to her own players (as described in the preface), Professor Jo Hasell was unflagging in her careful readings of the numerous drafts of this manuscript. Alongside sustained personal encouragement, her incisive criticisms of the text and valuable suggestions for basic upgrades throughout the critical stages of its development proved to be extraordinarily significant indeed!

NOTE

1. See References.

Introduction

Higher Education is in need of visions. We urge educators . . . to commit
to a cherished value or a compelling vision and then to articulate a purpose
that challenges the commitment of others. The callings, causes, and cries
that make up the innermost commitments of people can become educational missions that chart new paths for higher education.[1]

WHAT'S THE PROBLEM?

Why are colleges and universities "in need of visions"? What's wrong with
the current path that much of post-K–12 is following? Why are we being
urged to develop "educational missions" and "chart new paths"? What special role might the social sciences play in carving out and in paving those
paths?

Throughout the twentieth century, more and more critics of post-K–12 both
and in and outside the academy got increasingly vocal. Those critics included
public officials (elected and appointed), professors and administrators of colleges and universities, businesspersons, interested citizens, parents, students
(current and former), and even the comic strip *Doonesbury*.[2] Most were and
are "friendly" critics, and I plant myself firmly in that camp. Friendly critics
believe strongly in higher education and are committed to its core values.[3]
They concur with the widely held assessment that when it comes to their research mission, U.S. universities are without rival—they are the ultimate
standard of the world. But on the other hand, friendly critics feel passionately
that, on the whole, universities fall short when it comes to their two remaining missions—undergraduate education in particular and, in certain respects,
public service.

1

Obligations to Students—*Quality Education*

Without any doubt, the most frequently voiced complaint throughout the twentieth century was that universities do not do the right thing by their undergrads. And when critics explained why undergraduate education was pretty dismal, they said it was because professors were too busy doing research to pay attention to the needs and interests of students.[4] Hence, students were commonly advised that if high-quality teaching meant a lot to them, they ought to steer clear of post-K–12 schools where professors made research a priority. In their own defense, however, professors claimed that their research actually made them better teachers.[5] They asserted they could pursue research dollars and international reputation alongside being an effective teacher. The professor serving two very demanding masters came, over the course of the twentieth century, to be known as the "teacher-scholar."[6]

In any case, the point is that throughout the past century, the prevailing view was that students had options. If, for example, they felt their state's flagship research university placed too much emphasis on research, they could instead attend one of its comprehensive universities or its four-year public colleges. In recent years, however, that particular option has shrunk dramatically for reasons spelled out in subsequent chapters. For now, suffice it to say that, among other factors, reductions in state funding have meant that growing numbers of public and private universities and colleges, once aloof from the competition for external research dollars, have recently felt compelled to jump into the race. For good or for ill, more and more four-year schools of all stripes seem convinced that Dennis Tsichritzis is on target when he argued that in the new century any university or college failing to compete effectively for external research dollars "will slowly drift downward to the level of the community college."[7]

Assume for a moment that, in the future, fewer and fewer students will in fact have the option of going to a four-year public school where the quest for external research funding is not, or is not becoming, a principal pursuit of their professors. Even if students' choices are narrowing, why is that such a bad thing? If teaching and research do in fact complement one another, is it not fortunate that more and more students would be able to enjoy the benefits of learning under the tutelage of the teacher-scholar? Wouldn't growing numbers of students be better off as a result of it? The answer turns on what is meant by a *quality* undergraduate education.

During the 1990s, the Carnegie Foundation for the Advancement of Teaching spent several years taking the pulse of America's universities. Its diagnosis (called the Boyer Commission Report) was that many undergraduates—even at the private and public schools judged as America's "best" universities (including the most prestigious based on their reputation for research)—endured an "education" that was often mediocre and almost always monotonous:

The experience of most undergraduates at most research universities is that of receiving what is served out to them. In one course after another they listen, transcribe, absorb, and repeat, essentially as undergraduates have done for centuries. . . . The traditional lecturing and note taking, certified by periodic examinations, was created for a time when books were scarce and costly. . . . The delivery system persisted into the present because it was familiar, easy, and required no imagination.[8]

Robert Barr and John Tagg pinned the tag "Teaching/Instructional Paradigm" on that all-too-familiar mode of doing undergraduate education.[9] There's a snug fit between the teaching paradigm and what William Rainey Harper (who in 1890 became the University of Chicago's founding president) asserted was the grand purpose of undergraduate education. In no uncertain terms, he declared its purpose was "to stock the student's mind with knowledge."[10] A hundred years later, the Boyer Commission echoed Harper's credo: "the absorption of a body of knowledge once was . . . the hallmark of a good education."[11] A well-educated person was someone who knew lots of "stuff" — who had a broad range of information and knowledge. And that, simply put, was the essential meaning of a *quality* education for undergraduates.[12]

There was, furthermore, a rather cozy match between that particular indicator of quality education and the twentieth-century role of teacher-scholar. The teacher side of that role meant that he or she was viewed as a guru (sage-on-the-stage) actively transmitting expert knowledge to the undergraduate who, by comparison to the professor, was relatively passive. It was extremely convenient for the teacher side that the requirements for being a guru were far less demanding, less insistent, and much more manageable than those on the scholar side. Consequently, the teacher-scholar was well able to concentrate large amounts of uninterrupted time and creative energies on the latter, while giving satisfactory attention to the former.

But today the fly in the ointment (or the wrench in the gearbox, or the worm in the hard drive) is that the Boyer Commission, as well many other critics, believes that although the criterion of knowing lots of stuff may have been good enough for the twentieth century, it is woefully inadequate for the rapidly unfolding complexities of the twenty-first century. Despite the fact that observers differ widely as to the precise meanings of terms such as "information age" or "postindustrial" society, there is a broad consensus that navigating the new era successfully requires something far more significant than simply knowing lots of stuff, as vital as that might be.

Universities cannot call themselves successful unless they provide students with the fundamental skills that they require in the twenty-first century.[13]

Harper's ancient credo can no longer be perceived of as the prime indicator of a quality education. The Boyer Commission charged that schools continuing to operate in that previous mode "shortchange" their students and, what is more, actually "fail" them.[14]

> Tuition income from undergraduates is one of the main sources of university income, helping to support research programs and graduate education, but the students paying the tuition get, in all too many cases, less than their money's worth.[15]

If the old criterion of a quality education is losing credibility, and if universities short shrift students by perpetuating it, what then is the contemporary criterion of a quality education that schools are now obliged to supply their students? Virtually every critic before and since the commission converges on the response.

> The skills of analysis, evaluation, and synthesis will become the hallmarks of a good education.[16]

Barr and Tagg agreed totally, and asserted that the most favorable conditions for the cultivation of that style of quality education included the soil and nourishment of what they called a "Learning Paradigm."[17]

Within a learning paradigm, the student able to *demonstrate* that she or he actually possesses those and related "human capital" skills is taken to be the prime objective of undergraduate education. Accordingly, the absorption of course content (facts, figures, personages, dates, ideas) is transformed into the vehicle, or the means, to achieve that more significant purpose—that far superior indicator of a quality education. In effect, the commission sought to turn things topsy-turvy by urging professors, colleges, and universities to shift from an instructional to a learning model. Professors were asked to set aside their safe, conventional, tried-and-true ways of doing undergraduate teaching for something quite novel—ways that (in the classroom, though not in the professor's own research) remain for the most part foreign and unfamiliar. By any measure, such a shift would be what the report itself calls a "radical reconstruction," bordering on being "revolutionary." It would be a drastic reordering of priorities. And the commission recognized that startling fact by calling their recommendations the basis for "reinventing" undergraduate education.

Accordingly, the argument I make in subsequent chapters is that the typical twentieth-century teacher-scholar—focusing enormous amounts of creative energy and huge blocks of time on research and publication—simply does not have the psychological or intellectual resources left over to fulfill the extensive demands of an emerging learning paradigm.[18] In effect, post-K–12 is faced with the dilemma of trying to implement a twenty-first-century model of quality undergraduate education (the cultivation of human capital skills) at the same time that most of its professors remain preoccupied fulfilling a twentieth-century role—the teacher-scholar whose task was to fill up undergrads with knowledge.

And complicating the conundrum still further is the fact that increasing numbers of professors are already in the process of evolving beyond our typical understandings of the teacher-scholar role. They are adapting a somewhat different set of behaviors and a distinctive identity that some observers call the role and identity of "entrepreneur."[19] That incipient role is the vehicle whereby certain professors adapt to the external pressures identified above, namely, the incessant demands to gain external research funding from government agencies, private foundations, and commercial interests. Accordingly, it makes sense to infer that the embryonic role of entrepreneur is a microevolution occurring simultaneously within the macroevolution that is now reshaping post-K–12. The role of entrepreneur is taking on a series of forms within a broader milieu that's also very much in flux—an environment that's being referred to increasingly as the "entrepreneurial university."[20] The front line of this emerging enterprise is, of course, the sciences (the life sciences in particular),[21] technology and engineering, medicine, and related fields, that is, the "sciences et al."

Life on the front lines of the entrepreneurial university was captured vividly by a recent report on the education of medical students at Harvard. And, because most other medical schools around the United States seek to emulate Harvard, there is every reason to expect that those schools also are or soon will be following suit in this matter. Although "Harvard Medical School has more than 6,500 fulltime faculty members, it is struggling to recruit professors to teach students, both into the classroom and in the hospital wards."[22] The clash between scholarship (and the professional reputation, advancement, and salary enhancement it proffers) and teaching (that typically offers none of the above) was, of course, present and accounted for throughout the twentieth century.[23] The big difference between then and now is that in the new century (for reasons described in later chapters) administrators increasingly "expect faculty [not just in the medical school, but throughout the entire enterprise]. . . to generate the resources necessary to support their activities."[24] In effect, administrators and public officials are coming to view professors less and less as employees, or hired hands, and more and more as independent contractors, that is, entrepreneurs. The expression "freelance consultant" captures the developing mood.[25]

The implications of both the micro- and the macroevolutions do not bode well for the demand that post-K–12 should develop a twenty-first-century approach to quality undergraduate education. The chief reason for anxiety is that the teacher-scholar operating within the context of the typical twentieth-century research university was ultimately dependent for support (especially between grants) on university resources and their administrative gatekeepers. Hence, the teacher-scholar, whether because she wanted to or simply because he had to, took quite seriously the types of obligations inherent in the teaching paradigm.

By contrast, although the entrepreneur might perhaps wish quite genuinely to carry on certain sage-on-the-stage duties, she or he has far less time, energy, and obligation to do so than did the teacher-scholar. And, needless to say, the entrepreneur is hardly a candidate to participate in the construction of innovative ways to do quality education in the new century. The competing pressures, as well as the incentives, for entrepreneurial success preclude much if any immersion in the kinds of efforts necessary to invent and perform that demanding task effectively. As Diane R. Fingold (the person responsible for staffing courses at Harvard Medical School) put it,

> In the past, faculty used to view teaching as an honor and a privilege. . . . Now [they're] trying to stay alive. . . . And [after struggling with their survival activities they're unable] to try to summon the energy to teach. They have nothing left to give.[26]

Yet another emerging feature of the "new reality" that does not augur well for efforts at innovation is the incipient evolution of still another role (besides entrepreneur) taking its place alongside teacher-scholar. Randall Collins described it as the role of "credentialer"—the professor unable and/or unwilling to compete successfully for external research dollars.[27] Just as the entrepreneur is an internal adaptation to the realities of reduced university funding, the credentialer is likewise an internal adaptation to that same reality in combination with one more reality. And that is the certainty of huge increases in college student enrollments. Their numbers are already swamping us, and many more are projected—especially from minorities and the working class. The credentialer would spend the great bulk of his or her entire time and energy processing huge numbers of students that are, in effect, viewed as little more than "widgets." Processing widgets on that large a scale would mark a quantum leap beyond anything expected from the typical twentieth-century teacher-scholar.

For some years now, university administrators have cast a longing eye at computer technology as a potential means to achieve meaningful cost efficiencies in order to cope with the anticipated surges in enrollment.[28] Accordingly, it appears likely that the credentialer will be under considerable pressure to develop ways to save dollars via inventive computer technology.[29] As a result, the "cybercredentialer" would possess even less time, creative energy, and incentive than the teacher-scholar or the entrepreneur to worry about cultivating the sorts of human capital skills urged by the Boyer Commission. Nonetheless, administrators can readily justify an increase in the numbers of credentialers as long as filling the student's head with stuff remains the chief criterion of a quality education. Although the teacher-scholar promoter might disagree,[30] a strong case can be made for the view that a dedicated and talented credentialer is able to perform the sage-on-the-stage scenario as well as anyone. And if the cybercredentialer makes it possible to process mushrooming student enrollments more efficiently, administrators have little reason to concern themselves with the potentially unnerving consequences of establishing and implementing a wholly new criterion of quality education.

In sum, no one would contest the fact that professors have a profound moral obligation to undergraduates. What's in dispute today is the character of that obligation. In the past, its nature was unambiguous—pass on important knowledge so that students can grasp and retain it. Although some professors might prefer continuing to construct their obligation in precisely those conventional terms, a growing chorus of critics believes their obligation ought to be *re*constructed. More than anything else, say the critics, professors have the moral obligation to cultivate students' human capital skills, including the capability to analyze, evaluate, and synthesize, and thereby to demonstrate their problem-solving capabilities.

Obligations to Society—*Social Science that Matters*

In making their assessments of what's wrong with post-K–12 education, critics tend to target the institution as a whole, adding that the system in its entirety requires reorganization.[31] The notion, however, of the university as any sort of coherent whole has been more mythical than real for a very long time. In 1963, Clark Kerr, then head of the vast University of California system of higher education, observed that after many decades the *uni*versity had gradually morphed into the *multi*versity.[32] Today's multiversity consists of many disparate parts that seldom even speak with one another. The parts are arranged into a status hierarchy, and there is little doubt that the sciences (because they attract vast sums of external research dollars) are at the top of the heap.

The Boyer Commission sought to overcome that fragmentation by uniting all the university's segments (sciences, social sciences, humanities, and the professional schools) by their common pursuit of a "shared mission," namely, the reinvention of undergraduate education.[33] Although the goal of a comprehensive pursuit of reinvention is, in the long term, essential, my view is that in the nearer term it appears much more feasible to expect each segment of the university to test for itself how to implement such a mission. One reason for that more pragmatic strategy is that each part has its own history of development, and surely its own contemporary objectives. Hence, each segment would need to experiment with distinctive ways to reinvent undergraduate education that are relevant to its own sphere of interest. The ideal situation would, of course, be for several parts of a university to launch independent, though interdependent, reinvention efforts at the same time.[34] Each segment could then be continually learning from the others and, where mutually beneficial, develop joint partnerships. Absent that ideal, and recognizing that reinvention must start somewhere, my suggestion is that the social sciences should take the lead. They would then serve as a template for the other parts to observe regarding the pitfalls to avoid and the initiatives that might perhaps hold promise.

The most distinguishing element that the social sciences bring to the table of undergraduate reinvention is their historic mission to serve the public interest through the resolution of social issues. In the 1960s, Alvin Gouldner and S. M. Miller declared their personal and professional commitment to the mission that was set down originally around the turn of that century.

> It is the historic mission of the social sciences to enable mankind to take possession of society. This is a big job and will take a long time. . . . [The ultimate objective of this job is] to bring society under control.[35]

Subsequent chapters explain that the elusive phrases "taking possession of society" and "bringing society under control" refer to the participation of professor, student, and citizen alike in social inventions aimed at the resolution of urgent social issues. Those phrases highlight the type of social science that tries to make a *difference* in and to society. Another way to put it is that advocates for that type of social science believe that we ought to be actively engaged in the task of creating a more just or equitable society. Chapter 1 describes the flowering of the social sciences at the University of Chicago around the turn of the twentieth century, though they'd been gestating for some time. Because, during the nineteenth century, the sciences had made enormous strides in contributing to human betterment, President Harper expected that the social sciences would follow suit. They would do so, of course, in their distinctive manner. Harper believed strongly (as did the social scientists he recruited) that his new university was "in every sense an institution of public service."[36]

By that he meant that alongside enhancing her or his professional reputation, every professor had a moral obligation to contribute to an entity well beyond, and much broader than, one's scholarly peer group. Specifically, the professor was duty-bound to make life better in some fashion for his or her surrounding society and its citizens. The nineteenth-century sciences supplied, believed Harper, the ideal model by doing the kind of research that did indeed benefit the public interest of citizens and society. Harper expected that, in analogous fashion, the social sciences would carry on the kind of research that might also serve society—their research would be, unmistakably, in the public interest. The specific problems that concerned Harper and the social scientists he recruited pertained for the most part to the horrific conditions of urban life confronting the European immigrants and the rural Americans (black and white) migrating to big American cities including Chicago.

Unfortunately, it turned out that the social sciences were unable to serve society by helping to resolve those kinds of social issues. Because they failed to contribute to human betterment in the expected ways, they were unable to make a difference.[37] In reaction to those frustrating and disappointing (perhaps even embarrassing) circumstances, the social sciences began gradually distancing themselves from their historic mission. Harper's vision that the social sciences would be the university's focal point or hub for serving society through the resolution of social issues was, throughout the course of the twentieth century, pushed further and further into the background. The abdication of their historic mission by the social sciences was perhaps the principal reason why (much later on in the century) eminent scholars outside the social sciences overlooked them entirely when writing about the obligations of universities to attempt to resolve the social issues confronting the broader society.[38]

Those national figures shared Harper's conviction that, whatever else it might be, the university is, at its core, an institution of public service. But in spite of that noble ideal, each figure lamented the fact that late-twentieth-century universities were ignoring their obligations to serve the social needs and interests of the larger society. As far as those scholars could tell, universities were not doing the type of research that might contribute toward resolving urgent social problems. Historian Arthur Cohen wrote that Bok believed that the universities "should work directly to solve social problems; . . . act to reduce poverty, homelessness, drug abuse, and chronic unemployment."[39] And in their turn, Duderstadt and Boyer each identified similar kinds of social problems as matters that the university had a moral obligation to address but was failing to do so. It is indeed bizarre that although the social sciences had spent the entire twentieth century doing research pertaining to those and to many other social issues, the social sciences are not even mentioned by any of those scholars as being the potential reservoirs for their resolution. Despite decades of investigation, neither academics nor citizens seem to perceive the social sciences as the analog, say, of the life sciences. Academics and citizens perceive the latter as a significant means to make life better for untold millions of people around the world.

For that and several other reasons, subsequent chapters explain that some scholars have recently concluded that the social sciences ought to renew their historic mission by doing research that is more directly linked with social action, or change.[40] I agree with their assertion that human betterment, that is, making a difference, should once again occupy a central position on the social science agenda. Furthermore, I would also add that the social sciences should—at schools around the country—reestablish the position they once held at the University of Chicago a century ago as the campus focal point or hub for the resolution of social issues. The historic mission of the social sciences blends perfectly with the historic service mission that Harper expressed for the university, and it defies common sense that their union is presently invisible to scholars from other domains of learning.

Nonetheless, it's paradoxical indeed that although academic leaders appear oblivious to the historic mission of the social sciences, undergraduates never exposed to a social science course tend to hold the mistaken impression (conveyed perhaps by the media) that the social sciences are in fact all about trying to "change things." Nevertheless, in their very first course, they're shocked to hear "there is little [the social sciences] can reliably offer as to what to do that will change that condition, based on social science knowledge per se."[41] Their misguided impression that current social science equals human betterment is, nonetheless, a central motivation for many students wanting to major within that sphere. My view is that the social sciences should capitalize on the students' inclination toward human betterment, rather than dampening their interest, as we now tend to do.

Building on student interest in resolving social issues turns us once again to the Boyer Report, and to its pivotal proposal for reinventing the undergraduate experience:

"Make Research-Based Learning the Standard."[42]

Every professor has, in the course of pursuing her or his own career, undergone years of excruciating, and often frustrating, experience with the profound reality that human capital skills can be cultivated in only one way: the person must pose a question or problem and then launch into the thorny and uncertain process of trying to answer or solve it. The report used the term "inquiry-based" learning as another way to talk about "research-based" learning. Some schools already exploring innovations in undergraduate learning label such experiences as "discovery-based" learning. The influential twentieth-century pragmatic philosopher John Dewey (followed later by a number of other "progressive" thinkers) argued that learning happens best in the context of "reflective thinking."[43] And one learns how to think (analyze, evaluate, synthesize) by doing—specifically, trying to solve a problem, that is, seeking to answer a question.

With that in mind, it becomes feasible for the social scientist to fulfill her or his obligation to students to cultivate their human capital skills while concurrently discharging his or her obligation to society to contribute to human betterment. Fulfilling both responsibilities at the same time becomes viable by drawing on both the spirit and the actual language (radical reconstruction, reinvention) of the Boyer Report as a basis to reorganize the entire undergraduate experience of social science majors. The undergraduate experience would be devoted to the design of research aimed to change the conditions of social life in certain limited ways. And, when appropriate, the student would get actual hands-on experience by participating in the research and in making sense of the actual findings. But, at other times, the execution and interpretation might be done via simulation or a hypothetical mock-up of what might transpire if the project were actually carried out.[44]

Plainly, in order to do that type of demanding work, the student would necessarily have to comprehend the existing literature. And just as clearly, in order to carry on the work successfully, the student would of necessity be cultivating his or her human capital skills.

Furthermore, and very importantly, the student would gradually become imbued with the same spirit as her or his professor: *I have an obligation to contribute to an entity larger than my family and me. I am duty-bound to strive for human betterment—to try to make a difference—through the resolution of social issues.* In reaction to the trenchant criticism that college-age youth today are looking out solely for numero uno, and thus have no interest in the well-being of anything beyond themselves, many colleges and universities have recently become a part of a national organization called Campus Compact.[45]

That national coalition encourages "service-learning," in which the student applies classroom content to real-life needs and problems occurring in the community.[46] Although surely a step in the right direction, service learning is, at most schools, simply an optional add-on feature that each professor may or may not elect to implement. More basically, the rise of Campus Compact symbolizes the concern of a growing number of academics and citizens alike that post-K–12 in general is failing to do its part to confront the next generation with its responsibilities for the resolution of social issues. Put yet another way, post-K–12 ought to figure out how students might take part in the mending and/or weaving of the social fabric, that is, the building of the "public household."[47]

Furthermore, it could be alleged that the social sciences have faltered by failing to take the leadership role in this regard. Coming up with inventions for resolving social issues, that is, creating a more just and equitable society, is after all a matter that falls squarely within the domain of the social sciences. And it's indeed curious that although they have, in one form or another, studied those kinds of issues for a century, the social sciences are not designated as the campus hub for enhancing the students' sense of responsibility to entities beyond themselves.

WHAT HAPPENS IF WE DON'T ADDRESS THE PROBLEMS?

Failing to Make a Difference in Society

The preceding discussion highlights a grave consequence of the social sciences continuing to ignore their historic mission—their obligations to help resolve society's urgent social issues. The twenty-first century cannot be solely about the economic well-being of the growing numbers of persons attending college and becoming credentialed. Those degree-holders must also develop a sense that they are indeed obliged to contribute to their society and to the citizens that surround them. Society in the new century shall no longer be able to afford the luxury of college graduates lacking a keen feeling for the public household.

Hence, if the social sciences recommit to their historic mission, the outcomes are likely to be beneficial in both a current and a future sense. The students would be, alongside their professors, seeking to make a difference in society while they're still in school. Furthermore, chapter 7 describes a "Lifelong Learning" structure, making it potentially feasible for graduates to carry on those same kinds of activities throughout their postcollege years. But, if social scientists persist in ignoring their historic mission, students, citizens, and society are likely to be the worse off for it—both now and in the future. And, what is more, suggest chapters 1 and 2, the social sciences will themselves, in an era of rapid social change, also be the worse off for it.

Failing to Cultivate Students' Human Capital

Next, ignoring their obligations to students by failing to cultivate their human capital skills could also have a range of grave negative consequences. The first would be to deny to students the intrinsically rewarding experience that virtually every professor now enjoys, namely, possessing and developing human capital skills. There is simply no defensible reason why every undergraduate is not also entitled to precisely that same intangible and precious gratification.

On a more pragmatic note, Collins and others have suggested that, in future, the greater the numbers of students that receive a college degree, the less valuable it will become. As with any other commodity the degree is, in effect, subject to inflation. Degree-inflation is likely to have its greatest negative impact on the increasing numbers of minorities and working-class persons expected to enter post-K–12 during the years ahead. That is so because most of them shall—despite affirmative action programs benefiting a comparatively few gifted minority students—be attending less prestigious (based on faculty research, not on the growth of student human capital) colleges and universities.[48] Hence, if degrees in general lose their value owing to inflation, the less prestigious degrees are likely to suffer the most.

Because there's no way we could, or would ever want to, deny any qualified persons access to the degree, and because the numbers of slots at schools whose prestige rests on internationally recognized research are finite, the only plausible solution is to attach the components of *value-added* and *value-for-dollar* to the degree, regardless of its school's research-based prestige. Such components are, of course, the cited human capital skills that many observers concur will be the single most significant resource for doing well in the information-age marketplace.[49] Potential employers are expected to become ever more demanding about the quality of the job candidates they actually hire. Because many more job candidates than now will hold a degree, the employer shall be able to scrutinize them much more carefully than now for evidence of value and value-added.[50] Their degree (regardless of its prestige level) will by itself become less and less *sufficient* for its holder to be taken seriously as a viable job candidate. In the future, it will become increasingly *necessary* for the job candidate to provide convincing confirmation that he or she also possesses (in addition to the degree) a high level of the cited human capital skills.

And, importantly, those same quality criteria are likely to intensify the competition among employees once they're fortunate enough to have made it into the work force. In arriving at their judgments as to retention, promotion, and salary, employers are likely to search more and more for a clear demonstration that the employee's actual job performance displays a significant level of the kinds of human capital skills that got him or her the job in the first place. Employees giving evidence that they're cultivating those skills, thereby enhancing their company's productivity and success, are likely to be rewarded. But those failing to develop those skills are likely to be shunted into less desirable positions or, very likely, not to be around very long.

A Crisis

We believe that the state of undergraduate education at research [and wannabe] universities is [in] . . . a crisis, an issue of such magnitude and volatility that universities must galvanize themselves to respond.[51]

Currently, most colleges and universities are able, by and large, to get away with certifying degree holders apart from convincing evidence of a *robust* degree— the issue of quality apart from grades.[52] Post-K–12 is likewise at ease with sending graduates out into society apart from any documentation that they're able and willing to contribute to an entity beyond themselves—to *give* something to society as well as to *get* economic success. Consequently, a number of critics would agree with the Boyer Commission when it described the current situation as a *crisis* to which universities must respond. Post-K–12 in general, and the social sciences in particular, can no longer afford to ignore the quality dimension of cultivating human capital skills. Nor, at the same time, can the social sciences afford to ignore their historic mission. Rapidly unfolding events require the social sciences to pay ever more attention to their obligations for both students and the larger society.

HOW CAN WE ADDRESS THE PROBLEM?

> The ground may be fertile, the times ripe, for the founding of a new movement of radical departures in higher education. The lessons learned from the . . . most recent reform period . . . will serve as teachers and guides for those departures that may be on the educational horizon.[53]

I've already begun to introduce some of the ways in which subsequent chapters ponder the question of how the social sciences might aim to discharge both sets of obligations in the new century. However, two very important issues remain to be highlighted. The first pertains to a new role that the professor might play in fulfilling those obligations. The second relates to the innovative arrangements, organization, or structure, within which the professor might play that new role.

The Role and Identity of the Coach

Earlier, we saw that a number of professors are already well into the process of evolving beyond the teacher-scholar role. That role was, after all, a twentieth-century construction that had not been particularly prominent during the nineteenth century.[54] The term "super-professor" is an expression that captures the essence of the teacher-scholar role. The super-professor was, not unlike the super-mom or the old-fashioned medical doctor, a generalist expected to do it all. Moreover, she or he did it typically with grand style, deriving enormous pleasure in the doing. The emerging role of entrepreneur appears to be sprouting out of the scholar side of that older role—it is a new specialty that can be seen as an adaptation to the demands of the twenty-first century. And, at the same time, the role of credentialer is emerging, too, as a new specialty—and also in response to external pressures. That role is, however, sprouting out of the teacher side of the teacher-scholar role.

Additionally, there may be another role as yet hardly visible on the horizon—the metamorphosis of an entity springing from the genes of the old-style teacher-scholar. This new role would inherit the most desirable genetic material—and yet be different—from its progenitor. A good deal has been written of late about the incipient development of what's been called the role of "coach" or "facilitator."[55] In contrast to the metaphors of sage-on-the-stage or guru, the coach is encapsulated by the imagery of the master (or mentor, or facilitator) stimulating her or his apprentice to perform a certain range of skills at the level of their absolute personal best, and perhaps then some.

Most writers on the theme of the coach have thus far focused on how this distinctive role might stimulate the student's human capital skills. In subsequent chapters I enlarge the coach's role to include cultivation of the student's commitment to the resolution of social issues. Hence, the coach would be actively involved with both sets of obligations cited above. He or she would be addressing the interests of students while simultaneously helping to tackle the social concerns of the society in which they live.

AN EXPERIMENTAL LABORATORY MODULE

In the 1960s and early 1970s, a handful of visionaries sought, in reaction to the numerous complaints being lodged against post-K–12, to create new ways of doing undergraduate education.[56] And because most states were then relatively flush with money, some advocates were even able to persuade a few legislatures to construct whole new campuses—complete with classroom buildings, libraries, dormitories, and faculty that took very seriously the mission to educate undergraduates in innovative ways. However, for a variety of reasons, enthusiasm for the alternative-university movement diminished substantially by the mid-1970s.

In hindsight, observers noted that although the movement was star-crossed from its inception, its advocates possessed at least one instinct that was on target.[57] They believed that genuine transformation of the undergraduate experience could not come about within the framework of the colleges and universities existing at that time. Advocates felt that the ancient teaching paradigm had a choke hold on both the philosophy and the organization of most of post-K–12. Accordingly, they contended it was necessary to create innovative arrangements alongside the conventional settings. The new would *not* replace the old but be, instead, simply an alternative to it.

And a number of today's advocates hold a similar, though not identical, point of view. Experimental laboratory modules should, they say, be invented starting from the ground up.[58] They would be distinctive social arrangements aimed at facilitating the efforts of the coach to address the obligations of higher education both to students and to the social problems of society. Although such arrangements would possess a great deal of autonomy, it is not requisite that such modules should be physically and spatially separated from the campuses now in place. Indeed, their function as a template for other parts of the university to observe and, ideally, to interact with, indicates they ought to be close at hand.

Later chapters suggest that if appropriate incentives are provided, and if safeguards are put in place to protect the professor while he or she is experimenting, some social scientists (as well as professors from other spheres of learning) might very well be willing to try their hand at creating that unique type of module. They would be drawn from as many of their cognate disciplines (e.g., anthropology, political science, social geography, social psychology, sociology, criminology, women's studies, racial/ethnic studies, family studies, area studies, and others) as possible and, where feasible, come from several institutions. They might be willing to experiment if they perceive it to be in their own self-interest *and* because they see it as the right or moral thing to do.

The self-interest feature is both tangible and intangible. Working as a coach in the module could be a distinctive means for obtaining ample financial support in an era in which state and federal resources are otherwise severely restricted. Furthermore, the search for ways to reinvigorate undergraduate teaching/learning, and to make university service more relevant, would likely pique the interest of certain foundations and government agencies with money to invest in such an ambitious project.

On the intangible side, working as a coach in the module unlocks intriguing possibilities for educating undergraduates in innovative ways that are intrinsically rewarding and highly satisfying. Turning things topsy-turvy by making the development of human capital skills supreme, while bringing facts, figures, and ideas into its service, could be neither a superficial nor a simplistic endeavor. Furthermore, being a coach opens the door to doing social science in ways that are similarly innovative and potentially gratifying. The coach would, in effect, be attempting to craft a novel synthesis of research, undergraduate learning, and benefit to society.

And, turning to the moral dimension, beneath the skin even of the most hard-bitten, "objective" social scientist lurks the soul of an authentic social progressive.[59] In spite of all that I've said thus far, the fact is that virtually every social scientist hopes that her or his research and teaching will in fact eventually make a difference to society.[60] Hence, a fair number of us that, for one reason or another, are restive with the status quo might be willing to experiment with a cross-disciplinary module aimed at doing precisely that. Such professors are likely to believe that the ferment bubbling today through post-K–12 should be seen as a chance for innovation rather than a cause for alarm. They're likely to feel that the current uncertainty and confusion as to which paths higher education should follow offer a unique opportunity to carve out some new directions. Roads that lead nowhere would be abandoned, whereas successful routes would be diligently pursued.

Integral to the moral dimension is the obligation that every professor feels for the current and future well-being of her or his graduate students. And graduate education today is in almost (though not quite) as much ferment as undergraduate education.[61] The Boyer Report made a strong pitch to fully involve grad students and postdocs in the reinvention of the undergraduate experience. Accordingly, the module would aim to do precisely that.

TECHNOLOGY IN THE MODULE

No discussion of innovation in contemporary post-K–12 could ever be comprehensive apart from careful consideration of how technology might fit—in this case into the experimental module. On the one side, observed Karen Cárdenas, computer technology "has become the bandwagon *du jour* of higher education. Faculty . . . are being urged to hop on board the bandwagon."[62] Extravagant claims about computer technology as a revolutionary force for education are not unlike those made earlier for radio and TV when each burst onto the scene.

On the other side, it's widely acknowledged that for good or for ill computer technology has already made token inroads into colleges and universities and that in one way or another such trends are sure to become more prominent.[63] However, the shapes that those developing trends might take remain quite murky. Technology is a restlessly stirring though dozing giant, and many speculate about two things: When (not if) shall it fully awaken from its slumber? And, what shall happen when it finally starts to flex its powerful muscles? But the biggest question of all is whether (to mix metaphors) the tail of technology shall be allowed to wag the dog of higher education:

> Technology is a means to an end. . . . No amount of technological expertise can substitute for students' ability to critically analyze a problem and to clearly articulate a response to it.[64]

Bravo! But critics charge that, technology aside, twentieth-century post-K–12 failed miserably to demonstrate those peerless indicators of superior educational quality. And post-K–12's continued allegiance to the conventional teaching paradigm would almost surely leave technology where it is right now—a situation that Northwestern University's Roger C. Schank mockingly dismisses as nothing more than "text online with a quiz."[65] Others use the unflattering term "clip art" to describe the popular PowerPoint technique.[66] It's thus hardly surprising that academics interested in the same human capital outcomes as Cárdenas are curious to find out if computer technology might help realize Dewey's conviction that quality education implies far more than transmitting knowledge.[67] The Boyer Commission, for instance, asserted that computer technology ought to be used "creatively" as one element within a comprehensive program aimed to help bring about the reinvention of undergraduate education.

Hence, one of the module's central aims would be to experiment with how technology might be useful in the pursuit of that overarching objective. Importantly, the module's coaches would, from the start, declare that rummaging about within the hazy depths of computer technology in search of a silver bullet that could somehow revolutionize university teaching/learning is wrong-headed. That is indeed setting the cart ahead of the horse. A more likely scenario is that the proposed shift to a radically different paradigm for student learning would subsequently call forth innovative software and hardware to meet the distinctive needs of coaches and *players* alike.[68] Accordingly, upon establishing its learning and service agenda, the new module would then aim to incorporate the reality of ever-evolving software and hardware into its organization and operation.

Support by Public Officials

To be sure, implementing a learning paradigm, complete with coach and supportive next-generation technology, would not be cheap. Nevertheless, it may turn out to be no more expensive (and perhaps even more cost-efficient) than the prevailing teaching paradigm, which is marred by a great deal of inefficiency and, more to the point, does not return value-for-dollar, much less value-added.[69] Presently, public officials do not believe that professors are answerable to them for the dollars allotted for undergraduate education. The high moral ground academics once held proudly by serving the public good has been relinquished.[70] Officials today perceive (rightly or wrongly) that academics tend to design and maintain universities primarily to serve their own best interests.[71]

At the same time, officials now face competing and insistent demands for money to meet urgent needs they view as unmistakably contributing to the public good—programs such as K–12, Medicare, Medicaid, prisons, transportation, health and human services, and so on. Hence, lacking evidence that faculty are answerable to them for the public good, it's not been too difficult for officials to continue to cut back on post-K–12 spending, or to simply assign it nominal amounts.[72] One of the results of relinquishing the mantle of the public good was that the college degree came to be viewed more and more as a *private advantage* rather than as anything else. Because the degree holder (not society) is now viewed as its principal beneficiary, the emerging belief is that he or she should then pay for it in the form of steadily rising tuition and fees.

Advocates argue that in order to make any sort of learning module a reality, interested academics must first take the initiative and reach out to public officials—elected and appointed.[73] Universities should get proactive by seeking to recapture their lost image as a public good, that is, intent on serving the public interest.[74] One way to begin to do so is to realize that, in the information age, the best interests of undergraduates cannot be framed the same ways they were during the industrial age. Merely stocking the student's mind with stuff will no longer cut it. A second way is to discharge the university's obligations to help weave the social fabric. The upshot is that advocates believe that if professors could demonstrate to public officials that they are indeed answerable to them for both sets of tasks, financial consideration might then once again be forthcoming.

FLOW OF THE CHAPTERS

Chapter 1 considers the early-twentieth-century roots of the social sciences in the United States and shows how and why, over the course of that century, social science increasingly ignored its origins.

Chapter 2 traces the historical evolution of higher education up through the late twentieth century, culminating in the recent surfacing of the entrepreneurial university. It also elaborates why, by and large, social science appears to be on the sidelines of that latest evolutionary epoch of post-K–12.

Chapter 3 examines what was known as the "alternative university movement" of the 1960s and early 1970s. It was, in a very real sense, a mutation in the evolution of post-K–12 that, for the most part, did not survive. That brief interlude in the evolution of post-K–12 was essentially a short-lived attempt on the part of some reformers to respond to the criticisms being leveled at universities that they were, among other things, indifferent to the needs and interests of students.

Chapter 4 explores why the role of coach may, for some professors, be a highly significant option alongside (not instead of) the roles of teacher-scholar, entrepreneur, and credentialer. The dual tasks of the coach are also briefly introduced there—namely, cultivating students' human capital skills and nurturing their involvement in and contribution to the resolution of social problems. Chapter 4 also identifies Ernest Boyer's notion of the "New American College" as the basis for creating and supporting both an experimental laboratory module and the role of coach within which it would operate.

Chapter 5 explores the stark contrasts between, on the one side, the conventional teaching paradigm and, on the other side, an innovative learning paradigm. A learning paradigm refers to the assumptions and the procedures that govern discovery-based learning (DBL). A learning paradigm is what it takes in order to fulfill the Boyer Commission's mandate to make research-based learning the standard. Within the context of a learning paradigm, the coach cultivates the players' human capital by engaging them in what the preface described as action research. The distinctive characteristics of this type of experience highlight why, in the new century, the best interests of both students and society alike might perhaps be furthered through students' active participation in such a singular paradigm.

Chapter 6 elaborates on action research and its implications for social inventions aimed at resolving social issues. It also considers both the organization and the operation of the experimental laboratory module. Particular attention is paid here (as well as in chapter 5) to some of the ways in which next-generation computer software and hardware might, in a cost-efficient manner, facilitate both of the module's intertwined objectives—student learning and student involvement with social inventions.

Finally, chapter 7 brings together the several themes of the entire book and explores more fully how professors might reach out to public officials in order to forge a new social contract within the context of a "Learn Grant Act" for the twenty-first century. In the course of negotiating that contract, the financial costs of an experimental module are weighed against those of an array of social science departments. The twin issues of value-for-dollar and value-added are pivotal matters in that regard. And so is the issue of labor savings within the module when compared to conventional social science departments.

Chapter 7 also explores how other spheres of the university (e.g., the sciences, humanities, and others) might cooperate with the social sciences in developing their own distinctive DBL modules. The chapter also considers the fact that grad students and post-docs share a vital place in both the current success and long-term prospects of any experimental module. Furthermore, the issue of lifelong learning is examined in terms of the participation of citizens of all ages in both of the module's dimensions—cultivating human capital and working toward a more just society. That chapter and the book close with a discussion of what it means to say that the module's degree is robust and that it is both market-driven and a moral obligation—it is both the *smart* thing and the *right* thing to do.

NOTES

1. Cited by Kliewer 1999:xxx–xxxi from Townsend et al. 1992:69–70.
2. For an assortment of *Doonesbury* cartoons re post-K–12, see Pescosolido and Aminzade 1999.
3. Marcy 2003.
4. Cuban 1999; Fairweather 1996.
5. Rhodes 1998:11.
6. Cuban 1999.
7. Tsichritzis 1999:102.
8. Boyer Commission 1998:16.
9. Barr and Tagg 1995.
10. Cited in Bulmer 1984:15.
11. Boyer Commission 1998:11.
12. Ruben 1995.
13. Duderstadt et al. 2002:64.
14. Boyer Commission 1998:5.
15. Boyer Commission 1998:5.
16. Boyer Commission 1998:11; see also Duderstadt et al. 2002.
17. Barr and Tagg 1995.
18. Some friendly critics believe, however, that the teacher-scholar can and should take on those demands, e.g., Fairweather 1996.
19. Duderstadt 2000; Powell and Owen-Smith 2002; Dee 2003a, b.
20. Yudoff 2002.
21. Powell and Owen-Smith 2002.
22. Mangan 2003:A18.
23. Cuban 1999.
24. Duderstadt 2000:51.
25. Duderstadt et al. 2002:14.
26. Mangan 2003:A18. See Duderstadt 2000:51 for graphic portrayal of the "plight of the young faculty member in medicine."
27. Collins 2002a.
28. Cárdenas 2000; Duderstadt et al. 2002; Cuban 2001.
29. Arenson 2003.
30. Perlmutter 2004.
31. Mahoney 1997; Sinnott and Johnson 1996; Patel 1995; Brint 2002a.
32. Kerr 1963.
33. Boyer Commission 1998:9.
34. I discuss this option further in chapter 7.
35. Gouldner and Miller 1965:vii.
36. Cited in Bulmer 1984:22.

37. Flyvbjerg 2001; Rossi 1969.
38. Bok 1982; Duderstadt 2000; Boyer 1994. Clark (2002:323), too, agrees that universities are expected to "assist in solving societal problems."
39. Cohen 1998:414–15
40. Whyte 1982; Flyvbjerg 2001; Greenwood and Levin 1998.
41. Collins 2002b:42.
42. Boyer Commission 1998:15.
43. Schon 1983; Rodgers 2002; Martin 2003.
44. Bates, Bates, and Poole (2003:63) refer to "expert systems," i.e., "computer programs that imitate an expert's decision process." This book addresses the matter in chapter 6.
45. www.compact.org.
46. See also AmeriCorps in the 1990s, Eggers 2003.
47. Bell 1990.
48. Sacks 2003; Chenoweth 2003.
49. Kuh 2001; Duderstadt 2000.
50. Marchese 1995.
51. Boyer Commission 1998:37.
52. Brown and Duguid 2000.
53. Kliewer 1999:xxx.
54. Cohen 1998; Cuban 1999.
55. Barr and Tagg 1995; Duderstadt et al. 2002; de Corte 1996.
56. Cardozier 1993; Kliewer 1999.
57. Kliewer 1999.
58. Kliewer 1999; Boyer 1994; Duderstadt 2000.
59. Olsen 1981; Moyers 2003.
60. See chapter 1, this book, and also Flyvbjerg 2001.
61. Bartlett 2003b; Coppola 2002.
62. Cárdenas 2000:203, italics in original.
63. Schank 2000; Duderstadt et al. 2002; Lanham 2002; Tomlinson-Keasey 2002.
64. Cárdenas 2000:195; Katz 2001.
65. Schank 2000.
66. Zemsky and Massy 2004a:B7.
67. To name but a few, see Newman and Scurry 2001; Hazemi, Hailes, and Wilbur 1998; Hazemi and Hailes 2002; Bates and Poole 2003; Brown and Duguid 2000; Duderstadt, Atkins, and Van Houweling 2002.
68. Schank 2000; Zemsky and Massy 2004a.
69. Barr and Tagg 1995; Lanham 2002.
70. Lovell 2000; Cohen 1998; Duderstadt 2000.
71. Duderstadt et al. 2002:18, 125; Cohen 1998.
72. Duderstadt 2000.
73. Lovett 2001.
74. Duderstadt 2000; Boyer 1994.

Chapter One

The Troubled Marriage of Social Science with Human Betterment— *From Bliss to Disenchantment to the Search for Reconciliation*

> It is the historic mission of the social sciences to enable mankind to take possession of society. This is a big job and will take a long time. . . . [The ultimate objective of this job is] to bring society under control.[1]

THE ORIGINS OF AMERICAN SOCIAL SCIENCE

During 2002, National Public Radio offered a series called *Present at the Creation.* The series helped us see how certain cultural icons came to be. How, for instance, did we get the surfboard, or Crackerjacks, or Jack Kerouac's 1957 novel *On the Road,* or Rod Serling's 1960s offbeat sci-fi TV show *The Twilight Zone,* or the word game Scrabble, or Tennessee Williams's play *A Streetcar Named Desire,* to say nothing of the lowly hamburger? And in their case, the social sciences in the United States came about in large part owing to the convergence of three features: an extraordinary place set within a unique period in history, a cast of gifted and visionary characters, and a distinctive mission.

An Extraordinary Place at a Unique Time

Although they'd been gestating in Europe and in the United States for some years, the social sciences came fully into being (their full flowering) at a particular place—in the bosom of the University of Chicago (UC)—at a particular point in time—around the turn of the twentieth century.[2] During the decades when the United States was industrializing (1870–1944), American universities were being transformed.[3] Scientific and technological research was the force that drove their makeover. The University of Chicago was

23

founded in 1890 with major funding from John D. Rockefeller Sr. and with moneys from other private sources in the city. Its founders were wholeheartedly committed to the goal of making UC a major player in the new game that the new-style universities (the first was Johns Hopkins in 1879) were starting to play in earnest—the game of worldwide eminence via scientific research.

A Cast of Gifted and Visionary Characters

The University of Chicago's founding president, William Rainey Harper, was determined that his new university should eventually outshine all others on both sides of the Atlantic. To further his goal, he raided rival colleges and universities and spirited away their most gifted scholars to UC. Among his first recruits was the social philosopher John Dewey, whom Harper recruited from the University of Michigan in 1894. In 1892, Harper had enlisted sociologist Albion W. Small to head his new social science department. Alongside Small, Harper appointed an anthropologist to his new department, as well as a specialist in "charity administration" (Charles R. Henderson) who was also the university chaplain. Harper then added two women to his social science department: a historian and a home economist.[4]

At that time, philosophy, religion, and the social sciences (sociology and political science, along with anthropology, economics, and geography) were closely intermingled at UC, a situation quite unlike the sharp departmental cleavages now dividing them throughout today's universities: "The University of Chicago during its early years was an institution whose [departmental] boundaries were still highly permeable."[5]

Those boundaries got even more porous when Dewey (with Harper's blessing) imported George Herbert Mead to UC from Michigan, where they'd been colleagues in the philosophy department. While together at UC, Dewey and Mead had a "personal connection" that "served as a conduit for the wholesale transfer of ideas."[6] Among other accomplishments, Mead was eventually recognized as the patron saint of twentieth-century social psychology.[7] And, because Mead helped him think like a social scientist, Dewey was able to participate in a "very productive exchange" of ideas with other members of UC's budding social science department—including Small and Henderson along with George E. Vincent and W. I. Thomas.[8]

Ever since the pre-Christian Greek thinkers, philosophy had always been about a quest for Truth. And starting in those ancient times, virtually every philosopher and theologian wondered: *What is a good society? Which social arrangements are more preferable than others?* Dewey held that logic or reason alone could not entirely answer those questions. Consequently, he became a leading exponent of what was called *pragmatic* philosophy. If one argued, for example, that social arrangement A is preferable to arrangement B, then one is obliged to devise some sort of empirical, that is, hands-on, test in order to support one's argument. Dewey, in effect, supplied the philosophical basis for what the UC social scientists wanted to do anyhow, namely, apply empirical research techniques to the cause of discovering the most desirable ways people ought to live. Dewey assisted them by his compelling arguments that their scientific approach to the study of social life was superior to the assumptions of the conventional philosophers and theologians that relied, respectively, on reason and on revelation (i.e., scriptures).

What Dewey got from Mead in return was a social science point of view regarding his all-consuming passion, the study of public education. As a result of the influences of Mead, Small, and their colleagues, Dewey concluded, "educational science is first of all a social science."[9] And, because he adhered so passionately to that point of view, Dewey sought to make social science an effective counterweight to the sway that psychology then held over K–12. To that end, he established his famous experimental Laboratory School on the UC campus in 1896.

During the same period that Dewey's pragmatic philosophy and the social sciences were cross-fertilizing each other, the social sciences were simultaneously engaging in a series of mutual interchanges with the UC divinity department. Its brightest star was Shailer Matthews—internationally known as one of the foremost exponents of the Social Gospel described below. Owing to the profound character of their two-way influences, the divinity professors became oriented toward empirical research, while the social sciences took on a "marked Christian inclination."[10] Indeed, the social sciences, religion, and philosophy were all housed together in the College of Religious and Social Science. That college's principal mission, noted a 1910 outside observer, was to train students for "the business of applied Christianity, such as the management of religious, charitable, and philanthropic organizations."[11]

A Distinctive Mission—*Human Betterment via Scientific Research*

Harper demanded that his new social science department engage in the highest-quality research and graduate training. At the same time, he fully expected that its work would be "socially useful." Both he and his professors viewed their work as a coherent whole consisting of several integrated features: "scholarly research . . . [graduate] teaching . . . [and] public service . . . [defined as] an interest in social betterment."[12] Accordingly, Harper believed strongly that his new university was "in every sense an institution of public service."[13] He dismissed any professors who failed the test of being "as committed to public service as he was."[14] In essence, Harper officiated at the wedding uniting social science research with human betterment. What is more, he and many others expected much fruit from their union, and an eternal state of bliss.

Harper was thoroughly imbued with the liberal Protestantism of his day, described frequently as the Social Gospel. Its advocates perceived a close fit between the social sciences and their own conviction that Christianity ought to transform society as well as individuals. In 1907, the internationally known social scientist and social reformer E. A. Ross (though not at UC, he was Small's close friend) published a widely circulated book called *Sin and Society: An Analysis of Latter-Day Iniquity.*[15] Ross argued that sin could not be limited to the individual. Sin should also be used, he said, to describe the many social arrangements of his day that were unjust toward, and oppressive of, the masses of less advantaged and powerless citizens.

And, in that same vein, Henderson wrote, "to assist us in the difficult task of adjustment to new situations God has providentially wrought for us the social sciences and placed them at our disposal."[16] Whether or not they agreed entirely with the finer points of that assessment, Harper, Small, Dewey, and Mead all shared the same religious background as Henderson (as did Ross), and each one believed fervently that social science should in one way or another result in the betterment of society, that is, a society that was more just and equitable. In 1897, as part of his campaign to establish his "science of education" at UC, Dewey asserted, "The teacher always is the prophet of the true God and the usherer in of the true kingdom of God."[17]

Furthermore, Small had previously studied social science in Germany, and while there "acquired an ethical view of social science embodying a promise of scientific social reform."[18] The idea that science and social change are inextricable was, of course, central to the work of the German Karl Marx—the highly influential nineteenth-century social science pioneer. As he so famously put it, "Philosophers have sought to interpret the world in various ways; the point is to change it."[19] Both in Europe and in North America, many advocates of scientific social reform adopted the sciences, medicine, and technology as their template. Throughout the nineteenth century, researchers in the sciences et al. had succeeded in making life remarkably better for the masses of citizens in numerous ways, most noticeably in human health and thus life expectancy.

In an analogous manner, Small, Henderson, Matthews, and their colleagues argued that the abysmal social and economic conditions of everyday life for the masses of citizens crowded together in the burgeoning cities on both sides of the Atlantic were analogous to the diseases and health problems at which the sciences had been chipping away throughout the nineteenth century. Consequently, those advocates wanted to construct a new science of society that would advance citizens' social and economic life, just as science was improving human health.

Furthermore, at the turn of the twentieth century, the horrific conditions of urban life for the great masses of people migrating to Chicago from U.S. rural areas and from Europe were as dreadful as in any big city. Hence, at its inception and for some time thereafter, the UC social science department, alongside the divinity professors and the philosophers Dewey and Mead, took the city as their own particular laboratory. All the parties involved aimed to develop a science of society that would contribute to the betterment of the social and economic conditions of Chicago's citizens.

UNFORESEEN DISENCHANTMENT BETWEEN THE PARTNERS

Alas, the marriage of social research with social betterment got off to a rocky start. Despite the high hopes that the partners might live together in harmony and on an equal footing, they never seemed able to get it just right. Initially, research was viewed as the maidservant of betterment. In the ensuing decades, however, their roles got reversed—research gradually became the master, and betterment got stuck in a subordinate status, with the partners growing increasingly distant. Nevertheless, despite their growing alienation, and although from time to time throughout the twentieth century there was talk of it, the two partners somehow never got around to a final divorce decree based on their mutual consent.

Research in the Service of Betterment—*Charles Henderson*

Henderson and his social science colleague at UC, Charles Zeublin, were both ordained ministers (as was Albion Small). George Vincent and W. I. Thomas were the sons of clergymen and, although Thomas later moved in a sharply secular direction, "the residue from liberal Protestantism was an important formative influence" throughout his life.[20] Henderson's vision for recasting society in the image of liberal Protestantism included training students in "social welfare administration." Welfare administration (later called social work or social service) was then a program within the social sciences department, and it was the particular responsibility of the department's faculty, who viewed themselves as sociologists.[21]

Unlike Marx, who approached social change from the bottom up (i.e., the oppressed citizens would take control of their own social circumstances in order to make life better), Henderson followed a top-down approach—the expert social scientists would work to make life better for the citizens that eventually came to be called "clients." Henderson also differed from Marx in another vital way—Henderson tended to think that a major part of the cause for the citizens' problems could be traced to the citizens themselves. For example, Henderson described the great masses of Chicago's poor citizens (whites and blacks alike) as the "dependent, defective, and delinquent classes."[22] Hence, as he began his research, one question that Henderson posed for himself, his colleagues, and his graduate students was how to change the citizens themselves so they would no longer possess those antisocial characteristics.

As the first step in answering that question, Henderson insisted that his students learn to do survey research.[23] Indeed, he was among the very first social scientists in the United States ever to use survey research as a method to gain information. The second step was that he and his students believed they could use that information as a basis to change the citizens. Henderson adapted his logic from the ways in which physicians were successfully treating their patients. The physician would first use certain techniques (e.g., stethoscope) to diagnose what ailed the patient. Next, the doctor would prescribe a cure that the patient should accept in order to get better. Henderson viewed survey research as his diagnostic tool. He and his students would first discover what was "wrong" with the citizens. Henderson and his students then saw their next task as "prescribing" ways for the citizens to move away from being "dependent, defective, and delinquent."

There were, however, at least three serious flaws inherent in their particular approach to social change/reform. The first was that Henderson, Zeublin, and their students had relatively little "passion for scientific understanding."[24] Their principal identity—who I am—was that of reformer rather than social scientist. As a result, their survey research was not informed by any general social theories, for example those of Marx or anyone else.[25] Furthermore, because they were in a big hurry to make life better for the citizens, they were frequently impatient with the inevitably time-consuming and sometimes plodding progression of research. Consequently, their research was often quite sloppy in its execution. Their zeal was, in short, focused principally on rapid intervention and to the solution of a particular problem in a particular place at a particular time. They had neither the interest in nor the patience for emulating, say, the example of the biologist, who had two equally significant objectives clearly in mind. First, he or she did rigorous (and time-consuming) research on a certain *specific* disease (e.g., diabetes) in order to learn how to prevent or cure it. Second, the biologist felt that his or her particular research should also contribute to the understanding of diseases in *general*—including but not limited to diabetes.

The second flaw integral to their social reform approach had to do with the definition of "disease." Although everyone in those pre-insulin days agreed that diabetes was a "bad" thing, what right did upper-middle class, liberal, white, Anglo-Saxon, Protestant males have to say that the masses of poor people were allegedly dependent, defective, and delinquent? Why should the researchers' own views of piety and morality be legitimated by social science? Because the answers to those questions became embarrassingly obvious in the years following, an exceedingly strong distaste began to incubate and to develop regarding any sort of social research aimed at telling people how they ought to behave. Among social scientists it became, over many decades, an article of faith that they had no business whatever telling anybody how they should live. Its corollary was that researchers ought to make zero value judgments regarding which human behaviors are "good" or "bad." In order to take themselves seriously, and to be considered respectable by the highly prestigious physical and natural sciences, social scientists gradually came to feel that they had to be "value-free."

The third flaw in Henderson's social reform approach sprang from the unforeseen conflicts that inevitably arose between the social reformers and the establishment—the privileged classes that benefited from the status quo. The conflicts ensued because it soon became quite evident to Henderson, Zeublin, and their students that not everything that was wrong with the poor masses could be attributed to their alleged moral deficiencies. The researchers might, for instance, document that a dozen or so landlords in certain poor neighborhoods were charging immigrants (who spoke poor or no English) exorbitant rents for substandard housing. As a result, the families had little or no money left over from their meager earnings to buy food or clothing so their children could attend school and thus avoid becoming delinquents in the first place. Consequently, the social reformers themselves sometimes tried to correct that situation by, for instance, exposing the injustice to public scrutiny via the newspapers. The reformers hoped that the negative publicity would bring social pressure to bear on the landlords, thus forcing them to lower their rents.

Needless to say, the privileged classes in Chicago were not the least bit amused by the spotlight of negative publicity. Their reaction was to complain to university administrators that the social scientists were interfering in matters that were none of their business: "Liberal and radical teachers at the university might find that complaints would be made about them to the president."[26] But Harper, and his immediate successor Harry Pratt Judson, never flinched, and staunchly defended their professors by responding that they were simply carrying out their duty to do research aimed at making life better.

Nevertheless, the painful reality that they should have anticipated from reading Marx became at once distressingly salient. As long as the social scientists were trying to figure out how to assist the disadvantaged masses in mending their defective and deficient ways, the privileged classes could conveniently ignore them. Attempts, however, to get the privileged persons to alter their social arrangements in the interests of the poor were quite likely to stir up impassioned resistance on the part of persons determined to maintain the status quo for their benefit.[27] E. A. Ross, for example, unlike his UC colleagues, was not fortunate enough to have had the protection of his school's president in the face of external onslaughts. In 1900, he was dismissed from Stanford University because he publicly condemned the labor policies of that school's founder and patron, Leland Stanford.[28]

Distancing Research from Betterment—*Robert Park*

After Henderson's death in 1915, his distinctive UC approach to social reform lost its foremost proponent. Not only was there no one to fill his shoes, the social gospel itself had (in the wake of the horrors of World War I) fallen out of fashion throughout Western societies. Hence, it was not too long before social welfare/work separated from the social sciences to become its own UC unit. The social scientists remaining in their department had no stomach for Henderson's particular strategies aimed at reforming the "defective classes," nor did they conceive of research as being nothing other than a mere diagnostic tool for human betterment. Thus began the long-term process of distancing betterment from scientific research, a process that led eventually to the ascendance of research over betterment.

In the years 1910–1916, Mead supervised a number of carefully executed social surveys of Chicago's urban life, including a highly publicized empirical investigation of the appalling conditions at the city's stockyards. His strategies and objectives were quite different from Henderson's. Most of all, he wanted to establish a "central statistical bureau to consolidate, coordinate, and gather data on local social conditions with a view to making it possible to plan social action and public policy on a scientific basis."[29] Mead, unlike Henderson, did not believe that simply releasing embarrassing data to the press (particularly so if the data were careless and sloppy) would shame the establishment into action. He also differed from Henderson in that he was far less likely to identify the ultimate cause of the plight of poor citizens as lying within the citizens themselves.

Instead, Mead felt that social scientists should focus less on the individuals and concentrate more fully on addressing the dreadful social conditions that spawned the problems in the first place. To realize that purpose, he believed firmly that the social scientist must collect his or her data in a rigorous and careful manner. Next, the social scientist would present those sound, scientifically based, findings to public officials (elected and appointed). Mead was convinced that the unassailable data would then persuade the officials take the types of formal actions necessary to alleviate the horrendous urban problems plaguing Chicago. Mead's "public enlightenment" model of social reform was embraced and carried forward most energetically by Robert Park, who joined the UC social science faculty in 1913. Like his new colleagues, Park, too, had been influenced by liberal Protestantism and by many of the tenets of the Social Gospel.[30]

Park had studied pragmatic philosophy with John Dewey at Michigan and then worked for ten years as a journalist before returning to the further study of pragmatic philosophy with William James at Harvard. After earning his PhD in Germany, he worked for a while in the United States as Booker T. Washington's private secretary. At UC, he combined his commitment to pragmatism with his journalism experience in a two-stage manner. First, because he deplored the sloppy research techniques utilized by Henderson and his students, he (along with Ernest W. Burgess) worked very hard to upgrade the scientific excellence of the social research done at UC. Second, like Mead, Park believed that *sound* social research does indeed yield incontrovertible scientific "facts." Hence, he argued that the task of the social scientist is to publicize (via newspapers and other media outlets) those facts with one ultimate, overriding objective: not to shame, but "to shape public opinion."[31]

However, Park's strategy for human betterment (though quite unlike Henderson's) ran smack up against the brick wall of stolid indifference. By and large, the public enlightenment model simply failed to work. Reading and/or hearing about the appalling social facts of urban life did not seem to move either the public officials or the advantaged citizens to take deliberate and serious actions to change things. The citizenry appeared either to be indifferent to the data or else unsure of how to solve the frequently large-scale social problems they represented. Although a bit of ameliorative social legislation was passed as a result of UC social research, Park's vision of achieving anything close to what he called "social control" over society through influencing the press—and, through it, public opinion—bore only the faintest resemblance to the social realities of his day.[32]

Nevertheless, the long-term process of distancing betterment from scientific research was visibly in place. Mead, and especially Park and Burgess, imposed a certain degree of daylight between the two previously intimate partners. Although they still shared the same bedroom, they now slept in separate beds. Furthermore, research was no longer viewed as the servant of betterment. Indeed, scientific research gradually assumed a position of greater significance (and thus more prestige and status) than betterment. After all, asked Park, apart from doing valid scientific research, how could one possibly presume to offer compelling proposals of any kind for effective social policies and programs?

Widening the Daylight—*The Dichotomy of W. I. Thomas*

After many years of hard labor, Thomas, along with his colleague Florian Znaniecki, finally published in 1918 their massive and landmark work, *The Polish Peasant in Europe in America.* That classic work established the two foundational elements—the mode and the mood—of social science that remain to this day. First the mode—research must be held to the highest possible standards of rigor. There could no longer be any room whatsoever for the sloppiness that had characterized the work of Henderson and his colleagues. Second the mood—Thomas's approach to research was "detached, unemotional, and scientific, marked by penetrating curiosity and the desire to understand human behavior rather than moral fervor and the desire to change society."[33] Thomas shucked off the old Social Gospel zeal of his youth and replaced it with a passion to understand and to comprehend the way the social world works. By no stretch of the imagination, however, was Thomas indifferent to the urgent needs for urban social change. His liberal Protestant background made him quite sensitive to the enormous social, political, and economic needs of the disadvantaged Polish people he was studying. Nonetheless, he himself felt no burning desire (as did Henderson, whom Thomas once described as "sainted") to intervene in order to ameliorate their plight. Instead, Thomas viewed his work chiefly as a significant *contribution* toward solving their problems:

> The Chicago social sciences . . . embodied 'a tradition that asserts that effective sociological analysis per se is a relevant contribution to the efforts of collective problem-solving, because a clearer understanding of social reality serves to stir the visions of men and women.'[34]

Although Thomas agreed with Park that social research should contribute to problem solving, a sharp distinction existed as well: Owing to his journalism background, Park specifically targeted the press and its influence on public opinion as the venue for change. Thomas, on the other hand, was not concerned with the particular vehicle for betterment. He was content simply to make his contribution to scientific understanding and then to assume a much more laissez-faire posture regarding the actual medium for solving social problems. The instrument for achieving social betterment could, he believed, come from any number of places including, but not limited to, the press.

What Thomas did, in effect, was to shift the married partners into separate bedrooms located at different parts of the house. Thomas and his colleagues believed that even though the social scientist might feel a sense of concern about the impact of his or her research on human betterment, she or he was responsible solely for understanding and emphatically *not* for its application.

Thomas thus moved beyond Mead and Park by making it explicit that the two previously intimate partners could indeed exist in wholly separate spheres. Research in particular had its own life—it did not require betterment in order to survive. But, on the other hand, because betterment did require research, and was thus less independent, it held relatively less status and prestige. The gradual reversal (initiated by Park) in their priority and significance now became a stark reality. Thomas had created a very sharp sense of duality or dichotomy between social research and social betterment in which the latter was viewed as being entirely dependent on the former.

The Divorce of Research from Betterment—*William Ogburn*

For his part, however, William F. Ogburn (who joined the UC sociology department in 1929) wanted betterment out of the house! He demanded a separation followed by a final divorce decree—a "great gulf fixed" between research and betterment. Social science, he affirmed, is not "interested in making the world a better place in which to live."[35] He parted company with Park by declaring that the social sciences have no responsibility whatever "in spreading information, or in dispensing news." Science, he argued, is for "one thing and one thing only . . . discovering new knowledge."[36] Consequently, it is not too much to say that he actively sought to replace Thomas's strained dualism between research and betterment with a type of monism in which understanding alone matters.

Despite the fact that Ogburn said the social scientist should be unmoved by social problems, he did nonetheless consent to chair President Herbert Hoover's Research Committee on Recent Social Trends. The highly influential head of the UC political science department, Charles E. Merriam (who shared Ogburn's views regarding the mission of social science), was vice-chair of the committee that issued its final report in 1933. Both Ogburn and Merriam were strong advocates of the increasingly popular use of quantitative techniques in social science. Hence, they believed unflinchingly that using numbers is the surest means possible by which to gauge social reality. As an example, they said that education could be measured by numbers of years in school. Second, they argued that such numbers must be further subjected to certain statistical procedures. Numbers of years in school could be analyzed by techniques resulting, say, in a mean, median, or mode. Hence, in their report *Recent Social Trends,* Ogburn and Merriam calculated the median education for U.S. white males in 1910, 1920, and 1930. They then concluded that among those men what they called their "objective and value-free" data revealed an upward trend. Their committee's report pioneered research into what is still today called the study of "social indicators," among which educational trends remain a chief example.[37]

Ogburn and Merriam were entirely convinced that their quantitative data were compiled and analyzed in a "purely objective manner. All commitment, bias, and . . . partisanship were excluded rigorously from their study."[38] They believed they'd set themselves 180 degrees apart from previous studies in social science (including *The Polish Peasant*) that had relied heavily on the case-study technique and on other sorts of qualitative procedures, including the ethnographic techniques and field studies that for many years had been used widely in anthropology. The work of Ogburn and of Merriam had an incalculable influence on the emerging generation of "sociologists and political scientists [who now] saw themselves first and foremost as scientists."[39] And within the scope of their fresh self-image, little if any room was left over for the quaint notion that social science might necessarily bear any integral connection at all with human betterment. When, for instance, the UC social scientists Robert S. Lynd and Helen Merrell Lynd published in 1929 their widely heralded case study of Middletown (Muncie, Indiana), Ogburn dismissed it as "too interesting to be science."[40]

HOPES FOR RECONCILIATION

By no means, however, did Ogburn's belief that betterment should, once and for all, be entirely divorced from research win the day in twentieth-century social science. To be sure, some social scientists did and do agree with Ogburn's position re a pristine, value-free social science, but they were and remain in the minority.

The great bulk of today's social scientists believe that scientific research and social betterment ought to dwell in the same household for two vital reasons, each of which can be traced back to the pioneering days of Harper, Dewey, and Small. First, it is the right or *moral* thing to do. Social science has the indisputable obligation for human betterment built into its very warp and woof or, to use a contemporary metaphor, its DNA. Second, it is the *smart* thing to do. Harper reasoned that just as the sciences had made themselves useful to society, the social sciences could and would do the same thing. It is, in short, in the *self-interest* of the social sciences to participate actively in the processes of human betterment. If the social sciences are useful to society, it follows that society will support them—both financially and intangibly. The late social scientist James Coleman observed that the coalescing of moral obligation with self-interest is an infrequent but happy circumstance.[41] Few people today, either in or outside the social sciences, would argue openly against some sort of rapprochement between social research and human betterment.

Having said that most social scientists believe that research and betterment ought to dwell in the same household, there are, nonetheless, incredibly vast differences among them regarding how much intimacy is preferable. Should they go back to sleeping in the same bed—a sort of Henderson style in which betterment assumes a relatively more prominent position than scientific understanding? Or, if they're in bed together, should they instead be viewed as equals—do they exist on the same plane of significance? Or is it instead preferable to have separate beds? Or even separate bedrooms, located perhaps at different parts of the house? Separate beds and/or bedrooms imply a continuation of the present situation, in which research assumes a more prominent position than human betterment. Betterment would, moreover, continue to be perceived as dependent on research.

THE PECULIAR SPIN OF BASIC SOCIAL SCIENCE

The scenario that currently prevails in the social sciences—separate beds and/or bedrooms—expresses the theme established initially by Mead, Park, Thomas, and their colleagues. The majority of today's social scientists believe that the researcher's fundamental task is to collect data in the most rigorous fashion possible. Others (media, public officials, social workers, policy analysts, and program planners) are, in their turn, expected to pay attention to, and thus utilize, their social science data in order to make human betterment happen. It is, in effect, a *hands-off* approach to betterment, in which the researcher maintains a clear distance between scientific understanding and its application. It is frequently called *basic* social science, and the late social scientist Marvin Olsen defined it quite explicitly as the "pursuit of knowledge for its own sake."[42] On the other hand, the *applied* social scientist "views himself or herself as a practitioner who contributes to solving or eliminating social problems."[43] Notwithstanding that tidy distinction, today's basic social scientist is rarely a disciple of Ogburn. He or she, like Mead, Park, and Thomas, very much wants his or her research to be used in some manner by practitioners and/or public officials for the betterment of society.

Indeed, the best-known work of Ogburn's student Samuel A. Stouffer lies much closer to Mead's image of the proper marriage of research and betterment than it does to Ogburn's preference for their divorce. During World War II, Stouffer and his colleagues were hired by the U.S. government to do survey research on military personnel, resulting in a series of well-known volumes called *The American Soldier.*[44] Stouffer and his colleagues who studied the military before, during, and after World War II were interested simply and solely in objectively describing the way things were. It was left entirely to military officials to apply their data—that is, to utilize the social science data to develop policies and programs aimed at making life better for U.S. service personnel. The ways in which the officials did or did not use their data was *not* the responsibility of the researchers. Nor was it their personal concern that ultimately life might or might not actually get better for service personnel, though they of course hoped it would, for example, through racial integration in the military.

The construction of betterment as a separate and distinct enterprise—typically having its own set of specialized professionals—can be traced directly to Mead. Recall that he envisioned a specialized organization that would serve as a clearinghouse for data that had been previously collected by social scientists. He suggested that, in their turn, the professional specialists in the organization might use the data as basis to devise social policies and programs. In effect, Mead anticipated the evolution of the role of *policy analyst* that would serve as a conduit between the researcher and the public official (appointed and/or elected). And, in that vein, Stouffer and his colleagues transmitted their data to policy analysts who made recommendations (including risk-reward ratios of each program) to military officials holding the legitimate authority to actually make things happen, or not.

Earlier in this chapter, I used the term top-down as a way to talk about this approach to making life better. It assumes that certain experts (researchers) collect data about the ways to change things. They then pass on their information to another set of experts (policy analysts) who assess the data with an eye toward deriving specific programs that might bring about the changes implied by the research findings. Next, the policy analysts pass their recommendations on to public officials (elected and appointed) who possess the actual authority to make things happen. Sometimes, of course, a researcher might go directly to the officials with recommendations for change, thus bypassing the policy analyst. Finally, at the bottom of this chain of action are the ordinary citizens who would be most affected by the changes. The top-down approach to betterment fits hand in glove with basic social science, as defined above.

The Mead and Stouffer image of basic social science, and its integral link with the top-down strategy, is vividly illustrated by a recent *Washington Post* report. The journalist interviewed a sociologist who had just published an article in what the journalist called one of the discipline's two "best" (most prestigious) journals.[45] The article was based on sound survey research data collected in 1997 by the National Longitudinal Study of Adolescent Health. The sociologist told the journalist that his sophisticated statistical analyses of the data revealed that racial integration in American high schools does not by itself promote "cross-race teen friendships."[46] He also informed the journalist *"he hopes his work will be used"* by school officials to design extracurricular activities in which "more cross-racial friendships might ensue."[47] The aim, he said, is to "mix the kids . . . so they see each other working together' and see that 'these people are just like me. . . . Are we getting them meeting and talking together? . . . Are we fostering those ties?"[48]

That this social scientist was avidly interested in human betterment is beyond any doubt. He was quite keen on stimulating public officials to invent social arrangements that might enable youth from differing racial/ethnic backgrounds to form meaningful emotional bonds. In making his recommendations for changes, he was skipping the policy analyst and appealing directly to school officials, as well as to the *Post*'s readers. And he hoped they would initiate the sorts of changes that might involve the persons at the bottom of this chain, namely, the high school students. His basic assumption was that cross-racial friendships among students would result in a better school, hence, ultimately, a better society.

Unmistakably, nonetheless, the burden for inventing some sorts of changes in the interests of betterment was clearly *not* his. Furthermore, he gave no hint that any other social scientist was about to design an experiment testing the soundness, that is, validity, of his fundamental conclusion. A test of his conclusion that certain activities might in fact *change* cross-race teens from simply being fellow students into becoming genuine friends was left entirely to chance. As a result, it is not certain that anyone would ever carry out such an experiment.

Bear in mind that this social scientist was doing precisely what his professional peers expected him to do. Adhering strictly to the towering partition between accurately describing the way things are versus actively participating in the way things *ought* to be is the established and legitimate means for a social science professor to gain status and prestige—alongside tenure, promotion, and higher salary. The rationale for those distinctions in status and rewards goes back to Park and Thomas, namely, that scientific research is more significant than betterment—research can stand on its own, but betterment cannot. Research is said to be an incremental contribution to knowledge and is thus considered scientifically important, even if it is not immediately useful in any practical sense. In short, despite the fact that today's basic social scientist believes that research and betterment ought to remain married, it is a marriage of unequal partners who dwell in different spaces within their own household. Furthermore, the communication between them is, in actual fact, a one-way monologue—*from* research *to* betterment.

Notwithstanding, economist James Spengler way back in 1969 cast some doubt on the good sense of that model of one-way communication. "Scientific inquiry," he said, "has two immediate outcomes."[49] First, scientific inquiry helps us explain something—it enables the researcher to understand what's going on in whatever realm she or he is studying. And there's no doubt that such understanding is enormously satisfying to the researcher and a thing of beauty to behold in its own right. But equally pleasing and exquisite is Spengler's second outcome—actively linking that understanding with the "redirection of some course of events."

Importantly, in the sciences (especially the life sciences), both features tend to be built into the same experiment, even if it's a basic study, that is, one having no immediate practical application.[50] A life scientist, for instance, studying the growth of animal cells might introduce substance X into their development. The result of doing so confirms her hypothesis that X would alter that cellular development away from its conventional course. No drug company, however, rushes to fund more of her research because it's unclear how her results might be useful to them, that is, how it might be applied. Nonetheless, although it is basic, it contains both of Spengler's features: The changes she demonstrated inform the understanding of cellular development—apart from those changes, there could not have been a deeper level of understanding. A genuine two-way dialogue exists between both coequal features—one feature (understanding) is *not* considered more significant than the other (change). And the publication of her work would surely enhance her prestige—her professional reputation.

Next, a biologist studying the development of brain cells infected with Alzheimer's disease reads her study. His research focus is how that dreaded disease actually "travels through the brains of living patients 'like a flow of lava.'"[51] He gains several fresh ideas and insights from her use of the substance X because to him it seems promising in terms of designing a drug that could impede the course of Alzheimer's across human brain cells. In that sense, his work is applied and is funded by drug companies for obvious reasons. At the same time, his research on using X for brain cells invaded by Alzheimer's also provides additional fresh insights about the understanding of cellular development in general. Hence, when he publishes his findings, his prestige too is enhanced.

She subsequently reads his report and gains from it several new perspectives that she'd not previously understood about cellular development in general. Those insights stimulate her to apply for federal funds to investigate the fresh angles she gained from his work. In her request for money, she cites his applied research as evidence of the validity and thus the increased believability of her prior basic research ideas about cellular development in general. The upshot is that his ideas have become intertwined with hers and are integral to her subsequent basic research. Her basic work informed his applied work that, in its turn, informed her basic work, and the cycle of *understand-*

ing and *redirection* continues in that ongoing fashion. Furthermore, and very importantly, each of them derives a great deal of personal satisfaction from having had some small part in the fight against the scourge of Alzheimer's. Each has contributed actively to the quest for human betterment, and each embodies Horace Mann's entreaty "Be ashamed to die until you have won some victory for humanity."[52]

The preceding scenario highlights the observation that today in the sciences "the distinction between basic and applied research is rapidly losing its relevance."[53] One crucial reason for the growing insignificance of believing that the two spheres retain clear-cut boundaries is that the time lapse between basic research findings and applied research findings "continues to shrink." Owing especially to the peer-reviewed online dissemination of valid research results, insights from basic work and from applied work get intermingled much more quickly than ever before.[54] And, as both sets of ideas become blended together rather rapidly, it becomes well nigh impossible to separate who ultimately contributed which specific insights. The upshot is that today, in the sciences, the division between basic and applied is getting exceedingly difficult to unscramble, except in the sense of a strict and formal definition (memorized and quickly forgotten by sophomores) that, in the real world, turns out to be quite vapid indeed.

There is, moreover, something even more fundamental than speedy diffusion leading Powell and Owen-Smith to conclude that the "old divide [between basic and applied research] has been rendered moot."[55] They speak principally of the life sciences, for example, molecular biology, genetics, and biochemistry. At one time, it made sense to describe "public" science as applied, and basic science as "private."[56] The former was aimed chiefly at the marketplace, the latter at academia and its scholarly disciplines. Today, however, the image of public/private is archaic because "academic and commercial life scientists are now members of a common technological community."[57] The emergence of the entrepreneurial university means that the academic and the commercial communities that were once quite distinct from each other have now become virtually indistinguishable. Life scientists located in universities look and behave very much like their colleagues working in commercial entities, while those situated in the latter look and behave very much like those working in the former. Indeed, they frequently move back and forth between the two settings. Powell and Owen-Smith describe this as the "new world of knowledge production in the life sciences."[58]

Nevertheless, at the same time that those profound changes are happening in the life sciences, the distinctions between basic/private and applied/public in the social sciences remain as rigidly fixed as ever. Despite the fact that Alvin W. Gouldner cautioned forty years ago that the ways in which the social sciences construct the differences between basic and applied are "misleading if not inaccurate," no one gave much heed to what he said.[59] Gouldner objected to the premise—prevailing then and now—that basic social science research has no essential need for applied research, and that the former is ultimately more significant than the latter. He reasoned that the scientific *understanding* of social life—and the struggles necessary to implement actual *changes* within social life—feed forward into each other over time. Actually trying to change something (whether the course of Alzheimer's or the process of household poverty) helps the researcher to understand it much more fully than would otherwise be possible. That understanding would, in its turn, guide future efforts to bring about change, and those efforts would in their turn promote greater understanding, and so the cycle continues.

Notwithstanding, the social sciences continue to insist that understanding has no ultimate need for definitive, or demonstrated, redirection. The received wisdom was and is that what is necessary *and* sufficient for good social science is to try to understand and describe something, quite apart from any built-in efforts at redirection—as underscored above in the case of the cross-racial friendship study.

APPLIED SOCIAL SCIENCE—
MAKING A DIFFERENCE IN SOCIETY

During the middle third of the twentieth century (the period in which most social scientists were being influenced by either the moderate views of Park and Thomas or by the extreme position of Ogburn and Merriam) a smaller number (such as Gouldner and Miller) were casting about for some alternative. They wanted somehow to reduce the distance between social research and human betterment envisioned by the hands-off approach. By no means, however, were they seeking a reunion of research with betterment that was as sloppy in its methods, or as distasteful in its moralisms, as was Henderson's. Although there were and are many sharp differences among this array of alternative approaches, what seemed to unite them is that, to one degree or another, they were quite uncomfortable with the notion of basic social science research as defined above. They perceived themselves as reaching out for something that was distinctive vis-à-vis the peculiar spin of basic social science. It seems safe to say that, to one extent or another, they hoped to get research and betterment once again into the same bed, only this time as equals—each on the same plane of significance as the other, and each having something important to say to the other.[60]

When, in 1883, Lester Ward affixed the label "applied" to social science he was, as far we know, the first person to do so.[61] Nonetheless, it was the anthropologist A. R. Radcliffe-Brown who, during the 1930s, made "applied" a household word throughout the social sciences.[62] Recall that the applied social scientist "views himself or herself as a practitioner who contributes to solving or eliminating social problems."[63] Gouldner reported that the first identifiable organization that could be labeled as applied (the Society for the Psychological Study of Social Issues) appeared in 1929 "in response to the Great Depression."[64] Alongside applied anthropology and applied psychology, the term "applied sociology" soon came into common usage. In 1950–1951, the Society for the Study of Social Problems was formed.[65] Not too long afterward, the phrase "applied sociology" was equated with terms such as the "uses" or "usefulness" of sociology.[66] Political science likewise developed a comparable area of applied concern, especially with regard to issues such as urban planning and world peace.[67]

Jay Weinstein observed that by the close of the twentieth century, a number of applied social scientists were engaging in the actual day-to-day struggles of trying to make a "difference. [They are found] in state and county agencies, in private corporations, in consulting businesses, in communities, with nonprofit service providers, and in other kinds of organizations."[68] Weinstein states that applied social scientists seek to achieve human betterment through what earlier in this chapter was called a "bottom-up" approach. Although they too (like many basic researchers) fight against "injustice," Weinstein says they do so "as guerrillas, insinuating [social science] theory and method into micro contexts."[69] Integral to their bottom-up strategy is their belief in a *hands-on* approach to the implementation of betterment. In contrast to the *hands-off* approach of basic researchers, applied researchers tend to become part of the actual processes of trying to make life better.

Weinstein's expression, trying to make a "difference," captures the fundamental theme embraced by all applied researchers. It also covers those of us that, although we are *not* applied, believe that social research should indeed make some sort of difference.[70] Both the applied researchers and their "cousins" share the encoded gene that social science should be relevant in the sense that it should make an actual difference in society. Olsen's plaintive query *"Will anyone listen to us?"* is a variation on precisely that same theme.[71] The sciences would hardly put such an odd question to themselves. To do so would be perceived as utterly bizarre. The sciences commanded society's attention throughout the nineteenth and twentieth centuries and will continue to do so throughout the twenty-first. Harper wanted his UC social scientists to fashion a realm of study that might also command a significant degree of attention from the larger society. Basic social science, however, failed to achieve his vision, and by 1981 Olsen warned that "the public will not continue for much longer to tolerate or support a field that makes no appreciable contribution to the welfare of society."[72]

In short, applied researchers point the way by arguing that the peculiar spin of basic research works against the self-interest of the social sciences because it fails to construct a "tolerable marriage" between research and betterment. Applied researchers have the right instincts because they feel that absent such a marriage, society at best ignores social science, and at worst begins to withdraw support—financial and otherwise. Thus, for reasons of self-interest, and owing to a sense of moral obligation, the applied social scientist hopes to override the dichotomy imposed long ago by Thomas, Park, and their colleagues.

In effect, the applied researcher tries to make a difference and become relevant, and thereby attract the attention of the public, by focusing on a real-world problem. As an example, Stephen Steele and his colleagues reported that a group of parents and educators in a certain locale were puzzled and concerned over the high rate of suicide among their adolescents. They asked, "Why is this happening to our children?" Accordingly, the group hired applied researchers to figure out how to reduce their adolescent suicide rate. The researchers' "first and foremost concern," said Steele et al., is to reduce the suicide rate by applying the insights and tools of social science: "Validating theories of suicide, although very important, is secondary."[73]

Hence, at least some (not all) applied researchers propose a marriage restoring, in a limited way, the view of Henderson and his colleagues that research ought to serve betterment. Nevertheless, in their intense desire to be relevant and thus contribute to immediate human betterment, today's applied researchers may stumble into certain pitfalls.[74] The most serious of these is that their research tends not to enlarge the scientific understanding of what they're studying. Their work (e.g., on suicide) is not driven by Spengler's model of both redirection *and* understanding. Although the basic social scientist targets understanding to the virtual exclusion of redirection, at least some applied social scientists focus on redirection to the neglect of understanding. And, over the long term, their failure to strive for that understanding could seriously undermine their goal of human betterment. Life scientists, for example, have been remarkably successful in preventing and curing diseases in large part because they try to understand the patterns and processes of cell life in general. Had they targeted only one disease (e.g., diabetes, polio, HIV-AIDS) to the neglect of cellular understanding in general, it's questionable that they would ever have been as successful as they were and are in achieving human betterment.

Another serious pitfall is that the "applied [social scientist] tends unwittingly to become a supporter rather than a critic of existing social, economic, and political conditions."[75] However severely and justifiably we might criticize Ross, Henderson, and their colleagues for their many flaws and shortcomings, we could never say they feared confronting the establishment. Indeed, they envisioned their campaigns against the social evils of their day as bearing some semblance (violence aside) to the medieval Crusades of the church. Today's applied researchers, however, particularly if paid by government, business, or private agencies, find themselves in a rather awkward situation. How long may one continue to bite the hand that feeds one before that beneficent hand is withdrawn?

APPLIED RESEARCH IN THE GREAT SOCIETY

The 1960s was, for numerous reasons, a unique and tumultuous decade. Not least among its singular features was President Lyndon Johnson's dramatic policy vision to construct the Great Society. Central to Johnson's vision was his War on Poverty. That war was one important phase in the long-term struggle by government to overcome economic disadvantage—a struggle begun in nineteenth century Europe and carried forward into the twentieth century in part at least by the early University of Chicago social scientists. It should therefore come as no surprise that a considerable number of applied social scientists got hired by the government to help wage the war: "At long last," observed Peter Rossi in 1969, "social science has come on center stage in American society. . . . Sociologists, psychologists, political scientists are wanted in government, industry."[76]

However, unlike many of today's applied researchers who favor a *bottom-up* approach to human betterment, the Great Society's researchers followed a *top-down* approach. Their job was to design policies and programs in Washington, D.C., that could then be handed down to state and local officials. The officials would, in their turn, receive the programs from above and implement them for the presumed benefit of the layer below them, namely, the poor citizens in their city or county.

Among the war's social scientists was David Gottlieb, who spent three years in the Office of Economic Opportunity (OEO) and, more specifically, in the Community Action Program (CAP). Gottlieb observed that in CAP there was "an abundance of social reformers and social workers but there were few social scientists."[77] In effect, akin to the days of Ross and Henderson, the majority of persons engaging in the task of human betterment were not even applied researchers. They were instead "reformers"—persons interested in social change quite apart from the demands of doing rigorous research. In contrast, Steele et al. defended today's applied researchers by declaring they do *not* use "shoddy methods."[78] But because the reformers and social workers in CAP paid far more attention to curing problems than they did to the rigor of their research methods they, like Henderson, were guilty of doing sloppy work.[79] Not only that, Rossi added that the underlying social theories they occasionally used as a basis for their work were poorly conceived and quite superficial.[80]

The inevitable and unfortunate outcome of their careless research was their failure (not unlike Henderson's) to achieve human betterment. Among the harshest critics of OEO and CAP was the political scientist (and later U.S. senator) Daniel P. Moynihan who in 1973 became an adviser to President Richard Nixon—Johnson's successor. CAP was a fiasco, charged Moynihan, in terms of its splendid mission to eliminate poverty.[81] He went further by arguing that social scientists have no business whatsoever doing any kinds of hands-on research aimed at changing things. According to Rossi, Moynihan endorsed an Ogburn-like image of the researcher: "Social scientists should [according to Moynihan] stick to what they know best: the measurement of social trends and the evaluation of the effectiveness of social action programs."[82] Although Moynihan acknowledged grudgingly that research and betterment might perhaps dwell in the same household, he absolutely did not want them in the same bedroom, much less in the same bed.

BLENDING UNDERSTANDING
WITH REDIRECTION—*PETER ROSSI*

By no means, however, did Rossi buy into Moynihan's attempt to restore the degree of distance and daylight that prevailed pre-1960s between social science research and human betterment. Rossi reasoned that if the Great Society researchers had made a mess of things (as had Henderson and his colleagues), the proper response should be to try once again to get it right. Getting it right did not mean endorsing the peculiar spin of basic research, which he called mere "description" and "bookkeeping." And he was equally disenchanted with applied research, which he labeled as nothing more than "evaluation." Consequently, he suggested a third solution that was neither basic nor applied as defined above. His ideas were in the same ballpark as Spengler's—a blend of understanding with redirection. Rossi argued that *sound* research and *effective* betterment should get a whole lot closer together and be much more intimate than they'd been for a long time. His proposed schema would locate the two partners, or players, on the same level playing field. Each would have something important to say to the other; each would influence the other in substantial ways.

As an example of what he had in mind, Rossi pointed to the "income-maintenance" experiments that the federal government was launching at the tail end of the 1960s.[83] Cross-disciplinary teams of social and behavioral scientists (economists, sociologists, psychologists) had convinced government officials to test an innovative program aimed at alleviating household poverty in America. Specifically, the social scientists compared an "experimental" group of poor, married-couple households (receiving extra government dollars) with a matched "control" group of married-couple households (*not* receiving extra dollars) located within the same community. Those types of experiments were carried on in several cities throughout different regions of the United States. The researchers were testing a number of interrelated questions, including the effects of receiving extra government dollars on the likelihood of marital dissolution. One of the bitterest complaints about the welfare rules of the period was that a poor mother and her children could obtain government dollars *only* if they lived apart from any male. Thus, charged critics, those existing policies inadvertently encouraged marital dissolution because the mother could get welfare benefits only if the husband exited the household.

So, reasoned the social scientists, why not test the effects of giving extra dollars to intact marriages—poor couples where the spouses were still living together? And why not compare the results with equivalent intact couples *not* getting any extra dollars? Virtually all the social scientists and policy analysts fully expected that the couples in the former (experimental) group would experience significantly lower marital dissolution rates than couples in the latter (control) group. The reason for their expectation was obvious—husbands in the experimental group would not have to leave home in order to trigger additional household benefits.

Plainly, those experiments were neither basic nor applied, in the strict senses defined above. They were instead founded on the premise adapted from the life sciences, namely, that one way to understand something is by trying to change it. The experiments also sprang from the prevailing social science theories of the day, and the researchers believed their findings would add to the general understanding of the complex linkages between economic resources and marital stability. At the same time, that enhanced understanding would be inseparable from the degree to which the researchers did (or did not) bring about human betterment. If they could demonstrate that more dollars led to more marital stability, they felt they would have blended an increased level of understanding with an increased degree of human betterment.

Much to everyone's amazement and utter astonishment, however, the actual outcomes of the experiments were precisely the opposite of what they'd predicted! After several years, couples receiving the extra dollars were in fact more likely to split than couples *not* getting the extra dollars.[84] The horrified reactions of some policy analysts and public officials in the early 1970s to those wholly unexpected findings revealed that even well-crafted social science could collide with the establishment. It is indeed ironic that whether social scientists did sloppy work (Henderson and his colleagues, many Great Society reformers), or whether they did innovative, rigorous, and highly respected work (the income-maintenance researchers), they may in either case risk ruffling the feathers of those with power and money. In that early 1970s situation, the government's core conservative constituency accused President Nixon of frittering away tax dollars and undermining "the family" at the same time. Needless to say, the government quickly abolished those rather costly experiments. It did so as part of its comprehensive dismantling of the Great Society as a whole, including its most controversial programs (OEO and CAP) aimed at waging war on poverty.

When, in the late 1960s, Rossi applauded the income-maintenance experiments, he could anticipate neither their results nor their political fallout. Those unforeseen consequences do not, however, invalidate his argument that a sensible means for blending research with betterment is to do field experiments that build real-world change into their design. To take another type of example, the above-mentioned researcher who suggested that certain kinds of high school programs might enhance cross-racial friendships could be asked to do an experiment comparing and contrasting different schools. In one set of schools, he might work with officials and students establishing the sorts of programs he appears to have in mind. In another set of schools, no such programs would exist. He and his colleagues could then observe both sets of schools over time to see if his earlier expectation is confirmed. Whether it was confirmed or not, his additional work would have contributed to further understanding and also perhaps to actual human betterment. Both types of contributions would move us well beyond his original basic social science report.

To draw on still another example, I listened not too long ago to a social scientist describing the results of her rigorous studies on the social characteristics associated with violent crime in urban areas. In the question period I asked if, in the wake of uncovering those characteristics, she was now perchance planning a next step? Did she intend to carry out some sort of field experiment that might seek to modify those characteristics, thus perhaps reducing the levels of violent crime? In that manner, would she not, I asked, thereby enhance both the believability of her earlier conclusions and also contribute to human betterment at the same time? Not expecting such a naive query from a fellow traveler, she looked at me rather quizzically and asserted (almost dismissively) that she was decidedly *not* designing such an experiment: "My role," she asserted, "is simply to discover what's going on out there. My results are published, and it's up to others to apply them." Translated, *I've fulfilled my professional obligations. It's now up to policy analysts, program planners, and public officials to choose whether or not to apply my results. They must decide whether my conclusions are sound enough to propose legislation and/or to design programs.*

She was, of course, affirming the credo of basic social science, that a great gulf is indeed fixed between basic and applied research. Nonetheless, the income-maintenance programs above suggest how vital it is to try to bridge the gap between understanding and redirection. Consequently, those programs should never have been suspended owing merely to their politically incorrect results. To the contrary, the unanticipated results of those experiments ought instead to have become the basis for a series of subsequent experiments. Researchers should have been allowed to explore the question "What was it about getting the extra dollars that caused couples to split?" A team of life scientists, for example, doing innovative experiments aimed at subverting the course of HIV in the bloodstream recently reported that so far they've been unable to undermine it.[85] But rather than think of those outcomes as failures, the team felt that the setbacks gave them a much greater understanding of what's actually going on. The setbacks are in fact steps on the path to greater understanding and thus to anticipated success in eventually managing that disease.

That the income-maintenance programs were in fact quashed speaks to Gouldner's point that a huge stumbling block to doing social research aimed at actually changing something is the *resistance* it's likely to generate among influential groups unhappy with the results.[86] That "social law" was pivotal to Marx's nineteenth-century theories, and Henderson and his colleagues likewise stumbled onto that same law early in the twentieth century. Furthermore, that law forces the *nonbasic* social scientist of any stripe into a conundrum. If she or he does research that is indeed relevant to society—research that makes a difference by resulting in human betterment or making things different—he or she may run into a lot of stiff opposition. Relevant research can, in short, be quite risky to one's professional health.

"Nobody's Listening"—*A Downside of* *Basic Social Science Research*

Basic research is, by comparison, relatively risk-free, and a number of critics say that's why the majority of social scientists have for a long time followed that path of least resistance.[87] However, basic research has its own major downside, namely, irrelevance—no one pays any attention to it. The "social science bag" is Gottlieb's colorful take on the way basic scientists view their modus operandi inherited from Thomas, Park, and Ogburn.[88] Social scientists do their research and "point [it] out and then leave it to social engineers . . . to translate our research papers into social policy and programmatic guidelines."[89]

Alas, even on those rare occasions when a translation is done, the next and critical step en route to human betterment virtually never happens, as Park disappointingly discovered long ago when his work was met with stolid indifference. "One would be hard-pressed," Gottlieb noted ruefully, "to identify any social policy or program which was brought about primarily as the result of social science input."[90] Notwithstanding, back then and still today social scientists routinely testify, for example, in front of legislative bodies in hopes of influencing pending legislation. A number of them appeared, for instance, before Congress as it was negotiating the 1996 Welfare Reform Act.[91] The same thing occurred again in 2002 and 2003 as Congress debated the terms of the act's renewal.

Nevertheless, both sets of legislative processes were governed by the axiom that Ralph K. Huitt enunciated based on his actual participation in the Great Society. He concluded that social science data and/or its translation might indeed sometimes be used by public officials—but *only* if it "recommends" what they "want to do."[92] Political expediency, for example, not extant social science data, drove President Clinton and Congress to design their 1996 reform legislation.[93] Indeed, a number of social scientists and policy analysts spoke out strongly against the "reform" precisely because it ignored their data. In effect, nothing seems to have changed very much since Gottlieb observed that no matter what social scientists have to say, they will not "be taken seriously by those in a position to implement social policy and social change."[94]

To be sure, the sciences are by no means immune from intense political pressures of that sort. For example, the G. W. Bush administration was marked by ongoing struggles between scientists and opponents of stem cell research.[95] Because opponents feared that such research might foster relaxed practices toward fetal abortion, they lobbied the Bush government not only to withhold funding from stem cell research but also to ban it outright. No one, however, seriously believes that stem cell research shall ever come to a screeching halt (as did the income-maintenance programs) either in the United States or in other countries.[96] The reasons are obvious: the research carries significant implications for *both* scientific understanding *and* human betterment. Cures for devastating chronic diseases such as Parkinson's, Alzheimer's, and multiple sclerosis, among others, may result from stem cell research.

But if political expediency (the Huitt axiom) drives social legislation, why did such expediency play comparatively less of a role in Bush's cautious efforts to cope with the political hot potato of stem cell research? His core constituency dearly wished him to ban it outright. Indeed, that coalition includes many of the same groups that lobbied him successfully to pressure Congress to insist on much stricter marriage requirements for the 2002 and 2003 welfare reform bill than those set in the 1996 version.

One obvious answer to the question is that advocates for stem cell research have their own potent lobby, embracing such notable figures as Nancy Reagan, whose late husband (and former president), Ronald, was afflicted with Alzheimer's.[97] Their son, Ron, is also a prominent national spokesperson endorsing stem cell research. Furthermore, that lobby possesses the crucial leverage that both Rossi and Gottlieb observed was and is missing from social science research, namely, a track record of research that *works*. Public officials simply cannot afford to ignore scientists the way they disregard social scientists, because for two centuries scientists have demonstrated convincingly that they can in fact *disturb* the course of things and *change* them in the interests of human betterment. Because social scientists, to state the obvious, lack such a historic record, Gottlieb strongly backed Rossi's proposal to do experiments that blend understanding with actual change.

Both researchers feared that apart from a strategy making it useful to society, social science would become progressively marginalized by, and grow increasingly irrelevant to, policy analysts and public officials alike. During the late 1960s, Spengler concluded (in rather colorful terms) that social scientists "take in each other's wash," that is, they talk only to and write almost exclusively for one another.[98] This isolation of the social sciences from the real world has not diminished during recent decades, nor is it peculiar to the United States.[99] In the UK, for example, a thirteen-member commission was charged with the task of reporting on the current and future situation of the social sciences in Britain. Their 2003 report stated that

> business and government are dissatisfied with "much of the help they get from social scientists" who can be oblivious to their needs, give "ideological pre-ordained answers," and cannot present useful conclusions.[100]

Despite its dismal assessment, the commission held "great expectations" that the future of social sciences in the UK might somehow get turned around. It hoped that "the social sciences could one day influence and serve all of society, not just a few academic disciplines."[101]

Unfortunately, it would seem that events surrounding the 1996 U.S. Welfare Reform Act do not bode well for such lofty expectations either here or in the UK. That act was arguably the most radical federal attempt to address the issue of household economic disadvantage since the income-maintenance proposals some thirty years earlier. During the late 1960s, however, social scientists held a seat at the table of public policy, and thus debated with reformers, analysts, and officials over how to blend research with human betterment. By contrast, today's social scientists have, for all practical purposes, been relegated to the outer lobbies of Congress alongside the tourists.

Banished to the sidelines, many social scientists complained that the proposed welfare reforms could be characterized as a "war on the poor."[102] Indeed, most of us were convinced that "reform" was likely to have disastrous consequences for poor mothers and their children. Nonetheless, the catastrophe that most of us expected has not yet come to pass. Masses of homeless mothers and their children are not roaming the streets waiting in Depression-era lines for stale bread and cold, watery soup. To be sure, the situation of poor mothers and their children is plainly a mixed bag. Although welfare rolls were reportedly cut in half by early 2002, many disadvantaged mothers are employed at the kinds of jobs that are highly vulnerable to downturns in the economy—minimum-wage jobs lacking vital benefits such as health care.[103]

The bottom line is that whether those new government policies and programs eventually turn out on the whole to be good, mixed, or bad, one thing is quite clear. Public policies and programs regarding household economic disadvantage—an issue that has lain at the core of social science research since its inception—are now shifting markedly, and by and large nobody's listening to what social scientists have to say.[104] Isabel Sawhill (a respected social scientist and policy analyst who is located at the "liberal" Brookings Institution in Washington, D.C.) observed in 2002, "A new conversation on poverty' has begun reflecting a political consensus that would have been hard to imagine in 1995 or 1996."[105] Whether or not such a consensus is indeed emerging, it is plainly not the result of either research or advocacy on the part of social science taken as a whole. Apart from a few exceptions, most social scientists were exceptionally dubious about the 1996 reforms. Moreover, it was worrisome enough that social science was marginalized when the reform programs were first debated in the mid-1990s. But it's even more upsetting for social science to remain immaterial to the body of broad public policy that might be emerging in the early twenty-first century as to the conditions of household economic independence. That situation of gross nonsignificance seems just as preposterous as would be a scenario in which stem cell policies and programs were devised apart from the theories and research of life scientists.

And yet that very situation seems to be unfolding for social science today. Officials can afford to ignore social science for many reasons, and one is that, unlike the life sciences, it possesses no track record of research that works. We cannot, in fact, point to anything we have "cured." To be sure, if social scientists try to do research that works, we risk offending the establishment, as was the case of the income-maintenance experiments. The early-1970s Nixon government was not about to invest in research and programs that actually increased the incidence of the "disease" (marital dissolution) that they in fact were trying to "cure."

The upshot is that social science is marginalized for any number of reasons, two of which overlap the difficulties that plagued Henderson and his colleagues. The first is achieving a consensus as to the definition of the disease requiring a cure. Is marital dissolution a "disease" that should be "cured"? Or should we instead construct the termination of any seriously committed relationship as a transition that's likely to require smoothing out but *not* as a problem to be cured?[106] Social scientists differ markedly among themselves as to which particular behaviors are bad (deviant) and which are good. Citizens, policy analysts, and officials likewise hold widely varying perceptions of what is deviant behavior and what might perhaps be positive, or at least neutral.

The extraordinary complexity inherent in getting persons on all sides to agree on the nature of the disease and how, if at all, it should be cured invariably causes social science to bump up against a second leftover obstacle from the Henderson era: if the establishment and the social sciences construct a problem and its solution in very different ways, how can social scientists possibly avoid alienating the powers that be, especially if they turn out to be funding agencies? Let's assume that, for example, a social scientist regards a social problem in a certain way and, à la Rossi, designs an experiment testing to see if that "problem" can be "solved." Let's say the issue is adolescent sexual behavior, and the powers that be consist of federal funding agencies. The realm of adolescent sexuality is a classic example of the Huitt axiom that social science data can be useful to public officials—but *only* if it "recommends" what they "want to do." In recent years, under pressure from the religious right, federal agencies have constructed nonmarried adolescent sexual intercourse in and of itself (apart from unwanted pregnancy, disease, coercion) to be a "social problem." As a result, they've had no hesitancy in decreeing its solution ahead of time, namely, abstinence. Hence, for several years, researchers have been invited to submit proposals to federal agencies aimed at increasing the likelihood of adolescent sexual abstinence, and thereby "prove" that abstinence is "better" for both the adolescent and society.[107]

The upshot is that a researcher currently stands no chance of being funded if she contends that the core social issue lies not with sexual intercourse per se. Let's assume that she instead argues that the underlying problem is the conventional gender-based definitions of what it means to be male and female in American culture. Those definitions, she contends, impair the negotiations (including those that are implicit) between girls and boys regarding their sexual and contraceptive behaviors. If she were to propose a Rossi-style field experiment in which the indicator of success would *not* be the incidence of intercourse but rather the degree to which adolescent girls and boys effectively negotiate their sexual and contraceptive behaviors, the secretary would toss it at once into the recycle bin.

A NO-WIN SITUATION

In short, owing in part to the peculiar mode of operation called *basic* research that's dominated social science for many decades, the discipline has been unable to demonstrate a track record of research that works—that is, that's useful to society. But if, in the interests of being useful and relevant, it seeks to break free from the social science bag and follow Rossi's route of blending understanding with actual redirection, it then runs the risk of biting and enraging the hand that feeds it. Hence, one could say that social science is caught in a no-win situation—damned to one kind of hell if it doesn't try to blend research with betterment, but damned to a different hell if it does. As Randall Collins noted, "the politicized character of social science limits its salability as practical skills."[108]

That quandary notwithstanding, what Spengler said thirty-plus years ago—as the death knell of the Great Society was sounding—is infinitely more compelling now than it was then:

> As a rule, delivery is required. Controllers of the power of the purse demand results of social as well as natural scientists. They cannot long be put off by promises of serendipity. . . . [109]

Today, the pervasive demand for accountability is a much more all-encompassing phenomenon throughout government and at all levels of education, as well as in business, than it was in the 1960s and 1970s. Back then, some public officials evidently still believed that social scientists could deliver cures for the social ills targeted by the Great Society. Frustrating and disappointing experiences taught them otherwise, and so today officials for the most part simply pay no attention to what social scientists do. They no longer expect, much less demand, "delivery."

No one, however, wants to be ignored, and so a number of distinguished social scientists took part in a symposium protesting the fact that the social sciences are simply unnoticed by government officials and the media. In commenting on their distress over being invisible or at best perceived as nondescript, Weinstein acknowledged that they were genuinely concerned about human betterment. Symposium participants, said Weinstein, plainly wanted their research to "affect social life for the better."[110]

But at the same time they are *basic* social scientists—they clutch tightly, in Gottlieb's phrase, to the social science bag. That is, they wanted their basic research to be used by others to help "shape social policy."[111] To attain that end, they wanted to get "the attention of policy makers," and to help "journalists [and the public] see things sociologically."[112] Weinstein concluded that the social scientists worked out a "near-perfect consensus . . . that the results of [social science] research, packaged properly . . . should change social policies to conform to scientific truth."[113]

Nevertheless, Weinstein faulted them for their adherence to the decades-old strategy of Mead and Park. He accused basic researchers who fail to participate in the day-to-day struggles of betterment as "preferring to operate on a least-effort principle. They seem to believe that they have been 'trained' to do only one thing: 'my research.' And they believe that in so doing, they should be able to change society."[114]

It does seem rather odd that despite their noble hopes to connect research with human betterment, eminent basic social scientists of the twenty-first century have not yet devised any more effectual strategy for doing so than the type of dichotomy espoused early in the last century by Mead, Thomas, Park, and Burgess. And although those early pioneers seemed content with their strategy, today's social scientists appear to lament its apparent ineffectiveness. Weinstein suggested that many of the symposium participants were "miffed, if not outraged, by the way journalists, politicians, and the public treat their work."[115] He added that the social scientists identified the "right-wing think tanks" as the single most formidable obstacle to the translation of their research into viable policies and programs. Those same right-wing policy analysts were highly influential in shaping the 1996 Welfare Reform Act, much to the dismay of most social scientists. Today's right-wing analysts are the heirs of those 1970s analysts who successfully urged the government to terminate the star-crossed income-maintenance experiments. They are, moreover, closely allied with those analysts who attempted, but with much less success, to convince the Bush government to sandbag stem cell research.

Stem cell researchers are quite *pragmatic,* in the Dewey sense. They're able to demonstrate many past linkages, and to project a believable future link, between their research and actual human betterment. Their research *works.* In contrast to that pragmatic style, said Weinstein, the symposium participants seemed to believe that their brand of social science research "had special powers to cut through a tenacious and popular political ideology."[116] That allegation was a bit of a caricature, because it implied that basic social scientists are oblivious to their own ideology. They are in fact keenly aware of their liberal philosophy.[117] Not only that, they're quite convinced that the basic research they do would empower their beliefs to overcome the ideology of the other guys *if only they could get the hearing from the media that their stellar research deserves.*[118] Failing, however, to attract the level of media and political attention that Park and others sought long ago, it could be said that much of contemporary social science continues to find itself stuck in the "shoals of irrelevance."[119]

Whatever their distress levels at being ignored by media and politicians, there's no sign on the horizon that some type of rapprochement between basic and other social scientists might be just round the corner. In addition to the applied researchers, *other* may also subsume humanist social scientists,[120] as well as critical social scientists,[121] and also clinical social scientists.[122] The *other* camp also includes a significant set of critics from inside and outside the social sciences known as feminist theorists.[123] Although there are some important differences within and among this broad band of groupings, they are united by their intense disapproval of the peculiar spin of basic social science. They censure its failure to make any difference in society, and they lament its inability to matter and thus be pertinent to citizens and officials alike. Those several groupings complain bitterly that basic researchers have lost sight of a major reason social science was created in the first place, namely, to enhance human betterment.[124]

A further regret of those other groupings is that virtually no dialogue exists between them and basic social scientists. Basic researchers typically ignore the applied journals that might possibly supply insights that could perhaps strengthen their own research. On the flip side, applied researchers seldom read the basic journals searching for insights they might test in the field. In accounting for the gulf between the two sides, Weinstein reaffirmed what many others (e.g., Gouldner, Olsen) have observed for a long time. Because basic researchers control every one of the social science disciplines, persons in the other groupings feel that the elite pay lip service—but little else—to their interests.[125]

Hence, it should come as no surprise that the elite established a status and prestige hierarchy in which the peculiar spin they put on basic research far outranks applied, as well as all other forms, of research. The major leagues of the social sciences are reserved for professors devoting themselves entirely to basic research. Everyone else is relegated to the minor leagues—they are, in effect, second-class citizens. Because tenure, promotion, and salary stem principally from basic research, only the most courageous professor can risk (though some do) having his or her work tainted with opprobrious labels such as "applied." And the absolute kiss of death is to be characterized as either a social worker or as a reformer. Basic researchers hold a gut feeling of intense aversion to the residue of the Henderson model of social reform muddled up with sloppy research and unjustifiable personal moralisms.

UNDERGRADUATE LEARNING AND THE
HISTORIC MISSION OF THE SOCIAL SCIENCES

Social science and social scientists have not yet turned to the question of what is a good society and which social arrangements are to be preferred to others. I think we have reached the stage of maturity where we can turn again to these problems, for a completely value-free social science is a social science of little value.[126]

More than thirty years ago, Rossi urged social science to recover its early-twentieth-century roots—to struggle once again with what a good society is and which social arrangements are to be preferred over others. The tumults internal to the social sciences in recent decades—stemming largely from the ranks of the alternative groupings of researchers—have, ironically enough, moved social science closer to the place Rossi advocated.[127] Ogburn's endorsement of a final divorce decree between research and betterment is now considered naive at best. Even the most hard-bitten basic researcher senses the two spheres must somehow be reconciled, because Rossi was right—value-free amounts to being of little value to society.

The unsettled question remains, however, the specific terms of their reconciliation. To be sure, that's not a novel question at all. It's been puzzled over ever since social scientists first became disenchanted with the Henderson-style marriage. A central theme in the story of twentieth-century social science is the struggle over how up-close and personal their marriage should be. Nevertheless, despite the fact that it's always been a vital question, the union of research with betterment has seldom been viewed as "extremely urgent" or "top priority" or "job number 1" by elite basic researchers—those who manage the fate of the social sciences.

One principal reason the question has not been all-consuming to them is that although social science never got to be as socially useful as Harper and Small intended it to be, it's nevertheless had a safe and secure home within the confines of the twentieth-century ivory tower. We've benefited enormously because we do in fact *talk* a great deal about human betterment. As a result, administrators have given us generous amounts of respect and financial support, and students have filled our classes. The awkward reality that we've not been very effective at delivering betterment has been tolerated in hopes that one day we might indeed fulfill that reason for our existence.[128]

But the more things appear to stay safe, secure, and stable, the more tentative and uncertain they become, as social scientists know very well. Several external and powerful forces are now laying siege to post-K–12. One outcome of those forces, explains chapter 2, is that the reasonable amounts of respect and financial support enjoyed by the social sciences in the twentieth century are no longer a sure thing. Lacking that security, social science could, in coming years, wind up as even more of a sideline than it is at present.

Consequently, those external forces, alongside the distressing circumstances of much of the contemporary undergraduate experience, may well offer a distinctive opportunity for at least some (not all) social scientists to move from the shoals of irrelevance to more solid footing within post-K–12. At the same time, seizing such an opportunity might improve our standing in the eyes of the larger society. As noted in the introduction, professors from a number of the social science disciplines might voluntarily assume the identity and role of coach. They could then work together with interns (grad students and postdocs) and students within the context of an experimental laboratory module. One side of the coach's mission is to fulfill his or her obligation to cultivate human capital skills among the students electing to participate in the module. The flip side of the coach's mission is also built into the module. The coach, alongside interns and students, aims to fulfill the historic purpose of the social sciences: to take possession of society and bring it under control.

Those cryptic phrases capture the bottom-up approach to human betterment described above. Such an approach would not, however, follow the modus operandi of most applied researchers. It would instead aim for understanding just as much as for change. To achieve both objectives, the module would seek to facilitate all its participants (coach, intern, undergrad), and eventually citizens of all ages, in their struggles to assume greater control of their own lives and the community in which they live. It would be neither more nor less than what Dewey envisioned for his laboratory school in particular and for U.S. education in general. It would be, as he put it, "democracy in action."[129]

Although the objective of human betterment seemed quite straightforward a hundred years ago, we've seen how unbelievably prickly it got to be from the very start, and it remains so to this day. There is no simple or clear-cut way to go about it. If there were such an obvious route, it would have been explored decades ago. Hence, what greater challenge to offer undergraduates and interns than this? What more appropriate means to cultivate their human capital skills than by posing what heretofore has been an intractable problem and by asking them—alongside their coaches—to begin figuring out ways to try to resolve it? What more timely strategy could the social sciences pursue in order to enhance their significance in the eyes of post-K–12 and society alike, and thereby help to overcome their current second-class status?

NOTES

1. Gouldner and Miller 1965:vii.
2. Bulmer 1984:8.
3. Cohen 1998.
4. Bulmer 1984:33.

5. Lagemann 2000:54.
6. Lagemann 2000:53.
7. Bulmer 1984; Straus 1964.
8. Lagemann 2000:53.
9. Lagemann 2000:50.
10. Bulmer 1984:39.
11. Slosson 1910/1977:438.
12. Bulmer 1984:23.
13. Bulmer 1984:22.
14. Lagemann 2000:46.
15. Bulmer 1984:9; Ross 1907/1973.
16. Cited in Bulmer 1984:35.
17. Cited by Lagemann 2000:20.
18. Bulmer 1984:33.
19. Cited in Aronowitz 2000:xvi.
20. Bulmer 1984:39.
21. Lazarsfeld 1962/1993:264–65.
22. Bulmer 1984:35.
23. Bulmer 1984.
24. Bulmer 1984:25.
25. However, Levine et al. (1975) argued that some of the ideas of Georg Simmel played a part at that time.
26. Bulmer 1984:25; and see Collins 2002b:42 for a discussion of the general issue.
27. Gouldner 1965:15–17.
28. Furner 1975, cited by Bulmer 1984:9.
29. Bulmer 1984:24.
30. Bulmer 1984:31.
31. Bulmer 1984:70.
32. Bulmer 1984:24.
33. Bulmer 1984:46.
34. Janowitz 1974:xv, cited in Bulmer 1984:23.
35. Bulmer 1984:182.
36. Bulmer 1984:182.
37. Rossi 1969.
38. Bulmer 1984:80.
39. Bulmer 1984:80.
40. Cited in Bulmer 1984:182.
41. Coleman 1990.
42. Olsen 1981:565.
43. Olsen 1981:565.
44. Stouffer 1962; Bowers 1967.
45. Huget 2002.
46. Huget 2002.
47. Huget 2002, italics added.
48. Huget 2002.
49. Spengler 1969:454.
50. Powell and Owen-Smith 2002; Wade 2003.

51. Goode 2003.
52. Antioch University home page, www.antioch.edu.
53. Duderstadt 2000:135.
54. Harmon 2002.
55. Powell and Owen-Smith 2002:107.
56. Merton 1973.
57. Powell and Owen-Smith 2002:107.
58. Powell and Owen-Smith 2002:108.
59. Gouldner 1965:7.
60. Gouldner 1965.
61. Ward 1883.
62. Gouldner 1965:6.
63. Olsen 1981:565.
64. Gouldner 1973:16.
65. Lee 1986:xii.
66. Lazarsfeld et al. 1967:x.
67. Archibald 1965:274–276.
68. Weinstein 2000:346.
69. Weinstein 2000:346.
70. Flyvbjerg 2001; Whyte 1982.
71. Olsen 1981:570, italics added.
72. Olsen 1981:565.
73. Steele et al. 1999:4.
74. Denzin 1970.
75. Olsen 1981:565.
76. Rossi 1969:469.
77. Gottlieb 1969:445.
78. Steele et al. 1999:4.
79. Gottlieb 1969:445.
80. Rossi 1969:470.
81. Moynihan 1969.
82. Rossi 1969:474.
83. Rossi 1969:477.
84. Hannan et al. 1977.
85. Pollack and Altman 2003.
86. Gouldner 1965:15–21.
87. Rossi 1969; Spengler 1969; Gouldner 1973; Lee 1986; Weinstein 2000.
88. Gottlieb 1969:447.
89. Gottlieb 1969:448.
90. Gottlieb 1969:444.
91. Weaver 2000.
92. Huitt 1969:482.
93. Weaver 2000.
94. Gottlieb 1969:444; Flyvbjerg 2001.
95. Pollack 2002; Revkin 2004.
96. Brainard 2004.
97. *Washington Post* 2003.

98. Spengler 1969:452.
99. Flyvbjerg 2001.
100. Harold Orlans. 2004. *Footnotes.* January 2004:4. Taken from *Commission on the Social Sciences* (March 2003). *Great Expectations: The Social Sciences in Britain* (www.the-academy.org.uk/). An earlier version can be found in *Change,* Nov/Dec 2003.
101. *Footnotes* January 2004:1. See also Agger 2000.
102. Clawson 1997:vii.
103. Hays 2003.
104. Flyvbjerg 2001.
105. Toner 2002.
106. Scanzoni 2004.
107. See "Availability of Funds for Adolescent Family Life Demonstration Projects." *Federal Register.* April 2, 2004.
108. Collins 2002b:42.
109. Spengler 1969:451.
110. Weinstein 2000:344–45.
111. Weinstein 2000:344.
112. Weinstein 2000:344.
113. Weinstein 2000:344.
114. Weinstein 2000:346
115. Weinstein 2000:345.
116. Weinstein 2000:345.
117. Collins 2002b:42.
118. Gamson 1999.
119. Duderstadt 2000.
120. Lee 1986; Fishman and Benello 1986; Scimecca 1981.
121. Fay 1987; Flyvbjerg 2001; Mills 1959.
122. Lee 1986:xii.
123. Zalk and Gordon-Kelter 1992.
124. Gouldner and Miller 1965:vii.
125. Brooks 2004.
126. Rossi 1969:479.
127. Wallerstein 1999, 2000.
128. Flyvbjerg 2001.
129. Lagemann 2000:51.

Chapter Two

Universities in Transition— Social Science in the Impoverished Backwaters

SEA CHANGE OR TIDAL RHYTHM?

We must recognize the profound nature of the rapidly changing world faced by higher education. The status quo is no longer an option. We must accept that change is inevitable and use it as a strategic opportunity to control our destiny, retaining the most important values and traditions.[1]

A number of observers believe that twenty-first-century higher education in North America (as well as in Europe) is caught in a "sea change." Though by no means as cataclysmic as a "perfect storm," a sea change represents a severe and typically unforeseen shift in the environmental conditions of winds, waves, temperature, and rain. Instead, however, of longing for an unattainable return to earlier conditions, some observers reason that the most appropriate response to a shifting environment is to craft innovative ways to operate effectively in an unstable milieu.

Although some academics concur with that point of view, others do not. Instead of a sea change, they assert that post-K–12 today is simply experiencing its usual tidal rhythms. The ocean, they remind us, covers the beach every day at a predictable hour, dumping lots of shells, weeds, driftwood, and dead fish. It overwhelms our sandcastles and creates big pools of water but slowly begins to recede. And it's not too long before the beach looks pretty much the way it did yesterday around the same hour.

Professors in the tidal-rhythm camp say that because post-K–12 has always faced challenges from its environment, modest adjustments are nothing new. What's happening now, they say, simply reaffirms the old adage: The more things change, the more they stay the same. They add, "This too shall pass . . . if we demand that the university hold fast to its traditional roles and character."[2]

And, of course, a large amount of social change—perhaps most—is in fact measured by ever-creeping increments. On the other hand, the historian Arthur Cohen classified the development of American higher education (starting in the seventeenth century) into five distinctive eras. To be sure, each era overlapped considerably with the periods before and after it. And within every era there were many incremental, and sometimes barely visible, ebbs and flows.

THE ERA OF UNIVERSITY TRANSFORMATION—*1870–1944*

Still, the third era was indisputably a genuine "sea change."[3] Cohen called the years 1870–1944 the era of "university transformation." The gargantuan force rolling over everything in its path during that period was the growth of the United States into a technologically developed nation and a major industrial power. A second, and resulting, force was the quest by universities for worldwide eminence—particularly within the sciences. Recall from chapter 1 that the University of Chicago (UC) was founded expressly to compete with universities on both sides of the Atlantic for scientific eminence. Universities of that era electing to compete for scientific eminence and scholarly prestige became known as "research universities." In the decades prior to 1890 the task of research—the discovery of new knowledge—had been added incrementally to the professor's role at universities such as Johns Hopkins, Columbia, Harvard, and Clark. Despite that fact, stocking the undergraduates' (mostly elite white males) minds with knowledge remained the professor's pivotal task throughout post-K–12.

Nevertheless, UC president Harper began, in dramatic fashion, to turn that priority set on its head, thereby helping to bring about a *transformation*—a sea change. In his new university, Harper declared, "the work of investigation [is] primary, the work of giving instruction secondary."[4] In effect, Harper rewrote the job description of the professor. Bear in mind, however, that his revision of that role made a fundamental distinction between graduate and undergraduate teaching. Although the professor was obliged to continue stocking undergraduates' minds, he or she could no longer be content to do that for graduate students. The number one priority of graduate teaching became instead to produce researchers:

> It is only the man who has made investigation who may teach others to investigate. Without this spirit in the instructor and without his example, students will never be led to undertake the work.[5]

What's more, he put teeth into his new job profile by declaring that promotion and salary would be based "more largely" on the professor's research than on his undergraduate teaching. Pre-Harper, the typical U.S. professor would likely feel that "who I *am* is a *teacher* who also happens to be doing some research." But post-Harper, the successful professor would likely feel that "who I *am* is a *researcher* who also happens to be doing some teaching." To be sure, Harper was not the first university president, nor was UC the first university, to adopt the revolutionary idea that universities were primarily "in the business of discovering new knowledge" and only secondarily committed to being the "inheritors and purveyors of the store of existing knowledge."[6] But Harper ranked far above all other university presidents of his time, first, in terms of his skills at fomenting the revolution, and second, in his ability to guarantee that, once in place, it would resist successfully any efforts to revert back to the old-style university through some sort of counterrevolution.[7]

THE GOLDEN AGE (1945–1975)—
A BOLD NEW SOCIAL CONTRACT

Although the emergence of the research university was indeed a spectacular sea change, the subsequent transitions into the fourth and fifth eras, while quite significant, were somewhat less of a genuine makeover. They were instead a series of noteworthy developments in the maturation of post-K–12 in general and of the research university in particular. The fourth era (1945–1975) was called "mass higher education." Cohen also called it "higher education's golden age," and that was indeed the case for a number of reasons. That era was launched in large part by a report called *Science, the Endless Frontier.*[8] Prepared around the close of World War II by a commission of academics, government officials, and influential citizens outside of government, that report upgraded the mid-nineteenth century social contract known as the Land Grant Act.

The report reaffirmed the previous social contract and expanded it beyond the sciences, medicine, and engineering to cover all other parts of the university, including the social sciences. The federal and state governments agreed to support the universities in their pursuit of knowledge. Professors were entirely free to choose the type of research or scholarship they wished to pursue, and also to teach in any ways they deemed appropriate. In exchange for such generous support and an extraordinary degree of self-determination, professors consented to a *gentleman's agreement*—a tacit understanding with government. And that was "the hope that significant benefits would accrue to American society" from their research and teaching.[9] Government became, more than ever before, the "patron" of higher education.

Among other things, that updated social contract stimulated an era of stupendous growth throughout the entire post-K–12 enterprise—in the numbers of students and professors, in the creation of new campuses, and in the construction of new classrooms, office and laboratory buildings, and dormitories. Moreover, all of that was made possible, of course, by the vast outlays of dollars from federal and state governments. A big chunk of those dollars was funneled indirectly to colleges and universities via the GI Bill for returning World War II veterans. The GI Bill paid for, among other things, their tuition, books, and housing costs. That period of unprecedented expansion contributed to the broad expansion of higher education beyond the province of elite white males. A college degree gradually became widely accessible to lower-middle-class and working-class white men, and then later to women, and finally to minorities.

And, as those dollars came flooding into state schools, a number of schools elected to evolve into something they had not previously been, namely, research universities. Many of those schools became known as the state's "flagship" universities. They resolved to compete with the elite private schools by plunging into the chase for national eminence via research—chiefly in the sciences, medicine, and technology, but also in the social sciences, humanities, and the nonscience professional schools. Although James S. Fairweather described this frenetic competition as the "mimicry of elites," he was being neither cynical nor sarcastic.[10] Fairweather simply told it the way it was and is—he captured the reality that throughout post-K–12, the maximum levels possible of status, prestige, influence, and money were and are reserved for research universities. Schools seeking those highly desirable rewards were and are persuaded they have no options but to behave like (i.e., mimic) the schools that already possessed the high levels of prestige and status—private schools such as the University of Chicago, Stanford, and Princeton, or public schools that had gotten into the prestige-ratings game very early in the twentieth century, for example, the University of Michigan. Recall, for example, that in the preface I described my arrival at Indiana University–Bloomington at about the time it was being entirely made over from what it had been previously (my senior colleagues called it a "cow college") into a fully developed research university—intent on competing successfully in the strenuous race for research dollars, and for the status and prestige they make happen.

The vast numbers of government dollars flowing into post-K–12 during that fourth era brought about yet another significant evolutionary development. State schools that "had begun as post-high school academies, normal schools, [public] liberal arts colleges, schools of agriculture, [schools of] industrial arts and home economics, and of engineering and business administration" morphed into comprehensive universities.[11] Comprehensive universities began to offer undergraduates a complete menu of courses and majors—a bill of fare that before that time had been provided solely by the state's flagship universities.

The latter didn't seem to mind the competition for students because there were plenty to go around and, in any case, the flagship schools were preoccupied mutating into research institutions. Comprehensive universities got busy stocking undergraduates' minds over the full range of the knowledge spectrum. Instead of focusing narrowly on only one area (e.g., home economics or K–12 education), the comprehensive institution now offered the student virtually the same broad array of majors as she or he might get at the state's flagship school. In addition, most comprehensive universities began to offer master's degrees, and some even provided doctoral degrees in a few fields, for example, education.

THE POST-GOLDEN AGE (1976–1998)— *THE SOCIAL CONTRACT UNFULFILLED*

Cohen chose the phrase "contemporary era" to describe his fifth time frame (1976–1998).[12] That tag fails, however, to capture the important events and trends that were then occurring throughout post-K–12. We can, nonetheless, readily infer what was happening when we recall that "golden age" was the name of the fourth era. If post-K–12 had indeed attained the pinnacle of its existence during the fourth era (in terms of money, expansion of students, faculty and facilities, and officials' and citizens' feelings of amity and goodwill), then the fifth had to be marked by one of two trends. There was either a plateau effect—a leveling out of the good fortunes of higher education—or a decline in its fortunes. It turns out that both features surfaced during the fifth era—first the plateau effect, and later on the decline.

Many observers noted that anything that had gotten as huge and as dominant as post-K–12 was bound to be subjected to microscopic scrutiny. Chapter 3 describes, for example, how the 1960s student activists took a long and hard look into the inner sanctum of the research university and didn't much care for what they saw.[13] Among their numerous complaints was that professors invested so much time and energy striving for national eminence for themselves and their school that they had few creative juices left over to pour into students. Activists charged that professors were so busy mimicking the elite in order to gain international recognition that their level of stocking the students' minds had descended into second-rate status. To be sure, that complaint was not new—it had in fact surfaced repeatedly throughout the twentieth century.[14]

What was markedly different, however, about the 1960s was the extensive media attention attracted by activist complaints about teaching, as well as by a range of additional activist complaints over what they termed as the "corporate" university. Notwithstanding the fact that most citizens and public officials (elected, appointed) deplored the unruly and disruptive campus protests by students (covered in minute detail by TV cameras) that occasionally turned ugly, there seeped slowly into the public consciousness the barely perceptible sense that professors and universities might perhaps be accountable first and foremost to themselves. The interests of the student, community, and the larger society appeared to end up a distant second when compared with the university's quest for scientific and scholarly eminence.

Harper's conviction (shared by most early twentieth-century professors) that the university was "in every sense an institution of public service" seemed like a quaint relic from the ancient past—a shibboleth intoned at commencement to assure parents and also used when administrators went hat in hand to legislators asking for more money. In essence, public officials and interested citizens were starting to wonder if professors and universities were holding up their end of the bold social contract devised at mid-century.

Payback Time

As the fifth era wended its way, what at first was merely a nebulous sensation slowly got more and more substantial and less ill defined.[15] It got increasingly common for officials and other friendly critics to apply unfamiliar and unsettling buzzwords such as "assessment" and "accountability" to universities.[16] Another frequently heard term was "quality," alongside its sister expressions "productivity" and "value-added." The critics observed that during the last third of the twentieth century business, government, and K–12 were, more than ever before, being subjected to a broad array of extensive and intensive pressures for accountability. And so, puzzled the critics, by what divine right does post-K–12 get to be let off the hook of the increasingly widespread practice of answerability? Why is it free of the obligation to demonstrate that it too is indeed a good steward of the public trust, to say nothing of the public purse?[17]

But, for its part, "much of higher education did not take kindly" to the insinuation that what they did for the benefit of students and society could somehow be assessed in a manner similar to a corporation measuring its efficiency and quality in the production, say, of its widgets.[18] Academics responded that the essence of the research and teaching enterprise discharged by professors was and is far too intangible and much too subtle to be conceived of as some sort of readily measurable "product" or "outcome." They invoked an ethical aura over the ways they did their work, claiming that any modifications imposed on their efforts by outsiders would simply compromise the integrity of both research and teaching. In effect, professors responded to officials and others puzzling over accountability with *Trust us.*

We're the experts, and we know what we're doing regarding the education of students and regarding the contributions we're making to human betterment via our research. We know what's appropriate for post-K–12, and any problems with the status quo could be solved if public officials would simply give us more money and greater autonomy.

Although that might seem like a perfectly sensible response, officials and other critics weren't buying it. The academics' arguments that they were the ultimate arbiters of quality teaching, research, and service "were convincing few people outside the academy."[19] The basic reason for the outsiders' skepticism was the perceived failure of post-K–12 to make good on its long-standing promises. It was not, in the view of many outsiders, honoring the terms of its social contract. In order to get financial support and professorial autonomy, universities had promised virtually anything society wanted to hear but had delivered a whole lot less:

> For decades, they had promised that if only enough funds were forthcoming, they could equalize opportunity, produce better citizens, ameliorate social problems, train workers for any emergent field, enhance the development of industry, and enrich the culture of the broader community. By the end of the century, *it was payback time.*[20]

Recall from chapter 1 that way back in 1969 Joseph Spengler had warned the social sciences that payback time could not be delayed indefinitely. He asserted that those who "control the power of the purse demand results" from social scientists and other academics. The results refer, among other things, to the contributions to human betterment that social science had promised since the days of Harper and Small. It's not by chance that most of the items on Cohen's list are unfulfilled promises made by the social sciences, for example, equalize opportunity, create better citizens, relieve social problems, and enrich community culture. On the flip side, it's no accident that he didn't cite a comparable array of unfulfilled promises made by the sciences and technology.

And, very likely, that's because officials and citizens perceive (rightly or wrongly) that for the most part the sciences are delivering on many of their promises to enhance human betterment—especially in areas such as health and medicine, as well as technology. Hence, when critics complain that professors are accountable solely to each other—and not to the public—for what they do with their public moneys, the sciences can demur in a relatively convincing manner if the specific grievance is about contributions to the larger society.[21] Notwithstanding, when the critics target what the introduction called quality undergraduate education, they indeed have the scientists as well as all other academics in their crosshairs.[22]

Check/Checkmate

Social scientists are, in short, extremely hard-pressed to raise plausible objections to the critics' complaints either about undergraduate education or their service to the larger society. Although chapter 1 suggested that the elites who control the several social science disciplines are distressed over their apparent irrelevance to society, they evince little willingness to march aggressively in the direction of greater social significance. They are loath to venture beyond the public enlightenment model that Thomas, Park, and their colleagues devised so long ago.[23]

Furthermore, in the atypical event a social scientist might, in some fashion, seek to unite understanding with redirection in order to achieve human betterment, he or she could wind up facing one or more of the several of the perils noted in chapter 1. Recall that if, in the interests of being useful and relevant to society, a social scientist might try to break free from the "social science bag" and to follow Rossi's route of blending understanding with actual redirection, he or she runs the risk of biting and enraging the hand (external funding sources) that feeds him or her. Second, in trying to do any type of research that "matters," she or he runs the risk of ignoring criteria established by the elite for prestige and status. And, by ignoring those criteria, the social scientist places his or her hopes for tenure, promotion, and salary increases under a cloud of doubt.

In any event, public officials were, during the fifth era, becoming increasingly impatient with the "trust us" mantra chanted by many professors as a comeback to their demands for accountability. And so for a while during that period, public officials tried to get post-K–12 administrators to pressure faculty to "do something" to show they took seriously the officials' insistence on faculty answerability.[24] The "something" turned out, however, to be certain limited practices that were relatively superficial and quite easy to get a handle on—things such as teaching more classes and/or more students, being more available to students for advising by spending more time in one's office, and so forth. And the perennial complaint regarding mediocre teaching was ostensibly dealt with by requiring every professor to have her/his course formally evaluated by its students at semester's end. The results of that entire array of practices (put in place, allegedly, to ensure accountability) were decidedly mixed, largely because over the years academics became exceedingly adept at tweaking such directives to make it seem they're compliant with the letter of the law, while at the same time cleverly circumventing its spirit.[25]

Despite those adroit maneuvers and simplistic practices, officials have by no means been duped into believing they've actually gotten professors to change their ways in any fundamental senses. The upshot is that officials are just as mindful as professors that the two sides are presently deadlocked in a stalemate. Clara M. Lovett—president emerita of Northern Arizona University—describes the prevailing relationship between public officials and professors as adversarial and antagonistic.[26] She believes that the "clash of cultures" between officials and professors has resulted in a number of unforeseen and unfortunate consequences. The most tragic of these, she says, is that the "we-they mindset" felt by each side has ignited so much hostility, suspicion, and mistrust that the best interests of students and society invariably get blocked out.

Events, however, throughout the larger society soon began to overtake the convoluted chess game between officials and academics. The post-golden age witnessed a steady and seemingly inexorable falling off in real dollars funneled to higher education by both the federal and state governments.[27] In 1990, state appropriations to the Pennsylvania State University, for example, made up 21 percent of its total budget. By 2000, the state proportion had dropped to 13 percent.[28] For the University of Washington, comparable figures went down from 35 percent to 28 percent. And at the University of Wisconsin, comparable figures went down from 36 percent to 31 percent. That descending slope is being repeated in virtually every state, leading Duke University's Stuart Rojstaczer to suggest that the seemingly boundless largesse of the golden age (with its golden goose) is "gone for good."[29]

Officials justify their steady reductions in funding for post-K–12 by pointing to the increasingly urgent demands for state dollars from K–12, Medicaid, Medicare, children and families, transportation, prisons, and so forth. In recent years, citizens' resistance to higher taxes, as well as the high costs of combating terrorism, have also been added to the officials' list of legitimate competing demands.[30] And there's no doubt that the rival claims for finite state resources are real, persuasive, and eminently worthy. At the same time, it's equally true that in light of how academics balk at officials' demands for accountability, officials were slowly drained of their golden-age inclination to view post-K–12 as having a unique entitlement to the funding trough.[31] There is a

> growing frustration on the part of many state leaders about what they perceive as higher education's lack of accountability and its unwillingness to consider the changes characterizing other parts of society.[32]

Loss of a Singular Status

But perhaps the most unfortunate consequence of the impasse between officials and academics during the winding down of the fifth era is that higher education surrendered an element far more valuable than any amount of dollars per se. Post-K–12 appears to have relinquished the lofty symbolic meanings affixed to it throughout much of its history in the United States. Those special meanings were captured by Harper's simple faith that the university is "in every sense an institution of public service." Divested of its principled advantage (its high moral ground), and thus its unique status, officials now tend to view post-K–12 in much the same light as its rivals for funds, and so they toss its appeals into the same in-box with those of its competing supplicants. It is, furthermore, placed at the bottom of the in-box. As a budget assistant to the governor of Washington state put it, "Once all the other decisions are made, the Legislature will look at the table, see what change is left, and that's what goes to higher education."[33]

Today, post-K–12 is, for the most part, perceived as simply another pesky interest group much more absorbed with self-interest than with the greater good of the larger whole. Or as one professor put it, "Politicians with their fingers to the wind have figured out what we would rather not admit—that the people paying the bills don't like or respect us as much as they once did."[34] The disillusionment of public officials arises from feelings of trust betrayed. As they construct the situation, post-K–12 has not, by and large, been faithful to the solemn vows it undertook by signing on to the mid-century social contract

THE DECLINE OF THE RESEARCH UNIVERSITY AND THE RISE OF THE ENTREPRENEURIAL UNIVERSITY—*ERA 6*

Although Cohen did not label the sixth era in the story of American higher education, he did, nonetheless, capture its incipient spirit. As the fifth era was winding down, the sixth was coming into being and, like the third era, it was indeed a genuine sea change. It was the emergence of the entrepreneurial epoch:

> The institutions remained opportunistic: they followed the money and took on whatever projects an agency was willing to fund. They indulged themselves in internecine warfare over student admissions, curricular emphases, and faculty promotion criteria. The idea that higher education could reform itself or even that it maintained consistency in its goals and processes was outstandingly archaic in a system as large as this one had become.[35]

In all fairness to post-K–12, a principal reason the institutions were compelled to follow the money wherever it led was because of the steady reductions in funding—especially by state legislatures. But those reductions arose in large part because universities had abandoned the high moral ground they'd previously occupied. They'd squandered an advantage once perceived as their virtual birthright. Furthermore, they've been unable and/or unwilling to try to reclaim some of that lost ground by, say, entering into a meaningful dialogue with officials over the issue of their accountability.

Mark G. Yudoff (chancellor of the University of Texas higher education system) suggested that the upshot of this complex amalgam of social forces is that the public research university as we knew it in the twentieth century is now "dead."[36] Other observers recognize that same trend, and describe what's happening as "the fall of the flagships."[37] Another observer spoke of the "disappearing state in public higher education" and warned that even with the end of the recession of the early 2000s, officials will not repeat what they've done in prior years, namely, increase significantly their support of public colleges and universities.[38]

Yudoff's stark and dramatic assessment reflected the fact that public officials have in essence cut—or at least severely crimped—the singular umbilical cord that once generously sustained the post-K–12 enterprise. Perceiving a lack of commitment on the part of many professors to the old social contract, they've reacted by likewise pulling back from its terms. Hence, in order to survive and thrive, universities have had no choice but to look elsewhere for sustenance. One obvious source is student tuition that, in the fourth and fifth eras, public colleges and universities kept relatively low. More recently, however, most states have been raising tuition and fees at a pace far exceeding the rate of inflation.[39] A striking example of this trend occurred in 2004 when "tuition at the nation's pubic universities rose an average of 10.5 percent . . . the second largest increase in more than a decade. It is the first time that the average tuition" at the nation's public universities has surpassed $5,000.[40]

The second—and, in the long run, perhaps far more significant—source of alternative sustenance is the external funding, or the money trail cited by Cohen. Imported dollars may come from the government agency or the private foundation and, increasingly, from commercial and business organizations. Dennis Tsichritzis observes that agencies, foundations, and companies alike want to use their money to "buy" what he calls "innovation."[41] On the flip side, university researchers (just like researchers working under the aegis of independent firms) want to "sell" their services in order to satisfy the buyers' wants. In that same vein, chapter 1 noted that, among the life sciences, distinctions between being situated within a university vis-à-vis being situated within the marketplace are getting increasingly hazy.[42] Researchers move back and forth all the time between the two settings.

Although such a marketplace was indeed developing during the fourth and fifth eras, both sellers and buyers in today's marketplace are impelled by a much greater sense of urgency than ever before to *deal*. Instead of being the grand patron of university research, as it was in the twentieth century, the government has now instead become a procurer of university research in the same senses that it acquires any other types of goods (office equipment) and services (lawn maintenance) from any other sources.[43] The unique partnership between government and universities that once lay at the heart of the old social contract now seems as out of date as the time period in which it was conceived and nurtured.

The upshot of those striking transformations is that the research marketplace in the sixth era is a considerably more frenetic and consequential place than it ever was in the fourth and fifth eras. Sellers—especially universities—"cannot afford to stay out" of the marketplace as they might have done in the twentieth century.[44] The basic reason they're compelled to plunge in and to succeed is that schools failing to compete effectively "will," predicts Tsichritzis, "slowly drift downward to the level of the community college."[45] "Downward" implies two linked components. First is money. Public colleges and universities need desperately to replace the plentiful dollars that once flowed into their coffers from the public till. They now face a huge imperative to keep on increasing their levels of extramural funding.

Second, and exceedingly vital, are the national prestige and status rankings. Although once obscure to the public and of interest only to academics, the annual rankings of colleges and universities compiled, for instance, by *US News & World Report* are now featured on sources as diverse as CNN, *USA Today,* and NPR.[46] The incessant media hype leads parents and their college-bound children to take it as an immutable article of faith that the big-name schools (i.e., the most prestigious based on research and scholarship) provide the best undergraduate education.[47] And, at the same time, being successful at selling their wares in the new marketplace is how universities of lesser prestige and status obtain the resources necessary to get a big name. The outside dollars, in effect, enable them to mimic the elite. Tsichritzis's fundamental argument is that it's impossible for schools ever to remain at any fixed point in the fierce competition for external dollars and for status. And if they're not moving up, there's only one other way to go.

The Holy Grail of Innovation

Just as sellers feel much more keenly than ever before the incessant need to market their wares, Tsichritzis argues that buyers are likewise under greater pressure than ever before to purchase innovation. Recall from chapter 1 that the sciences are on the trail of both understanding and redirection or change. The change might be basic (with no apparent practical application), or it could have immediate pragmatic implications. We would expect that, in most cases, in order to be construed as an innovation, the change is likely to carry certain pragmatic implications, even if the possibilities are limited, and even if they are not yet readily perceived. Characterizing change as innovation presumes that the change is—or will be at some indeterminate future point—an advance over whatever exists right now. Innovation suggests progress of some sort; the change is presumably for the better. Better, of course, than the present, namely, the status quo. The sciences thrive in the twenty-first-century marketplace because they have been and continue to be all about innovation—that is their stock-in-trade.

The notion of innovation is well understood in the commercial realm. Yesterday's immense room-size mainframe computers were replaced by today's unpretentious laptops. Though far superior to the old dinosaurs, the laptop itself is highly vulnerable to being replaced by smaller and more sophisticated equipment that is far more capable of meeting the user's ever-changing needs.[48] But government, too, is in the market for innovation. Recently, for example, NASA requested bids to design the next generation of space vehicles. More than one hundred universities (sellers) applied, and the $16 million contract was finally awarded to a consortium of seven universities headed by the University of Florida.[49] But quite apart from commercial interests (computer hardware), and technology (spacecraft), innovation is also a prime objective of government agencies charged, for instance, with improving the health of U.S. citizens. Those agencies, along with drug firms, are intensely interested in buying biological and chemical research targeted, say, on treating and/or preventing afflictions such as HIV-AIDS, the many types of cancers, Alzheimer's, and so on.

One reason today's commercial interests feel so keenly the pressure to purchase innovation is the rapid obsolescence of many of today's products and technologies. Private firms that rely for profits on what they offer today—apart from simultaneously investing in what their firm might offer tomorrow—stand to lose their competitive edge. Second, Tsichritzis notes that although in the past companies expected to derive innovation from their own research and development division, the notion of corporate research and development (R&D) is itself becoming increasingly less common.[50] Instead, companies are finding it more cost-effective to outsource their demand for innovation to universities or to independent research firms. Hence, companies whose internal resources once enabled them to stay out of the marketplace now find it both necessary and useful to plunge into the frenetic competition. The increasing array of buyers— urgently demanding innovation—has had its predictable effect on greatly expanding the numbers of sellers among universities, private firms, and, more recently, independent contractors via the Web.[51] The sciences (whether in or out of the universities) are well positioned to take advantage of the growing demand for more sellers. In recent years, they've expanded and intensified their long-standing efforts to get research moneys from external sources, and they remain at the forefront of university efforts to mine those sources.

Contrariwise, the concept of innovation is, needless to say, wholly extraneous to contemporary social science, if not utterly foreign. It is decidedly not part of our everyday vocabulary. Redirection in general and innovation in particular are issues found neither at the core nor at the periphery of the peculiar spin of basic social science. Although the closest label we possess, noted chapter 1, is "application," that notion is seldom if ever viewed as some sort of innovation that we might be interested in "marketing."[52] There are several reasons for that set of circumstances, and chapter 1 identified some of them. Regardless of the array of reasons, the point is that unlike the sciences, the social sciences are hardly in the business of selling innovation. And, as painful as that reality might feel, it nonetheless places the social sciences at a distinct disadvantage in today's research marketplace—a market insistent on innovation and disposed to buy little else.

The Evolution of a Distinctive Role and Identity

Recall that the emergence of the twentieth-century research university went hand in glove with Harper's reconstruction of the role and identity of the professor. The nineteenth-century priority of teaching over research was reversed. It follows that within the old-style research university, "researcher" became the professor's prime identity and role. In analogous fashion, the evolution of what many observers call the "entrepreneurial university" is being accompanied by yet another reconstruction of the professor's identity and role. During the glory days of the conventional research university, the well-worn cliché "Publish or perish" was said to be the driving force behind the professor's activities. But in the entrepreneurial university, that maxim is, in a very real sense, *so* twentieth century, and perhaps even passé:

> In many fields, the real pressure is not to publish, but to be a successful entrepreneur capable of attracting the resources to support not only one's own activities, but also one's students and department.[53]

In effect, a slowly growing number of professors—scientists in particular— are electing to make the role and identity of *entrepreneur* an inherent and essential element of their personal and professional makeup.[54] Within the emerging entrepreneurial university, the maxim for success is becoming Hustle or atrophy—compelling Publish or perish to move over and share the limelight at center stage.

Today's professor qua entrepreneur no longer has any choice—no twenty-first-century option—but to "hustle" in order to keep on accumulating research dollars from today's distinctive marketplace.[55] Negative connotations aside, the term "hustle" or "hustler" also conveys a positive meaning, as in baseball when we say "the infielder hustles." Whether ballplayer or entrepreneur, a "hustler" is a person who works or moves energetically and rapidly and with a lot of drive. To be a successful academic entrepreneur one must hustle, and that means searching continually for several different sources of funds at the same time. The fact that she or he gets a "hit" (succeeds in landing an external grant or contract) in no way diminishes the hustler's never-ceasing marketplace activity. The successful hustler hires students (graduate and sometimes undergraduate), nontenured PhDs, and postdocs in order to fulfill the terms of the grant or contract she or he has obtained, while at the same time remaining occupied at mining additional funding sources. As a successful entrepreneur in our chemistry department said to me while speaking of his never-ending quest for money, "We're always on the edge of a cliff." Or, remarked a nontenured PhD physicist working in another shop, "I'm only sure of one year at a time, because I'm totally dependent on the grants and contracts that I, and others in our group, manage to get." Or, as another observer observed about the typical medical school professor required unremittingly to obtain large sums of money in order to meet a host of departmental needs (quite apart from his own research costs): *"Not an easy life."*[56]

UK scientist Phil Dee used the label PI (principal investigator) as another way of labeling the frenetic hustler feature of the entrepreneur's role.[57] Although the old-style researcher in the old-fashioned research university would, from time to time, do PI-type activities, the PI feature was seldom intrinsic to his or her identity. But, argues Dee and many others, "success in [today's] ruthless battle for the top of the heap" cannot be gained apart from incorporating the PI feature into one's psyche.[58] Hence, it may not be too far off the mark to suggest that the identity of the successful professor in the entrepreneurial university might perhaps be captured in this manner: "Who I *am* is an *entrepreneur/PI* who also does research and, much further down the priority list than in the twentieth century, is also an undergraduate teacher." The twentieth-century teacher-scholar was fundamentally an employee of the state (hired hand) and ultimately dependent on it. During those times when he or she was unable and/or unwilling to get external funding, he or she could count on the state for sustenance.

Conversely, today's entrepreneur/PI, whether tenured or not, is much closer to being an independent contractor or consultant—an employee of the state much more in name than in reality. Interestingly enough, Richard Lanham tells us that the

> professors who staffed the medieval university were individual entrepreneurs. They lived by fees paid to them by the students for their lectures.[59]

The university or city provided the hall but little else. Boring lecturers got few students and thus made less money than lecturers who were scintillating and entertaining. In effect, market forces drove the demand for professors and determined their relative compensation. Later on, that entrepreneurial model was replaced by the employee model of the last several centuries. But who's to say the hired-hand model is necessarily the best arrangement for today's professors, students, and society? The ongoing emergence of the twenty-first-century entrepreneurial model may perhaps be a case of déjà-vu all over again.

State-Located, Independently Supported

The entrepreneurial university, alongside the entrepreneur/PI, has, in effect, fashioned an alternative umbilical cord to replace the conduit (the lifeline severely crimped if not yet cut by today's public officials) that nurtured the old-style twentieth-century research university. The University of Michigan (UM) is one among many examples of today's public entrepreneurial university.[60] UM has been remarkably successful in siphoning off enormous amounts of dollars from today's emerging research market, in which selling innovation is the key to continued successes. UM's successes coupled with reduced state funding led it to "restructure our finances so that we became, in effect, a privately supported public university."[61] Or as another university president put it, during his tenure "his university had changed from state-supported to state-assisted to state-located."[62]

"Money makes the world go 'round," declares the old saw. In this instance, money (less from the state till coupled with much more from commercial, foundation, and government sources) is, like it or not, transforming the twenty-first-century university along with some of its professors. Money is a huge part of what above was called a sea change—analogous to the influences of industrialization and technology on the universities of the late nineteenth and twentieth centuries. What is more, in this new environment the sciences are for the most part doing quite well at managing their own destinies. Most units within the sciences are becoming very proficient at fashioning their own umbilical cords to sources of sustenance. They have, in effect, been successful at molding a workable alternative to the old social contract.

Fretfulness in the Wake of Success

The success of the academic entrepreneurs does not imply they're free of angst over the new style of university they're conceiving and cultivating.[63] At the same time, they neither regret its creation nor believe that any limits whatsoever should be placed on its continuing development. And, in any case, pleas from any quarter to reign in the enterprise would, needless to say, be sheer folly. The entrepreneurial university is here to stay, and the sciences et al. will remain at center stage in its maturation and enlargement.

Not only that, the ranks of schools determined to mimic prestigious public universities have begun to swell, and can only swell further. Recall that during higher education's golden age many schools morphed into comprehensive universities, offering as wide a range of major fields and course options to undergraduates as did the state's flagship schools. Furthermore, a growing number began to compete at the master's and doctoral levels. But today's comprehensive universities and four-year state colleges, no less than their sister flagship schools, are feeling the pinch of legislative downsizing in funds made available to post-K–12. The upshot is that they, too, are now entering the twenty-first-century research marketplace—they likewise yearn to become sellers of innovation and thereby try to mimic the elite. Consequently, they're determined to follow the money as diligently as do their sister flagship schools.

A headline, for example, in the *Chronicle of Higher Education* stated, "Power-Building President Seeks Stature" for Miami's Florida International University (FIU).[64] For almost twenty years, Modesto Maidique has sought to transform FIU (launched in 1972) into another UCLA—a distinguished, high-profile, urban campus. Although not yet there by any means, external research funding during his tenure has increased fourfold to $61.2 million, enrollment has doubled to more than thirty-two thousand students, and he has added some twenty doctoral programs. The feverish quest to become a serious player in the game of mimicking the elite drives every facet of FIU's existence. And because big-time sports is associated with big-time research," FIU is now preparing itself for NCAA Division I competition.[65]

Nonetheless, when the journalist tactfully inquired about "academic quality," Maidique admitted that thus far in FIU's development that issue has remained secondary. He pledged, however, to attend to academic quality during the "next phase of his plan." Not to be left behind or outdone, most other comprehensive universities (and some colleges) in Florida and throughout the Sunbelt—and indeed the entire United States—are reenacting the FIU scenario. Also known as "wannabe" schools,[66] those comprehensive institutions are, in effect, leapfrogging over the rapidly vanishing entity of state-supported research university in hopes of competing successfully for money and status among the ranks of the up-and-coming privately funded, state-located, entrepreneurial universities.

But the question that Maidique so deftly sidestepped is precisely the issue now troubling many academics throughout North America and Europe.[67] The entrepreneurial university cleverly sweeps the long-standing issue of accountability under the rug by seeking and getting funds from sources beyond the control of state officials. It is axiomatic that if A is dependent on B (e.g., the legislature) for resources, and thus subject to its control, A may gain autonomy from B only to the degree that A accesses resources apart from B. Although that is precisely what the entrepreneurial university is all about, many insiders nonetheless worry that, as a result, it is moving even further away than did the twentieth-century research university from Harper's simple faith that post-K–12 is first and foremost an institution of public service. That historic faith was, after all, the engine that powered the old social contract—in both its nineteenth- and mid-twentieth-century modes.

Although no professor would ever quarrel with that historic faith, the devil is in the details of what it means, and especially in who gets to decide those details. Outsiders and some insiders argued persuasively that even the twentieth-century research university was not keeping the historic faith in the ways it ostensibly served its students, its community, and the larger society. And, if outsiders perceived the research university as being unresponsive to their demands for accountability, they view the emerging entrepreneurial university as being incredibly less receptive. Its capability to disregard external pressures stems from its pipeline to alternative funding sources. Critics tend to view its independence as a mixed blessing. On the positive side, its freedom permits it to pursue and explore a wide range of research opportunities in an unfettered manner. And many of those projects (though by no means all) do in fact expand our understanding of the world and also contribute significantly to human betterment. Furthermore, the research funds make it possible to hire and train students—principally graduate, but also some undergraduate—in the ideas and methods of demonstrably important fields. The funds also help maintain the researchers' departments, to say nothing of the many perks the department would not otherwise enjoy. In addition, the moneys employ professional researchers who for one reason or another opt not to follow the typical tenure-track career path.

But how much freedom and independence are too much of a good thing? How far can the entrepreneurial model go before it loses entirely its moorings to the historic significance of service to undergraduates, community, and society? How far before the distinctions are entirely obliterated between the entrepreneurial university and a collection, say, of independent research firms, or wholly autonomous contractors?[68] And, after all is said and done, would it make any conceivable difference to anyone if the twenty-first-century entrepreneurial university no longer made any pretense at all of maintaining a viable connection to its historic faith?

FLOUNDERING IN THE IMPOVERISHED BACKWATERS

Those are the kinds of questions that worry an array of academics and friendly critics alike.[69] Related to those thorny matters are the inevitable inequities that arise between the sciences and other parts of the university that simply cannot compete with them as sellers of innovation. Because they cannot contend for resources at the same level, one observer has cautioned that when compared to the sciences other programs—including the social sciences—"with fewer opportunities for external support can become impoverished backwaters."[70]

Even as far back as the golden-age era, Clark Kerr, the head of the University of California system of higher education, observed that the *uni*versity had morphed into the *multi*versity.[71] Although a core set of values and objectives—alongside a shared vocabulary and guiding vision—may long ago have bound together the *uni*versity's several disparate parts, Kerr said that such a notion became archaic in the twentieth century. Replacing it was the reality that within the research multiversity, each discipline had its own unique language and a set of interests that were quite foreign to those of to other disciplines. The upshot was that professors rarely scaled disciplinary boundaries in order to talk to one another. Indeed, even within the same department, research interests were frequently so narrow and specialized that colleagues seldom shared in-depth conversations with one another about their own work. The cohesiveness and mutually enriching conversations happening among professors from the several social sciences, philosophy, religion, and social service at the University of Chicago around the turn of the twentieth century was, by its close, little more than a revered relic from the ancient past.

Despite the rigid demarcation of disciplines that characterized the research multiversity, the fact that a pecking order existed among them (led by the sciences) was soft-pedaled. Although distinctions in status and prestige among the broad range of disciplines were clearly visible, the differences were construed as a type of open social class system. It was believed that any discipline could achieve at least some degree of upward mobility by dint of dedication and hard work. But, within the emerging entrepreneurial multiversity, the previous relatively fluid class system is being replaced by a much more rigid caste system. The earlier, more egalitarian class system was buttressed by the terms of the old social contract. Because each discipline was perceived as intrinsically important in its own right, and none was viewed as inherently more worthy than any other, each was allotted an equitable (though by no means equal) share of public moneys.

However, as today's officials steadily reduce the level of public funds available to higher education, disciplines that are most dependent on it (e.g., the social sciences) could end up suffering an inordinate amount. Because, moreover, they're unable to compete at the same level with the sciences in the new marketplace, they may find themselves locked more tightly than ever before into a lesser status from which they have no realistic hopes of ever escaping. Further complicating the matter is the developing tendency of today's administrators to forsake an essential principle of the twentieth-century social contract. Edward J. Ray, provost at Ohio State University (OSU), reported that up until recently, "any new money that came along [from the state] was spread across programs evenly 'like jam.' . . . The first good idea that came in the door got funded."[72]

OSU has, however, now replaced its conventional mode of an even distribution of dollars with an uneven style that Ray called "selective investment." Every OSU unit is now "taxed" (required to give back moneys) and, in turn, the funds are distributed to those units showing the greatest promise of successfully mimicking the elite. Each unit must explain in detail how it would use a windfall of internal dollars to increase its national prestige ranking among all public universities. Administrators at the University of Florida proposed a similar strategic plan for precisely the same reason—to embellish the university's national rankings. Many additional wannabe universities around the United States are devising comparable strategies in order to "squeeze into the top tier" of the research elite.[73]

For the most part, the enriched units at OSU "are using their money to recruit expensive, senior scholars."[74] Each of the recruited scholars had previously established a successful track record in the research marketplace, and the explicit requirement is that they will continue to remain successful entrepreneurs. The quest to mimic the elite in terms of prestige and status is obviously inseparable from success in the marketplace. As a result of their hoped-for success, the privileged units would soon, according to OSU administrators, no longer need nor receive enriched state funding. They would be on their way to the level of independence and self-sufficiency that now characterizes some units at many elite institutions. The successful units would be in the vanguard of OSU's projected metamorphosis into the top-ten tier among twenty-first-century public entrepreneurial universities.

Among the thirteen OSU units initially picked for investment, seven were in the sciences, engineering, or medicine. The six OSU nonscience units receiving the enrichment dollars were economics, English, history, law, political science, and psychology. The long-term success of the new model will, of course, be based on the extent to which each of the thirteen units is able to achieve a relative degree of independence from state funding. If one accepts Tsichritzis's premise that the marketplace is driven by the desire for innovation, it then follows that the units most capable of supplying that commodity would probably be the most successful. And that, in turn, implies that the seven units from the sciences are the most likely to do quite well.

But will enrichment enable the remaining six OSU units to avoid floundering in the impoverished backwaters? For economics, political science, and psychology, the key might perhaps be the extent to which each could somehow break free of their peculiar basic social science spin that disengaged understanding from redirection, and thus from innovation. To be sure, each of those three fields now contains certain subparts that already seek to engage in redirection (as does law), and one might surmise that fact was one reason those four units got enrichment dollars. The rationales for English and history are less apparent. What is beyond dispute, however, is that the surest way for any of the units to avoid being stuck in the impoverished backwaters is to navigate their way out via the entrepreneurial channel. Although the maintenance of the pecking order between the sciences and the others is not in any doubt, it is less clear whether and which of the others can, over a number of years, sustain the kinds of activities necessary to keep on selling their brand of innovation in what promises to become an increasingly competitive national/global marketplace.

AND WHAT OF THE OLD-STYLE TEACHER-SCHOLAR?

Harper was among the very first administrators to aggressively raid other universities for researchers and scholars who could embellish the University of Chicago's quest for worldwide eminence. But, by the time the twentieth century drew to its close, the practice had evolved into its own art form. In order for universities to compete successfully for money in the marketplace, they must first vie with one another for "stars," namely, professors who possess the greatest eminence in their field. In most fields—especially the sciences—the stars have been highly successful at getting grants and contracts. Academics are, in short, not only selling their wares to external buyers, they're also selling themselves to universities willing to bid the highest price for their services. Like any other market, this national academic marketplace means that some professors are more valued than others.[75] The more valued they are, the higher their salary and the greater the perks they're able to command.

At OSU, for instance, the average salary for all full professors in 2000 was $92,200.[76] However, one of the stars hired under its new selective investment model was promised a $220,000 annual salary. A chemist under that new model got $165,000 plus a $2 million start-up package. A historian received $130,000 plus a $12,000 annual research and travel stipend, and a lighter teaching load than the supposedly "less valuable" nonstars in the department.

Furthermore, among elite private universities, the amounts of star moneys for salaries and perks are in a wholly other, and far more elevated, stratosphere altogether. The *New York Times* was not above using a well-known baseball rivalry to describe the competition between, for example, Harvard and Princeton:

> It may not have been comparable to the Yankees buying Babe Ruth from the Red Sox, but Princeton University's trustees this morning approved the acquisition of a major league scholar of African-American studies who has been on the roster of rival Harvard for more than a decade.[77]

Furthermore, Roger Schank observed that when stars are negotiating their deals over salary, equipment, and support services, their teaching load also shows up on the table. A star "may teach as little as one course every two years. On the other hand, his colleague [nonstar] may teach as many as four courses a quarter."[78] Not only that, the star gets to work with small graduate seminars, while the nonstar is required to manage huge sections of undergraduates, often at the introductory level. During the era of the state-supported public research university, such huge inequities in money and teaching load between stars and nonstars were tolerable owing to the premise that a rising tide lifts all boats. The reasoning was that administrators would, out of sheer decency, gradually respond to pressures to bring the salary and the teaching load of nonstars into closer alignment with those of the stars. And that stratagem seemed to work—at least in part—during the years when the twentieth-century umbilical cord was in place. The decency argument made sense within the framework of the old social contract.

But within the market-driven entrepreneurial multiversity, such an argument is far less compelling because it necessarily diverts finite resources from the overarching objective of becoming world-class. At OSU (and similar places) dollars are routinely removed from poor units that have few prospects of escaping poverty and given instead to units that are already better off. They get the added funds because they possess solid prospects for actually getting to be even more well off than they are right now. That strategy is based on the mindset that we should take from the lower class and give to the middle class so they can eventually become upper class. Furthermore, among the units with prospects, there is no longer any compulsion (or resources) to bring the salaries and perks of nonstars into line with those of the newly recruited stars.

The inevitable result of this wholly market-driven approach to faculty rewards was captured by a *New York Times* headline, "Ohio State U Faculty Fed Up with Low Salaries." The journalist cited a professor from the department of psychology (a unit slated for investment) who was leading a public campuswide forum protesting low faculty salaries.[79] According to the professor,

"Many faculty are grossly underpaid, earning less than public high school teachers." And, he added, "Faculty are getting creamed when it comes to salary." It's virtually certain, however, that none of the stars OSU recently recruited via its selective investment strategy was among the professors at the forum protesting low faculty salaries. During the era of the old-style research university, big-time or "hot-shot" researchers coexisted rather amicably with ordinary mortal professors, despite the chasm in their salaries and perks. The nonstars were reasonably compensated because they too (similar to the stars) were perceived as valuable in their own right, although for very different reasons. They provided the bulk of undergraduate teaching and advising, did most of the department's service in the form of routine committee work, and paid close attention to the unit's everyday administrative details.

THE TEACHING PROLETARIAT— *CREDENTIALERS AT WORK*

But given the market-driven characteristics of the twenty-first-century entrepreneurial university, Randall Collins contends that the professor who is not an entrepreneur is in a much more precarious position than was the nonstar within the old-style setting.[80] Collins bases his argument on the premise that the teacher-scholar has two sets of wares to sell, and each is sold in a wholly different marketplace. Alongside the wares peddled to buyers in the research marketplace, she or he also distributes a commodity to buyers (students) in the teaching marketplace. The principal nature of that commodity is stocking the student's mind with knowledge.

Around the turn of the twentieth century, when colleges and universities were inhabited mostly by elite white males, the acquisition of those stores of knowledge was, on the one hand, viewed as a vital objective in and of itself. Familiarity with Greek, Roman, and English literature, an appreciation of painting, sculpture, and classical music, a grasp of philosophy and the history of Western civilization, along with a sense of the elegance of mathematics and the mysteries of science were seen as intrinsically satisfying. Those and similar pursuits (e.g., Latin, Greek, and French languages) made up the *content* of the gentleman's education. An *educated man* was one whose mind was stocked with that type of knowledge. It was believed, moreover, that such content had a liberating effect on the student—it actually lifted him to a higher state of being.

At the same time, the special knowledge those elite men gained was also judged to have a particular utility. It was assumed that the eternal verities and the sound wisdom gleaned from the timeless erudition to which they were exposed enabled those privileged men to be highly effectual once they took their rightful places at the helm of commerce, government, and other parts of society. Although they never used the term *credential* (far too ignoble), that's in effect how the content of their classical liberal arts education was perceived. The unique content to which they were exposed helped to legitimate their access to the prime leadership roles they occupied following commencement.

The numbers, however, of elite white men enrolled in colleges and universities around the turn of the twentieth century was substantially less than 1 percent of the total population.[81] Moreover, Collins reminds us that by 1910, less than 10 percent of the total population held even a high school diploma.[82] He also observes that a major reason why the numbers of college students mushroomed during the twentieth century was the belief in higher education's credentialing function. The conviction spread throughout most segments of the population that the college degree was in fact a necessary credential—but not with the same sense of entitlement assigned previously to the degrees of elite while males. It was instead a voucher—the ticket—into the fierce competition for high-prestige and high-paying jobs. The upshot has been a proliferation of buyers for the college degree qua ticket—so many in fact that Collins asserts our society is now confronted by an inflation of credentialed persons. And, like monetary inflation reducing the value of currency, credential inflation is reducing the value of the college degree. Because so many people have it and/or are getting it, the degree *qua* degree is giving up its scarcity, and thus (like the high school diploma) its relative value.

Nevertheless, there is no sign whatsoever that runaway credential inflation is about to slow down any time soon. On the contrary, during the next couple of decades the demand for the highly prized ticket is expected to escalate still further. In August 2000, Education Secretary Richard W. Riley predicted that during the subsequent ten to fifteen years U.S. college enrollment would grow by 19 percent, or 2.4 million students.[83] Even more striking is the prospect that racial and ethnic minorities could account for some 80 percent of that increase.

During the many decades that the significance of the college degree as a requisite credential skyrocketed, the issue of the *content* of the college degree fell into general disarray.[84] The classic liberal arts curriculum detailed above lost its priority status. It was replaced gradually by more practical courses such as those offered by the professional schools—business, education, engineering, computer science, journalism, and others.

> The academic year 1969–70 was the last year in which a majority of American four-year college and university students graduated from arts and sciences fields. . . . [By 1997–98] more than 58 percent of bachelors' degrees were awarded in occupational fields.[85]

And, of course, students in the liberal arts college are no longer required to fulfill the core classic curriculum in a rigid manner, but are instead given a considerable deal of leeway in the range of electives from which they might choose. Given that the principal objective of the college degree in the fourth and fifth eras gradually became to credential vast numbers of nonelite students for the marketplace (and not to assure he or she had a grasp of Latin or of Greek and Roman history), why not, went the logic, allow the curricula—at least to some degree—to float toward students' needs for marketplace readiness?

That particular question regarding content leads to a second and related issue. How do we verify that the student has in fact learned the type of content she or he actually needs in order to do well in the real world? Back in the old days of the classic liberal arts curriculum, it made sense to give graduating seniors a set of field exams testing their knowledge in areas such as literature, history, languages, philosophy, and even science. Today, however, such a requirement for the public college or university credential would be laughable. Furthermore, well into the fifth era, many graduate programs required applicants to take a Graduate Record Examination (GRE) in the discipline (e.g., chemistry, history) they intended to pursue. The objective was to discover how much content about their chosen discipline they'd absorbed as undergraduates. Today, by contrast, virtually no graduate program (even at elite universities) requires its applicants to take a discipline-specific GRE.[86] The obvious reason for this is that today's undergraduates can select from an almost endless potpourri of courses even within their own major. Hence, there is simply no way for a graduate program to settle on the essential core of knowledge that every applicant should be reasonably expected to possess.

What's happened, in short, is that now (as compared with Harper's time) there's no longer a universal answer to the questions, "What is an educated person? How can we tell when we're looking at one?" As the twentieth century wore on, that question became answered less and less in terms of the *content* of a college degree and more and more in term of the degree *qua* credential. Although saying that *an educated person is someone who has a college degree* begs the question of what *educated* means, it no longer makes any difference. As content has diminished steadily in significance, the credential has by comparison loomed bigger and bigger.

In all fairness to academics, the nebulous character of content during the fourth and fifth eras was one of several reasons they stoutly resisted officials' demands for accountability. Assessing a first-rate professor of undergraduates in Harper's day was far more straightforward because, among other things, there was general agreement among them as to which intellectual issues should appear on the field exams. Teaching was much more of a public enterprise in the sense that although the professor might order his or her classroom in any way she or he saw fit, he or she was at the same time responsible to their colleagues to ready their students to grapple eventually with a set of intellectual issues everyone considered vital.

The situation back then was in certain limited respects similar (though in many other respects quite different) from the recent insistence that K–12 students must demonstrate a minimum level of proficiency in, say, reading and arithmetic. Teachers and their schools are now held accountable—and rewarded or punished—for how well their students perform on statewide standardized tests on both of those subjects. Prior to the recent testing requirements, the prevailing K–12 practice rested on the notion that teaching is a private matter between teacher and student: *I hereby certify that she can read (or do arithmetic) because she has passed my course.* That earlier idea was replaced by the current belief that teaching is a public matter in the sense that *I am now responsible to officials and citizens to enable her to demonstrate in a manner convincing to them (by passing the state exams) that she can indeed read (or do arithmetic).*

Unlike K–12 teachers, college professors have thus far vigorously and with great passion successfully resisted any and all attempts by officials to devise any up-to-date and highly limited versions of the field exam in which students would be required to demonstrate how much content they have or have not absorbed during their college years.[87] On the other side, the late Ernest Boyer was for many years a leading exponent of the goal to make college teaching more public.[88] He reasoned that just as research is a public not a private enterprise, teaching too should be constructed by that same learning-as-community mind-set. Although he did not espouse the idea of the old-style field exam, he insisted that professors should somehow devise contemporary ways to make teaching more of a community endeavor.

By and large, however, Boyer's efforts and those of other academics to interject a note of community-based learning into college teaching have, at best, met with minimal success. The only universally accepted measure of public accountability that academics finally assented to is the use of student rating forms at semester's end.[89] In effect, the credo surrounding the professor's civic accountability existing in Harper's day has given way to a much different reality—a state of affairs that Harper, Dewey, and his colleagues could never have imagined—even in their worst nightmares. Public accountability has been reduced from issues of intellectual rigor to its lowest common denominator—*Did the students like the course? Did they find it interesting and perhaps enjoyable?*

If that is indeed the ultimate public criterion of a good teacher, then it's no surprise that we now have "a growing and increasingly beleaguered teaching proletariat. The material conditions of their lives are poor, and their career tracks are highly uncertain."[90] These are the nonstars (the mortals) located, says Collins, at schools other "than the top of the research elite." They are either unwilling and/or unable to sell their wares at an increasingly fast tempo in the research marketplace. And, precisely because they're not entrepreneurs, their value in the research marketplace is marginal at best. When, moreover, they turn their attention and energies to the alternative teaching marketplace, they discover that there too their value is becoming more and more problematic. If the principal objective of teaching is to get students credentialed, with virtually no public discussion about or *demonstration* of the nature and quality of educational content, then officials are perfectly justified in wondering aloud as to what value to place on credentialing.

And, even more to the point, how should they reward the credentialer? How can officials validly distinguish a poor from an effective credentialer? A *Chronicle* essay about outstanding professors who win teaching awards concluded that actually gauging "greatness" in a teacher is virtually impossible.[91] Ken Bain, however, takes a sharply contrasting point of view. He believes that one can indeed identify what makes a college teacher "great."[92] In any event, the point is that the failure of post-K–12 as a whole to develop public criteria regarding the intangible aspects of quality teaching leaves officials with little choice but to come up with their own rather crude indicators. For example, certain state officials devised a program that pays faculty according the numbers of students they're able to graduate, that is, credential.[93] At the national level, however, the George W. Bush administration attempted to get beyond mere graduation rates. It proposed linking federal dollars for post-K–12 to certifiable criteria that college students have in fact learned important stuff by the time they graduate.[94]

What's happened, in effect, is that academics' adamant refusal to go along with outsiders' efforts to make them more accountable has boomeranged. For instance, the more that academics insisted, first, that each department has the sole right to decide which courses should be offered, and, second, that the professor has the ultimate authority over course content, the more the curricula were taken out of the public realm and put instead into the private sphere. (Not-so-friendly critics snidely label it the realm of the rarefied.)[95] In response to calls for public assessment of the quality of teaching—assessment going beyond the current naïve measures—most academics have responded that the professor is the ultimate judge of such complex issues. They contend, moreover, that in the interests of academic freedom, such issues must only be left to her or him.

And, although those appear to be sensible responses, the upshot has been to shroud college teaching behind an aura of inscrutability. The only thing that everyone (including students) can plainly see and understand is its credentialing function. Moreover, as far as officials and citizens can tell, apart from the numbers they're able to graduate, one credentialer is ultimately as good as any another. Because there's no publicly validated means to distinguish an effective from an ineffective credentialer, there is no reliable way to assign market value. The result is that the individual credentialer is simply one more face within the masses of the teaching proletariat.

One might assume that, given the usual laws of supply and demand, the ever-increasing numbers of students wanting to buy a college degree would enable the credentialers to raise their prices. For one thing, however, unlike the research marketplace, and unlike the medieval university marketplace, buyers and sellers in today's teaching marketplace do not deal directly with one another when it comes to money. There are obviously several intermediate brokers, including public officials and college administrators. Whatever benefits colleges and universities might accrue from hiking tuition, the additional moneys are seldom shared with the credentialing proletariat. Second, there is no shortage of persons holding doctorates willing to enter the proletariat. There is indeed an abundant supply of tenured credentialers able and ready to meet student demand.

Third, post-K–12 routinely hires large numbers of graduate students and increasing numbers of non-tenure-track adjunct professors (many with doctorates) to meet the bourgeoning demands for credentials.[96] Those growing trends have corresponded with a gradual decline in the overall proportion of tenure-track professors at public universities.[97] Finally, the rapid growth in recent years of the for-profit university—whose principal reason for existence, so far at least, is to credential the nontraditional student—expands the total numbers of credentialers available to the entire range of interested buyers. Those for-profit entities are, among other things, experimenting with the use of innovative technologies aimed at reducing the total numbers of credentialers needed to meet the growing demand for what they have to sell. Not only that, for-profit entities are beginning to set their sights on what has thus far been the virtual monopoly held by conventional post-K–12 over traditional (aged eighteen to twenty-four) students.[98]

In short, although officials, citizens, and students obviously consider credentialing vital, the credentialers themselves have so far been unable to make much of a compelling case (apart from the quantity of students they're able to process) as to why any one of them should be rewarded in a distinctive manner. The upshot is that the market value of the credentialer is low and expected to get even lower. Although the projections for the life experiences of the entrepreneur within the emerging twenty-first-century university seem quite promising, the prospects for the credentialer, says Collins, appear far less rosy. Scientists have the least to worry about because they are uniquely situated to take advantage of a broad range of opportunities for entrepreneurship. At the same time, the majority of social scientists (except, as Collins notes, for those few at elite institutions) are at a much greater peril of facing relative impoverishment.

NAVIGATING OUT OF THE IMPOVERISHED BACKWATERS— *SPOTTING AN EMERGING MARKET*

Chapter 1 portrayed the social sciences as being in peril of getting stuck in the shoals of irrelevancy owing in large part to their peculiar spin that divorced understanding from redirection. Chapter 2 has expanded that theme by suggesting that those same shoals could be simultaneously construed as the backwaters of impoverishment. The conundrum confronting the social sciences is that although their peculiar spin served them reasonably well within the twentieth-century university, post-K–12 is not standing still. The ground beneath the social sciences is shifting toward an entrepreneurial model in which buyers are looking for sellers capable of delivering innovation, that is, change or redirection.

Although it sounds neither flattering nor dignified to say that academics market their wares to certain audiences, that uncomfortable (and often unspoken) reality has confronted professors for hundreds of years. One characteristic of a successful entrepreneur in any realm is the capability to identify and target an emerging market, that is, a market where certain kinds of needs, interests, desires, and trends are only just coming into view and are not yet fully formed. Because the entrepreneur has an intuitive sense that in the years to come the new market is very likely to expand and come up with a certain set of demands, she or he begins to position him/herself to try to satisfy those demands. The successful entrepreneur places oneself at the leading edge—on the cusp of efforts aimed at meeting that incipient market's requirements.

The introduction laid out two features that advocates for changing post-K–12 have so far characterized simply as pressing needs. One has to do with the quality of undergraduate education. The second has to do with the matter of resolving urgent social issues. Although the second feature has been the unique province of the social sciences ever since their inception, they have not by and large had much of a track record in meeting that need. For a variety of reasons described in the introduction, as well as in subsequent chapters, both needs are, throughout the course of the twenty-first century, quite likely to evolve into demands. In short, it could be said that both needs may lie at the core of an "emerging market" for post-K–12 change. The possibility is that growing numbers of citizens shall eventually come to demand *both* quality undergraduate learning *and* sustained efforts at the resolution of urgent social issues. Meeting both sets of demands simultaneously could perhaps offer at least some social scientists a means to steer a course out of the impoverished backwaters. It could very well be in their own self-interest to begin positioning themselves to satisfy that emerging market. By establishing themselves as major players within that market, they might perhaps be able to earn greater levels of both tangible and intangible rewards than they could, say, simply by remaining a part of the beleaguered teaching proletariat. Furthermore, satisfying both sets of demands within that emerging market is indisputably the right thing to do. Hence, being enterprising within that type of marketplace implies a union of the pursuit of self-interest with the fulfillment of certain moral obligations. It is both the smart thing and the right thing to do.

NOTES

1. Duderstadt 1999:39.
2. Duderstadt 1999:50.
3. Cohen 1998:2–8.
4. Bulmer 1984:15.
5. Harper, cited in Bulmer 1984:15.
6. Bulmer 1984:15.
7. Bulmer 1984:16.
8. Duderstadt and Womack 2003:53.
9. Duderstadt 2000:111.
10. Fairweather 1996:186.
11. Cohen 1998:189.
12. Cohen 1998:291.
13. Gitlin 1989.
14. Cuban 1999.
15. Wilshire 1990. Zemsky (2003) describes how deeply that perception has sunk into today's public consciousness.
16. Cuban 1999; DeZure 2000; Ruben 1995.
17. Dziech 2002.
18. Cohen 1998:435.
19. Cohen 1998:436.
20. Cohen 1998:436, italics added.
21. Bok 1982:65.
22. Handelsman et al. 2004.
23. Deutscher 2002.
24. Cuban 1999; Cohen 1998.
25. Cuban 1999.

26. Lovett 2001.
27. Hirsch 1999; Williams 1999.
28. Selingo 2003a.
29. Rojstaczer 1999.
30. Janofsky 2002.
31. Lovett 2001.
32. Duderstadt 2000:58.
33. Selingo 2003a:A23.
34. Dziech 2002:B9.
35. Cohen 1998:415.
36. Yudoff 2002. In its place has risen what Duderstadt (2000:49–52) and others call the entrepreneurial university.
37. Gose 2002.
38. Selingo 2003a.
39. "Responding to the Crisis in College Opportunity." January 2004. National Center for Public Policy and Higher Education. www.highereducation.org.
40. Winter 2004.
41. Tsichritzis 1999:100.
42. Powell and Owen-Smith 2002.
43. Duderstadt 2000:118–19. See also Bok 2003a.
44. Tsichritzis 1999:102.
45. Tsichritzis 1999:102.
46. Troop 2003.
47. Mathews 2001; Dash 2004.
48. Ishii 1994.
49. Ciotola 2002; Miller 2002.
50. Tsichritzis 1999:102.
51. Recently, a growing number of companies have found it increasingly cost-effective to post their needs for innovations on the Web. Sellers—usually independent contractors—are offered generous cash incentives for solutions that work. See Paul Kaihla, "Building a Better R&D Mousetrap." *Business 2.0,* pp. 50–52. September 2000.
52. Collins 2002b:42. But exceptions to that conclusion may be found in a new publication—the *Stanford Social Innovation Review*—published by the Center for Social Innovation at the Stanford Graduate School of Business. www.ssireview.com.
53. Duderstadt 2000:153.
54. Clark 2002:328ff.
55. Duderstadt 2000:153.
56. Duderstadt 2000:51, italics added. And see Mangan 2003.
57. Dee 2003a, b.
58. Dee 2003a.
59. Lanham 2002:165.
60. Gose 2002.
61. Duderstadt 1999:51.
62. Rhodes 1999:169.
63. Bok 2003a.
64. Basinger 2001.
65. Sperber 2000.

66. Arnone 2003.
67. See Hirsch and Weber 1999, passim.
68. Powell and Owen-Smith 2002.
69. Bok 2003a; Hirsch and Weber 1999.
70. Duderstadt 2000:172.
71. Kerr 1963.
72. Wilson 2001:A8.
73. Arnone 2003.
74. Wilson 2001.
75. Burke 1988.
76. Wilson 2001.
77. Steinberg 2002.
78. Schank 2000.
79. Dippold 2002.
80. Collins 2002a.
81. Cohen 1998.
82. Collins 2002.
83. Steinberg 2000.
84. Bloom 1987.
85. Brint 2000b:231.
86. Schank 2000.
87. See the chapter 7 discussion of the Academic Learning Compact recently imposed by the trustees responsible to the Florida legislature for overseeing the state's public universities.
88. Boyer 1990; Shulman 2004.
89. See Seldin (1997) for arguments re additional means to assess teaching, namely, the "teaching portfolio."
90. Collins 2002:B20.
91. Bartlett 2003c:A8.
92. Bain 2004a, 2004b. I shall explore more of this in subsequent chapters.
93. Burd 2003a.
94. Burd 2003b.
95. Anderson 1996; Sykes 1988.
96. Chait 2002a; Fogg 2004b.
97. Chait 2002a.
98. Duderstadt et al. 2002; Lanham 2002; Tomlinson-Keasey 2002.

Chapter Three

Mid-Twentieth-Century Efforts at University Reform— *Mutations that Didn't Quite Make It*

Chapter 1 described the twentieth-century development of the social sciences and suggested that, as far as the larger society is concerned, they're barely visible and perhaps even irrelevant. Chapter 2 portrayed the twentieth-century evolution of higher education and suggested that in the upcoming twenty-first century the social sciences may find themselves, for the most part, floundering in the impoverished backwaters. An additional theme of chapter 2 is the perception held by most friendly (and all unfriendly) critics of the whole of post-K–12, namely, that it's failing to live up to its obligations as set forth under the old social contract with society.

Chapter 3 extends that latter theme by describing how a minority of reformers (professors, students, administrators, citizens, public officials—elected and appointed) undertook a laudable effort to fulfill some of those obligations. The reformers included personnel from virtually all the disciplines—including the social sciences. Their time frame was the decline of higher education's golden age, though hardly anyone at the party sensed it was over. Indeed, it was the largesse itself that brought the reformers' dreams to pass. Nonetheless, following a brief but heady period, the reformers' experiments came, for the most part, to naught.

Hence, if we're to create a future for the social sciences that includes reinventing the undergraduate experience, we must first briefly consider several wide-ranging questions regarding those earlier reform efforts. Why did they happen? What were they like? What did the several experiments share in common? And, perhaps the most intriguing of all—why, for the most part, did those reform efforts go under? Finally, as we try to shape a future for the social sciences, what lessons can we learn from the past?

AN ALTERNATIVE MOVEMENT AT AN EXCEPTIONAL TIME

The alternative higher education movement of the 1960s and early 1970s was the most recent (though by no means the first) attempt to reform at least some parts of post-K–12 in the United States.[1] Burton Clark described analogous experiments from an even older time period that resulted in distinctive colleges such as Antioch, Reed, and Swarthmore.[2] And Joy R. Kliewer presented a brief overview of several previous (mid-nineteenth and early twentieth century) experiments also aimed at doing post-K–12 in a variety of ways.[3]

It should come as no surprise to discover that the 1960s and 1970s alternative movement took root in the coalescing of a broad set of remarkable social, economic, and political forces.[4] Recall from chapter 2 that, among other things, those years represented the home stretch of post-K–12's golden age. Despite that reality, dollars were still flowing freely into higher education, and optimism over its future remained unbounded. There were, however, some dark clouds looming on the horizon, and one of those turned out to be the hostile reactions of student activists to what they perceived to be the excesses of the research university.

Their principal complaint was that many professors were so obsessed with what Fairweather called "mimicking the elite"—and thus embellishing their professional reputation via research—that they failed to invest either in quality teaching or in developing the personhood of their students. In his now legendary oration on the UC-Berkeley campus in December 1963, Mario Savio electrified hundreds of fellow-student listeners by declaring that Berkeley was nothing more than a "corporate firm."[5] Its "manager," mocked Savio, was Clark Kerr (president of the entire University of California system). Furthermore, Savio ridiculed the university's regents by calling them the firm's "board of directors."[6] And the faculty, he charged, are simply a "bunch of employees, and we [students] are the raw material." Savio then implored the students to declare their independence from such a dehumanizing assembly line and to affirm that, as he put it, "We're human beings!"[7]

Savio and his colleagues thus ignited the multifaceted 1960s student Free Speech Movement that spread rapidly to many other campuses throughout the United States. Their objective of getting "oppressive" universities to mend their errant ways melded at once with several other freedom movements of the decade such as black civil rights, the second sexual revolution, and the second feminist revolution, which this time included men. Mixed in to the ferment were generous portions of the counterculture, the anti–Vietnam War movement, and the gay/lesbian liberation movement.[8] Although their passions gradually subsided over time, each movement left behind at least a minimal residue of one sort or another. For its part, the student unrest was a loud and clear wakeup call that something was very much awry with the old social contract between post-K–12 and society.

Despite the fact that the most disruptive (and occasionally violent) forms of student protest (e.g., destruction of university property, including in one or two isolated instances dynamiting a campus building) never accounted for more than a tiny handful of student activists, some nonstudent advocates (administrators, professors, public officials, interested citizens) nonetheless came to believe that the activists' complaints held significant implications that went far beyond their limited numbers. Among the grievances that resonated most with the nonstudent advocates were matters such as mediocre teaching, ignoring student personhood, and bottling up student freedom and individualism. The vast majority of those adult advocates then set about to work *within* the structure of mainstream colleges and universities in order to try to make them receptive and responsive to those and related student complaints.[9]

At the same time, a few of those adult advocates along with some student activists worked *outside* the mainstream. They

> converged upon mountaintops, held retreats in the woods, and occupied classrooms and board rooms for days at a time, to give life to new and radically different institutions of higher education. Scores of innovative or experimental colleges . . . [and a few universities] burst onto the scene.[10]

Kliewer followed Arthur Levine by defining innovative as "any significant departure from traditional practices in American higher education."[11] And to help us grasp more firmly what she meant by "departure," Kliewer came up with five overlapping dimensions.[12] Those several principles capture both the spirit and the substance of those experimental colleges and universities. The features answer the question as to what characterized the alternative movement in general. They describe the set of guidelines held and followed by the majority of the adult advocates and student activists. The dimensions are summarized in figure 3.1 and represent that movement's overarching norms and principles.

Free at Last

Borrowed from a stirring oration delivered during the 1960s by the Reverend Dr. Martin Luther King, Jr., "free at last" captures the way adult advocates and student activists felt about the kinds of innovative schools they were creating. They believed their innovations enabled them finally to escape the rigid hierarchy and authoritarianism that characterized most of post–World War II higher education. Each of the five dimensions revolved (like planets circling the sun) around what the advocates and activists perceived to be the core mis-

1. Inter/cross-disciplinary teaching and learning, and curricular activity.
2. Students engineered, that is, took charge of and helped fashion, their own academic programs, including courses and majors. They participated in both short-term and long-term planning for curricular development.
3. Egalitarianism and communitarianism (shared governance among professors and students in decision making), and collaborativeness among students, faculty, and administrators. The absence of formal titles and grades (replaced by narrative evaluations). Competition between students for grades was replaced by working together in shared projects.
4. Learning was constructed in terms of the pedagogic ideas and democratic ideals of John Dewey. The classroom was in and of itself no longer the focal point of student activity. Instead, learning was said to arise out of the hands-on student doing of projects, experiences, internships, and theses.
5. Faculty research and publication were in fact made subordinate to teaching. Faculty were imbued with an intensity, a spirit of vocation about teaching that "permeate[d] these communities."*

*Grant and Riesman 1978:33, cited by Kliewer 1999:xviii.
Figure 3.1.

sion of the college or university: to *serve the best interests of the student.* Declaring their independence from that previous hierarchy and authoritarianism was their way of assuaging their fundamental grievance, namely, that universities and colleges were organized by academics in order to achieve their own best interests.[13] They wanted to create a genre of post-K–12 that was student centered rather than faculty centered.[14]

For example, advocates and activists reasoned (figure 3.1, point 1) that although disciplinary boundaries were of obvious and enormous benefit to the reputations of professors, their outcomes for students tended to be a narrow and myopic view of what were in fact wide-ranging intellectual, social, and moral problems. Accordingly, within those innovative schools, professors from divergent disciplines would team up to offer courses, say, on "concepts of human nature" (a psychologist and biologist), or "the energy crisis" (natural and social scientists), or "the problems of perception" (an artist and a philosopher).[15]

Figure 3.1, point 2, was a response to the activist objection that once inside the disciplinary boundaries—already quite narrow to begin with—faculty tendered courses that further limited the intellectual outlook of students. Such courses, it was charged, reflected the current research interests of professors but not the broader curiosities of students. By contrast, at the innovative schools, students "were encouraged to take ownership of their education."[16] For one thing, that meant that a student might tailor a course and/or an entire major to suit his or her interests and work with certain interested professors (and perhaps other students) to get the program approved. More broadly, it meant that students were freed from the demands of conventional majors and the typical requirements for graduation. Not just individuals, but groups of students, could get together with professors in order to formulate their majors and to participate in overall curricular planning.

Accordingly, it's plain to see that the third point (figure 3.1) underlies and overlaps with the first two. Within those innovative schools, academic rank was muted and titles were taboo, and "campus decision making and policy drafting was often a dynamic, participatory, open-to-all arena."[17] The ancient credo that professors possessed superior wisdom was juxtaposed with the novel premise that students, too, might perhaps have some good ideas they could share with their professors. The activists and advocates felt strongly that professors had for decades used their claim to superior knowledge as a way to maintain their authority, even at the price of students' well-being. Hence, in an attempt to balance the competing interests of students and faculty, innovative schools aimed to "substitute equality for hierarchy, participant democracy for bureaucracy."[18] Recall from prior chapters that figuring out how to imbue the educational process with democracy was a pivotal theme in the early work of John Dewey.[19]

It's unclear how many of the innovative schools explicitly credited Dewey with points 3, 4, or 5. In any event, the principle of hands-on learning (figure 3.1, point 4) was also straight out of Dewey. That decisive principle reflects his unflagging zeal to try to synthesize the pursuit of ideas with the kinds of actions necessary to implement them—to merge thought with doing. Chapter 1 described it as his pragmatic philosophy. To that end, Dewey established in 1896 his well-known K–12 laboratory school at the University of Chicago. Accordingly, Kliewer's portrayal of the experiential, hands-on learning that occurred at the innovative colleges and universities of the 1960s and early 1970s would surely have earned Dewey's endorsement: "Students [in the innovative schools] were expected to venture out into the world, to take part in local work, social causes, or community-building experiences that would enhance and expand their readings and seminar discussions."[20]

Finally, point 5 in figure 3.1 echoed Dewey's concern that teaching should be much more imaginative and meaningful than simply stocking the student's mind with "stuff." Although Dewey didn't use the actual phrase, he is perhaps the foremost twentieth-century pioneer of what the introduction described as *quality* education. Quality was defined there as nurturing students' human capital skills, that is, analysis, evaluation, and synthesis.[21] Chapter 4 describes it as higher-order learning. And although the innovative schools didn't employ those particular phrases, "creativity in undergraduate teaching was a hallmark" of those places.[22]

The activists complained bitterly that the considerable talent, ingenuity, and energy that professors poured into their research—in their quest for high professional regard—drained them of the juices requisite for imaginative teaching/

learning. Hence, the innovative schools mandated their professors to embrace the teaching/learning enterprise with the same, if not more, resourcefulness as they might have given unstintingly to the enhancement of professional reputation. Recall that President Harper was instrumental in reversing the prime identity of the university professor—researcher replaced teacher as identity number one. Hence, advocates for the innovative schools aimed to get those priorities into the order they believed to be appropriate: *Teacher* would once again, they hoped, become the professor's principal identity.

A University to Do It All

Given that Savio had excoriated Clark Kerr in 1963, it is poignant indeed to realize that for some years prior to being roasted, Kerr (along with Dean McHenry) had in fact been devising a unique type of university that, once it appeared, Savio probably applauded.[23] Long before the student activists made the tension between professional reputation and learning a media event, Kerr had already made up his mind to create a new type of university aimed to reduce that strain. When the University of California–Santa Cruz finally opened its doors in the fall of 1965, Kerr called it a "collegiate university" whose essence was the residential college: "The idea, in Kerr's legendary words, was to 'make the campus seem small as it grows larger.'"[24] Kerr and McHenry (its first chancellor) envisioned Santa Cruz as addressing each of the five issues displayed in figure 3.1. It would, furthermore, aim at the same time to become a strong research university. Santa Cruz would strive, in effect, to do it all!

USHERING THE GENIE BACK INTO THE BOTTLE

Kliewer, along with V. R. Cardozier, explained how and why Santa Cruz, along with several other innovative schools of that era, managed to survive to the present time.[25] The vast majority, however, of the experimental schools begun during that turbulent period eventually went under. And among the schools that did survive, most (not all) were willing and/or pressured to adapt markedly to the economic, demographic, and social realities of the *post-*golden age. The essence of their adaptations was a shift in direction—they veered away from the ideals listed in figure 3.1 and moved instead toward emulating the mainstream universities and colleges. Kliewer reports that among the survivors, two serve as examples of schools that shifted most markedly toward the conventional mainstream.

One school that survived by adapting to external realities was the University of Wisconsin–Green Bay. Another school that adapted in the same manner was

Santa Cruz.[26] In the latter case, Kliewer remarked that by the mid-1990s, "the early dreams and visions for UC–Santa Cruz have faded."[27] A subsequent turn-of-the-century confirmation of her assessment regarding faded dreams came in 2000 when Santa Cruz added letter grades to its long-standing practice of providing written narrative evaluations of students.[28] In contrast to those two schools, and at the other pole of the array of survivors, Kliewer notes that several schools "persevered with nearly all of its early principles or founding philosophies intact."[29] As examples, she cited Hampshire College (Massachusetts), Pitzer College (California), the New College of Florida, and the Evergreen State College (Washington).

The severe economic downturn of the early 1970s, marking the close of the golden age, was especially punitive for the innovative schools. They were after all terribly cost-*in*efficient, which was OK as long as dollars were abundant. But when sources of public and private moneys began to dry up, the innovative schools were the first to suffer and, in many cases, to close up shop.

Furthermore, keep in mind that the students attending the innovative schools were in the 1960s and 1970s interested primarily in participating in a unique college *scene.* The college degree qua credential, though obviously important, was not necessarily more vital than their quest for the sorts of meaningful undergraduate experiences captured by figure 3.1. And as long as the economy was booming and jobs for college graduates remained plentiful, it made little difference whether one had majored in history or chemistry or, say, in the mystical experience—from St. Augustine, to medieval Christian Heretics, to Zen Buddhism, to Thomas Merton, and to Hallucinogenic drugs.

But when the economy tanked and the job market tightened in the 1970s, parents and students turned overwhelmingly to what the vast majority of undergraduates had in fact been doing throughout the 1960s and 1970s— attending mainstream schools to study a useful major and thus buy their ticket into a well-paying job. The sharp downturn in student enrollments at innovative schools, added to the reduced funding from public and private sources, took its toll in closing many of them and in forcing the remainder to get less ethereal.

A second element that relentlessly drove innovative schools toward the mainstream was also rooted in the economic woes of the 1970s and early 1980s. As many innovative schools closed down and they lost their jobs, their out-of-work professors became painfully aware that job *in*security was part of the high price they paid for their eagerness to experiment with the ideals in figure 3.1.[30] That distressing lesson was not lost on those few faculty fortunate enough to hold their positions at those innovative schools still struggling to keep their doors open. Hence, they edged ever closer to the mainstream. At the same time, the newly unemployed professors, along with the newly minted PhDs, avoided the innovative places and looked instead for positions at more mainstream schools where the promise of job security was considerably greater.

A third and equally powerful element that in the mid- to late 1970s deterred professors from joining the innovative schools (and caused professors that worked there to become less inventive) was the unforeseen and unintended consequence of "faculty immobility."[31] Professors at the innovative schools soon discovered they had neither the time nor creative energy, or the institutional resources of money and support services, to pursue their professional reputation. They had no opportunity, in short, to try to mimic the elite scholars from their own discipline. Having few, if any, publications, they found themselves stuck in a "professional dead end."[32] They had no bargaining chips whatever to compete effectively within the national marketplace described in chapter 2. Given that professional reputation was and is such a vital part of what it means to be a professor, it's plain to see that feature as being one more reason why many innovative schools gradually moved toward the mainstream. Their shift was essential if they were to retain current professors and recruit new faculty.

The upshot of those (and related) forces was that by the mid- to late 1970s most of that brave and hardy band of pioneering professors and students had abandoned their quest for a distinctive college experience. They instead joined their peers in settling for a conventional genre of post-K–12. Apart from the notable exceptions mentioned above, the alluring and seductive genie of the 1960s and early 1970s — expressed by the ideals in figure 3.1 — was for the most part once again shut up within the bottle of the mainstream post-K–12 experience.

Reactions of the Mainstream Schools—
The Illusion of Reform without the Substance

That is not to say, however, that the conventional, or mainstream, schools remained stolidly indifferent to the yearnings of the student free speech movement that universities and colleges should reform—that they ought to live up to the terms of the old social contract by creating more meaningful undergraduate experiences. The mainstream schools were, after all, the ultimate cause of the student unrest, and many of them had to contend with the (infrequently violent) disruption of their business as usual.[33] Larry Cuban's detailed account of how the faculty and administration at Stanford University responded to the student unrest seems fairly representative of the reactions of many conventional post-K–12 schools throughout the United States during the 1960s and 1970s.

First of all, reports Cuban, Stanford administrators appointed a 1967 steering committee that contained twice as many professors as students. The committee's charge was to come up with proposals to make the Stanford undergraduate experience more relevant and meaningful. A professor who'd served on the committee told Cuban that "we were free to discuss a curriculum we thought was best."[34] Let there be no doubt, however, that the ideals in figure 3.1 never showed up anywhere on the committee's table. That same professor, for example, confided to Cuban, "there was . . . certitude among faculty about what was best for students."[35]

Cuban reported that at Stanford and elsewhere, one principal concession to the students' desires for freedom, and thus for greater control over their own education, was a reduction in the numbers of required courses and a significant expansion in the range and numbers of elective courses—including some credits for community internships. It turns out that the competing policies of students being free to choose their own courses versus being required to submit to a prescribed curriculum had in fact been batted about in many colleges and universities at least since the 1870s.[36] Throughout the decades, schools routinely went back and forth by allowing students a certain degree of elective choices but later on withdrawing some of that freedom, to be followed by allowing more choices, and so forth.

The 1967 Stanford steering committee found the middle ground regarding student freedom of curricular choice through what seemed to be an elegant, astute, and expedient compromise: "Let the objective of curricular planning be to encourage the faculty member to teach what he likes to teach and the student to learn what seems vital to him."[37] The committee was enormously pleased with their Solomon-like decision, and convinced themselves that it furthered the best interests of both sides. The historic ideal of faculty autonomy was reinforced— the professors continued to be entirely free to offer courses on the thing that was, after all, the nearest and dearest to their hearts, namely, their own research interests. And at the same time, the belief in student freedom was also upheld— students could pick and choose from an almost endless hodgepodge of course offerings. Nonetheless, at Stanford and elsewhere, on those occasions when the "research interests of the faculty fail to coincide with student's course interests, ways are invented to make sure the faculty wins."[38]

The second concession made to students' yearnings for greater influence on their college experience appeared, at first glance, to pose a much greater threat to faculty autonomy. Recall that the 1960s activists had complained bitterly about mediocre teaching. Hence, in order to address that specific grievance, in the early 1970s Stanford approved a policy that had been kicking around in post-K–12 long before the 1960s—the "idea that for tenure and promotion decisions 'some formal procedure of teacher evaluation be used.'"[39] Consequently Stanford, along with virtually every other university and college in the United States, had by the close of the 1970s devised a teacher rating form that all students were expected to complete at the end of each course they took. The forms consisted typically of a series of standardized multiple-choice questions that the faculty devised and that they claimed accurately evaluated the professor's teaching skills. Second, faculty claimed the forms validly assessed whether, as the Stanford committee put it, the student had learned what seemed "vital" to him or her.[40]

New Bottle—*Same Old Innards*

It is simply *not* possible to overstate the enormous political significance (as opposed to the negligible pedagogical importance) of that particular innovation. Its political significance is not because the new practice relieved students of being subjected to mediocre teaching—it in fact failed to achieve that lofty goal. The new practice was a defining moment in post-K–12 precisely because it conjured up the illusion, but failed to achieve the reality, of genuine transformation. It constructed the false impression that the new schema had finally put an end to instructional mediocrity. It was, in short, a solemn means of assuring public officials, parents, and students that "all is now well," when in reality virtually nothing had changed. Cuban described the introduction of rating forms by mainstream schools, as well as the start-up of the two corollary practices described below, as instances of "change without reform" and the "taming of reform."

Alongside the rating forms, most schools began, for example, to establish highly publicized (often announced at commencement), annual cash bonuses for the professor deemed to be the "teacher of the year." And, although there are several criteria for such prizes, a professor failing to score highly on the rating forms need not waste his or her time applying. Furthermore, many schools set up teaching centers to assist faculty to become "better" teachers. Although the actual substance of "better" was and is seldom debated publicly, there is little doubt that "better" is understood to mean that, ultimately, the teaching center aims to help the professor raise his or her scores on the rating forms.[41]

Cuban observed that the rating form and its two corollaries (bonuses and teaching centers) had an immense influence on quelling complaints from students, parents, and public officials over mediocre teaching.[42] Administrators and faculty could point to the forms and convincingly assure their constituents that *you need have no fear regarding poor teaching. We now have the tangible safeguards in place ensuring that your children are the beneficiaries of excellent teaching.* Despite the hype, Cuban reported that at Stanford the teaching scores were never taken seriously when decisions were being made about salaries, tenure, and promotion.[43]

Stanford views itself, after all, as the "Harvard of the West," and it is patently one of the world's elite universities. The remaining elite schools in the United States acted no differently than Stanford when it came to the seeming paradox of using the rating forms and at the same time disdaining them.

Furthermore, once they entered the competition for national eminence, the state flagship schools, followed later by their sister comprehensive schools, were obliged to mimic the elite in this as in every other matter. Although the schools of lesser status and prestige assiduously copied the elite by solemnly honoring the evaluation forms in the breach, it was plain to see that their exemplars had not achieved their lofty heights by fussing over mere teaching scores. In short, no matter what it might proffer to parents at commencement, the more intensely that any university or college strives for national/global eminence, the more it treats the practice of the rating forms as a relatively trivial matter. To be sure, because of its public relations significance the practice is viewed as an essential and nonnegotiable formality—but little more.

Cuban took great care to assert that professors do not intentionally spin the practice of the rating forms. Academics are not in the same category as, say, the wily politician or the devious advertising mogul that purposely sets out to concoct an illusion at the expense of the gullible voter or consumer. Nevertheless, the unintended consequences are pretty much the same. The rating forms are hyped up to construct the impression of producing a quality product—they're used to verify excellence in teaching. That is the case even though no one bothers to debate the meaning of excellence, except to assert that excellence is what the forms measure. Accordingly, the forms mollify the customer, even though the product being peddled may not after all be in the customer's best interest.

It must be added, in all fairness, that a big part of the reason for treating the prevailing teaching evaluation practice as perfunctory, and thus in the end inconsequential, is that the forms in no way pretend to address the genre of discovery-based learning (DBL) described throughout this book. Michael Theall et al. highlight the fact that the rating forms were, after all, designed initially in the 1970s.[44] The form's entire purpose was to assess the professor's effectiveness at transmitting information, that is, stuff. Theall et al. remind us that at that time few voices were heard contesting the received wisdom that transmitting stuff is the preeminent objective of undergraduate education. During the sunset of the industrial era, there was no apparent reason to chip away at the credo that DBL, although requisite for graduate students, was in the case of undergraduates quite dispensable. Had it been discussed at all, DBL would have been deemed to be an unaffordable, and ultimately unnecessary, luxury item.

The upshot of that point of view was that, from the moment of the rating forms' inception, most professors damned them with faint praise. Virtually every academic then and now would agree with Frank Rhodes that, in the best of all possible worlds, undergraduate education *should* be about higher-order learning.[45] But, given that for the most part it never has been, and given that the 1970s rating form is, from a political standpoint, an extraordinarily useful fact of life, the typical professor swallows his or her intellectual pride and simply tolerates it. Few, if any, professors, however, believe for a moment that the forms get anywhere near assessing the sorts of human capital proficiencies described in subsequent chapters.[46]

Cuban's fundamental thesis is that the elite schools, along with their wannabe imitators, maintain "an institutional tradition of reform complete with symbols and the common practice of improvised incrementalism."[47] The fond hopes of advocates seeking for genuine reform of the mainstream schools via teaching evaluations, cash bonuses, and teaching centers have not been realized. Their strategy was to labor for structural change *within* conventional post-K–12 in order to facilitate student interests. However, those advocates were no more successful in achieving their goals than were most of the advocates electing to go *outside* the prevailing system in order to experiment with innovative schools. The frustrating experiences of both sets of would-be innovators cause Cohen to conclude that throughout post-K–12

An industry of innovation is apparent. But it must be satisfied with small victories: an occasional new course requirement, modified student admissions practices, changed patterns of faculty recruitment. More than that the system successfully resists, co-opts, or absorbs—eventually changing but with the glacial majesty befitting a venerable structure.[48]

A "GENTLEMEN'S AGREEMENT"

The apparent intransigence of many professors toward authentic reform may be one reason why today's students are not much interested in post-K–12 transformation. They are not marching on administration buildings to object, for instance, to the emergence of the entrepreneurial environment described in chapter 2. This most recent evolutionary development is arguably far more inimical to students' long-term interests than was the old-style research university against which Savio so vehemently protested. If not rallying for change, how then are contemporary undergraduates passing their time while growing numbers of their professors strive mightily to become and remain successful entrepreneurs?

The answer is, of course, that students are busily pursuing what for them is today the entire point of college—obtaining the credential deemed requisite for a well-paying job. The issue of the *content* of their education appears, when compared to its *utility,* far less significant. In contrast to the brief interlude of the 1960s and early 1970s, when a minority of students were obsessed with the burning issue of content alongside utility, that issue is seldom if ever raised.

The principal (and bitter) lesson they garnered from that era is that it does little good to struggle against faculty interests. Even when professors seem to be making significant concessions to student interests, they're really not.

Hence, the only sensible student response is to withdraw from the fray and simply go along with whatever type of post-K–12 their professors choose to hand them. Picturing two circles that intersect over the most minuscule amount of space possible gives one a visual sense as to how little overlap exists today between the world of professors and the world of undergraduates.

Furthermore, their minute intersection is presided over by what Roger Schank called "an implicit gentlemen's agreement . . . [under which students affirm], You give me the grade, I'll get the degree, I'm out of here."[49] And, according to observer Morris Berman, Murray Sperber described the student-faculty bargain in similar, though more dramatic terms, as a "tacit, 'nonaggression pact' between students and faculty to stay out of each other's way."[50] Sperber is, in fact, quite cynical about the plight of today's undergraduates—especially at universities that emphasize big-time sports alongside big-time research. He alleges that one of the consequences of the lavish spectator sports sponsored by many universities is to deflect attention away from the abysmal content of their undergraduates' educational experience. Sperber compares that situation to what the ancient Roman rulers achieved by offering extravagant circuses to their masses of citizens. Those entertainments made the citizens forget their complaints against their rulers, and thus effectively staved off the types of discontents that could potentially undermine their rulers' authority.

The essence of the gentlemen's agreement between academics and students is derived from the Solomonic decision of the 1967 Stanford steering committee: *Design the university to give both sides what they want.* Students get the credential, and professors get the chance to pursue diligently their professional reputation.[51] Throwing big-time sports into the bargain also benefits both sides—perhaps money and status for the university, and surely amusements for the students.[52] The upshot is that because today's students are in no way exposed to the worst excesses of the hierarchy and authoritarianism that characterized much of post-K–12 prior to the 1960s, most of them seem quite content with the status quo. That is so despite the fact that when researchers examine the particulars of what actually happens to students, optimism over the quality of their college experience appears far less warranted.[53]

In any case, one could say that the situation of undergraduates today is analogous (though not identical) to the unintended consequences of the 1960s liberation movements aimed at undermining racism and patriarchy. There's little doubt that the worst excesses of the oppression and discrimination against both minorities and women prevailing in the 1960s have now been alleviated. It is, however, just as indisputable that today's dominant society all too often somehow manages to operate against the best interests of both minorities and women. Similarly, although today's undergraduates possess many more choices (in terms of "open admissions, pass/fail grading options, independent studies, African American studies, Women's Studies, coeducational dorms," internships, service learning)[54] one would be hard-pressed to counter the assertion of, among many others, the Boyer Commission—that is, that the typical U.S. undergraduate experience is decidedly *not* in the best interests of most students.[55]

Importantly, few critics reproach either professors or students for dutifully playing their respective parts in what is, over the long haul, a star-crossed silent bargain.[56] The true "villain" (if such there be) in this scenario resides within the nature of the beast—the essence of the research, and now entrepreneurial, university. Schank and Cuban simply documented what Cohen said and what everyone already realizes: After a hundred years of trying, it's obvious that the beast cannot be tamed, nor—given the contributions that the sciences make to society—should it be. Professors are busy embellishing their reputations via grantsmanship, research, and publication, while students are intently pursuing their highly valued ticket to the world of work. Why would anyone want to infringe on what appears to be a beneficial and cozy arrangement all the way around?

THE "DISRESPECTED STUDENT"

The reason to step in, says Schank, is that their cozy deal "disrespects" the student.[57] Their bargain disregards the mandate that, in the information age, post-K–12 must concentrate much more single-mindedly than ever before on fully cultivating our most valuable resource, namely, people. Or as the Boyer Commission put it, research universities and their wannabes have "shortchanged" students:

> They have failed, and continue to fail, their undergraduate populations. . . . In all too many cases, [they get] less than their money's worth. . . . All too often they graduate without knowing how to think logically, write clearly, or speak coherently. . . . And with larger and larger numbers of their peers holding the same paper in their hands, even that credential has lost much of its potency.[58]

The disrespect stems from the failure of much of post-K–12 to pay attention to the reality that higher-order learning is becoming increasingly *in*dispensable for undergraduates—just as it has been among grad students for the entire twentieth century. Undergrads require higher-order learning to navigate effectively within the twenty-first-century marketplace and also for their participation in what the introduction called the weaving/repair of the social fabric. Students in our new century need a high level of human capital proficiencies in order both to *get* (labor force achievement), and to *give* (to contribute toward the resolution of the urgent social issues around them). Unhappily, Schank believes that most students have at best only a vague sense of the implications for their future well-being of the differences between stocking information versus the nurturing of human capital skills. Failure to appreciate that distinction is, unfortunately, most prominent among the increasing numbers of working-class and minority persons that are the first of their kin ever to attend college.

Regardless of their background (privileged or less privileged), today's entering college freshmen soak up the existing gentlemen's agreement like a sponge. When they first enroll they are not, however, presented with a *limited* warranty and asked to study it carefully and sign it. Such a document would make the nature of their gentlemen's agreement explicit rather than implicit. The document would state briefly and plainly that their chosen school makes no claim that it offers higher-order learning. No warranty is given that students will participate in a value-added experience.[59] There's no hint that, by the time they leave, they may or may *not* have ventured further up the ladder of human capital skills than where they're at right now. They're not informed that their academic experiences may or may *not* fit them to participate at an optimum level, either in the marketplace or in the civic society of the new century. In terms coined by John S. Brown and Paul Duguid, they're not cautioned that their degree may not be "robust."[60]

The proposed disclaimer would readily affirm that, at present, the credential is indeed both necessary *and* sufficient to obtain the best-paying jobs. It would nonetheless caution that as more and more citizens obtain the degree, there is the very real possibility that it (like the high school diploma before it) will become progressively more ravaged by credential inflation. The upshot of such a long-term process is that employers would be able to draw much more selectively than ever before from a rapidly expanding pool of degree-holders. Consequently, the employer would be able to start asking awkward questions.

Does, for example, the job candidate possess a sufficient level of problem-solving skills? Where is the evidence that she or he is able, among other things, to analyze, evaluate, and synthesize complex issues? Moreover, how does the candidate show that he or she has developed the capabilities to think well and to write well? Does the candidate comprehend that as the demands of the more desirable jobs become increasingly sophisticated and complex, she or he must possess a much greater command than ever before of the sorts of human capital proficiencies described, for instance, throughout this book? In effect, a disclaimer would warn students that over time their degree, although remaining quite *necessary,* might by itself become less and less *sufficient* to obtain one of the more desirable jobs. The proposed disclaimer would also add that once in a desirable job, the credential-holder might (in order to keep it) be called on to demonstrate, on a day-to-day basis, higher levels of human capital skills than were ever expected in the past.

Accordingly, their school's tentativeness about offering the prospective student a disclaimer of this sort implies, at the very least, a disregard for her or his long-term best interest. Their school's lack of candor means, in effect, that the student is less likely to be able to make a fully informed judgment regarding the momentous step she or he is poised to take. And, what is more, few of today's students (and their parents) even realize it. Nevertheless, only a handful of academics would dare even to entertain the mere thought of such a disclaimer because it would be an implied admission that, for the most part, we've failed to live up to the old social contract.

That older contract, like the current one between professors and students, was also a gentlemen's agreement. Professors made a silent bargain with public officials that, in exchange for dollars, their colleges and universities would, alongside doing research, look out for the students' best interests. But even prior to the 1960s, critics of the university charged that the earlier deal was entirely too vague and allowed professors far too much wiggle room. By demanding greater accountability from professors regarding the content of undergraduate education, the friendly critics were and are doing nothing more nor less than trying to remove the older deal from the murky realm of the implicit and to make its terms much more transparent.[61]

THE SOCIAL SCIENCES AND AN
EMERGING MARKET FOR INNOVATION

One reason the mid-twentieth-century advocates failed to change post-K–12 in any significant manner was the absence of a robust market for reform, that is, innovation or significant change. Plainly, advocates at both the innovative and mainstream schools believed fervently in the great need for students to have a richer undergraduate experience. And, at the innovative schools, that meant their experiences should be shaped according to Dewey's ideas and ideals. But a market is always two-sided. It implies there are potential benefits to the seller for the kind of retooling necessary to satisfy the buyer's interests. In other words, although the benefits for that era's students (a richer educational experience) seemed apparent to some, how would significant retooling have benefited mainstream post-K–12 schools and their professors? Given that there were no compelling answers to that question, the small market for innovation eventually collapsed—especially when economic conditions deteriorated.

But why was the market for change was so limited? Here too a compelling case for change was never made. Why would the types of experiences expressed, say, in figure 3.1 be in fact better for students (and thus the larger society) than, say, the typical experiences students encountered at the mainstream schools? After all, during the industrial age, one set of credentials was just as likely as any other to provide access to the most desirable jobs. And now? Does the postindustrial (information) era provide the basis for responding to both questions in a persuasive manner? Does this new era help to generate a market for post-K–12 to begin offering discovery-based learning? Furthermore, is there a complementary external pressure to create a market for university change due to urgent social problems? Following two centuries of grappling with the social issues generated by rapid and continuing economic and technological changes, the new century may make it imperative to take a fresh look. The external conditions might finally be coming into place for at least some social scientists to fulfill the historic mission of their field by enabling humankind to take possession of society.

In short, the fact that mid-twentieth-century efforts to change the organization and culture of post-K–12 went (for the most part) nowhere should not be seen as proof positive that genuine restructuring is simply a mere fantasy. The key, however, to any sort of meaningful reorganization would appear to be a two-pronged, emerging external market casting about for innovation. What is more, supplying the innovation should be seen as benefiting sellers as well as buyers. Such happenings would make change at least a possibility. Their absence would almost certainly guarantee business as usual.

NOTES

1. Kliewer 1999; Cardozier 1993.
2. Clark 1970.
3. Kliewer 1999:8–9.
4. Gitlin 1987.
5. Gitlin 1987:291.
6. FSM-A the Free Speech Movement Archives home page, www.fsm-a.org/.
7. FSM-A the Free Speech Movement Archives home page, www.fsm-a.org/.
8. Gitlin 1987.
9. Cuban 1999; DeZure 2000.
10. Kliewer 1999:xv.
11. Kliewer 1999:xviii; Levine 1980.
12. Kliewer 1999:xviii.
13. Cuban 1999:86.
14. Duderstadt 2000.
15. Kliewer 1999:6.

16. Kliewer 1999:7.
17. Kliewer 1999:7.
18. Gaff 1970, cited by Kliewer 1999:7.
19. Lagemann 2000:35.
20. Kliewer 1999:7–8.
21. Boyer Commission 1998:11.
22. Kliewer 1999:8.
23. McHenry 1993.
24. Kliewer 1999:138.
25. Kliewer 1999; Cardozier 1993.
26. Kliewer 1999:212.
27. Kliewer 1999:157.
28. Rogoff 2001.
29. Kliewer 1999:212.
30. Kliewer 1999:13.
31. Kliewer 1999:139–40.
32. Kliewer 1999:139.
33. Gitlin 1987.
34. Cuban 1999:35.
35. Cuban 1999:35.
36. Cohen 1998.
37. Cuban 1999:37.
38. Schank 2000:16.
39. Cuban 1999:30.
40. Theall et al. 2001.
41. But see Bain (2004a, b) arguing that teaching is far more than teaching scores.
42. Cuban 1999:76.
43. Cuban 1999:41.
44. Theall et al. 2001:3–5.
45. Rhodes 1998.
46. Hutchings 1999.
47. Cuban 1999:88.
48. Cohen 1998:1.
49. Schank 2000:9.
50. Berman 2000; Sperber 2000.
51. Boyer 1994.
52. Duderstadt 2000.
53. Astin 1993; Hebel 2003; Mathews 2002.
54. Kliewer 1999:4.
55. Boyer Commission 1998.
56. Anderson 1996 and Huber 1992 are among several notable exceptions to that generalization.
57. Schank 2000.
58. Boyer Commission 1998:6.
59. Marchese 1995; Nemko 2003.
60. Brown and Duguid 2000:234.
61. Lawrence 1995.

Chapter Four

Let All the Flowers Bloom—
A Landscape of Diversity among Professors in the New Century

The dawn of the twentieth century was a time of extraordinary optimism for the infant social sciences. At the University of Chicago, social scientists had a firm hold on their identity and their mission. Before long, however, they began losing their grip and spent the remainder of the century struggling to regain it. And, by the way, a funny thing happened as they went about their business. Social, political, economic and, mostly recently, technological conditions surrounding the social sciences kept on changing—Harper's twentieth-century research university was morphing into something quite different. The entrepreneurial university was coming into being. Within this newer and different setting, the social sciences are at a much greater disadvantage vis-à-vis the sciences than they ever were within the twentieth-century incarnation of post-K–12.

THE WANNABES

Alongside that overarching set of circumstances is the fact that within social science itself, some professors are considerably less well-off (in terms of status, prestige, money) than others. The highly skilled practitioners (stars) of the peculiar basic social science model, located typically at the handful of elite schools, are much better off than their distant social science cousins found at "lesser" schools. Because those cousins are keenly aware of their comparative disadvantage, many are determined to mimic their elite kin. Furthermore, even within the same department, stars are in a much more advantageous position than their mortal colleagues. Nonetheless, attempts to mimic the elite are invariably costly and difficult and often result in frustration and failure for what one friendly critic called the "wannabes," namely, departments and institutions feverishly bent on enhancing their national prestige rankings.[1]

One upshot of patchiness in the quest for eminence—or of an unwilling-ness to pursue it in the first place—is that in future, many social scientists (along with other academics in general) may find themselves edged into what Randall Collins called the "teaching proletariat."[2] Because he believes their situation is so egregious, Collins asks if we might expect them to "revolt" against, say, public officials and administrators who, increasingly, are requir-ing them to work under less than optimal conditions.

Collins responds, however, that such a revolution "is not very likely." The reason, he says, for professors' quiescence in the face of relative disadvantage is their personal identification with the research elite. Even though they're unable and/or unwilling to emulate the elite, most willingly defer to them. From the moment they step through the doors, graduate students in the social sciences are pounded by the message that their most virtuous professional task is to take the elite as their role model. Hence, the student is urged to em-ulate, as fully as possible, the elites' professional behaviors. That is so despite the fact that the student may have no intention whatever of working in either an existing entrepreneurial setting or in a university morphing toward the en-trepreneurial model. Paradoxically, even if the student might perhaps aspire to the elite status, she or he is made well aware that the chances of actually being successful in their quest for the Holy Grail are slim indeed.

Bear in mind, however, that even if a graduate student aims to enter a set-ting where teaching remains the primary activity (community college or a four-year college that is not yet a wannabe), she or he must first earn the PhD. And, in order to get that degree, she or he has no choice but to run the gaunt-let at an entrepreneurial university—actual or wannabe. According to a *Wash-ington Post* report, today's private liberal arts colleges are under severe pres-sure as they try to replace the large numbers of faculty recruited during the boom years of the 1960s and early 1970s who are, or who soon will be, retir-ing.[3] The colleges' most vexing problem is to recruit professors who, by the colleges' standards, are capable teachers: "Many of the best young academ-ics," said one of the college officials, "demand more research time than these teaching-focused schools are used to offering." Another official added, "younger scholars have expectations different from what their elders had and . . . are less interested in small schools than in big research universities." The college officials went on to say that the students' graduate school mentors strongly advised the neophyte PhD against ever going to a "teaching institu-tion." If, despite that advice, the new PhD was forced to start her or his ca-reer at a teaching institution, he or she is then urged to work especially hard in order to "publish your way out of it."

Most graduate schools have, in short, been highly effective at instilling the belief that each new PhD they mint must, to the furthest extent possible, pursue a professional reputation in a manner established and legitimated by their discipline's elite. Although most new and current social scientists recognize they will never enter the ranks of the privileged few, they seek nonetheless to emulate, or mimic, elite behaviors as fully as possible. In the social sciences, the highest levels of prestige and money flow from conforming to the peculiar basic social science spin that the select few place on their research activities.

That elite model with its peculiar spin is, after all, the most prestigious and most monetarily rewarded. And, although it's not the only game in town, it is far and away the best-liked and most widely admired by social scientists. And Collins's argument is that because the vast majority of social scientists accept the legitimacy of the game, they're hardly likely to disrupt it or try in some fashion to modify the rules. Despite the fact that their conformity to the game's rules may perhaps relegate many of them to the ranks of the teaching proletariat, they nonetheless continue to go along with it. Indeed, they persevere even though the current gap between the proletariat and the bourgeoisie, that is, entrepreneur, is likely to widen into a yawning chasm.

THE MISGIVINGS OF GRADUATE STUDENTS

To say that graduate schools are highly effective both at inculcating the image of the elite professional and at convincing grad students to strive for it by no means implies that all of them are being herded blindly into the ranks of the entrepreneurs. University of Michigan chemistry professor Brian Coppola reported that, for a number of years, he's helped to organize an annual retreat attended by graduate students and professors from various institutions and from a range of disciplines.[4] The major objective of those informal give-and-take encounters, held at a rustic off-campus site, is to enhance the grad students' professional development. And, after participating in those encounters for a long time, Coppola has come to feel that, over the years, the character of the bond between professor and grad student has, in his words, "degenerated." His troubling conclusion is based on the considerable angst expressed by some of today's grad students over what they see in their professors qua entrepreneur and by what those perceptions might portend for them personally.

To be sure, the kinds of issues that some grad students find so distressing today were indeed perceptible in the twentieth-century research university. Within the new entrepreneurial milieu, however, those perennial concerns have gotten a great deal more salient and all-encompassing than ever before. Because they're so much more pervasive than in times past, those sorts of anxieties are harder for the grad student to escape or avoid by, for instance, the older strategy of simply switching advisers. Furthermore, those same feelings of unease have now taken on a far more profound intensity than in times past. Because so much more is at stake today for the professor qua entrepreneur, objectionable and distasteful matters that were, in the past, bearable for the grad student have now gotten greatly exacerbated. The upshot is that some of the unsavory stereotypes that academics once upon a time plastered onto businesspersons are now coming home to roost:

> Students see themselves as being used as workers for hire by thinly stretched research directors who are under increased pressure to compete for diminishing resources. Accurately or not, the students . . . would describe their advisers as unremitting followers of ethical egoism: We have no duty except what is best for ourselves. The students see faculty members subordinating their own disciplinary work to personal advancement and self-aggrandizement.[5]

Coppola's stinging indictment is that the professor qua entrepreneur is so consumed by his or her acquisitive interests and activities that she or he fails to take the time and energy requisite to address the grad students' "biggest concern: Do I have to give up being me in order to become you? I need to know, because I don't like what I see."[6] Although grad students are bombarded continuously with demands to scrutinize and improve the research base of their discipline, Coppola observes that "open discourse about the nature of academic life . . . and where and how to improve it" is typically nowhere to be found in the graduate experience.

Entrepreneurs tend to view such discourse as superfluous at best. The student is expected to embrace, apart from any mental reservation, the once-for-all delivered faith pertaining to the mimicry model. The faculty view the student as a pre-professional (not unlike the novice admitted to a religious order) obliged to give unquestioning assent to the ways in which the professionals have organized their department's agenda—ways designed to enhance its national prestige ranking. Inviting students to critique those ways—the very essence of the department's life—unleashes the potential for disrupting and perhaps altering that life. What's more, faculty worry that any variations in that life could get in the way of their academic excellence as measured by the department's national rankings.

Many academics would, of course, protest most vigorously to the preceding portrayal of their associations with graduate students. To be credible, however, the protesting professor must, first of all, affirm that she or he has in fact engaged students in serious dialogue regarding the evolving character of the academic enterprise, as well as conversations about the student's upcoming career path within it. Protesting professor A might, for instance, have said to students, *Although I am indeed (or am becoming) an entrepreneur, I seek to be enlightened in my dealings with you, and that includes informing you that you have no binding obligation whatever to follow in my footsteps. Other roles besides entrepreneur may be open to you, and I'll try to help you prepare for them.* Professor A would, at the same time, admit how difficult it is for any entrepreneur to pay scrupulous attention to the interests of students (especially their existential concerns), except insofar as student interests contribute to the professor's success and thus reputation.

On the other hand, another protesting professor (B) might take an entirely different tack by saying, *It's because I remain a teacher-scholar, and not an entrepreneur, that I find it quite natural to give serious attention to your concerns over the shifting nature of academic life. And I'm very much in tune with your aspirations to achieve something other than being an entrepreneur.*

In view of professor A's candor as to how tricky it is to tread ceaselessly the fine line separating the obsessions of entrepreneurial success from enlightenment toward their apprentices, a grad student might determine that she or he shall not (in terms of forthcoming career plans) ever get caught in such a dilemma. Accordingly, a student reacting to A might well ask, *What career options—other than entrepreneur—are actually available to me?*

And with regard to professor B, a grad student might put a twist on the same question: *Let's get real: In point of fact, what choices do I have but to be squeezed into a role that I find less than compatible with who and what I am? It may have been possible for you in the past to avoid the entrepreneurial path and to stay the course as a teacher-scholar, but today the winds of change are blowing. Forces out there are coalescing to modify the options (along with the pleasant life style) once enjoyed by professors.* Simply raising such complex and emotionally laden issues turns out to be the easy part. Grappling with them is, however, quite something else. One alternative to academia that appears more readily available to grad students from the sciences than from the social sciences is to take jobs outside the ivory tower in private firms, governments or the United Nations, or nonprofits. As she wrestled with the agonizing conundrum facing grad students in the sciences, one young scientist asked,

> How do you know if you really aren't cut out for a career on the academic hamster wheel? After all, there are whole departments out there filled with people just bumbling along, researching the chemical structure of newt toenails or somesuch.[7]

EVOLUTION OF THE TEACHER-SCHOLAR, OR SUPERPROFESSOR, ROLE

University administrators and professors spent much of the twentieth century constructing and promulgating the teacher-scholar role.[8] Larry Cuban reported that the Stanford faculty grappled for many decades prior to the 1960s with the thorny issue of how to reconcile the quest for scholarly eminence and international reputation with the teaching of undergraduates. Moreover, it's fascinating to realize that a 1969 report to the Stanford faculty described the ideal *undergraduate* teacher in terms strikingly similar to the way in which William Harper had, at the turn of that century, characterized the ultimate *graduate* teacher: "It is only the man," said Harper, "who has made investigation who may teach others to investigate. Without this spirit in the instructor and without his example, students will never be led to undertake the work."[9]

Remarkably akin to Harper, the Stanford report, many decades later, arrived at an equivalent assessment—this time, however, for the *undergraduate* teacher: "Although the best teacher is a catalyst for the student's discovery, he teaches in such a way that the student can learn to do without him."[10] The report added that the professor who is absorbed in self-motivated discovery, that is, who is a researcher or scholar, is the person best able to inspire that same sort of intellectual curiosity in undergraduates. He or she is also the person best able to inspire a love of learning and the unique sense of curiosity and excitement that can come only from activities associated with pursuing and unearthing new knowledge. Recall that the Boyer Commission described that style or approach as discovery-based learning for undergraduates. And although in the late 1960s that particular style may have been the manner in which at least some of the Stanford faculty constructed undergraduate teaching, Cuban nonetheless reports that teaching of *any* style was admired and surely rewarded far less than a reputation for outstanding research.[11]

The disappointing reality is, however, that a demonstrable discovery-based strategy for undergraduate learning was largely obscured by the more conventional approach to college teaching that the Stanford faculty shared with the great bulk of twentieth-century post-K–12 professors. Although the ideal of inspiring self-motivated discovery in the undergrad was viewed as highly desirable, it was, much more to the point, *dispensable.* By contrast, stocking the student's mind with stuff was thought to be *indispensable.*

Today, we might label the teacher-scholar as the "superprofessor," not unlike the legendary "supermom" who can, allegedly, do everything. The hype that *you should be proud of professors at your university because they can do it all—teaching, research, and service—*was foisted onto public officials (most of whom were not fooled), and onto parents, students, and citizens (most of whom were). And when critics charged that many professors neglected their teaching because they spent too much time fretting over their professional reputation, the standard academic rejoinder was that research actually made them better teachers.[12] Because they're on the cutting edge of their discipline, went the spin, they're able to give the student the very latest and most significant knowledge. Never mind, as Roger Schank observed, that star researchers—especially in the sciences—are not obliged to spend any time at all with undergraduates (though some may elect to do so).[13] The dollars they get from sources external to the university permit them to hire someone else (grad students, adjuncts) to do their share of undergraduate teaching, in much the same way as well-to-do Northern males could, for a time, avoid conscription by hiring a proxy to fight in their place during the U.S. Civil War.

In any case, when grad students peer into the shadowy mists of the future probing for career options other than entrepreneur, most are typically aware of no game plan other than to gaze fondly back in time, hoping to recoup desirable features of the teacher-scholar syndrome. The numerous risks, however, of drawing from the past in order to plot one's future—especially in such rapidly shifting times—are obvious. Chapter 2 described the weakening of the old social contract that buttressed the remarkable freedom and flexibility enjoyed by the twentieth-century superprofessor. Although he or she was expected to be both a teacher and a researcher, the actual mixture of these elements varied from professor to professor, not only across institutions but also within departments. The professor who viewed him- or herself as primarily a researcher need not necessarily possess star quality in order to be comfortably supported by his or her institution. On the other side, the professor who saw her- or himself as a teacher could (once tenure was granted) also do reasonably well (at other than elite schools), especially if she or he also did a substantial amount of the departmental teaching and housework.

However, because the umbilical cord of the previous social contract is being increasingly crimped, today's grad student (or professor) hoping to blend teaching, research, and service in quite the same way as before finds him- or herself in an increasingly awkward situation. The familiar and comfortable middle ground (with its delightful sinecures that one colleague called a "gig") between the elite entrepreneur and the teaching proletariat is, in the years ahead, likely to be compressed, that is, squeezed into a smaller and smaller area. The inevitable upshot of such a trend is that less and less social space is likely to be available in post-K–12 for professors who want to be researchers who are also teachers—or teachers who are also researchers—in the fashion of the late twentieth century. The unequivocal message the grad student or professor receives today is that, to avoid plummeting into the unenviable ranks of the teaching proletariat, he or she is obliged to pursue the entrepreneurial mode and lifestyle. Assuming, however, that he or she possesses the considerable talent and abundant motivation necessary to practice it successfully, that choice unavoidably entails certain accouterments that at least some academics (would-be and actual) are uneasy about taking on.

THE ENTREPRENEUR AS A SPECIALIST

Nevertheless, although a number of graduate students and professors may be unwilling and/or unable to pursue it, the identity and role of entrepreneur represents a significant evolutionary development in the role of professor.[14] The entrepreneur is a *specialist* at garnering external dollars in the pursuit of knowledge and/or innovation. The entrepreneur qua specialist is no more a superprofessor (a generalist) than the orthopedist, cardiologist, or neurosurgeon is a superphysician. Nor does it make any greater sense to mourn the decline of the twentieth-century superprofessor than it would be to lament the demise of the twentieth-century family doctor routinely making his round of house calls while clutching his ample black bag that held the cure for any and all ills. There is no doubt whatever that the growing demand for entrepreneurs will stimulate a bountiful supply of gifted students and professors (especially in the sciences) willing and able to meet the demand. They presumably feel quite capable of facing up to the challenge of being a hustler (in the best sense) while at the same time struggling to maintain an appropriate level of enlightenment toward grad students.

In short, a process of evolutionary development is already in the works with regard to the role and identity of the twentieth-century professor. The direction of change has been away from the teacher-scholar, or generalist, and toward greater role specialization. One observer described it as the "decoupling" of entrepreneurship from other long-standing activities of the professor.[15] The trend toward role specialization is the result of continual adaptation to ever-shifting environmental conditions. To be sure, the superprofessor is by no means an extinct species. It is simply on the endangered list. That role is likely to be with us for some time to come—at least for as long as the remaining shards of the old social contract continue to make it less than imperative for her or him to become economically self-sustaining.

THE CREDENTIALER AS A SPECIALIST

Although the entrepreneur—the economically self-sufficient specialist at garnering external moneys—is the most prominent example of an adaptation to an environment in flux, it is possible to conceive of the emergence of the credentialer as likewise being an adaptation to rapidly changing economic conditions. It could be said that the credentialer, too, is responding to external forces over which he or she has little or no control. The twenty-first-century credentialer can be thought of as the specialist servicing the vast numbers of undergraduates expected to burst the seams of colleges and universities during the next several decades.[16]

Although Collins paints a rather dismal image of the circumstances of the teaching proletariat, not all professors or graduate students are or would be necessarily devastated at the prospect of being proletarian. Using Collins's own criteria as a guide, it's obvious that, for example, teachers in K–12 have been proletarian for a long time. And, despite the persistent complaints of K–12 teachers over slumping salaries and stifling bureaucratic control, most are diligent in their work and enjoy what they do.[17] They do not believe, in short, that being proletarian excludes the possibility of a meaningful and productive professional life.

Furthermore, professors at community colleges and at many public four-year colleges have, for many years, been subject to pressures comparable to those long felt by K–12 teachers—pressures that faculty at wannabe post-K–12 schools are only now beginning to feel to any significant degree. Despite the fact that the professors at community and four-year colleges have been proletarian for some time, most are hard working and derive considerable satisfaction from their activities.[18] Although freely acknowledging that they are very much a part of what the preface called the ed biz and that, as a result, their main task is to process as many widgets as possible, they nevertheless seek, as fully as possible, to differentiate widgets from gems and to encourage the gems to polish their minds and exploit their talents.

Needless to say, the professor at a wannabe school is accustomed to perceiving him- or herself as having more prestige and status than both the K–12 teacher and the professor at the community and four-year colleges. The teacher-scholar's sense of his or her own importance stems from identification with, and mimicry of, the elite situated at the top of their discipline's status hierarchy. The prospect of being shunted into the ranks of the teaching proletariat—and thus having to identify with persons lower in the status hierarchy—is by no means agreeable. Nonetheless, some teacher-scholars, willing or obliged to relinquish that twentieth-century role (including its claim to prestige and status) may nonetheless be able to discover a set of unique compensations from becoming a credentialer.[19] Chapter 5, for example, suggests that, among other things, the twenty-first-century credentialer might perhaps accumulate rewards (both tangible and intangible) via the use of innovative instructional technologies.[20] The upshot is that being a credentialer may not necessarily be as grim a situation for every academic as Collins makes it out to be.

In any event, the role of credentialer is just as much a budding reality as is the role of entrepreneur. Both are very much with us, and it's virtually certain that both will expand their numbers well into the foreseeable future. The credentialer makes no more pretense of being a superprofessor than does the entrepreneur.[21] He or she, too, is a specialist and, as such, also represents an evolutionary adaptation to shifting environmental conditions. Those conditions pivot around the reality of bourgeoning numbers of students demanding a college degree. For their part, students want their degree on terms that for them are as trouble-free as possible.[22] And, for their part, public officials want the process of supplying the degree to be as economically efficient as possible. Finally, the credentialer, for her or his part, is able and willing to concentrate fully on supplying the requirements of both sets of interest groups.

Furthermore, as unlikely as it appears at first glance, the credentialer may, paradoxically enough, have something else (besides being a specialist) in common with the entrepreneur. And that is that public officials are likely to perceive that each of them (when compared to the superprofessor) earns her or his keep—although from very different bases. Chapter 2 noted that officials complained perennially that twentieth-century teacher-scholars did not and do not teach enough students. One outgrowth of that allegation is a recent proposal by the federal government to "reward [via additional dollars] colleges [and universities] for retaining students and graduating them on time."[23] That particular congressional proposal is based on a program already existing within the state of Pennsylvania.

Some researchers (not all) argue that graduation rates are a "poor measure" of colleges.[24] And, although such programs have obvious drawbacks, they nonetheless represent an opportunity for credentialers to respond, at least in terms of quantity, to the recurring calls of public officials for faculty accountability. Many officials deem it an important policy objective to ensure that the numbers of students who actually graduate from college should be as high as possible. Florida officials decreed recently that the state must "increase the number of undergraduate degrees by 46 percent in less than a decade."[25] If and when that becomes official state policy, it makes perfect sense for officials to provide incentives to schools and professors that are effectual in achieving their policy's stated goal.

Chapter 2 noted that it's often difficult to differentiate (and thus evaluate and reward) one credentialer from another. Nonetheless, certain clusters of credentialers may be highly successful (with, say, the aid of innovative instructional technology) at conveying large numbers of students (especially minorities and working-class persons) over the arduous route from matriculation to commencement. Hence, some officials have declared they're prepared to take note of successes in raising both the incidence and the rates of graduation, and seem quite willing to reward those accomplishments.

In sum, diversity in the identity and role of the professor is by now very much a part of the twenty-first-century post-K–12 landscape and is likely to get even more prominent. Presently, we can identify at least three broad species of academic. The role of the entrepreneur and the role of credentialer are materializing to vie with the role of teacher-scholar. It is futile to lament the long-term trend away from the twentieth-century image of the generalist struggling mightily to do it all. The newly emerging construction of the academic's role is that of the *specialist* highly proficient within a particular realm of activity. Rather than mourn the alleged decay such a trend represents, we might, without turning a blind eye toward the imperfections of each, more profitably celebrate the positive features inherent in the three "flowers" currently "blooming" throughout post-K–12.

THE EVOLUTION OF YET ANOTHER SPECIALTY

Having acknowledged the reality of diversity as a response to changing economic, social, political, and technological conditions, one could infer that its subsequent course is very much an open matter. It seems quite arbitrary to assert that grad students and professors would be limited simply to three career paths. And if greater variety is a possibility, might we, peering through the dim haze of the future, pick out certain emerging environmental conditions pointing to some adaptations that might perhaps be in order? Do certain needs exist out there that are going unmet? Is there or will there be a demand that some professors—especially from the social sciences—might conceivably be willing and able to supply? Might there be space in post-K–12 for perhaps one additional specialist or flower to bloom? Is there now, or will there be, an emerging market for additional role innovation?

Prior chapters noted that a growing chorus of vocal critics has, for decades, worried that colleges and universities pay insufficient attention to the *quality* of the educational experience they provide for their undergraduates. We observed that, at the outset of the twentieth century, the quality issue was framed principally in terms of a certain type of classical content. By century's close, however, concern over the quality of college content was far less in vogue than simply viewing the degree as the indispensable ticket to the best-paying jobs. From time to time, however, certain facets of the quality issue managed to nudge their way onto the radar screen and capture a degree of sustained public attention, at least for a brief moment.

A *Chronicle of Higher Education* report, for example, explored "Why Johnny Can't Write, Even Though He Went to Princeton."[26] The report described how Princeton, along with a number of other elite schools, was trying yet again to cope with the dirty little secret that everyone is privy to: no matter which college (elite or otherwise) the student attends, few today ever hone the proficiency of writing. That is so, even though Eric Schneider (associate director of academic affairs at the University of Pennsylvania) remarked, "Writing is the edifice on which the rest of education rests. . . . If we don't do that well, you have to wonder what we do well."[27] And if "wondering what we do well" regarding undergraduates is causing some level of anxiety at the nation's most prestigious schools, it follows that virtually every other school is, or at least should be, wondering the very same thing and feeling quite nervous about it, too.[28]

What concerned the Ivy League officials was not the absence from Johnny's academic arsenal of some portion of essential content or stuff (e.g., the rise of the autocratic Napoleon out of the radically egalitarian French Revolution). They were instead dismayed over Johnny's inability to demonstrate a particular proficiency. Their concern was about process, not product. The officials' concerns led them to debate the matter and, in most cases, to experiment with certain innovative schemas aimed at cultivating the proficiency of writing. Nevertheless, Ivy League officials are not convinced that they have as yet devised a satisfactory resolution to this deficiency in Johnny's education.

In any case, given the anxiety of the Ivy League personnel over this perceived shortcoming of their schools, one might ask whether, in recent decades, the construction of *quality* education is perhaps shifting. Could it perhaps be morphing *away* from product to process, that is, away from the transmission of knowledge and *toward* the cultivation of one or more types of student proficiencies? Has the definition of an educated person altered from someone whose mind has been stocked (though with what is indeterminate) to someone who instead possesses certain proficiencies, among which good writing is fundamental? Apart from a few isolated instances, "no" is the safe answer to both questions.[29] Supplying product, that is, subject matter—though today drastically different in character from the classical model—remains the principal preoccupation of most colleges and universities, whether the cosmopolitan Ivy League school, the local community college, or the vast range in between.[30]

THE COACH—*A SPECIALIST IN DISCOVERY-BASED LEARNING*

Cultivating Players' Human Capital

Advocates for proficiencies such as writing take great care to distinguish their broad rationales, objectives, and activities from the much more specific skills in which most professional schools (e.g., business, accounting, journalism, computer science) typically train their students. Lauren Resnick, for instance, utilized the intriguing phrase "higher-order skills" to capture the significance of the kinds of proficiencies she and like-minded advocates have in view.[31] Although "lower-order learning" describes content transmission, no advocates for higher-order proficiency desire to undercut the importance of facts, figures, names, dates, and ideas, that is, product. Instead, they seek to ensure that the prevailing urgency for content transmission should somehow incorporate the cultivation of students' higher-order proficiencies into its makeup. Or, more likely, the other way around—process, that is, higher-order learning, should encompass product, that is, lower-order learning. As Richard Lanham put it, it is not content or stuff that matters so much, it's what humans *think* about stuff that matters.[32] Such advocates believe that quality undergraduate education ought to include both stocking the student's mind *and* cultivating higher-order proficiencies. Their fear is that, for the most part, the issue of proficiency development is relegated to the back burner of most of post-K–12. It is, by comparison to content, relatively expendable. Professors pay it reverential homage, while in fact focusing the great bulk of their attention and energy on stuff, that is, content transmission, because that is deemed to be *obligatory*.

Despite that reality, the Ivy League's concerns over student writing might also be taken as one expression of a discernible move afoot throughout North America and Europe to deepen our conversations about quality undergraduate education.[33] An overarching objective of this concerted effort is to try to get proficiency development onto the front burner—to have it constructed as lying at the heart of a high-quality undergraduate education.[34] A 1993 Princeton University task force compiled the set of proficiencies displayed in figure 4.1, thereby discharging its obligation to arrive at a set of indicators signifying what is meant by a quality education, an education that genuinely cultivates the student's mind. The task force suggested that possessing these overlapping kinds of higher-order proficiencies is what designates a person as truly educated. It is no coincidence that these proficiencies are the basis, that is, the nuts and bolts, of what the 1969 Stanford task force (above), along with the 1998 Carnegie Commission, envisioned as discovery-based learning.

The final item in figure 4.1 was not on the Princeton list. I borrowed it instead from a 1998 address by Virginia governor James S. Gilmore III, in which he invited the trustees of his state's universities to justify their students' credentials:

> Do the degrees they receive confirm that they are proficient writers, critical thinkers, and ethical citizens? That is, after all, what you contracted to provide.[35]

The Princeton task force made it abundantly clear that its proposed proficiencies were nothing more than a highly desirable set of *goals* for which the

The ability to think, speak, and write clearly
The ability to reason critically and systematically
The ability to conceptualize and solve problems
The ability to think independently
The ability to take initiative and work independently
The ability to work in cooperation with others and learn collaboratively
The ability to judge what it means to understand something thoroughly
The ability to distinguish the important from the trivial, the enduring from the ephemeral
Familiarity with different modes of thought (including quantitative, historical, scientific, moral, and aesthetic)
Depth of knowledge in a particular field
The ability to see connections among disciplines, ideas, and cultures
The ability to pursue lifelong learning*
The ability to behave in an ethical manner

*Rhodes 1998:11

Figure 4.1.

university should strive. By no stretch of the imagination did it make believe that Princeton (or any other school at any prestige level) actually had the mechanisms in place to demonstrate that its undergraduates do in fact possess any or all of those higher-order capabilities. Furthermore, after praising the task force for its efforts, Frank Rhodes cautioned his audience against being carried away with the implications of cultivating those particular proficiencies in students:

> Let me be clear, however, dedicated teaching and advising are not to be done in place of research and scholarship. . . . We need our best scholars to be our best teachers, and we need them to give the same creative energy to teaching as they give to scholarship. We need to identify, support, and reward those who teach superbly. There is no antithesis between teaching and research. Great teaching, in fact, can be a form of synthesis and scholarship.[36]

No more eloquent apologia has ever been crafted to praise and uphold the highly revered model of the twentieth-century teacher-scholar—the gifted generalist able to do it all with style, elegance, and excellence. Hence, it seems doubtful that Rhodes would look kindly on the current trend toward role specialization springing from the tacit assumption that all academics are not created equal and that some can in fact do certain things better or less well than other professors.

Furthermore, just as the Princeton task force made no pretense whatever that higher-order learning proficiencies were actually being nurtured at their school, the heads of several other celebrated schools (Yale, Columbia, Bard College, the University of Illinois at Urbana-Champaign) danced around the question of their successes in cultivating those very same sorts of capabilities.

When a journalist asked each university head, "What should a student get out of college?" the officials' responses matched very closely the array of proficiencies displayed in figure 4.1.[37] Notwithstanding their affirmation of the pivotal character of those proficiencies, no university head, when asked if her or his school does in fact cultivate these capabilities, even hinted that he or she had the least bit of evidence to validate that graduates actually possessed them. For example, the strongest assurance that the Yale president could offer was a rather tepid "we hope our students emerge with" those proficiencies. Interestingly enough, when the same journalist asked certain employers what they sought from the college graduates they hired, they, just like the college heads, targeted the human capital skills of figure 4.1.

It would be a rare, and some might say nonexistent, event for all academics (along with employers) ever to agree over any one thing. But if there is any notion at all on which virtually all professors would share an almost universal consensus, it is the credo that those and similar proficiencies exist at the very core of what it means to be educated. Moreover, the reasons for this unusual display of academic accord are not hard to uncover. Because professors have spent their entire lives cultivating these very same capabilities, they are near to the essence of their being. One might go so far as to say they're an extension of their being.

Those kinds of proficiencies are the tools of the professor's trade—the implements whereby new information and knowledge are generated. In contemporary terms, they are the professor's human capital, the wherewithal to engage in research, scholarship, and much more. The "much more" includes virtually every other realm of life, both personal and public. Furthermore, most academics would subscribe to the thesis that persons and society are much better off to the extent that such human capital proficiencies are widely disseminated throughout the population. Hence, it's no mystery why, when asked what, by the end of the day, a student should have derived from college, academics point to those sorts of proficiencies. When all is said and done, the proficiencies do indeed signify what an educated person is.

That being the case, it's rather astonishing to find that the heads of the most prestigious schools, along with most other academics, are so tentative regarding the degree to which their students are in fact developing these higher-order human capital resources or capabilities. Accordingly, the question posed here is whether—Rhodes's persuasive apologia notwithstanding—their cultivation requires some sort of specialist. Are those proficiencies so vital for the welfare of persons and society in the twenty-first century that their nurturing can no longer be left to chance, as seems now (for the most part) to be the case? And, if their development can no longer be left to chance, does that buttress the case for a specialist whose principal mission would be the care and feeding of human capital proficiencies?

Although James Fairweather does not explicitly endorse the invention of yet another specialization, he moves very close to doing so. He does this by elaborating at length on H. H. Crimmel's description of the large amount of energy and extraordinary type of effort it takes for any professor to generate the sorts of proficiencies displayed in figure 4.1.[38] Crimmel used the weighty phrase "intellectual supervision" to capture the kinds of distinctive activities required of any professor in order to nurture the capabilities of figure 4.1. "Intellectual supervisor" is a vividly graphic means of communicating what the coach does as she or he seeks to cultivate higher-order learning. From this perspective, "faculty members may become more like coaches or consultants than didactic teachers, designing learning experiences and providing skills instead of imparting specific content."[39] Furthermore, if there is a coach, it follows there must be *players:* "In these new learning paradigms, the word *student* becomes largely obsolete, because it describes the passive role of absorbing content selected and conveyed by teachers."[40]

Most advocates for innovative undergraduate education tread gingerly around the issue of enlarging the umbrella of role diversity among professors. The matter of creating yet another specialty (i.e., coach) is seldom considered in any serious fashion. Instead, most academics contend that the conscientious superprofessor should strive earnestly to modify (e.g., become more coachlike) her or his teaching in order to ensure the cultivation of those proficiencies in students.[41] Moreover, as to how far the teacher-scholar role should actually be modified, advocates such as Rhodes envisage a relatively limited degree of modification. Others, such as Fairweather, envision a great deal more in the way of significant alterations in both university structure (especially the reward system) and in the superprofessor's work life.

In short, it seems likely that, if polled, the majority of academics would at present respond that calling for a specialist of this sort is premature and that trying to experiment with such a notion would be role diversity run amuck. Most would probably feel that it would be *in*appropriate to try to create one more species of flower. But if a new and different role is deemed to be unnecessary, then it's fair to check out whether that majority is quite safe in assuming that one or more of the three existing roles is up to snuff when it comes to the vital task of cultivating higher-order proficiencies among undergraduates.

Starting with the entrepreneur, it seems apparent that he or she possesses neither the time nor the incentive to add such a demanding pursuit to an already extraordinarily overburdened agenda. Having said that, it is nonetheless very much in the entrepreneur's self-interest to try to cultivate human capital proficiencies in the graduate students (and the occasional undergraduate) that work with her or him. For that select set of students, the entrepreneur is in fact an authentic intellectual supervisor. Successful supervision is measured in large part by the extent to which the student develops human capital proficiencies and then in turn is able to use them to contribute added value to the entrepreneur's research project(s). And, at the other end of the spectrum, the credentialer likewise has neither the time nor the incentive to pursue the all-consuming activity of being the intellectual supervisor of undergraduates. That is obviously not what he or she is being paid for, any more than is the entrepreneur.

Furthermore, being an intellectual supervisor may be of no interest either to the entrepreneur or to the credentialer. Not all professional athletes, for example, have any desire to coach the younger players in their sport. And if perchance the professional athlete did have such a desire, she or he may simply not possess the gifts requisite for being an effective coach, no matter how talented a player he or she might be. By the same token, being either a successful entrepreneur or an excellent credentialer is no guarantee whatever that one has the talent to coach undergraduates in developing their higher-order learning capabilities.[42] Consequently, if neither of those two specialists is the heir apparent for concentrating on this demanding activity, then the ball is left in the superprofessor's court.

The problem is, of course, that the ball's been stuck there for many decades.[43] When the twentieth-century advocates pled for quality teaching, they were in effect urging teacher-scholars to modify their ways. But superprofessors, as explained chapter 2, fiercely resisted officials' efforts to achieve some degree of accountability over their teaching activities. Hence, when Virginia's Governor Gilmore asked his universities' trustees if they could confirm that their students possessed certain human capital proficiencies, he was not so naïve as to believe that the officials would take the time to respond. The typical late twentieth-century superprofessor held that the main focus of his or her teaching was to stock the student's mind with stuff and to find out how much of it the student retained by the time of the test. An especially conscientious professor might in addition seek to transmit knowledge in ways that somehow nourished students' human capital proficiencies. But there was little or no systematic attempt to evaluate the success of that particular nurturing, much less a concerted effort to reward the professor who might possess the distinctive talents of being an intellectual supervisor.[44]

Most importantly, today's teacher-scholar is feeling enormous pressures to imitate or mimic the entrepreneur in order to avoid banishment to the ranks of the credentialers. Adding the all-consuming activities of intellectual supervisor would almost surely derail any hopes of eventually becoming an entrepreneur. Finally, she or he might simply lack the desire and/or talent for being a coach, in which case the entrepreneurial option becomes even more compelling.

If it is in fact vital for growing numbers of twenty-first-century undergraduates to demonstrate they possess higher-order human capital proficiencies, and if none of the existing professorial roles are sufficiently attuned to nurture those proficiencies, then it's plausible to wonder whether we ought to enlarge the umbrella of diversity. We might consider whether it makes good sense to create a role and identity for the professor called "coach." The resulting intellectual supervisor would thus be an additional flower or adaptation. He or she would be a specialist invented in response to a rapidly changing external milieu that might gradually perhaps be creating a demand for students to command those sorts of proficiencies. Such a demand might conceivably arise out of a deepening sense that those human capital proficiencies appear increasingly *in*dispensable for the benefit of both citizens and society in the new century.

Enabling Players' Skills at Resolving Social Issues

When Gouldner and Miller described the historic mission of the social sciences as enabling humankind to take possession of society and bring it under control, they did not elaborate the meaning of their cryptic phrasing. However, the phrasing's context showed it to be in synch with the views of Rossi and Spengler that social science should be about the blending of scientific understanding with social redirection. Recall from chapter 1 that Rossi argued that sound research and social action aimed at human betterment should get a whole lot closer together and be much more intimate than they'd been for a long time. His proposed schema would locate the two partners, or players, on the same level playing field. Each would have something important to say to the other; each would influence the other in substantial ways.

Chapter 1 showed that when social science was first launched there was, in certain quarters, a demand that the linkages between understanding and betterment should be explored and actually implemented. The question today, over a hundred years later, is whether there is any demand for social scientists once again to absorb themselves and their students in actively exploring the links between social research and human betterment. But, if there's not much demand just now, is there any possibility that such a demand might perhaps pick up (like the potential demand for undergraduate human capital) in the decades ahead? And, if such a demand develops, would it reinforce the argument that we ought to encourage greater role diversity among professors who are also social scientists? Could we suggest, as we did for higher-order learning, that the current roles of entrepreneur, credentialer, and superprofessor are simply not up to the complexities of exploring the tortuous links between social research and human betterment? Assuming those three roles don't readily permit such linkages to be explored, would then the specialist called coach be responsible for cultivating higher-order learning *and* for exploring the links between research and betterment? If so, there would then be two connected rationales for encouraging an additional flower to bloom—higher-order learning *and* social research aimed at social redirection.

Recall from chapters 1 and 2 that, throughout the twentieth century, post-K–12 never shied away from making big promises. And today, public officials and citizens typically perceive that the pledges made by the sciences, medicine, and engineering to improve, say, physical health and well-being were or are, for the most part, being fulfilled. The sciences asked for and got vast sums of money to try to solve an array of problems that matter a great deal to everyday citizens. And, in their turn, citizens have constructed the sciences as being reasonably good stewards of those huge stores of money. Although they hold serious misgivings over the potential excesses of scientific research, many citizens have a pretty fair picture of what a scientist is and does and, for the most part, admire and respect what science has done for the good of humanity. When, for instance, life scientists announced in 2003 that the "human genome is complete," few citizens had any clue whatever regarding the technical implications of that declaration. Most of us were not at all clear as to what that assertion might in fact mean. But all citizens readily appreciated the added explanation in plain English that the genome "data are perceived as the foundation of a new era of medicine."[45]

When, however, we shift from the realm of science to the sphere of social science, the contrasting images are both sharp and instructive. Historian Arthur Cohen wrote that Harvard University president Derek Bok believed that universities "should work directly to solve social problems; . . . act to reduce poverty, homelessness, drug abuse, and chronic unemployment; . . . and be more engaged in moral development for everyone."[46] Despite the fact that the social sciences actually studied those and other social issues throughout much of the twentieth century, most citizens have virtually no impression that the social sciences have been particularly adept at solving those or, for that matter, any other types of social problems.

Recall that the social sciences surfaced in the wake of the many dramatic nineteenth-century scientific successes and were expected to try to emulate those successes as fully as possible within the realm of social life. Almost at once, however, unforeseen stumbling blocks got in the way of the social sciences, and they were never able to fulfill the lofty expectations assigned them at their birth. One outcome of the chasm between those fond hopes and their lack of fulfillment is that many, if not most, citizens have at best a very hazy image of what a social scientist actually is and does. And, it would be gullible indeed to believe that most citizens have even the slightest inkling whatsoever regarding any benefits the social sciences might perhaps have provided to humanity. Compared to the sciences, the social sciences remain far more detached and quite aloof from the everyday concerns of the vast bulk of citizens.

If, for example, one visits the numerous science museums dotting the United States, one comes across little trace of what the social sciences are doing today. Instead, one finds displays from physical or cultural anthropology of exotic tribes and cultures—typically from an earlier era. And while PBS, the Discovery Channel, and the Learning Channel devote numerous hours of programming to the sciences, how much time is ever allotted to the nitty-gritty of what the social sciences actually do in the twenty-first century? A TV documentary on a health problem such as breast cancer invariably shows scientific research as being pivotal to its eventual solution. But among the TV documentaries devoted to social issues (e.g., underemployment, stresses on dual-earner parents), how frequently does the producer explain how ongoing social science research might in fact be connected to their potential solution? The most the producer is likely to do is to interview an elite social scientist reciting a social policy suggestion derived from the basic social science spin of chapter 1. If, moreover, one logs onto the *New York Times* online science section, one may click onto the link to social science. Unfortunately, the reports that appear there tend, like the science museums, to limit themselves either to ancient archaeology or to present-day tribal cultures. The intelligent and informed readers that browse that site derive few, if any, clues regarding the vast range of additional issues confronted by contemporary social science.

That rather depressing state of remoteness and inaccessibility has not, of course, been by design. The elite scholars holding sway over the social sciences, and imposing on them their peculiar basic social research spin, wish fervently it were otherwise. Nonetheless, it's not unfair to conclude that one upshot of that basic social science slant is that outsiders seldom perceive the social sciences as being good for something, or as making a difference, or as mattering.[47] And that particular outcome has had a number of unfortunate consequences. Among the most significant of these is the virtual invisibility of the social sciences. And, as a case in point, we may turn to the late Ernest L. Boyer—among the most thoughtful critics of American higher education of the late twentieth century. His 1994 essay on how universities might serve society underscored the obscurity of social scientists to their fellow academics, to say nothing of the real world.

Recall from chapter 1 that Harper asserted, at the outset of the twentieth century, that his University of Chicago was in every sense an institution of public service. Woodrow Wilson (later Princeton's president) made an even more audacious declaration in 1896: "It is not learning but the spirit of service that will give a college a place in the public annals of the nation."[48] Furthermore, Stanford president David Starr Jordan "declared in 1903 that the entire university movement in this country was progressing toward 'reality' and 'practicality.'"[49] But Boyer's lament was that by the early 1990s post-K–12 had long since cast off that spirit of service and squandered the public goodwill that accompanied it.

> Higher education's historic commitment to service seems to have diminished. I'm troubled that many now view the campus as a place where professors get tenured and students get credentialed.[50]

Post-K–12 is, he asserted, obliged to renew its historic mission to serve both community and society. When, moreover, he offered examples of the types of service that universities ought to render to society, he identified an array of issues that the social sciences have, in fact, investigated for many decades. Oddly enough, however, Boyer omitted even the slightest reference to the social sciences as being the potential movers and shakers in any concerted efforts by universities to serve society via grappling with those problems. Surprisingly, he did *not* view the social sciences as being in the vanguard of university efforts to enhance human betterment.

A similar type of bizarre exclusion of social science from the resolution of social issues appeared in Bok's discussion of the "social responsibilities of the modern university."[51] He identified many of the same social ills as did Boyer and likewise lamented the fact that the university as a whole was doing little or nothing by way of directly confronting those ills. But like Boyer, Bok made no reference whatsoever to the social sciences as being the distinctive spearhead—the leading edge—of any subsequent university efforts to meet its "social responsibilities."

More recently, Duderstadt concurred with Boyer and Bok that post-K–12 ought to breathe new life into its historic concern with public service. Post-K–12 should, he observed, begin to weave concern over social problems into the tapestry of its unfolding agenda. Despite his concurrence with Bok and Boyer regarding that particular objective, he differed from them as to the fundamental reason why universities ought to pursue public service. Both Bok and Boyer believed that post-K–12 should move in that direction because it is the *right* or *moral* thing to do. But Duderstadt's rationale for such a move was based principally on *self-interest:*

> Universities must evolve [in the direction of wrestling with social issues] if they are to continue to earn public support. They must re-establish their relevance to this new social agenda or run the risk of being marginalized.[52]

He asserted that twentieth-century post-K–12 (read social sciences) did its "least impressive work" in addressing social ills.[53] Nonetheless, sheer self-interest, he reasoned, would compel twenty-first-century post-K–12 to stride beyond the level of mediocrity, and oblige it to explore a whole range of pressing social issues. Among these he included "revitalizing K–12 education, improving race relations, rebuilding our cities." Notwithstanding, he, like Bok and Boyer, entirely disregarded the social sciences and failed to place them at the vortex of such innovative explorations. Instead, he joined his colleagues by stating in rather ambiguous terms that the university should in *general* assume those sorts of hefty obligations.

The plight, for example, of economically disadvantaged children and their mothers was at the top of Boyer's list of problems he believed the universities should address. He also pinpointed the distressingly familiar matters of household poverty and the homelessness of mothers and children as pressing social issues:

> Given such conditions, can colleges and universities honestly conclude that the crises confronting America's children are someone else's problem?[54]

Next on Boyer's list was K–12. He described the well-known problems they confront, for example, the alienation, disinterest, and lack of a true love for learning on the part of all too many children and adolescents—including those from the more advantaged social classes. He asked if "colleges really believe they can ignore the social pathologies that surround schools and erode the educational foundations of our nation?" The problems of cities and urban America also showed up on Boyer's inventory. He cited an urban official's warning that "universities cannot afford to remain shores of affluence, self-importance, and horticultural beauty at the edge of island seas of squalor, violence, and despair."[55]

A New American College

Boyer did not, however, lay the universities' failure to deal with these and other social issues at the doorstep of the social sciences. Neither did he fault their peculiar basic social science spin as being part of the reason for the passivity of post-K–12 in the face of those kinds of pressing social problems. And, even more indicative of their apparent irrelevance, he does not even refer explicitly to the social sciences as being part of the solution. It's simply as though they weren't there at all—they're seemingly invisible. They have, since Harper's day, slowly but surely faded away into the ivy. Like his two colleagues, Boyer argued that post-K–12 in *general* should get more responsive to urgent social issues. Furthermore, his notably distinctive tack was to propose that post-K–12 ought to consider inventing a novel arrangement that he called the New American College. His new college would offer interested professors the option to pursue a much greater range of diversity and role specialization than existed throughout the twentieth century.

Although he did not make use of the particular labels, Boyer argued in effect that it might not be realistic to prevail on the entrepreneur, credentialer, or teacher-scholar to assume the prime responsibility for grappling with the kinds of complex social issues he identified. Indeed, we can no more expect the superprofessor to assume that obligation than we might count on him or her to take up the activities of the intellectual supervisor for undergraduates. For many years, Boyer was among the foremost advocates urging teacher-scholars to shift higher-order learning from the periphery and closer to the center of their undergraduate teaching activities. But, in his 1994 essay, he seemed to edge away somewhat from that generalist construction of the professor. He argued instead that just as some schools focus on research while others emphasize teaching,

> We also need institutions that define professional service as a central mission. The goal of such colleges would be to bring knowledge into intimate relationships with the small, daily problems of real people and real neighborhoods.[56]

Professors in those new colleges would, Boyer argued, "apply knowledge to real-life problems." Recall from chapter 1 that the applied social scientist "views himself or herself as a practitioner who contributes to solving or eliminating social problems."[57] Notwithstanding, that one-way street is not what Boyer seemed to have in mind. He did not, for example, assume that basic research would inform applied research without applied work also influencing basic work. Boyer instead advocated a model similar to that proposed by Rossi and by Spengler, namely, we should assume that scientific understanding and the redirection of social life influence one another over time. The new type of professor would, in his new college, be a specialist that Boyer, citing MIT's late Donald Schon, called a "reflective practitioner."[58]

If, for instance, the income-maintenance experiments described in chapter 1 had been allowed to continue for an indefinite period of time, the social scientists working on them could have been labeled quite correctly as reflective practitioners. That is, they began their work by intruding into the real, everyday world of poor married couples. The researchers gave money to households (defined as being caught up in a social problem) but withheld it from others (caught in the same problem) and then observed the consequences of their intrusion. The outcomes of their research provided them with a wealth of unexpected understanding that, if permitted to, they could then have used to keep on trying again and again to change the real world. As time went on, they would have been able to observe their results, ponder their fresh understandings, and then introduce further kinds of changes into the real world, and so on. Hence, the social scientist as a reflective practitioner is analogous to the life scientist who, in the laboratory, examines animal tissue beset by a problem (HIV, cancer), then intrudes on the tissue's cellular development with a certain biochemical, next observes the results, and thereby gains further understanding enabling him or her to fashion another type of intrusion, and so on.

Boyer argued that his new college would be organized on a "cross-disciplinary" basis, and also that "undergraduates . . . would participate in field projects, relating ideas to real life."[59] For our purposes, we could say that the players would participate with their coaches (from a range of social science disciplines) in being reflective practitioners. In essence, the coaches and players would, through mock-ups and actual investigations (when feasible) of one sort or another (chapters 5 and 6), seek to gain understanding regarding a particular social issue. Based on their understandings, they would then (as fully as possible and when feasible) act to implement certain changes of one sort or another. They would next observe (or simulate) the consequences of their actions and, among other things, regard those consequences as data supplying additional understanding, and so on.

Their efforts would, it is hoped, accomplish at least two objectives. First of all, the coaches and players would be trying to connect social science understanding with social betterment. Second, the players would be engaged in higher-order learning that is in fact discovery-based. There is no better means to cultivate one's human capital proficiencies than via problem solving—in this case, investigating social conditions perceived as a problem, that is, less than desirable, and aiming to change those conditions for the better in some (albeit small) manner. To be sure, actually changing social situations is no simple matter for all the reasons described in chapter 1 and elaborated further in chapters 6 and 7.

Nevertheless, that is the mission of the social sciences, and if we don't finally get serious about it, we run the several risks described in earlier chapters, including the acute invisibility presented in this chapter. Boyer argued that his new college, with its reflective practitioners, "would be committed to improving, in a very intentional way, the human condition."[60] For now, let's say that intentionally improving the human condition is one way of describing what it means to weave/repair the social fabric, or construct the "public household."[61] It's also another way of describing what it means to enable humankind to take possession of society and bring it under control. We must, at the same time, point out that critics pleading for universities to get active at resolving social issues may not appreciate fully what an overwhelming task it is to try to change social situations. But, in their defense, perhaps the principal reason why they don't entirely comprehend that reality is that the social sciences have not made weaving the social fabric their main agenda item. The upshot is that as far as the critics can discern, certain urgent social issues are out there and the universities are doing little or nothing about them.

Building on chapter 4, chapters 5, 6, and 7 explain that, within an "experimental module," that is, a new American college, cross-disciplinary teams of social scientists would take on the role of coach and seek to engage their players (along with grad students, postdocs, and sometimes citizens) in DBL. Such a strategy aims to weave the social fabric at the same time that the players' human capital skills are being cultivated. Implementing that strategy is obviously a big job and would in fact take a long time. Nevertheless, both of those long-range objectives are increasingly being constructed as *needs* that universities in general should be supplying. Given enough time, it's conceivable that those particular needs could in due course morph into pressing *demands*. In effect, a market could develop in which buyers would be looking for sellers who can deliver innovation of precisely that sort.[62] Moreover, if it develops, the social sciences would have a big stake in becoming a major player in such a market. To be otherwise seems unthinkable—especially given their already minor and marginalized position within both the academy and society.

NOTES

1. Arnone 2003.
2. Collins 2002.
3. Argetsinger 2001.
4. Coppola 2002.
5. Coppola 2002:B17.
6. Coppola 2002:B17.
7. Arney 2003. See also Marino 2001; Dutta 2001; Dee 2003a, b.
8. Cuban 1999:38; Cohen 1998.
9. Harper, cited in Bulmer 1984:15.
10. Cited in Cuban 1999:38.
11. Cuban 1999:41.
12. Fairweather 1996:109ff; Rhodes 1998; Cuban 1999.
13. Schank 2000.
14. Powell and Owen-Smith 2002.
15. Duderstadt 2000:315.
16. Rooney 2002.
17. Sizer 1992.

18. O'Banion 1997.
19. Brooks 2004.
20. Lanham 2002.
21. Fogg 2004b.
22. Schank 2000.
23. Burd 2003a:A31.
24. Burd 2004.
25. Sikes 2004.
26. Bartlett 2003a.
27. Cited in Bartlett 2003a.
28. Mansfield 2003; Kluge 2003.
29. De Court 1996; Boyer Commission 1998.
30. Mansfield 2003.
31. Resnick 1987.
32. Lanham 2002:176.
33. e.g., De Court 1996; The Glion Declaration 1999; Pescosolido and Aminzade 1999; Ruben 1995.
34. Ruben 1995; O'Banion 1997.
35. Melton 1998.
36. Rhodes 1998:11.
37. Flaherty 2002.
38. Fairweather 1996:112; Crimmel 1984; Bain 200a, b.
39. Duderstadt et al. 2002:64.
40. Duderstadt et al. 2002:64, italics in original.
41. Bartlett 2003c; Bain 200a, b.
42. Crimmel 1984.
43. Cohen 1998.
44. Fairweather 1996.
45. Wade 2003.
46. Cohen 1998:414–15; Bok 1982, 1990.
47. Flyvbjerg 2001; Collins 2002b.
48. Cited in Boyer 1994.
49. Cited in Boyer 1994.
50. Boyer 1994.
51. Bok 1982:84ff.
52. Duderstadt 2000:31.
53. Duderstadt 2000:145.
54. Boyer 1994.
55. Cited in Boyer 1994.
56. Boyer 1994. He quotes Ellen Condliffe Lagemann, but he does not add a citation.
57. Olsen 1981:565.
58. Schon 1983.
59. Boyer 1994.
60. Boyer 1994.
61. Bell 1990.
62. Brown and Duguid 2000:207ff.

Chapter Five

Discovery-Based Learning—
The Coach Cultivating
Players' Human Capital

> Undergraduate education in research universities [current and wannabe]
> requires renewed emphasis on a point strongly made by John Dewey . . .
> learning is based on discovery guided by mentoring rather than on the
> transmission of information.[1]

Discovery-based learning (DBL) is nothing more or less than inciting
William Harper's revolution among undergraduates. The professor must,
Harper insisted, infuse graduate students with the spirit and the substance of
what he or she has long struggled to cultivate. They're obliged to engage their
apprentices in a process of learning by doing, enabling them to become
skilled in addressing the important research questions within their area. And,
without any doubt, the Carnegie Commission's call to engage undergraduates
in a similar endeavor is a revolution of the same magnitude, whose consequences could just as far-reaching. To be sure, Harper never dreamed of educating undergrads in that manner. He held the conventional view of undergraduate learning shared by his contemporaries and, regrettably, by many
professors still today. This chapter contrasts that rather limited perspective
with what has been brought to light by the most recent research on undergraduate learning. And, if we reflect on it for a moment, it isn't the least bit
startling to realize that undergrads can learn in a manner identical to grad students. Indeed, as Dewey observed, everyone at every age learns in precisely
that same fashion. His thesis was that higher-order learning demands that the
learner has "accomplished something or . . . [is] able to do something."[2]

And, by the end of the twentieth century, the University of Louvain's Erik
de Corte arrived once again at that same elementary, yet profound, conclusion. He did so after reviewing the large body of recent research literature
from both sides of the Atlantic exploring the issue of undergraduate learning.[3]

He found that the work was permeated by three overarching themes. Each theme has been alluded to in prior chapters and will be developed more fully in this chapter. Chapter 6 explores how those themes might enable students to participate in figuring out inventions to address social issues.

First of all, cultivating human capital skills requires "a fundamentally new conception of learning and teaching" (i.e., as problem solving).[4] Second, it "implies a major alteration in the position and the role of the students" (i.e., as active players).[5] Third, it "requires drastic changes in the role of the teacher" (i.e., as coach, facilitator, mentor).[6] And, based on their analyses of that same vast literature, Americans Robert Barr and John Tagg considered all three points (and more) when they urged post-K–12 to replace their ancient "teaching/instructional paradigm" with what they called a new "learning paradigm."[7] One observer compressed that massive amount of research about reinventing learning into the ten overlapping and interconnected points displayed in figure 5.1.[8] These mutually reinforcing notions provide an initial grasp of some of the more salient contrasts between a teaching paradigm and a learning paradigm.

A HISTORIC BASIS FOR THE
TEACHING PARADIGM—*TELLING AND TESTING*

Arthur Cohen reminds us that the "history of higher education . . . teaches appreciation for the power of tradition. . . . The system successfully resists, co-opts, or absorbs—eventually changing but with the glacial majesty befitting a venerable structure."[9] The glacial-like character of higher education is plain to see when it comes to the tenacity of the teaching paradigm (TP). At its core lies the premise that the entire point of having students around is to "instruct" them—to pass on knowledge. The operant word is *input*—the professor is duty-bound to "cover the course materials," to "expose" her or his students to what's "important" for them to "know." And because professors are the transmitters of information, they are situated at the center of the teaching enterprise and are thus

From teaching to learning organizations
From passive students to active learners
From faculty-centered to learner-centered
From linear, sequential curricula to hyperlearning experiences
From just-in-case learning to just-in-time learning to just-for-you learning
From credit-hour or seat-time credentialing to learning assessment
From solitary learning to interactive, collaborative learning
From classroom learning to learning communities
From campus-based to asynchronous to ubiquitous learning opportunities
From student or alumnus to lifelong member of a learning community

Figure 5.1.

much more active than students that, by comparison, are relatively more passive. The proverbial sage-on-the-stage imagery captures that reality quite well. Cohen tells us that TP has dominated post-K–12 ever since the seventeenth-century founding of the very first colleges in America. The Protestant clergy who ran those colleges borrowed it, of course, from Europe, where the paradigm had thrived at least since the Middle Ages.[10]

Within the European (and later American) churches (whether Protestant or Roman Catholic), the legitimacy and significance of TP was conveyed to children for perhaps the first time when they entered catechism or confirmation classes. Successful completion of the classes ushered the child into a new and respected social status and, with that, they were given permission to receive Holy Communion, or baptism, or church membership. Never mind that most children were illiterate. All they had to do was listen to the priest or pastor explain the unintelligible sounds of the catechism, memorize them, and finally recite the answers to the questions their cleric might direct at them.

Many European universities were during that period influenced heavily, if not controlled, by a church of one persuasion or another. The European universities—followed later by the American colleges—relied almost exclusively on TP because the professors believed it was the innate, or natural, or obvious means of educating (male) students. Educating in the sense of stocking the student's mind with stuff. But not knowledge in the everyday, ordinary, run-of-the-mill, *secular* sense in which, say, the master printer might, as described below, mentor his apprentice. Instead, the knowledge passed on by the professors was *sacred,* in the sense that all of their knowledge came from God, either through the church or through scripture. Their task was to fill up empty vessels with ultimate (unchanging) truth.

The professor's lecture was seen as existing virtually on the same level as the clergyman's homily. Moreover, just as the experience of listening to the sermon was thought to be beneficial because of the information he passed on, the university lecture, too, was constructed in that same unique and sublime manner. Accordingly, students were expected to attend very carefully to the professor in order to be able to repeat the truths he'd told to them via the lecture. By repeating them, the students demonstrated that they'd actually "learned" those truths and, as a consequence, they were perceived as better off than persons who were not learned. Moreover, the students were now in a position to pass those truths on to others that were less enlightened.

AN ANCIENT MODEL OF MENTORING— *LEARNING BY DOING*

Bear in mind that ordinary folk and privileged classes alike were thoroughly familiar with an alternative, and ancient, model for learning. And that was, of course, the informal but essential mentoring that had gone on for centuries, in which younger males worked with men within their extended family and from their community to learn by doing it how to maintain livestock, grow crops, fish, and hunt for game. Similarly, younger females worked with women both in and out of their extended family to learn by doing it how to perform their numerous household tasks including, of course, bearing and caring for children. And, adjacent to their dwelling, girls learned by doing it how to grow vegetables, milk cows, and care for poultry and other barnyard animals.

Furthermore, beyond the realm of extended families and the broader community, the notion of generational mentoring became formalized in the shape of the apprentice system. A peasant boy might be indentured to a master, for example, a blacksmith, harness maker, carpenter, stone mason, wheelwright, builder, gunsmith, printer, and so on, for a set number of years, receiving during that time hardly more than basic food and primitive shelter. Plainly, the boy hoped that he would learn his master's skill by doing it, and thus be able eventually to survive on his own. And, for her part, a peasant girl might be bound over for some years to a wealthy household in order to learn, by doing it, how to perform the myriad tasks that the privileged classes expected their domestic servants to perform.

Besides the fact that one possessed secular and the other sacred knowledge, another important distinction between clergy/professor on one side, and the master/mentor on the other, was the responsibility for ensuring that the learner actually connected knowledge with action. The clergy or professor, for example, hoped ardently that his parishioner or student would use her or his knowledge to serve God in the world. Knowledge was never viewed merely as an end in itself (intellectual navel-gazing) but ultimately was seen as a means to serve God by doing good works in society.

The requirement, however, to see that such a link actually occurred rested almost entirely with the parishioner or student, not with the clergy or professor. The clergy were, of course, obliged to test the candidate prior to confirmation, and the professor was required to test the student. But neither monitored the everyday life of the candidate or student to make sure he or she actually obeyed the truth by putting it into action. At the same time, one could argue that the Catholic practice of confession was a mechanism for the priest to check up on his flock. And, among New England Puritans, the belief that "I am my brother's keeper" meant that every community member was expected to keep a sharp eye on other members in order to help make sure they actually obeyed the truth.

Notwithstanding, whether Catholic or Protestant, the ultimate obligation for linking knowledge with action lay with the parishioner or student, not with the professor, priest, or pastor. But, by contrast, because it was clearly in the master's self-interest to ensure that his learner connected knowledge with action, he took all necessary steps in a determined effort to make sure that such a link actually occurred. His self-interest was first of all economic, because a skillful apprentice was likely to earn money for the master, whereas a blunderer would surely cost him money. Second, his self-interest was also intangible, in the sense that status, esteem, and prestige were attached to a master that was known to produce, say, expert blacksmiths or fine violin makers. Masters took a great deal of pride in the fact that they had a reputation to uphold, both for the quality of their own craftsmanship and for the reliability and excellence of their craftsmen.

Roger Schank and his colleagues have for some time been exploring the issues of how people learn and "how we can teach."[11] He and Chip Cleary concluded that there are two broad theories, or perspectives, to help us understand what learning is and how it happens. The first they called the "transfer" or the "warehouse" viewpoint, which is simply another way to characterize TP. This point of view "proposes that one learns effectively by being told."[12] Plainly the churches, followed by the colleges and universities, were and are persuaded that good telling equals learning.

The second theory, say Schank and Cleary, is the "acquisition" model, and that's simply another way to describe the learning paradigm.[13] Here, the focus is far less on the "what" (the information itself) than on "how [students] will come to know [acquire the information]. How we learn [acquire] determines what [information] we learn."[14] Plainly, the informal mentoring that took place for eons among extended families and communities, followed later by the formal mentoring of masters, sprang directly from this second perspective. Mentor and mentored persons alike were persuaded that the *how* of learning something is through the doing it. Furthermore, parties on both sides were equally active in the doing of it.

SECULAR KNOWLEDGE AND LEARNING BY DOING

Cohen reminds us that during the latter part of the seventeenth century colleges and universities on both sides of the Atlantic became increasingly secularized. Knowledge was no longer limited to revelation, but sprang increasingly from reason (philosophy) and in particular from experimentation (science). A fundamental premise of secular and especially scientific knowledge is that it is *never* ultimate truth. Whatever is known today cannot ever be the last word. Nor will tomorrow's knowledge ever be considered final. The essence, after all, of being a researcher is to replace the information of today and tomorrow with new, more valid knowledge, realizing full well that the day after tomorrow another researcher will repeat precisely that very same process. Thus was laid the foundation of the research university and of graduate education—particularly in Germany, and later imported to the United States in the late nineteenth century.[15]

Furthermore, one can discern instantly the genetic link between secular knowledge and a theory of learning based on doing. The secular frame of mind and the theory of learning based on doing are intimate partners. By definition, a researcher does not acquire information by being told. The scientific bent of mind demands a healthy skepticism toward every bit of existing knowledge. In order to learn (acquire new knowledge), one must find out for oneself—one must *do* something. And that constant doing inevitably displaces today's knowledge with tomorrow's information.

Nevertheless, although professors and their investigations got secularized over many decades, the aura and mystique that for centuries imbued TP continued to rub off onto professors—especially in their dealings with undergrads. They constructed themselves as special people with important things to say. The transition from the sacred to the secular did nothing to undermine the notion of the professor as an admired icon—a sage on the stage, a revered guru. Hence, undergrads were obliged to attend carefully to what the guru said in order that they, too, could eventually say or write it, thus demonstrating that they were entitled to a special status. Although most secular knowledge was known to be short-lived and transitory, it was nonetheless viewed as sufficiently enduring for undergrads to memorize and repeat it via an examination.

Cohen reminds us further that during the late nineteenth and especially the twentieth century, colleges and universities opened their doors wide to vast numbers of undergraduates, ordinary citizens. TP, including its centerpiece, the lecture, came to be viewed as the most efficient means of educating the largest number of students at the lowest possible cost. Hence, added to its unique historic quality was the element of cost efficiency—a patently unbeatable combination. Hence, concluded the Boyer task force,

> The experience of most undergraduates at most research universities is that of receiving what is served out to them. In one course after another they listen, transcribe, absorb, and repeat, essentially as undergraduates have done for centuries. . . . The traditional lecturing and note-taking, certified by periodic examinations, was created for a time when books were scarce and costly. . . . The delivery system persisted into the present because it was familiar, easy, and required no imagination.[16]

And not just at research universities, but at wannabe schools as well. TP now permeates most of post-K–12—even many (not all) community colleges, where classes tend to be smaller than they are at four-year institutions.[17]

To be sure, chinks on the face of the TP glacier have been noticeable for some time. As far back as 1931, Hamilton Holt, then president of Rollins College, told a national conference of academics that the lecture method was "probably the worst possible scheme ever devised for imparting knowledge."[18] Holt mused that the lecture is

> that mysterious process by means of which the contents of the professor's notebooks are transferred by means of the fountain pen to the pages of the student's notebook without passing through the mind of either.[19]

THE SILVER BULLET OF TECHNOLOGY

More recently, some of TP's proponents have turned to information technology as a silver bullet, or magic amulet, that might somehow slow its meltdown. At Stanford University, quipped observer Ian Parker, "the use of PowerPoint is so widespread that to refrain from using it is sometimes seen as a mark of seniority and privilege, like egg on one's tie."[20] Schank added that, for the most part, the currently prevailing technologies (PowerPoint, filmed courses offered on closed circuit TV, and courses offered online) are constructed as ways to shore up the sagging TP, but surely not to replace it.[21] Based on the results of their recent research into the uses of technology at several universities, Robert Zemsky and William Massy describe PowerPoint as "essentially 'electronic clip art.'"[22]

In the emerging information age, students encounter virtually nothing that's the same as it was several centuries ago. TP is, nonetheless, a notable exception to that generalization. The fact that TP is a curious anomaly is, however, muted by the technologies that, on the surface, create the facade of making TP appear contemporary. For example, St. Joseph's University (Philadelphia) has completed a $30 million building that's "wired to the hilt."[23] In one classroom, adds observer Scott Carlson, "students sit behind glowing laptops that are plugged into . . . the campus data network." Carlson claims that wired classrooms with technologies permitting "unprecedented interactivity between students and professors, are changing the face of the lecture hall." Moreover, Carlson is quite correct when he asserts that a growing number of university administrators "see those wired classrooms as the future of higher education."

The huge problem is, of course, that administrators "struggle with the challenge of getting more professors to use [sophisticated] technology in the classroom."[24] George Mason University president Alan G. Merten is attempting to entice his professors to leap into the brave new world of instructional technology (IT) by offering them the unique opportunity to teach in his brandnew $20 million high-tech building. Merten's Innovation Hall is reserved for any and all professors (not departments) who commit to jumping into the realm of sophisticated, technology-based instruction. Making such a leap should not, however, be done apart from realizing that technology is a relentlessly demanding overseer. Ongoing upgrades in software/hardware are the name of the game, and the professor expecting to be successful in this unpredictable and fluid realm must keep abreast of the latest advances. Merten declares, for instance, that if a professor now in the hall ceases to stay innovative and remain on top of her or his work, "we'll throw you out and bring someone else in."[25]

The point is that it's easier said than done to conceive of today's typical superprofessor as being able to invest the huge amounts of time, thought, and creative energy requisite to become proficient and remain competitive in the ever-shifting and extremely fluid sphere of undergraduate IT.[26] Such an all-consuming activity generates zero pay-off in terms of one's quest to mimic the research elite in one's discipline and thereby to embellish one's professional reputation. Nevertheless, IT is a sleeping giant that's already stirring and thrashing about, and its continued incursion into undergraduate instruction throughout the new century appears inescapable.[27]

That being the case, one might picture, say, the credentialer who is technology savvy as being the specialist most likely to take Merten's leap of faith and to seize the opportunity to carve out a unique niche for him/herself. And, in that vein, New York University president John Sexton wants to "create or make new categories of faculty members. These include 'teaching professors' who are not judged by their research, *'cyberfaculty'* members who specialize in the use of the Internet."[28] Although Sexton's cyberfaculty would not be tenured, Karen Arenson reports they would be "higher prestige professors" than the lowly and rather marginalized "adjunct teacher."[29] The clear implication is that plunging ahead into this murky realm of technological innovation is likely to be one effectual means to thwart the dismal predictions that Randall Collins made for the typical credentialer.[30] The cybercredentialer who is talented and skillful in the realm of undergrad IT would surely become a valued and highly sought-after commodity by the rapidly expanding array of administrators who, like Sexton and Merten, are determined to achieve two vital goals simultaneously—to become more cost-efficient and to refurbish the ancient TP for the twenty-first century.

Nevertheless, despite fast-moving technological advances placing cyberfaculty at center console, the archaic TP would, under that scenario, likely remain supreme.[31] Given that he or she would remain the revered guru dispensing facts, figures, and ideas, the tech-savvy credentialer would continue to play a much more active classroom role than the students. One encounters relatively few advocates suggesting that technology might somehow play a pivotal role in facilitating some type of innovative learning paradigm.[32] Consequently, TP—in its low-tech, and increasingly in its high-tech, contours—is likely to remain a stubborn presence well into the foreseeable future.

THE TEACHING PARADIGM GETS AN INCOMPLETE

On the basis of his many years of empirical research on the undergraduate experience at America's colleges and universities, Alexander Astin concluded that the conventional belief that *what* undergraduates learn is more significant than *how* they might learn it remains largely uncontested.[33] The process of learning continues to play second fiddle to the outcome or product, that is, the stuff. Notwithstanding, he wonders if professors ought to consider the "possibility that the student's 'general education' consists of something more than the content of what is taught."[34]

Astin is, in effect, confronting the ancient credo that professors have fulfilled their obligations to students once they've supplied them with subject matter—information or knowledge. And although he doesn't employ the precise term, Astin's reasoning suggests that his "something more" is the higher-order learning captured by figure 4.1.[35] Needless to say, learning paradigm (LP) advocates never make the silly claim that information is irrelevant. More accurately, LP advocates argue that although information is obviously vital, the means—the how—of acquiring it turns out to be even more significant. Telling students about facts, figures, persons, dates, and ideas ought no longer to be the definitive objective of undergraduate education, as is now the case. The new aim of nurturing human capital skills would replace it:

> The skills of analysis, evaluation, and synthesis will become the hallmarks of a good education, just as absorption of a body of knowledge once was.[36]

In alarmed reaction, some academics might pounce on such a proposed re-ordering of priorities and disparage it as both extreme and risky. Students come to college, they say, to soak up vital information. And if we don't concentrate on presenting them with stuff, we shall have failed them by ill-preparing them for life.

Fair enough. Public officials and other friendly critics already resonate with that argument, namely, that college students should accumulate information. Recently, in fact, officials have gotten so worked up about the issue of how much stuff college students actually learn and retain they've begun increasingly to propose testing schemas analogous to those imposed for some years on K–12.[37] Officials reason that if the professor's objective is to transmit stuff, then officials, parents, and citizens ought to be able to hold the professor accountable for her or his successes (or failures) in doing so. Some officials suggest, for instance, that by the end of their junior or senior year they should be able test college students (just as they now test K–12 students) in order to determine how much stuff they've actually stored in their heads.

Ultimately, officials hope to link accountability for student learning to dollars.[38] The George W. Bush administration, along with some Democratic representatives, proposed, for example, that reauthorization of the 2003 Higher Education Act, "which governs how colleges and universities get federal money," include accountability measures of student learning.[39] Built into that accountability, say officials, would be indicators of value added.[40] Do students know more stuff when they leave college than when they entered it? And, from a related angle, can it be shown that college youth have actually stored more stuff in their heads than have, say, noncollege youth of the same age, gender, economic background, and race/ethnicity?

Fair enough once again. Moreover, to address that question in a nonthreatening manner, the National Center for Public Policy and Higher Education prepared its second report on college and university performance.[41] The center's 2002 report assessed every one of the fifty states across several dimensions. One dimension was "What do we know about student learning as a result of education and training beyond high school?" The disappointing (but hardly surprising) answer was, not very much. In that category of student learning, the report assigned an "incomplete" to every state, and for that reason it captured a lot of media attention.

> Few states, if any, know about the learning of their graduates of private colleges—or about the intellectual capabilities of their college-educated residents—regardless of where they were educated. Moreover, the information that states do gather about collegiate learning is specific to each state; it cannot be used to compare performance relative to other states. As Measuring Up 2000 made clear, it is only in the context of these kinds of comparisons that a state can know whether its level of performance is good or bad news.[42]

Given that post-K–12 has, for undergrads, deemed higher-order learning to be desirable but dispensable, it was not the least bit surprising to find out that the report was entirely silent about how successful or not schools have been in the realms of students' "critical thinking, communications skills, quantitative literacy, and problem solving."[43] Nevertheless, what thoroughly astonished officials, business-leaders, and citizens was the absence of any data regarding the precise thing that most of post-K–12 holds to be *in*dispensable—lower-order learning, that is, curricular content, knowledge, or information. The absence of any data as to how much stuff students actually know caught officials and business leaders entirely by surprise. The reason for their utter shock and amazement is that they're keenly aware that academics deem the transmission of stuff to be pivotal to their mission. Public officials, business leaders, and interested citizens found it "'outrageous' that a report card on higher education was mute regarding the knowledge and skills of persons that had completed at least some education beyond high school."[44]

At first glance, it seems unbelievably strange that on the one side, professors claim that knowing stuff is what college is all about, but on the other, they're indifferent to, and frequently resist, efforts to impose any sort of comprehensive examination on how much stuff their students might actually store and retain. That puzzle begins to be resolved, however, if we recall the expediency of the 1967 Stanford committee on teaching: "Let the objective of curricular planning be to encourage the faculty member to teach what he likes to teach and the student to learn what seems vital to him."[45] One upshot of that widely copied principle is that the vast majority of today's undergraduates are exposed to a hodgepodge—an infinite cafeteria line—of courses.

Furthermore, an ever-growing army of professors (with their distinctively narrow research interests) continues to pour more and more ingredients into the mishmash. Schank notes that such a chaotic potpourri is one reason why graduate schools no longer require (as they once did) their applicants to take the Graduate Record Exam in their specialty field of study.[46] Given the curricular chaos and virtual course anarchy undergraduates must contend with, it's impossible to reasonably expect that "such and such a fact" is the right stuff for a college graduate to know—whether it be in the humanities, history, the social sciences, or the sciences.[47]

The surest way to terrify undergraduates is to hint (even obliquely) that learning might imply some tiny smidgeon of retention: *Even though our course ends today with our final exam, at some point in the near future,* quips the professor in jest, *you'll be held responsible for the stuff you've just "learned" in this class.* In support of his assertion that *how* one learns is far more significant than *what* is acquired (for the test), Schank notes that students have adapted quite successfully to the TP typically practiced in both K–12 and post-K–12.[48] They've adapted, he says, by honing their short-term memory skills to an exceedingly fine edge. One obvious outcome of those short-term memory skills is that most students have gotten extraordinarily proficient at taking (cramming for) either multiple-guess or essay exams. But in no way can it be said, he adds, that today's college students are learning in the senses captured by figure 4.1.

That grave shortcoming might go unnoticed, however, if it could be demonstrated that students stored vital information beyond the close of today's final exam. If, for instance, the national center had reported that college graduates do indeed share a common core of important stuff about history, science, literature, and civic affairs, then advocates for lower-order learning would have a compelling argument in their favor. Schank, however, contends that, surprisingly enough, perfecting short-term memory skills to the exclusion of human capital skills actually tends to undermine the person's capability to retain the stuff beyond the test.[49] As counterintuitive as it seems, retention appears to be enhanced when telling stuff to students ceases to be the professor's principal objective.[50] As Dewey suggested a long time ago, retention is an inevitable by-product of cultivating the sorts of skills described by figure 4.1. In common sense terms, the surest way to retain and store stuff—whether driving a car, operating a computer, or understanding the sheer folly of World War I—is to *think* about it carefully and, simultaneously, to practice *doing* it. (In the case of World War I, the practice could be in the shape of games and simulation, as discussed in chapter 6.) If one is not a "reflective practitioner," stuff passes in one's ear (though it stays put long enough for the test) and soon exits through the other.[51]

Anyone who takes the time to ask an informal sampling of students and/or recent college graduates some simple stuff about history, for instance, is likely to come out at the same place as Anders Henriksson.[52] His wildly entertaining book was described as "a history of the world taken verbatim from term papers and exams at American and Canadian colleges."[53] He concludes that his data show that a "base of common knowledge [regarding history] isn't as wide as we commonly assume." Most college persons are simply unable to provide correct answers to straightforward questions such as "In what year did the U.S. Civil War end? World War II? When was the Russian Revolution? When did World War II start? When did American women get the right to vote in national elections? When was Napoleon defeated at Waterloo? When did Hitler become German chancellor?"[54]

And, more importantly, even fewer students are able to find an error "in each of these excerpts from [actual] student essays collected by Henriksson: Martin Luther Junior's famous 'If I had a hammer speech.' John F. Kennedy worked closely with the Russians to solve the Canadian missile crisis. Stalin, Roosevelt, Churchill, and Truman were known as the 'Big Three.' Athena the Hun rampaged the Balkans as far as France. Ferdinand and Isabella conquered Granola, a part of Spain now known as Mexico. Good times ended when England suffered civil war between the Musketeers and the Round Ones."[55]

My own experiences closely parallel Henriksson's. To draw from one of endless examples, during a recent class discussion of the 1960s civil rights movement a white student asked if "Martin Luther King was a slave." No other student (black or white) volunteered a response, and the perplexed expressions on their faces made it quite clear that no one in the class seemed quite certain (or even cared much) about this matter. From this and literally hundreds of other similar occurrences, my impression (and my nonrandom sampling of colleagues and students from around the United States and Canada does nothing to contradict it) is that many college persons appear to be uninformed re basic historical stuff.

That is so despite the fact they might recently have taken one or more courses in which they were required to pass an exam on which that same stuff had appeared. One very bright student remarked that he'd just completed a course on nineteenth-century U.S. history, and so I asked who Napoleon was: "Some French guy who lived in Louisiana," was his immediate response. Nor is history any different from the remaining areas, social sciences, humanities, sciences, and so on. For instance, a recent study by the National Science Foundation discovered that "70 percent of American adults do not understand the scientific process."[56] And, although the report didn't say so, one can't help wondering if the study found any differences between college and noncollege persons. Regardless of the field of study, students are extraordinarily adept at passing exams on the knowledge the professor thinks is important but then speedily allowing the information to leach into the trash bin.

WHO DECIDES WHAT STUDENTS ACTUALLY "LEARN"?

Schank argues that students' perfecting their short-term memory skills reveals their adroitness in determining how best to exploit the hodgepodge of courses served up to them.[57] They've simply adopted the pragmatic stance of not storing any information except what they're interested in or feel they can use either in another course or in real life.[58] Retaining information from calculus I, for instance, is highly useful for as long as it takes to complete calculus II. If, however, students can't use the stuff now or in the future, or if they have no particular interest in it, into the trash bin it goes.

I shall never forget the keen disappointment and frustration I felt when it first socked me at a gut level how students actually feel about much of the stuff that we believe is so important—vital enough, in fact, to insist they repeat it back to us. I was teaching an honors college section of twenty-five sophomores with stratospheric SAT scores and a nearly flawless grade point average (GPA) in both high school and college. Every one of them was in a highly demanding field, for example, premed, engineering, or the sciences. They'd enrolled in the course because it fulfilled their social science general education requirement. All of them freely and unashamedly acknowledged that they behaved precisely as Schank said they would: if they have no use for course content (whether in or out of their major field), it's promptly forgotten.

I recall most vividly how puzzled I was that even "the brightest and the best" possessed no authentic love for learning, no intellectual curiosity, and no passion for knowledge for its own sake. I was profoundly distressed by the fact they viewed the contents of their courses no differently than did the vast majority of their less gifted fellow students. They saw content primarily in utilitarian terms, as a necessary and often tedious step toward the accumulation of the credit hours requisite for getting credentialed.[59] Nonetheless, in their defense, I must say that the pragmatic stance of today's undergraduates is precisely what one would expect. Given the system in which they're required to function, and on the basis of the implications of recent theories about learning, students are behaving in an entirely predictable, that is, "rational," fashion.

According to Schank and Cleary, there are two "fundamental lessons [that are the basis of] learning theory." One is, "An interest is a terrible thing to waste"; the second is, "Students must be in control of their own learning."[60] Both lessons are buttressed by the broader proposition that genuine learning occurs best in a social situation that is *student* centered. TP ignores that proposition and its implications. It insists instead on the opposing postulate that learning is *professor* centered. Moreover, the first axiom derived from the latter postulate is that the professor tells the student what she or he should be interested in. The second axiom is that the professor is in control of what the student learns. In effect, professors wholly concur with the viewpoint that all knowledge is not created equal. But they retain the right and authority to decide which information is more equal than others: the most equal information is what professors expect students to learn for the test.

Unfortunately, many professors appear blithely unaware of recent "robust empirical evidence"[61] that agricultural people and masters/mentors alike have, for centuries, regarded as common sense. Growing numbers of studies are demonstrating that students are not "passive recipients of information . . . they actively construct their knowledge and skills."[62] They, like humans in every situation, pick and choose and tweak what they believe to be important. In short, today's students, as all persons have always done, claim the right and the authority to decide which information is more equal than others—they decide what they wish to learn and retain or not. To be sure, they will readily memorize (and promptly forget) the stuff imposed on them for the test—but they do not make it their own and retain it. Hence, my earlier frustration at students' refusal to retain what I believed was so vital reflected my feelings about a larger struggle for authority between professors and students that students inevitably win. They win because, of course, professors invariably acquiesce.

Professors give in because the alternatives to doing so simply make no sense at all in terms of enhancing their professional reputation. Trying to devise, for example, a tightly organized and coherent curriculum—including comprehensive examinations—would bloody the floors of most departmental conference rooms and waste enormous amounts of precious time and energy. Resolving the explosive issue (especially in the humanities and social sciences) of what is the right stuff we believe students in our field should know could drag on longer than the Thirty Years' War and be just as exhausting and indecisive. Adding fuel to the flames of the war is the professor's jealously guarded freedom to teach whatever he or she likes to teach. Moreover, in the event that public officials insisted on comprehensive field exams, many teacher-scholars would be diverted from teaching the specialized courses that they like (and that require little preparation because they have taught them hundreds of times) to the preparation of new courses focusing on the right stuff. Given the incessant demands of today's emerging entrepreneurial university, it would be sheer folly for teacher-scholars to make those kinds of risky investments of time and creative energy.

Critics of K–12 and post-K–12 alike argue that studies such as the policy center's demonstrate an alarming lack of "cultural literacy" on the part of U.S. citizens. Critics—including many public officials—assert that there ought to be a "definitive answer to the question, 'What should an educated person know?'"[63] And, in pursuit of what they believe to be an unassailable policy objective, officials and educators draw up "literacy lists" based on the premise that learning that type of distinctive stuff is the "only available ticket to full citizenship. . . . [And] the only sure avenue of opportunity for disadvantaged children."[64] Such beguiling phrases are now the stock-in-trade of politicians from both major parties, and the "leave no child behind" catchphrase is a rallying cry for supporters of the sorts of standardized testing that is now transforming K–12.[65] Because state and federal dollars are linked to students' achievement scores on such tests, K–12 teachers are spending ever-increasing amounts of time "teaching to the test," that is, diligently preparing students to get high scores on those tests.

Never mind that, given enough pressure, students of any age will memorize whatever they must for the upcoming test—especially if they're clued in (via some sort of detailed study guide or other method offered by many teachers and professors) about what's likely to show up on the test. Never mind that "knowing a random fact is simply that and no more."[66] Furthermore, never mind that students will promptly forget most of what they memorize because learning is socially constructed in the sense that persons retain only what interests them, and most of what they are forced to memorize in K–12 and college holds no appeal for them whatever. Finally, never mind that striving

> to know everything that makes up the "core" of our culture is an impossible and useless goal. When culture was younger and more tightly defined, it might not have been unreasonable to ask that an educated person recognize all the cultural icons. But the breadth and depth of today's culture makes that a ridiculous requirement.[67]

Despite how Schank and Cleary might feel about the issue of cultural literacy, the fact is that critics and officials have recently trained their guns on post-K–12. Energized by their supposed successes with K–12, critics and officials are determined to introduce accountability standards into post-K–12 and, if need be, to do so through some sort of achievement or comprehensive testing. Because officials are frustrated by previous efforts to impose accountability on superprofessors, some are now resorting to the carrot, for example, offering accountability incentives to the credentialer—especially if she or he agrees to go the cybercredentialer route.

DISCOVERY-BASED LEARNING—*PLAYERS AS AGENTS*

The alternative higher education movement of the 1960s and 1970s sensed intuitively what recent research into learning is now demonstrating, namely that in order to learn students "have to become more and more agents over their own acquisition processes."[68] Being an agent implies a certain degree of control or influence over the circumstances of one's life. In this case, being an agent means participating in decisions about one's learning experiences.[69] Participation, or collaboration, is simply another way to talk about being democratic. And figure 3.1 showed how thoroughly Dewey's principles of democracy and egalitarianism imbued those alternative schools. At the same time, the professors and students in those schools failed to recognize that, in order to thrive, a democratic, or collaborative, structure at any level requires clear and enforceable guidelines of accountability. They were so put off by the elitism and rigidity of conventional post-K–12 that some of them ventured perilously close to the opposite extreme—a chaotic state of affairs captured by a popular and enticing maxim of the time. Just do your own thing.

A major challenge facing the coach—in the context of the module (the New American College) described in chapter 4—is to foster an atmosphere for learning that is democratic, that is, both collaborative (participatory) and accountable, or responsible. The historic master/mentor is the prime archetype of how the coach might work within the module. Drawing on the first fundamental lesson of learning, the coach assumes that the student, or player, is there because she or he (like the apprentice) has a serious *interest* in learning—not, however, interested primarily in *what*, in simply storing information. Instead, the player wants to learn *how* to carry out the same kinds of capabilities that the coach/master now possesses: "skilled thinking and problem solving, resulting in competent performance in their domain."[70] The domain is, in our case, the repair/weaving of the social fabric. Plainly, those sorts of sophisticated human capital skills cannot be cultivated in a milieu that is chaotic or disorderly—one cannot presume that "doing your own thing" with little or no concern for the "things of others" would, over the long haul, be of much benefit to anyone.

The flip side of being interested in a particular domain is that one should have a sense of control over learning about it. According to the second fundamental lesson of learning, the player must feel that he or she has a certain degree of jurisdiction over the learning process. The players' responsibilities must, in short, be balanced by their freedom to shape the character of those responsibilities. The (oft maligned) entrepreneur and her or his apprentices are a contemporary template for the module's coaches and players to follow. The graduate apprentices join the entrepreneur's shop because, presumably, they have a keen interest in a particular domain. Their principal interest lies in learning how to do research in that domain, although in the process of doing so they fully expect to acquire a grasp of the stuff that's currently extant within it. There's a high level of mutual responsibility between the entrepreneur and the apprentice—the former is accountable to assist the apprentice in figuring out how to do research, and the latter is accountable to do it. A similarly high degree of mutual responsibility exists in the module between the coach and players—the former to assist the player in figuring how to do research in the realm of weaving the social fabric, and the latter to learn how to do it.

Furthermore, the entrepreneur has a keen interest in the apprentice becoming highly proficient, not only to further the shop's research objectives, but also to contribute to the entrepreneur's intellectual growth and professional development. The ultimate ideal is, in short, for the apprentice one day to become as good as, if not better than, the entrepreneur. In order to cultivate such a lofty degree of excellence and capability, the entrepreneur has no choice but to allow the apprentice to have a certain degree of freedom and autonomy in pursuit of the shop's objectives. Hence, by encouraging a high degree of freedom and autonomy, the shop becomes strongly collaborative. Chapter 6 elaborates the ways in which the module is comparable to this description of the shop. The coach must, within a context of mutual responsibility, provide a high degree of autonomy for his or her players. Hence, in being guided by the second fundamental lesson of learning, the module is likewise participatory and, in that sense too, democratic.

There are, of course, certain crucial differences between the shop and the module. One of the most important is that the shop is, unquestionably, a preprofessional experience for its grad students. They intend to enter the particular disciplines represented by the shop's entrepreneurs. On the other hand, for the undergrads, the module may or may not be a preprofessional experience. Like most social science majors today, the majority of the module's students are likely to enter an assortment of fields including (but not limited to) business, K–12, government service, and the nonprofit sector.

Consequently, those kinds of students would be attracted to the module for two principal reasons. First, it offers an apprenticeship in the kinds of transferable human capital skills they're hoping to carry with them after college when they enter any range of fields in today's rapidly evolving marketplace. Those portable skills are, moreover, certified to last a lifetime. Unlike stuff that is constantly under threat of becoming obsolete, those kinds of skills, like fine wine, only improve with age. The module would thus fulfill the classic liberal arts ideal, namely, preparing students to participate in a full range of labor force activities by outfitting him or her with a set of timeless capabilities.[71] And, as noted before and especially in chapter 7, we may expect that throughout the twenty-first-century information age marketplace, the demand for citizens who have high levels of those human capital capabilities is likely to get increasingly urgent. Second, even though most don't intend to become professionals in that realm, the module's students presumably have some interest in the issue of inventions that address social issues. Hence, in the process of gaining those portable human capital skills, they would also very likely have learned and retained a good deal of information about pressing social issues that concern them and their society.

At the same time, a portion of the module's undergraduates would, as do a number of today's social science majors, plan to enter one of the several professional fields linked in certain ways with social science. These tend to include what chapter 1 called the "applied" social science professions—for example, social workers, community coordinators, or policy analysts, to name but a few. The big difference is, of course, that the module's objective is to try to get beyond the conventional basic/applied distinction and to develop what was described as a synthesis of understanding and redirection. Moreover, chapter 6 explains how that synthesis is captured by the term "reflective practitioner." Chapter 6 also makes it clear that enabling players' skills at addressing social issues is part of the long-term objective of citizens' taking possession of society. Hence, the module is, for some students at least, indeed preprofessional, because it seeks to outfit them with both the vision and the tools to seek (in their professional life) to do social science that matters, that is, social science that aims to make some sort of difference in society.[72]

DISCOVERY-BASED LEARNING— *COMMUNITY IS FOUNDATIONAL*

The notion that in order to cultivate human capital skills in optimal fashion the apprentice/player must participate in some type of group setting (module, shop) contrasts sharply with TP. From its very inception, the latter rested, for all intents and purposes, on the grand ideal of the rugged individual operating in splendid isolation. One could surmise that such an ideal had its basis in the

Christian theology of the times that conceived of salvation in an individualistic sense. Even in Catholicism, it is the person alone who, in the final analysis, must function in harmony with the church.

Because the whole point of TP was and is to find out how much stuff the student qua individual carries around in his or her own head, peers were and are of necessity excluded from participation in the individual's written and/or oral exam. To be sure, students have always conversed with one another, and often studied together, in preparation for the test. Nevertheless, though the ingestion (like a meal) may have been done jointly, regurgitation must, eventually, be endured alone. The enormous gravity academics place on cheating during a test shows how loyal we are to the doctrine of the isolated student pulling stuff out of her or his own head, allowing for no inappropriate assistance.[73]

Historically, on the other hand, apart from the churches and schools, the demonstration of learning invariably took place in some type of group setting. That was surely the case for centuries among extended families and communities. Moreover, parallel to that group-based experience, it was common for successful masters to take in several apprentices at a time. Later on, the emergence of the guild system implied that a dozen or so apprentices might be located in a particular shop with ties to nearby shops of similar size practicing the same trade. Among other things, the presence of peers was believed to facilitate the kind of learning necessary to do the tasks at hand. The more experienced could assist the less experienced kin members and/or apprentices. Over time, it was hoped that the younger peers might in their turn contribute to one another, to newer peers and, eventually, to older peers.

Accordingly, it's no small matter that, on the basis of several decades of empirical research, Astin concluded,

> The student's peer group is the single most potent source of influence on growth and development during the undergraduate years.[74]

And "development," added Astin, includes the two most significant spheres in a college student's life, "intellectual and personal."[75] Alas, the great bulk of the academic establishment paid little attention to Astin's conclusion.[76] Many, if not most, professors find it almost impossible to resonate at a gut level with the anxiety that springs from considering the possibility that a student's peers might just possibly have greater intellectual bearing on him or her than does the student's professor.

Those sorts of intimidating feelings are not unlike the emotions stirred up within the hearts of many parents by Judith Rich Harris's widely circulated book concluding that peers actually have greater influence than parents on how children develop.[77] Her ideas were based on her secondary analyses of some fifty years of published research by academic psychologists and were originally published in an article by the prestigious American Psychological Association (APA) journal *Psychological Review*. In 1998, the APA even awarded her a prize for her article. And, although the *New Yorker* and the *New York Times* treated her book in a sensible manner, the mass media sensationalized it; for example, a quirky *Newsweek* cover inquiring ominously "Do Parents Matter?"[78]

Of course parents matter, but not as greatly as peers, concluded Harris. Likewise, professors obviously matter, but not as much, concluded Astin, as the peer groups with which the college student identifies. Professors strongly resist the notion that peers might matter more than they do for the same reasons that parents have trouble acknowledging that peer influence is as potent as Harris said. In both TP and in the prevailing "Parenting Paradigm," the professor or parent is perceived as the unique expert, leaving scant room for peers, other than at most to reinforce the expert.[79] Allowing a lot more leeway than that for peers is perceived by the expert—whether parent or professor—as reducing their distinctive influence and thus their status.

Furthermore, because the expert has a formal obligation to society for what her or his student/child does, that role carries with it a certain degree of legitimate authority over the situation. Peer influence is, however, a wild card that the expert has thus far been unable to hold in check. As a result, both professors and parents fear that peer influence might curtail their authority over the student/offspring. Finally, the worst-case scenario would occur when the peer is perceived as a potential threat to the professor or parent by actually undermining and/or contaminating the objectives he or she hopes to accomplish.

Fears of the experts notwithstanding, collaborative, or participatory, learning requires what numerous advocates on both sides of the Atlantic call a "learning community."

> Learning in this community goes on through a constant dialogue of free inquiry, mingling the voices of professors and students in open exchange as they strive toward intellectual excellence in a collaborative effort that supports and increases the human dignity of the participants.[80]

The upshot is that, rather than view the student's peers as at best tangential and at worst a threat to the goals of the expert professor, the module would construct all its participants—players, interns (grad students and postdocs), and coaches—as active players committed to a mutual learning process in which everyone is obliged both to give *and* to receive.

A community approach to learning by no means ignores the fact that the coach/mentor is virtually certain to possess a greater degree of expertise than the player/mentee in terms of human capital skills. Nor does it deny the reality that the coach is sure to know more of the existing information regarding the particular topic being studied by the module, at least initially. Once all parties are comfortable with those twin realities, the module need not be paralyzed with fear over any potential lessening in the status of its coach. The module is then free to concentrate on increasing the skills of its players, as well as those of the coach, to say nothing of the interns. An appropriate analogy for the module was described above in the case of the shop housing the entrepreneur and her/his students. It was also noted in connection with the master/apprentice. Specifically, a major indicator of the quality of the shop (whether the entrepreneur's or the master's) is the excellence of the students or apprentices produced by the shop/module—a few of whom might eventually come to outshine the entrepreneur/master/coach.

De Corte, like Astin, reports that the most recent research demonstrates the enormous significance of the "learning group" for the development of what we're calling discovery-based learning. The fundamental objective of any learning group is, he says, problem solving.[81] For its part, the module exists in order to address some of the social issues that have been the province of the social sciences for over a century. Chapter 6 explains that the module would be organized into small teams of players, and each team—along with its coach—would target a particular facet of a broader issue. The team's goal is to identify, and to try to resolve (even if minimally and despite inevitable failures), important questions regarding that facet. In order to pursue the resolution of its problem, the team invariably becomes a social context for the cultivation of the pivotal element of DBL, namely, human capital skills. The players would necessarily cultivate those skills as they work together to "exchange ideas, compare solution strategies, and discuss arguments."[82] Collaborating in such a manner tends to nurture the human capital capabilities (analysis, evaluation, and synthesis) of each player on the team at a rather profound level. The depth attained is far greater than could ever be plumbed by the typical student struggling alone.

Furthermore, De Corte underscores the fact that, as vital as that type of group interaction is, it is not sufficient for a learning group, that is, a team, simply to be a debating club. If players and their coach limit themselves merely to intellectual exercises (discussion, argument) over how to address a social issue (as occurs in some of today's conventional classes), their human capital capabilities tend to grow (if at all) at a much slower pace than if they actually put those skills into practice. An analogy from the life sciences lab might be having heated discussions over how to thwart the course of HIV but then failing to design an experiment aimed at actually doing it.

Accordingly, if those human capital capabilities are to be cultivated by the module in a significant manner, the coach and players must, in addition to verbally dissecting the issue, *do* something with it—they must take action of one sort or another aimed at resolving their problem.[83] Hence, it is in that sense that the players' learning (human capital capabilities) would be discovery based. As the players and coach do collaborative research (mock-up and/or actual) aimed at weaving the social fabric, their capabilities become developed to a far greater degree than is feasible simply by discussion or debate—no matter how stimulating, or just plain fun, such exchanges tend to be.

Incidentally, it's well worth noting that one of several complaints today's employers have about the college graduates applying for jobs is that they have no practical experience of working in a team context aimed at problem solving.[84] Their appraisal is hardly surprising given the fact that TP targets the individual student in isolation and insists there is a right answer that she or he must memorize and reproduce on the exam. By way of contrast, the pivotal role of team experience in the life of the module—including having to deal with the ambiguities and complexities inherent in trying to address thorny social issues—becomes one more reason why contemporary students might find the module both unique and attractive. First, the module helps to cultivate the sorts of human capital skills likely to become increasingly sought after in the information age. Second, at the same time, it provides invaluable practice in the type of team-based problem solving that employers find highly useful in addressing the complex challenges facing their organizations.

DISCOVERY-BASED LEARNING—
THE INFORMATION AGE AS "MAKING STUFF"

The module's emphasis on problem solving, that is, the creation of new knowledge, cuts to the chase of what the information age is all about. Although fundamental distinctions between the agricultural era, the industrial age, and the postindustrial era are easily understood, the differences between the information age and its immediate predecessor are not so readily apparent. The nineteenth and twentieth centuries were categorically *not* the *pre*-information age, if we take information to mean the explosion and widespread dissemination of knowledge.[85] Despite the fact that the world's store of knowledge had always been available to the privileged classes, they'd not gone out of their way to expose the great masses of the population to that information. The industrial age, however, blasted through that wall of limited access by forcing the elite to admit it was in their own best interest to have an educated workforce. And so the elite created a system of knowledge distribution known as K–12. Post-K–12 remained, for the most part, reserved for the (white male) children of the elite.

When, however, Harper and his contemporaries invented the research university, the old elite (e.g., John D. Rockefeller Sr.) who financed them failed to anticipate that they were thereby expanding the ranks of the elite. The new elite was made up of the researchers that the old elite bankrolled. By taking the quantum leap beyond the mere distribution of stuff to the task of producing it, the new elite became "knowledge makers."[86] *Knowledge is power* had forever been a commonsense adage. The masses went to college in the twentieth century to get knowledge and the "good life" it bought. But even as they were doing it, the ground beneath them was shifting. *Making knowledge is power* has become the more suitable twenty-first-century information age axiom. In this new era, students require the ability to "create knowledge instead of simply absorbing it."[87] One creates knowledge by unraveling complexities and solving problems. In effect, the ranks of the elite are being gradually expanded once again to include what have thus far been viewed as "ordinary" citizens. Their self-interest and the well-being of society demand that they, too, must now become knowledge makers.

Because the postindustrial information age is much more about making stuff than simply knowing stuff, it is to the distinct advantage of as many citizens as possible to have the sorts of module-based experiences described above. Citizens who have had those kinds of module experiences and who possess the human capital skills they engender are likely to do well in the increasingly competitive twenty-first-century global economy. Moreover, it follows that a society, the bulk of whose citizens are knowledge makers (rather than simply knowledge absorbers), is also likely to do well in a worldwide milieu that is very much in flux.

KNOWING STUFF AND THE PRACTICE OF TESTING

Because post-K–12 was all about knowing stuff, it followed that the practice of testing made perfect sense. Starting with the very first American colleges, telling, ingestion, and regurgitation became firmly established as the most valid and efficient model of learning.[88] And today?

> We assume there should be grades and tests because there have always been, and school is almost unthinkable without them. After all, how will we know who is the best, who succeeded and who failed, who did the work and who sloughed off without grades and tests? How will graduate schools know who to accept and how will employers know whom to hire? . . . Without tests, the system doesn't work.[89]

We saw, however, that a major glitch in that model is that, after upchucking its contents, the vessel is empty. There is, furthermore, a profoundly disturbing and heartbreaking consequence of the nearly universal practice of classroom testing. The practice constrains students to "do everything but love learning."[90] First, the practice leads students to conceive of the classroom as a highly competitive, win-lose situation—especially when tests are graded on the basis of some type of normal distribution—in which some students win and others lose. Second, as we saw above, students elect to differentiate among the bits of information that they sense should be memorized for the test. Despite the fact that in order to cover the material the professor exposes students to large doses of information, the students will restrict their cramming either to the limited range of stuff the professor has told them could be on the test, or the stuff they guess might be. Furthermore, even that reduced amount of stuff is allowed to leak the moment the test is over. Third, in recent years several research reports have indicated that, although it's been around forever, the incidence of cheating on exams is now on the increase among undergraduates. Cornell's Glenn Altschuler concluded that "recent surveys [suggest that] cheating has reached epidemic proportions in high schools and colleges."[91]

Fourth, testing, as it's practiced today, is integral to the gentlemen's agreement described in chapter 3 *(You give me the grade, I'll get the degree, I'm out of here)*. Professors feel enormous pressure to construct tests that are in sync with that silent bargain. And when they test in a manner that violates the spirit of that implicit deal, students immediately become overtly hostile. If, for whatever reason, their projected grade does not please them, they'll go to great lengths to cajole the professor into raising it. If, moreover, they're unhappy with the grade once it's been officially assigned, they'll spare no effort to insist the professor should amend it to a higher grade. Student obsession with grades places enormous pressure on professors to respond compassionately to their pleas for better grades and to pump them up.

There's also a practical consideration for either the credentialer or the teacher-scholar. She or he very much wants the students to endorse both her/him and her/his course via the evaluations described in chapter 3. According to a recent study by biostatistics professor Valen Johnson, there is a strong and positive correlation between the grading of students and the course evaluations that students assign to their professor at semester's end.[92] Johnson's rigorous research showed that "a student expecting an A or A– is about 35 to 40 percent more likely to give a faculty member a more favorable [evaluation]."[93]

Harvard University's Harvey Mansfield got a great deal of national media attention when it was revealed that he routinely assigned each student two grades. The official grade, he said, was aligned with "Harvard's inflated distribution, in which one-fourth of all grades given to undergraduates are now A's, and another fourth are A–'s."[94] However, each of his students also received a "private" grade based on their actual performance, and that turned out to be much less flattering. He did this "to show my contempt for the present system, yet not punish students who take my course."[95] The year following that highly negative national publicity, Harvard appointed a task force to resolve its grade inflation problem by "resurrecting the respectability of a B"—never mind revisiting the Neanderthal C.[96] Princeton's faculty made a similar move by voting to reduce the numbers of As at their school to 35 percent. They were alarmed by their own study showing that among all Ivy League schools, as well as MIT, Stanford, and the University of Chicago, 44–55 percent of all grades were As.[97] At Princeton, students had gotten As half the time, an increase over the early 1990s when they got As a third of the time.

By no means does everyone share the widely held view that there's been acute grade inflation throughout recent decades.[98] Astin, however, comes down squarely on the side of those who perceive an upward trend in grade inflation. His national data revealed that in 1966, some 15 percent of all college grades in the United States were in the A+, A, or A– range.[99] And in that same year, slightly above 30 percent of all grades were C+ or below. But by 1996, the patterns of the data had gotten entirely reversed: some 32 percent of all grades were now in the A+, A, or A– range, but less than 15 percent were C+ or below.

Friendly critic Alfie Kohn makes the telling point that whether grade inflation is genuine or not is fundamentally a peripheral matter that distracts us from what we should instead be deeply concerned about.[100] The essential question, he says, is *not* whether in fact grades have gotten pumped up but whether or not student learning has, over time, become greater than it was before. But as we saw above, the National Center for Public Policy and Higher Education reports that there is no reliable answer to that question. We don't know whether lower-order learning has gone up or down, and we surely have no sense at all whether higher-order learning has risen or declined. By comparison to those essential issues, the matter of grade inflation pales in significance. Despite our ignorance regarding those critical issues and whether or not grades are actually inflated, Kohn concurs with Schank and many other observers that today's students are indeed fixated on grades. Moreover, Kohn also agrees with Schank that our current reliance on exams as the fountainhead of grades "is likely to undermine the love of learning we are presumably seeking to promote."[101]

Students are decidedly not the bad guys in this dismal scenario. They're simply making do with a scheme imposed on them by academics—a system that puts a premium on cost-efficiency but not on learning. During the era of university transformation (1870–1944), the masses entered college in vast numbers never before seen. Cohen tells us that in order to cope with the disarray that followed in the wake of that rapid influx of students, administrators were forced to devise "uniform systems of accounting for the college experience."[102]

Prior to that era, there were no homogeneous, or standard, grades to document how much stuff each student might have stored. Instead, each professor prepared "written statements of a student's progress."[103] Progress meant how much stuff the student could repeat back to the professor, typically via a written essay that was sometimes embellished through oral recitation. After a while, however, that practice got censured as being too subjective, and thus biased. More to the point, that practice ate up huge amounts of time that the twentieth-century superprofessor could ill afford owing to the competing demands of pursuing his or her scholarly reputation. Hence, during the course of the twentieth century the practice of the narrative evaluation was gradually replaced by the now familiar technique of letter grades (e.g., A–F). Each letter was coded with a number (4–0), thus for the first time permitting the calculation of a mean, or average, grade point. Cohen contends that the GPA was the initial shot over the bow toward the construction of the college degree as a widely recognized credential. The numbers, he said, could be easily read and universally understood worldwide as a reliable and valid symbol of student performance.

"The other part of the credential," added Cohen, "was the standardized course unit or credit earned."[104] In 1919, the American Council on Education decreed that every accredited college should require a minimum of 120 semester hours before awarding a bachelor's degree. Hence, after agonizing struggles throughout the course of many decades, academics finally established the notion that a reliable credential demands that students pass an array of courses totaling 120 hours. They were typically required to have a GPA of 2.0, perhaps higher in their major. In reaction to that decree, Cohen remarked rather plaintively that

> Nowhere in these criteria was there are any comment about what or how much the students were supposed to be learning.[105]

The fundamental issue of learning assessment was (and is) left to the discretion of the individual professor. Holding a bachelor's degree in no way signified that the undergraduate had developed at least some level of intellectual curiosity or had nurtured a love for learning. All that was required for the degree was that one had piled up 120 credit hours.

Once more taking its cue from the shop of either the master or the entrepreneur, the coaches would ground the issue of player evaluation in the matter of the *production* of stuff instead of its mere repetition. Hence, the module would take the far-reaching step (as did some of the alternative schools) of shifting away from exams, grades, and credit hours and move instead toward what many observers call "learning assessment."[106] Assessment is simply another way to express the overarching consensus shared by learning paradigm advocates. And that is that our focus must shift from professor *input* to student *output*.

If, for example, we ask what's expected of the grad student in the entrepreneur's shop, we could say that she or he is evaluated on the basis of two interrelated criteria. The first is progress in developing the kinds of skills (both human capital and technical) necessary for doing the type of research that characterizes the shop. The second is the level of contributions toward resolving the research problems that concern the shop. Both skill development and contribution level must be viewed in relative terms, as a work in progress. Accordingly, the notions of constant achievement and ongoing effectiveness describe the continual improvement over time that the entrepreneur expects from the apprentice with regard to both dimensions.

Applying that same template to the social science module, its players would likewise be evaluated in terms of *relative* skill development—in their case, human capital skills. They would also be assessed in terms of their *relative* contribution to the resolution of the questions that confront their team. Analogous to the shop, the module's coaches and players would strive for continuous improvement over both sets of criteria. Although mistakes and shortcomings would inevitably occur, those would serve as stimuli for the coaches and players alike to keep on exploring how they might together become better able to achieve both their individual and group goals. One of the core concepts heard frequently among advocates for this type of quality undergraduate education is the concept of

> continuous improvement [which] implies a commitment by everyone in the organization to a recursive process consisting of planning and testing improvements, evaluating outcomes, learning from failures, implementing and sustaining successes, planning and testing improvements, and so on.[107]

Ruben added that the continuous improvement model was imported into post-K–12 from the business community. For some academics that fact is by itself sufficient to dismiss and doom it from the start, except that its reach extends much further than business. Schank and Cleary suggest that a continuous improvement model of one sort or other governs practically all human endeavors, including, as we just saw, the shop of the master and the entrepreneur. That model, moreover, surely governs the world of children in their life beyond the confines of K–12: "Doing, and attempting to do, is at the heart of children's natural acquisition of knowledge."[108] Furthermore, as Ruben indicated, there is no learning apart from failure—the so-called *oops* factor: "Failure," he says, "is critical in the learning process." Only within the isolated and "non-real" worlds of K–12 and post-K–12 does the "Myth of the Right Answer" prevail.[109]

In real life, there are nearly right answers, answers that were missing a step, and most important, situations in which there is no right answer at all.[110]

DISCOVERY-BASED LEARNING— *INNOVATIVE CONSTRUCTIONS OF SPACES, TIMES, AND TECHNOLOGIES*

So far we've seen how tough it is to conceive of the undergraduate experience apart from active gurus telling stuff and passive students reiterating the stuff via the test. Also seemingly inescapable is the grade and the amassing of credit hours that legitimate the credential. Furthermore, if we imagine those several elements as the threads of an intricate TP tapestry, we may then identify two additional threads—space and time—that are likewise woven into and inextricable from that tapestry. How can we visualize schools of any kind apart from the preset times at which the student and professor fly, like homing pigeons, to their predetermined classrooms? Fixed times and set classrooms appear to be the natural, the obvious and, perhaps more importantly, a highly cost-efficient means of fulfilling TP.

A room is, of course, a permanent physical space within a larger motionless structure that stays constant from day to day. And, as any prekindergartner knows, a class refers to a rigid meeting time (9:00–10:00 A.M.), for a certain course (Professor Jones, History 318, section 2138, room 216), that closely follows a prescribed syllabus. Once established, those class specs can no more be altered (over the length of a semester) than can the room in which they transpire. Moreover, as reliable as clockwork is the fact that students will sit in neat rows staring at the back of other students' heads and also at the professor talking at them. Increasingly common is, of course, the media-supported classroom, that is, one with a monitor on which appears (via PowerPoint) the professor's lecture, either in outline form or in its entirety. Notwithstanding, whether media-supported or not, join "class" with "room," and one comes up with the ultimate in constancy and predictability.

But what happens when we attach the term "wired" to classroom and get "wired classroom" (a computer terminal at the desk of every student)?[111] By itself, "wired" conveys the possibility of the uncertain and the unpredictable. Options are potentially increased, but we're not sure what those might entail, and whether they are positive or negative. By itself, "wired" is bound neither by the constraints of certain fixed physical spaces, nor by set days and times, nor by predetermined lecture notes. Some school spaces have, furthermore, gone "wireless," and that conveys a far more indeterminate situation. "Wired" or "wireless" says learning can happen anywhere, anytime, and within a range of circumstances. By contrast, however, "classroom" says this is the unique place and time where learning happens. The unwavering image it conveys is numbingly familiar even to the smallest child. Hence, one is compelled to ask, is the increasingly familiar expression *wired/wireless classroom* an oxymoron?

Not necessarily. In defense of the wired/wireless classroom, it could perhaps represent a transitional stage in the evolution of TP into something else.[112] Most academics, nonetheless, don't yet construct it quite that way. For the most part, today's administrators view what C. C. Strange and J. H. Banning call "computer-mediated communication" as a tool with the potential to improve TP's cost efficiency.[113] Nevertheless, experimenting with something new and different might eventually make the old seem bland and perhaps even dreary. Presently, however, "wired" or "wireless" linked with "classroom" implies nothing more startling than an add-on. Its proponents are *not* saying that classrooms and the TP they reinforce are obsolete. Instead, backed up by a lot of media hype and public fanfare, technology proponents hope to *add on* something new (e.g., terminals at every desk networked with each other and the professor) to the TP they believe is basically sound.[114]

Not too long ago, I spent several months wandering about our campus viewing wired/wireless classrooms on an unannounced and entirely random basis. My practice was to stand at the rear of the classroom in order simply to observe what was going on. Most often, the students sat politely in neat rows, staring either at their own monitors or at the professor, who stood facing them. As the professor explained what was on the monitor, most students were busily writing the information down in their notebooks. From time to time a student asked a question; frequently, the same student did so more than once. If the class had been designated as a "computer lab" led by a teaching assistant, the assistant would, in response to a question, sometimes walk to the student's monitor and provide instructions on how to perform a particular task. Toward the rear of the room, some students were reading the campus newspaper, while a few others were busily surfing the Web.

Sound familiar? It should, because it's simply the conventional classroom with the add-on of expensive technology whose full potential for imaginative innovation does not even begin to be utilized. Moreover, lest one might wonder if my "sample" is fatally biased, researcher Larry Cuban arrived at similar conclusions regarding Stanford University in particular and post-K–12 (as well as K–12) in general.[115] By and large, he says, computer technology has been "oversold and underused." His extensive research within a range of K–12 and post-K–12 schools showed that despite the millions of dollars spent during recent decades on computer technology, it has failed to revolutionize the teaching paradigm in the ways its proponents claimed it would. A tiny handful of notable exceptions aside,

Most teachers [and professors] continue to see the computer as an *add-on* rather than as a technology integral to their classroom content and instruction.[116]

The add-on strategy followed by most of today's academics is analogous to the mid-nineteenth-century situation when naval architects on both sides of the Atlantic began adding iron onto the hulls of wooden warships.[117] Their idea was, of course, to make their venerable vessels less vulnerable to their opponents' cannons that, owing to rapid technological advances, were decimating ancient-style wooden ships. Obviously, the ironclads' advocates felt their ship could win more battles than the old wooden vessel. The big problem was that the more the naval officers experimented with the ironclads, the more frustrated they got over how clumsy and cumbersome those ships were during actual battle maneuvers. Moreover, those aggravations finally led the British Admiralty to declare in a fit of exasperation that, despite its shortcomings, nothing could ever satisfactorily replace the wooden warship that, after all, had proven itself durable and reliable as far back as the ancient Phoenicians.

Similarly, advocates believe that adding on technology will make students better learners—at least in the lower-order sense.[118] Nevertheless, working with students in the context of a wired/wireless classroom has its own set of frustrations for professors, just as working with ironclads frustrated naval officers. Moreover, the professors' aggravations could lead to several kinds of reactions, depending on their role. Teacher-scholars have neither the time nor creative energy to cope with the unfamiliar hassles of the wired/wireless classroom because they're preoccupied with pursuing their professional reputation. Hence, they're likely to follow the tack of the Admiralty and argue quite convincingly that the conventional classroom has proven itself durable and reliable for centuries. Nothing, they say, could ever satisfactorily replace either it (though perhaps media-supported) or the TP that justifies it. Teacher-scholars, like the Admiralty, have a great deal invested in the status quo.

Credentialers are, for their part, much more likely to cope effectively with the frustrations of the wired/wireless classroom and gradually get better and better at managing it. If, after all, some of them are evolving into cyberfaculty, it's in their self-interest to be expert at making such a classroom work effectively and efficiently. They will thus invest the time and creative energy necessary to being as good a cyberprofessor as possible. Their rewards stem directly from that activity, just as the teacher-scholar's rewards come from quite another realm. There is, however, no apparent reason why cyberfaculty would question the very notion of the classroom itself, nor perhaps conclude that its time and space boundaries are far too limiting for what they need to do.

The coach would, however, do precisely that. The coach would argue that the temporal and spatial boundaries of the classroom (whether conventional, media-supported, or wired/wireless) place severe constraints on the learning paradigm described above. The coaches' strategy could be compared to that of the late-nineteenth-century German Navy. Their frustrations with the iron-clad led them to junk the wooden vessel entirely and to experiment with something extraordinarily innovative, based on the emerging technology of steel. The result was the steel warship. Accordingly, coaches would seek to replace the concept of the classroom itself by trying out new and different arrangements of time and space. The coaches would agree unreservedly with designer Graham Wyatt that the recent

> revolution in educational theory . . . [suggests] the term *classroom* unnecessarily narrows discussion and [that] the linguistically challenged *place of learning* more accurately reflects the fact that much learning can and should take place outside the traditional classroom environment.[119]

It turns out that around the United States, a few colleges and universities are, in fact, currently experimenting with "learning places." They are launching efforts to moderate the constraints of time and space that the concept of "classroom" imposes. For the most part, such experimentation is being carried out in the fields of mathematics and the sciences. In both fields, moreover, the underlying rationale for such innovations is that they are likely to contribute to enhanced student learning. To be sure, the sciences have had the model of the laboratory for a long time, and the lab was obviously constructed as a very different sort of place than the classroom. It was viewed as distinctive primarily because its centerpiece was the experiment (even if canned), and not the sedated routine of busily transcribing what the professor might be saying.

Nonetheless, what seems to be today's distinguishing feature (when compared to the past) is that as they design new labs or renovate existing ones, some scientists are making concerted efforts to incorporate the conclusions of recent learning theory into their designs. Designer Michael C. Lauber, for example, observes that recent research in teaching/learning theory demonstrates the importance of peer influences on learning.[120] As a result, he says, some new or renovated science labs are being designed to "increase the amount of student interaction in the lab."[121] Furthermore, the recognition of the significance of peer influence on science learning has also led to the design of "informal gathering spaces outside the lab."[122]

Additionally, the sciences are becoming more and more convinced that, alongside their research, their teaching likewise is substantially enhanced to the degree they can overcome archaic disciplinary boundaries. Hence, "New teaching facilities often seek to include all science disciplines under one roof . . . [including] floor plans that place different disciplines together."[123] Their spatial proximity facilitates research into important questions that "require interdisciplinary collaboration, such as neuroscience."[124]

Furthermore, adds Lauber, still another new design feature stems from the fact that, increasingly, scientists are incorporating growing numbers of undergrads into their cross-disciplinary research. Hence, at the same time that their new or renovated buildings are designed to accommodate interdisciplinary research, those designs also take into account not only the space needs of scientists, postdocs, and graduate students, but also the space needs of undergrads. Furthermore, the significance of the computer in today's emerging undergraduate science lab cannot be overlooked. Rather than being viewed in conventional terms as merely an add-on, Lauber reports that it is constructed as an "integral tool."[125] In short, the sciences are, at least to some degree, attempting to design their newer physical spaces in ways that are quite different not only from the classroom (conventional or wired/wireless), but also from their labs of a bygone era. Some of today's scientists appear willing to construct the kinds of spaces (in both the social and physical senses) for undergrads that reflect recent research and theory about learning.

LEARNING SPACES IN THE SOCIAL SCIENCE MODULE

In that same vein, the coaches construct their module as a place consisting not of classrooms, but of learning spaces. The innovators who participated in the alternative schools of the 1960s and 1970s felt intuitively the importance of getting beyond conventional ideas of physical spaces and times. UC–Santa Cruz was, for instance, designed in terms of a series of low-rise residence halls that combined living and academic functions into the same building.[126] Unfortunately, the entire cohort of pioneers from that era lacked two vital elements available to contemporary advocates for reinventing undergraduate learning. One is the rapidly evolving landscape of computer software/hardware, but even more significant are the ongoing advances in learning research and theory.

Wyatt's description of the Mathematics Emporium at Virginia Tech University helps to liberate our thinking from the constraints of conventional space, time, and technology uses.[127] The emporium is a renovated 58,000-square-foot former department store, and the large spaces that made up that store remain intact. Today, however, those large spaces enclose numerous pods (circular tables), and around each pod there are six hardwired computers. There are a total of five hundred computers in the emporium, which is open twenty-four hours each day. Math professors are there fourteen hours a day, and graduate assistants are present even more hours. There are typically hundreds of students in the emporium at any given time, and they "self-administer prepackaged, course-specific, computer-based instructional software [including tests] covering virtually all undergraduate mathematics courses."[128]

Student proceed at their own pace and go to the emporium as frequently or as infrequently as they wish. Professors and grad assistants are there to answer students' specific questions for any of the courses available to the students. In order to perform effectively, the "faculty have been obliged to learn new teaching techniques . . . working more as listeners and personal tutors than as lecturers."[129] Wyatt reports that although most professors have "risen to this challenge," Virginia Tech will, in future (especially if the practice is followed by other fields), invest much more time, effort, and money in "formal training for faculty, preparing them for their *new roles as coaches and tutors.*"[130]

The social science module would be analogous to, but also quite distinctive from, the emporium. It would be comparable because it, too, would aim to escape the constraints of time and space imposed by the classroom. The module would consist of physical spaces that could, until a more evocative term is devised, be described as a lab. Each lab might hold several sets of workstations, each with five or six semicircular networked terminals around which a team could gather. The workstation would also have a place for the coach and/or intern (grad student, postdoc) at those times when either or both were with the team. Because there is no set class time, the team could gather in the lab any time of the day or night. Times at which the coach or interns might meet with the team could be prearranged any number of ways, including by email. Instant messaging also keeps individual team members, coaches, and interns in continual contact when they're not in the lab. Furthermore, like the new science labs cited above, the module's coaches would represent a range of social science disciplines organized around the specific problems they're trying to address.

Because each lab has several workstations, any number of teams is likely to be present at any given time. Consequently, teams could and would consult freely with other teams, as well as with the coach and/or intern from those other teams, regarding the issue they're trying to resolve. Furthermore, as in the contemporary science labs, there would be, adjacent to the module's labs, informal gathering places for coaches, players, and interns alike. At other times, the teams might meet at an off-campus site (e.g., coffee house) if their objective is to dialogue about a problem and develop a mock-up of its resolution. When, however, their objective becomes more action-oriented and hands-on (see chapter 6), then the off-campus site could include any number of possibilities, such as a particular neighborhood, school, agency, or business, and so forth.

Ideally, prior to assuming their tasks, professors would have gained some experience at wrenching themselves away from TP and in trying to satisfy the unique and demanding role of coach. The big problem facing the experimental modules would be similar to one confronted by math professors in the Virginia Tech emporium. Specifically, at the present time there are not many schools where hands-on experience fulfilling the distinctive and difficult role of coach can be readily gained. The presence of interns within the learning spaces is one means to ease that shortcoming over time. Interns, along with the entire issue of module personnel, are explored further in chapter 7.

SUMMING UP

The mission of the module is to immerse undergraduates in discovery-based learning, or DBL. DBL has two indivisible components, one of which is the cultivation of students' problem-solving capabilities, also known as human capital skills (e.g., analysis, evaluation, synthesis), that is, higher-order learning. The second component is the doing of research (actual and/or simulated) by the student, that is, inquiry into resolving a research question or problem. For the social science module, that means a *social* problem, question, or issue. Moreover, the efforts to address the issue could be called enabling humankind to take possession of society. It is through their efforts at trying to resolve some of the issues inherent in weaving the social fabric that the students' human capital skills are cultivated. Contributing toward the mending and/or weaving of the social fabric can be thought of as producing or making knowledge. The capability of making knowledge is seen as the essence of the post-industrial information age. And persons who are skilled at doing that can be expected to do well in the twenty-first century—both in the marketplace and in civic society.

Problem solving and the cultivation of human capital skills are team-based. Peers learn from each other. And, although the coach is presumably more experienced in and capable than the players and the interns (grad students and postdocs) at such problem solving, the coaches fully expect to learn from and to grow alongside the players and interns. Hence, the coach collaborates with players and interns for two equally compelling reasons: One, it's in the best interest of the players and interns. Two, it's in the coach's best interest as well. Finally, DBL is not constrained by the spatial and temporal boundaries of the classroom. It can occur anytime anywhere, but the computer workstation sited within the lab is a convenient hub from which DBL emanates.

That said, would participation in those sorts of demanding activities inspire students to become intellectually curious and translate into a love for learning?

Whether or not it is passionate devotion, students are likely to find that their involvement in the module would (in addition to being tough and challenging) be satisfying, rewarding, and engaging. Perhaps even addictive, because it constantly stretches them to reach beyond where they are just now.

But why would a DBL approach stimulate intellectual curiosity and inspire a commitment to learning? The answer is found, quite simply, in the Boyer Commission's use of terms such as "inquiry" and "discovery." Most (if not all) humans have an inherent fascination with the new, and our curiosity is piqued if we become personally involved with its pursuit. The module is a place that would aim to discover or, more realistically, work toward the invention of, resolutions for certain urgent social issues (but never entirely resolve them). The preponderance of undergrads who currently major in the social sciences do so because they are, at least to some degree, interested in the resolution of social issues. Accordingly, the module would capitalize on their initial interest by offering such students the opportunity to participate in the never-ending process of finding, that is, of struggling to come up with some potential ways of addressing pressing social issues.

NOTES

1. Carnegie Commission 1998, italics in original.
2. Schank 2000:22.
3. De Corte 1996; see also Donovan et al. 1999.
4. De Corte 1996:128.
5. De Corte 1996:128.
6. De Corte 1996:128.
7. Barr and Tagg 1995; Bain 2004a, b.
8. Duderstadt 2000:304.
9. Cohen 1998:1.
10. Trow 1996; Castaldi 1994.
11. Schank and Cleary 1995:xi.
12. Schank and Cleary 1995:60.
13. For additional information re "acquisition," see De Corte 1996:113ff.
14. Schank and Cleary 1995:60.
15. Trow 1996.
16. Boyer Commission 1998:16.
17. Terry O'Banion (1997) reminds us, however, that some community colleges are making concerted efforts to experiment with ways to establish and maintain a learning paradigm.
18. Honan 2002; Cf. Detweiler 2004.
19. Honan 2002.
20. Parker 2001. See Turkle (2004) for an exceedingly thoughtful critique of PowerPoint and of other aspects of the widespread use of computer technology by

children/youth.

21. Schank 1994, 2000; Schank and Cleary 1995.

22. Zemsky and Massy 2004a:B7.

23. Carlson 2002.

24. Carlson 2003a. And see Carlson 2004a; Cuban 2001.

25. Carlson 2003a.

26. Cuban 2001; Schank 2000; Arenson 2003.

27. Cárdenas 2000; Newman and Scurry 2001; Lanham 2002; Tomlinson-Keasey 2002.

28. Arenson 2003, italics added.

29. Arenson 2003.

30. Collins 2002a.

31. Katz 2001.

32. Among the few are Duderstadt et al. 2002; Hazemi et al. 1998; Bates and Poole 2003; Hazemi and Hailes 2002; Patrides 2000; Brown and Duguid 2000; Lanham 2002.

33. Astin 1993:428ff.

34. Astin 1993:428.

35. Astin 1993:418ff.

36. Boyer Commission 1998:11.

37. Burd 2002a.

38. Burd 2003b.

39. Zernike 2002.

40. Marchese 1995; Massey 2003.

41. Miller 2002.

42. Miller 2002.

43. Ewell 2002.

44. Ewell 2002.

45. Cuban 1999:37.

46. Schank 2000.

47. Schwartz 2004.

48. Schank 2000.

49. Schank and Cleary 1995.

50. Schank and Cleary 1995.

51. Schon 1983.

52. Henriksson 2001.

53. Tierney 2002.

54. Tierney 2002.

55. Tierney 2002.

56. National Science Foundation 2002.

57. Schank 2000.

58. Mathews 2003.

59. Barr and Tagg (1995) report similar experiences with honors students. See also DeZure 2000; Bartlett 2003b.

60. Schank and Cleary 1995:43.

61. De Corte 1996:119.

62. De Corte 1996:119.

63. Schank and Cleary 1995:44.

64. E. D. Hirsch 1987, passim, cited by Schank and Cleary 1995:47.

65. Winerip 2003.

66. Schank and Cleary 1995:53.

67. Schank and Cleary 1995:63.

68. De Corte 1996:128.

69. Schank and Cleary 1995:43.

70. De Corte 1996:119.

71. Liberal Education 2004.

72. Flyvbjerg 2001.

73. Cf. Norman 2001.

74. Astin 1993:398, italics in original.

75. Astin 1993: 402.

76. But see Dennis et al. (2004) for a notable exception.

77. Harris 1998.

78. *Newsweek* 7 September 1998.

79. Scanzoni 2000.

80. Lawrence 1995:vii.

81. De Corte 1996:115. And see Bess 2000; Dennis et al. 2004.

82. De Corte 1996:122.

83. De Corte 1996:118–19.

84. Schank 2000; Duderstadt 2000.

85. Brown and Duguid 2000.

86. Florida 2002.

87. Duderstadt et al. 2002:64, 96–97, drawing from Lanham 1993. See also Powell and Owen-Smith 2002.

88. Cohen 1998.

89. Schank 2000:20–21.

90. Schank 2000.

91. Altschuler 2001.

92. Johnson 2003.

93. Ostby 2003.

94. Mansfield 2001.

95. Mansfield 2001.

96. Hartocollis 2002.

97. Hedges 2004.

98. Shoichet 2002.

99. Astin 2000:21.

100. Kohn 2002.

101. Kohn 2002.

102. Cohen 1998:149.

103. Cohen 1998:149.

104. Cohen 1998:149; see also Wellman and Ehrlich 2003.

105. Cohen 1998:150.

106. See Schank 2000; Schank and Cleary 1995; Barr and Tagg 1995; De Corte 1996. At the same time, see Rogoff (2001) explaining why UC–Santa Cruz, after several decades of not doing it, added the practice of grading.

107. Ruben 1995:21.

108. Schank and Cleary 1995:2.

109. Schank and Cleary 1995:21.

110. Schank and Cleary 1995:21.

111. Carlson 2002.

112. Lanham 2002; Tomlinson-Keasey 2002.

113. Strange and Banning 2001:181–98. See Carlson 2003a and our discussion of the wired classroom earlier in this chapter.

114. Duderstadt et al. 2002; Carlson 2004a, b; Cuban 2001.

115. Cuban 2001. And, based on their empirical research, Zemsky and Massy (2004a, b) came to the same conclusion.

116. Cuban 2001:164, italics added.

117. Archibald 1968; Hough 1969.

118. Duderstadt et al. 2002; Carlson 2004b.

119. Wyatt 2003:93, italics in original. See also Cornell 2002.

120. Lauber 2003:121.

121. Lauber 2003:121.

122. Lauber 2003:121.

123. Lauber 2003:121.

124. Lauber 2003:122.

125. Lauber 2003:122.

126. McHenry 1993.

127. Wyatt 2003:99–102. Detweiler (2004) reports that similar innovations may be found at Rensselaer Polytechnic Institute.

128. Wyatt 2003:99.

129. Wyatt 2003:100.

130. Wyatt 2003:100–101, italics added. See also Young (1998) for a report on a variety of student reactions to the emporium.

Chapter Six

Discovery-Based Learning—
The Coach Enabling Players
in Resolving Social Issues

[Let us] reorient the way we do . . . social science. . . . I suggest that we conceptualize this focus in terms of the discovery, description, and analysis of *social inventions for solving social problems.*[1]

IS THIS ALL?

German social scientist Karl Mannheim brings us full circle to chapter 1. In 1932, some thirty-plus years after it emerged fully at the University of Chicago, Mannheim described U.S. social science in these rather disheartening terms:

We must admit a very marked and painful disproportion between the vastness of the scientific machinery employed and the value of ultimate results. The subject title of most contributions evoke the highest expectations; yet, after having reached their conclusions, one is tempted to ask disappointedly, 'Is this all?'[2]

Some thirty-plus years later, Alvin Gouldner and S. M. Miller concurred that the dreams of Harper, Small, and their early-twentieth-century colleagues had failed to materialize; the social sciences were still struggling to discover their grand sense of purpose. Gouldner and Miller reaffirmed their purpose, but conceded how hard it is to realize:

It is the historic mission of the social sciences to enable mankind to take possession of society. This is a big job and will take a long time. . . . [The ultimate objective of this job is] to bring society under control.[3]

Fast-forward an additional thirty-plus years and we discover that not much has changed. Chapter 1 explained that the social science elites are distressed because today's politicians and policymakers pay them no heed. Making the situation even more dismal are the conditions described in chapter 2: On the one hand is the metamorphosis of the twentieth-century research university and, on the other, is the inexorable expansion of the twenty-first-century entrepreneurial university. The former provided a nest in which the social sciences could contentedly roost. The latter does not. Chapter 3 described some earlier (and largely failed) efforts at university reform that grew out of profound dissatisfactions with the research university—discontents that were perceptible throughout much of that century but finally bubbled over in the 1960s and 1970s.

Chapter 4 began laying the groundwork for a new stab at what the Carnegie Commission called "reinventing" undergraduate education, the very soul of which is discovery-based learning (DBL).[4] Chapter 4 added that role diversity among professors is essential to genuine reinvention. The twentieth-century role of teacher-scholar (superprofessor) is already being overshadowed by the role of entrepreneur. Furthermore, the role of credentialer (especially in its cyber forms) is likely to become increasingly prominent. Accordingly, chapter 4 suggested that the role of coach would be pivotal to DBL. Chapter 5 explained that the coach would be responsible for facilitating a style of learning by doing that's entirely at odds with the teaching paradigm (TP) that currently pervades most of post-K–12 on both sides of the Atlantic. Learning by doing is integral to DBL because the *doing* denotes the type of research that, in the case of the social science module, is aimed at enabling humankind to take possession of society.

And now, in its turn, chapter 6 elaborates some of the ways in which the social sciences might perhaps carve out for themselves a distinctive twenty-first-century niche within both post-K–12 and the larger society. Creating such a place includes, in my view, figuring out what it means to enable humankind to take possession of society and to bring it under control. My take on those cryptic phrases is that they have a lot to do with citizens becoming, over time, more active in shaping the social conditions of their everyday lives. Citizens would, in William Whyte's terms, play a vital part in the task of *inventing solutions to solve social problems.*

Another way of understanding those phrases is to say that citizens would gradually come to participate more fully in the mending and/or weaving of the social fabric. Or, put still another way, those terms represent activities that are nothing other than developing fundamental democratic processes aimed at achieving a more just society. And, rather than standing aloof (as is now typically the case) from what's obviously a never-ending job, the social scientist would fully participate. The job would be pivotal to the social science module alluded to in prior chapters and explored here and in chapter 7. Situating that job in the module implies that undergraduates (alongside grad students and postdocs) would be participating in a task that's endless—it's their initiation into the pursuit of what chapter 7 calls lifelong learning.

PHASE I—TRANSITION INTO A LEARNING PARADIGM

Throughout the last couple of centuries academics have repeatedly voiced sharp differences of opinion over how the several parts of post-K–12 ought to be arranged.[5] Continuing in that long tradition of creative differences, the module's advocates might propose a three-year degree of, say, eleven months each.[6] European universities have, for example, recently begun to cooperate in offering a three-year undergraduate degree. Much to their surprise, however, there has been a rather "cool response from [graduate schools] across the Atlantic."[7]

In any case, advocates would add that a significant feature of their module is its separation into two distinct, though highly interdependent, phases. Phase I is a transitional period for players during which begins the grueling process of wrenching them from the tenacious grip of TP. After all, the players will have spent some twelve years figuring out how to exploit that model to their own ends, and it's hardly a simple matter to wean them from a very familiar and quite comfortable way of schooling. Consequently, phase I is a halfway house that seeks to smooth out the changeover from the old to something quite new—a different experience that, for some players, would at first be unnerving. The module could agree to set the length of phase I at one year, though other modules might perhaps opt for two years, in which case the players' time in the module would then stretch to the typical four years.

Phase I is a bridge from the old to the new because players' experiences in phase I would be shaped by some form of learning paradigm. In phase I the players strive to comprehend the open-ended and arguable issues found at the core of the several broad spheres of learning that make up what J. M. Cameron called "The Idea of a University."[8] Simply for starters, a potential (though by no means definitive) list of such broad spheres might include the sciences, humanities, history, the social sciences, the arts and design, and mathematics.

If the module elected to set the length of phase I at one year, three of those spheres might be considered in the first half of year 1, and three during the second half. Within the social sciences module, phase II (two years) would then be devoted entirely to considering social issues in a manner that is much more specific and focused than in phase I. Chapter 7 explains that, ideally, each domain of learning might eventually develop its own distinctive phase

II module. Based on that strategy, all six modules could share responsibilities for phase I. However, each of the six spheres would shape its distinctive approach to phase II in ways that are appropriate to its own sphere of learning. Professors serving in phase I (like those in II) have opted not to fulfill the role of entrepreneur. What's more, they sense that critics wondering if the teacher-scholar role is "yesterday's news" might be onto something. They have no interest whatever in being a guru or in preserving any residue or remnants whatever of TP. They desire, at the same time, to be more than a credentialer and something other than what the term "cyberprofessor" typically conveys to the listener. Very simply, they wish to serve as coaches. Their duties are similar to, yet different from, those of the phase II coach. One of the similarities is that within each sphere of learning the coach would work with several teams each with, say, four to five players positioned around computer workstations within labs that are open 24/7. Working closely with both coaches and players would be interns — graduate students and postdocs.

Addressing the core issues that cut across and unite particular disciplines within each broad realm (sciences, humanities, etc.) makes explicit what has thus far been implicit — the module would be thoroughly interdisciplinary. Proponents of the 1960s alternative university movement were, like a number of academics and citizens, distressed over the twentieth-century evolution away from the notion of broad spheres of learning. They fretted over the concept of the narrow discipline preoccupied with establishing the status and professional legitimacy first of itself and then of its practitioners. That long-term development was no less apparent in the sciences, humanities, and so on than it was in the social sciences.

Interestingly enough, however, a second trend has emerged more recently — particularly in the sciences — that is 180 degrees away from the "joint tyranny of the department and the discipline."[9] Observers describe this latest development as "teams [of researchers from a variety of disciplines] assembled opportunistically to solve particular problems."[10] Some observers believe that this "'interdisciplinary [often entrepreneurial] momentum' is not a fad but a fundamental and long-term restructuring of the nature of scholarly activity."[11] Accordingly, the module would construct itself as being at the core of this emerging, problem-focused, interdisciplinary momentum.

Another feature of the module also becomes explicit at this point. Recall from chapter 5 that the notions of class and classroom, including the baggage now strapped to those ideas, would, within the module, be passé. Also set aside would be the vast menu (smorgasbord, hodgepodge, potpourri) of narrow courses that forever regenerates itself to accommodate the professional interests of both current and newly recruited faculty. In effect, the problem-focused *unit* would replace the hodgepodge confronting most students today.

The units would consist of open-ended and arguable issues located at the core of each broad sphere of learning.

Admittedly, the strategy of the problem-focused unit differs markedly from a number of current beliefs about the optimal means to broaden the intellectual horizons of undergraduates. Nevertheless, according to J. M. Bishop (chancellor of the University of California at San Francisco and winner of the 1989 Nobel Prize for Physiology or Medicine), "We have thoroughly botched the job of teaching science."[12] Making a mess of the teaching of science, he asserts, pervades both K–12 and post-K–12 alike.[13] The chaos occurs, says Bishop, because science professors have for the most part (like those in the other five domains) encouraged lower-order, instead of higher-order, learning. Scientists, for instance, have required their undergraduates to memorize "the amino acids found in proteins" rather than enabling students to "think critically about how science should be used." Bishop adds that everyday citizens "are largely ignorant of its ways, its achievements, its limitations."[14]

Harvard's Andrew Knoll made a strikingly similar indictment about the lower-order teaching of science in both K–12 and college.[15] And, the University of Miami's Susan Haack concurs that the teaching of science now leaves much to be desired. She argued that most U.S. citizens are "confused about what science can and can't do, and about how it does what it does; about how science differs from literature or art; about whether science is really a threat to religion; about the role of science in society and the role of society in science."[16]

In any case, the character of the scientific method is likely to be among the broad, open-ended, and arguable issues that players encounter while participating in the phase I science sphere. Another issue might be the historical development of science as a worldview in competition with other worldviews such as religion. Other issues could include the impacts of science on ecosystems, or the implications for human beings of genetic engineering, and so on.[17] Alongside the worlds of science, phase I would aim to get students thinking about and trying to understand the several other spheres of learning—again by struggling with some of their core issues. One of the matters that might be considered within the social sciences sphere would be a critique of the basic/applied research distinction cited in chapter 1. Another matter might be the essential differences and similarities between the social sciences and the sciences.[18] Another open-ended issue is "what is a good society and which social arrangements [especially pertaining to social class, race, and gender] are to be preferred to others."[19]

Moving on to history, Stanford's Sam Wineburg reasons that undergraduates ought to invest their time in mastering "historical habits of mind" rather than in memorizing events, dates, places, and facts about notable personages.[20] His fundamental rationale for cultivating students' human capital skills rather than their lower-order learning is precisely the same as that cited by the professors above regarding the teaching of science. In both science and history—as well as in the four remaining spheres of study—a vital goal would be to get students to view professors as "people who formulate and struggle with questions rather than merely assigning them on tests."[21] Moreover, to the extent the professor is coaching students to take part in that struggle, the latter would, says Wineburg, begin to perceive the former as "kindred spirits."

And, for her part, Princeton's Elaine Showalter makes the same sorts of arguments regarding the need for a "radical" shift from lower-order to higher-order, learning within her domain.[22] In a provocative essay describing how the humanities should be taught, she asserts that the humanities ought to make the transition from TP to a learning paradigm fitted, of course, to their own specific interests and needs.[23] To that end, one finds statements such as these in her essay: "I think that we should make our teaching as intellectually challenging and as much a topic of professional critique and review as our research." Furthermore, "rather than emphasize content, such courses stress the process by which critical work or literary production is carried out." And "in contrast to simply imparting information or presenting interpretation we can . . . lead [students] to fresh discoveries about . . . meaning and . . . research." She adds that the study of Shakespeare should be "a form of problem-based learning like that being used in medical schools or law schools." She concludes by saying "our ways . . . of teaching them [the humanities] effectively . . . need to be radically changed and improved. Their future in higher education will depend on how willing we are to start talking about that."

One of phase I's central objectives is to infuse undergraduates with the excitement of Harper's vision about making stuff—to captivate their minds (no less than the minds of grad students) with the essence of research, namely, discovery. In their life as scientists or scholars, researchers approach the knowledge in their field with the intention of comprehending it in order, ultimately, to discredit and/or replace it.[24] Not meant to be cynical, that stance captures the bottom line of the scientific method and of scholarship in general. Accordingly, the coaches believe firmly that players would be well served if they cultivated that same disposition in them. Why not shock them with the startling realization that the fundamental purpose of absorbing X is *not* to memorize it for its own sake? Wouldn't players (and in due course society) be infinitely better off if they took hold of the notion that the ultimate aim in understanding X is to figure out how, if at all, X might possibly be modified, expanded, or perhaps even replaced? Wouldn't players go on to be much more effective within both the marketplace and civic society if they invested their college years in learning—not to memorize stuff for the short term—but instead in figuring out how to critique and to modify stuff, that is, to become what chapter 5 called a knowledge-maker?

PHASE II—STRUGGLING WITH SOCIAL INVENTIONS

Phase I is about coaching students to start setting aside the passive role that, for many years, TP has obliged them to take on. Phase II assumes that the player is now reasonably comfortable with being an active agent of his or her own learning. What's more, s/he is getting relatively accustomed to collaborating with teammates in a serious fashion, determined to grapple with complex questions. Finally, the player is feeling a bit more at home with the notion of using computer technology, not simply as an add-on, but as a tool that is integral to DBL. Phase II of the social sciences module builds on and expands the players' phase I experiences by focusing their entire attention (for two years) on social issues. An overarching objective is to cultivate their higher-order learning by initiating them into the implications of being a "weaver" of the social fabric—an "inventor" of ways to address social issues—a maker of "stuff."

Accordingly, let's say that the players invest year 1 (eleven months) of phase II participating in six different hypothetical (simulated, mock-up, virtual) DBL experiences—three in the first segment of the year and three in the second segment. Those situations would range from the local and the regional to the national and the global. Next, during the second and final year of phase II, players would move beyond simulated DBL experiences. They would, for the entire year (eleven months), devote themselves entirely to in-depth, *intensive* participation with coaches, interns, citizens, and officials in an actual hands-on experience aimed at building a more just society. Solely for logistic reasons, the empirical experience is likely to be local or perhaps regional. It is, however, quite conceivable that if the practice of the module eventually becomes more widespread, a player might be able travel either to another school in the United States or to a school in another society in order to gain that hands-on experience.

One of the several hoped-for outcomes of operating in this manner is to produce citizens that have a keen interest in something outside themselves—beyond the self-interest of pursuing their degree and making lots of money. In response to the recurring criticism that post-K–12 does little to counteract students' preoccupation with their own self-interest, a number of schools are now introducing *service-learning* programs. Unfortunately, such well-intentioned efforts are, for the most part, wrongheaded. Aside from the fact that frequently they are no more than an optional accessory pursued by a handful of students, they reinforce the prevailing perception that school is something quite distinct from the real world.[25] Because their underlying rationale is to get students to "apply" their "classroom knowledge" to "real-world problems," they reinforce the erroneous impression that actually resolving social issues has nothing to say back to the world of basic social science research. Within that limited framework, basic social science research is believed to have a lot to say to application, but not the other way round. The module aims, by contrast, to create an alternative situation in which over time each dimension (research and change) would in its turn feed forward on to the other.

Phase II/Year 1—*Simulating Social Inventions*

One of the vast, open-ended issues phase I teams might consider is the wide expanse of social inequality. An example of a more specific question that a phase II team might then derive from that larger issue was alluded to in chapter 1: *what are the conditions under which economically challenged mothers are empowered to move away from economic dependence and toward economic independence, that is, self-sufficiency?* There are, of course, many other questions that could be derived, and the teams would be encouraged to come up with their own ideas. Players understand that they and their coach would discuss those proposals and that the form of the question that's eventually approved is likely to look quite different than it did at first. As in phase I, the distinctive physical and spatial environment described in chapter 5 is the backdrop for their work, but does not circumscribe it.

Coaches covet the players' inputs in hopes of stimulating their interest (Schank and Cleary's first lesson of learning theory) in what they're working on. Alongside their participation in the selection of the question and in refining the form it eventually takes, the coach might also aim to grab the players' interest via the "so what" query. What difference, if any, asks the coach, might it make to you, or to any children you have (or might have), or to your family and friends that some mothers are either economically dependent or self-sufficient? Furthermore, what difference, if any, might their situation make for our democracy? Should you care about their situation at all?

Schank and Cleary's second lesson of learning, that is, control, is the flip side of interest. The more fully players participate in the selection and refinement of the question, the more likely they are to feel that *we own this question.* And the more it becomes *their* problem, the more diligently they're likely to work at solving it. This is especially so if the coach refrains from trying to convince them ahead of time that it *does make a difference, you should care about it.* Indeed, the coach might suggest that the team has the option to try to demonstrate that economic dependency no longer exists in the United

States, and/or if it does persist, it makes little difference to them and/or to our democracy.

The coach would, of course, provide an initial set of readings and also facilitate ongoing team dialogue regarding the problem. At the same time, players are expected to search out additional readings and to confer continually among themselves, as well as with other coaches, teams, and interns as to the appropriateness of the sources they uncover and their implications for solving the problem. In phase I they learned (the hard way, by doing it) that their success, both as a team and as individuals, rests ultimately with them. With control come responsibility and obligation.

In order to make a compelling case as to why their specific question might (or might not) matter to them and/or society, they would need to have at least an initial grasp of what is meant by social inequality in general. They shall, moreover, require a tentative sense of how it might intersect with social class, gender, and race. They should also acquire some minimal insight into the nature of democracy and develop an understanding of the historic struggles required to bring it into being. In addition, they must become familiar with its strengths and weaknesses and comprehend what it takes to maintain democracy in a robust manner. Hence, as they explore social inequality in the form of mothers' economic disadvantage, their coach and interns would assist them in reflecting on the proposition that, because disadvantaged persons are hindered from contributing their abilities and talents to our democracy, its vigor may be linked inversely with inequality.

In pursuit of those ends, team members must begin to read and discuss the sources they've unearthed from the library, and the Internet (more about this below), and elsewhere in ways they've seldom if ever read and discussed before. Because they've no clue as to the "right answers," they can't hunt them down "in the book" in order to isolate and memorize them for the test. Nor can they ask the coach "will this be on the test?" Or, "how often do I have to come to class?" Obviously, there are no "right" answers, and there's no test, there's no "class," and the individual does not operate in isolation. Although the coach provides a set of start-up readings, none are assigned in the typical sense. Players must instead very carefully read (not skim superficially, as many do now) their entire range of sources—especially those they've uncovered—in hopes of devising their own solutions to "our" problem.

Read means first to *analyze* their sources, that is, break them down into their component parts. Next, read means to *evaluate* those segments, that is, the process of winnowing. They must judge (and be ready to defend) not only which parts are reliable, but also which are more significant than the others. Finally, read means to *synthesize* the most relevant segments (and thus set lesser parts aside) in the form of a logically coherent and compelling written document that purports to solve their problem, that is, answer their question.

In effect, the team is conducting an *inquiry* and, in the course of trying to resolve its question, its members are *learning* to cultivate their human capital skills—including their capability to write in a logically coherent and compelling manner.[26] While they're preparing their team document they consult fully and freely with each other, with persons from other teams, as well as with their coaches and interns. The consultations between coaches and players consist of a lengthy series of feed-forward stages in which players present their synthesis, at first verbally but very soon in written form. The coach then assesses their work and offers suggestions to improve it. The teams next revise their work accordingly, and the coach offers further suggestions, and so on.[27] At the appointed time, each team gives the coach the final version of the paper. The coach evaluates it and provides a set of written comments to the team, explaining the basis for the evaluation.

If inequality is indeed found to be detrimental to a democracy and to its citizens, then the question the team must try to answer in its next paper is how to decrease it—in this instance, by increasing mothers' economic independence. By now, we might expect that team members are at least partially convinced that inequality in general, and mothers' economic dependence in particular, do matter to them personally and to our democracy as well. And if they do in fact care about such things, at least to some small degree, then perhaps it might just possibly be worth their while trying to figure out if it could ever be minimized and, if so, how. All parties understand very well that the team can expect, at most, to make only the tiniest of contributions toward resolving contentious matters of such huge magnitude, innumerable facets, and enormous complexities.

No one would be more painfully conscious of those stark realities than the team members themselves. Among other sources, they'll need to immerse themselves in past work (including the vast literature describing efforts to reduce inequality) in order to come up with ideas they can discuss with their coach.[28] The coach (along with the intern) will be required to spell out again and again why the team's current set of ideas about increasing mothers' economic independence is inadequate to the task, why their written arguments fail to make a compelling case regarding ways to resolve the problem, and what they might do next in order to improve the quality of their ideas and the coherence of their logic.

Presumably, members are willing to keep on working that hard while enduring that many disappointments, first, because they're interested in the problem and, second, because of their feelings of control (via participation with their coach) over how to go about attacking their problem. We could assume further that interest and control contribute toward making their tasks seem worthwhile, enjoyable, and satisfying. Centuries before today's video games reminded us, our forebears understood that when humans find something to be enjoyable and satisfying, they keep on doing it in the face of numerous frustrations and failures.[29] Their persistence stems from, among other things, their desire to get better at it.

The adolescent struggling to get competent at tennis, gymnastics, or violin, is a classic example. As one becomes more successful over time, one's self image gradually begins to change. One starts to feel that one is actually growing into becoming reasonably good at doing something, for example, tennis, gymnastics, or violin. And because the ultimate limits of how good one might eventually get at doing the something cannot be known in advance, one tends to keep on working at it, intent on the gratifications that come with trying to get better at it over time.

Consequently, a major task of the coach is to facilitate the steady improvement of team members in rising to meet the tough and relentless challenges they face. The members should, over time, gradually come to sense that as a group, and as individuals, they're becoming better at doing their tasks. The self-image of each person should begin to change: *I'm improving at researching and developing papers that help resolve our team's problem. And I'm getting better at contributing to, and improving, our team's efforts. And I'm becoming a bit more effective at problem solving in general by getting better at trying to resolve questions regarding social issues. In effect, I'm becoming not only an agent and a collaborator but also, in a highly preliminary sense, I'm starting to become a maker or inventor of stuff, a weaver of the social fabric.*

The essential flip side of the coach facilitating growth of that sort within the players is his/her effort to get the group as a whole to construct itself as operating more effectively. Building the feeling that *I* can grow (me-ness) is inseparable from developing the sense that *we* can grow (we-ness): *Our team is getting increasingly effective at winning. Winning is not, however, a zero-sum softball game in which our team wins and yours loses. The fact that our team is becoming better at achieving our goals in no way diminishes your team's chances to do as well or even better. Indeed, our team shall do all it can to help your team do better work.* Within the module, the notion of winning is a "personal best" struggle in which the individual competes principally against her/himself and tries to improve on his or her own past record. Simultaneously, the concept of "group best" means that the team competes chiefly against itself—its fiercest competition stems from its own past record.

Phase II/Year 2—*Doing Social Inventions*

During phase II/year 1, players construct a series of papers in which they think through (but do not actually take part in) the complex processes of building social inventions from their start to their maintenance, and perhaps their dissolution. The coaches and teams would not, however, be content solely with mock-ups (as valuable as they are) of solutions to their research problems. The players should, in addition, be able to gain the opportunity to participate with citizens in asserting greater influence over their life circumstances, that is, inventing a more just society. In order to assert that the module is wholly committed to discovery-based learning, the players should have access to some type of empirical hands-on experience.

Keep in mind that the majority of the module's players are *not* there to ready themselves for careers in social-science-related fields. They participate chiefly because of the exceptionally high-quality education it offers—coaching in the sorts of portable human capital skills that they can transport with them into the information age marketplace. To be sure, they would also, presumably, have some degree of interest in carrying those same skills into any efforts they might make (later on as citizens) aimed at human betterment. Consequently, for them, as well as for the minority of players planning to enter a social-science-related field, the extensiveness that characterizes the first year of phase II would seem to be entirely prudent.

It's wise because the breadth and comprehensiveness that accompany a wide range of experiences permit the players to think through and simulate the solutions to a variety of social issues that extend far beyond the typical milieu of many colleges and universities. To be sure, certain urgent issues explored by the social sciences are often found within the less urbanized setting in which many schools are sited. Nevertheless, most social issues are typically much more intense and severe in sprawling urban areas and in large metropolitan centers. Furthermore, many other kinds of urgent social issues are regional, national, or even global in scope.[30] Consequently, it seems vital that year 1 of phase II should be *extensive,* in the sense of enabling players to wrestle with the challenges of trying to weave the social fabric throughout as wide a variety of settings as possible—regional, national, and international.

By way of contrast, the second year of phase II would be *intensive* in nature. Accordingly, each module would need to maintain at least one or more ongoing, long-term, empirical, hands-on projects, that is, local social inventions. For any number of obvious reasons, such a project should, ideally, be able to attract a significant amount of external funding from government and foundations, and perhaps even commercial enterprises. Coaches and interns would be pivotal in maintaining the continuity of such projects. Among numerous possibilities, the module's hands-on projects might perhaps select from among the pressing social issues that Bok, Boyer, and Duderstadt urged universities to consider—including the several facets of social inequality.

During phase II/1, each team would have been encouraged to select one of the module's ongoing empirical projects as the focal point for one of its six mock-up efforts. Such a strategy offers the potential for the team to test its II/1 simulation during II/2. And, although the team would surely make changes to its mock-up before it starts its actual field experiment, linking years 1 and 2 in this manner provides a singular opportunity for the team to get a firsthand feel for the soundness of its mock-up.

A Bottom-Up Strategy

Recall from chapter 1 that for the most part the elite social scientists of the twentieth century constructed the solution of most social problems in top-down terms. Most believed that professionals should proffer their expertise to politicians, policymakers, and clients on ways to solve problems—including the issue of increasing the economic independence of disadvantaged mothers. Regrettably, that strategy resulted in social science being overlooked almost entirely by politicians, policy analysts, and by academics from other spheres of learning. The elites' top-down strategy notwithstanding, the phrases "taking possession of society" and "bringing it under control" suggest a contrasting image. Those phrases, along with Whyte's "social inventions for solving social issues," imply some sort of bottom-up strategy in which citizens might have an active voice in shaping the conditions of their own lives. Hence, in the case of poor mothers striving for greater economic self-sufficiency, the team would try to figure out what a bottom-up strategy means, how it might be effective, and how it might mesh with eventually putting the social invention in place in the shape of a formal, though flexible, policy or program.

Karl Marx did, of course, view human betterment in bottom-up terms. He argued that the oppressed social classes should unite and rebel—typically in violent revolution—against the privileged classes that controlled society in an unjust and unfair manner. The injustice lay in the simple fact that the advantaged few made sure society's good things flowed in their direction with little or no interest in, or regard for, the masses of citizens. Marx urged disadvantaged citizens to use force to take *possession* of society (its political and economic systems) and thus to bring it under their *control* in order to distribute its benefits more equitably. He believed that in the process of struggling for justice citizens would, in effect, weave a new social fabric, that is, invent a new society in which they would be empowered.

Decades before Marx, the American Revolution was an obvious attempt to do precisely that: use violence to invent something new, a more equitable society, that is, a different social fabric. Once, however, their democracy was in place, the newly empowered citizens were expected to switch to nonviolent means in order to keep on improving their invention, that is, correct further injustices and make life better. The citizens' elected representatives were charged with the responsibility to mend the social fabric and, when necessary, to weave new segments into it. Both the mending and the weaving were aimed at inventing a more just society in the belief that justice is the principal ingredient necessary for human betterment and a robust democracy. The nineteenth- and twentieth-century feminist movement and the twentieth-century black civil rights movement were examples of bottom-up, nonviolent struggles to create a more just society. Using a variety of strategies, ordinary citizens pressured their elected representatives to do some much-needed mending and weaving. (On the other hand, the mid-nineteenth-century abolitionist movement did reluctantly endorse the violence of war in the interests of achieving a more just society.)

In his 1981 presidential address to the American Sociological Association, William Foote Whyte made an observation affirmed by many others before and since. Public officials and policymakers, said Whyte, view social science research in general as largely irrelevant. To counteract that prevailing perception of social science, Whyte said that social scientists should begin to do research resulting in "social inventions for solving human problems."[31] Some of Whyte's ideas for inventing a more just society sound remarkably similar to John Dewey's. Dewey, too, believed passionately in bottom-up, democratic change and, toward that end, argued vigorously that the public schools should do far more than merely imbue children/youth with democratic ideas and ideals. The schools must, he contended, also be the place where children/youth participate actively in the practices of democracy—they should get firsthand experience as to what it's all about. According to Ellen Lagemann, Dewey held that education ought to be

a means for nurturing new social capacities, especially the skills, orientations, and knowledge necessary to building and sustaining a democratic community.[32]

Whyte did not, however, follow Dewey in linking social inventions to the schools at any level. Nor did he address the key question of how and where social scientists might actually learn to do their social inventions—a process that Whyte later called "participatory action research," while others called it "action research" (AR).[33]

In order to fill that gap, the module would offer itself as a basic training ground on how to do social inventions. Phase II/2 is, in effect, a place for social scientists—in the company of students, interns, and citizens—to do in actual practice what was merely simulated in II/1. How might coaches, players, and interns make their transition away from the peculiar basic social science spin? How would they move instead toward the type of research (e.g., AR) that aims to synthesize understanding with social change? How might they actually go about seeking to invent a more just society?

Importantly, AR is *not* applied research, because the linkages between understanding and change are not merely one-way. The inventions influence understanding just as much as understanding influences the inventions. AR is a means for ordinary citizens to try to achieve greater control over (or take possession of) the social circumstances of their own lives. Undergrads would, as fully as possible, participate in this mission because it's in their own self-interest, as well as in the interest of society, to do so. Grad students and postdocs, too, would participate for both reasons and, presumably, because they would carry it forward into succeeding generations.

With regard, for example, to the long-range objective of reducing social inequality, AR would (as it does for all issues) aim at developing a bottom-up perspective. During the 1960s Great Society (chapter 1), some social scientists ventured quite close to that point of view:

> The theoretical basis of the Community Action Program [CAP] is the proposition that poverty in an affluent society is neither lack of individual economic resources nor 'relative deprivation,' but the lack of control by poor people over the institutions which serve them. . . . To break the cycle [of poverty] *both power itself and self-awareness of power are necessary.*[34]

Although the social scientists and policy analysts that devised CAP did indeed want poor people to be and feel empowered, their basic strategy was nonetheless to come up with their expert invention for empowerment and then deliver it ready-made to poor citizens. AR's much more excruciatingly demanding line of attack is for the researcher to work with disadvantaged (and also advantaged) citizens in hopes of developing their own inventions for empowerment—innovations that might perhaps later on be formalized by some type of program.[35] It's perfectly obvious, in short, that a bottom-up approach in no way excludes the notion of eventually putting formal social inventions/programs in place—either by legislative or other means.[36]

Although Whyte's bottom-up ideas sound like they came straight out of Marx (violence aside), the well-known Marxist philosopher Sidney Hook (one of Dewey's students at Columbia University) spent much of his career arguing that the notion of bottom-up social inventions sprang instead from a fresh synthesis of the fundamental ideas of both Marx and Dewey.[37] According to Hook, both thinkers were profoundly convinced that meaningful social change occurs when ordinary citizens—typically at the community level—become knowledge-makers or producers. The process of social change begins with citizens figuring out what's wrong with or lacking in their current situation, and also how to change it via some sort of social invention in which they actively participate.

Next, citizens seek to gain control (get power) over their situation by "testing" their invention—by doing hands-on "experiments." Moreover, as AR advocates see it, the social scientist would participate with citizens (not merely stand back and observe them) in their struggles for change. Social scientists would do so not only to help bring about greater social justice but also to gain firsthand understanding into the agonizingly difficult process of trying to do social inventions from the ground up—including the often fierce resistance to change on the part of those that perceive it as inimical to their own interests.[38]

Most social scientists would readily endorse the option of the researcher observing, say, poor mothers in a certain neighborhood while they struggle to achieve economic self-sufficiency. And many would even accept the option of becoming a *participant* observer, for example, a researcher moves with her child into a neighborhood consisting mostly of poor mothers and, like them, works at one or more minimum wage jobs, trying desperately to scrape by.[39] Most, however, would object to the AR perspective that the social scientists and the "stakeholders" (for example, poor mothers) should work together as "co-researchers."[40] Although many would concur that poor mothers require a sense of control over their life circumstances in order to become self-sufficient, most social scientists believe that the route to the mothers' empowerment stems from top-down government policies that are based on the results of research done by professionals but not citizens. Professionals are extremely ill at ease when the researcher with expert "outsider knowledge" and the stakeholder with expert "insider knowledge" combine their two sets of understandings in an ongoing process of investigation and redirection.[41] There are many reasons why the typical social scientist is leery of blending insider knowledge with outsider expertise, and one of the reasons is, said Whyte, that AR is invariably marked by "creative surprises" that decrease the professional's control over the research process.[42]

Not too long ago, I participated in an AR experiment that was indeed marked by a totally unanticipated surprise. The study was designed to try to enable poor mothers to develop a sense of control that might facilitate their attempts to become self-sufficient.[43] Several years before Congress passed the 1996 Welfare Reform Act, the state of Florida was testing its own "welfare-to-work" program. Mary Joyce Hasell (from the University of Florida School of Construction, Design, and Planning) and I were among many U.S. citizens concerned about how mothers would cope with the eventual termination of government assistance. Hasell had recently become aware of cohousing, namely, a type of community designed (both spatially and socially) by its residents in order to bring about and maintain mutual help patterns among their households.[44] Hence, we wondered if arrangements parallel (though not identical) to cohousing might perhaps be one means to enable poor mothers to cope with the eventual ending of public assistance, then called AFDC (Aid to Families with Dependent Children).

Accordingly, we got permission from a local Housing and Urban Development (HUD) director to carry out AR in a HUD project consisting of densely packed, one-family units in which all the women were African American lone mothers receiving AFDC dollars. After canvassing all the neighborhood households, we were able to interest some seven or eight mothers in participating in what we expected to be at least a two-year project. They agreed to take part in weekly focus groups and in-depth interviews aimed, we told them, at making it on your own. Earlier studies of black households in poor neighborhoods revealed that the residents frequently formed "fictive kin" networks—small clusters of households not linked by blood.[45] They were instead connected by social capital. James Coleman described social capital as patterns of giving and getting among network members.[46] Their ongoing reciprocity slowly generates a sense of trust among them. The members can then draw on that shared trust (as they would any type of capital, and as long as they repay) in order to facilitate their own interests.

The problem we explored was whether or not it was possible for mothers in this HUD neighborhood to form a fictive kin network (a social invention) that might facilitate the members' self-sufficiency. For example, as mothers began to spend more time in the labor force and/or in school, would they be able to help each other out, especially with child care, but also in other practical ways such as a ride to work? Furthermore, could the members provide emotional support for one another in order to cope with the discouragements and frustrations that inevitably accompany the difficult transition they would be expected to make?

Studies also suggested that, lacking fictive kin networks, residents of poor neighborhoods tend to keep their distance from one another. They do so out of feelings of mutual distrust and their fear of being exploited in some way. And in that vein, mothers in our focus group were emphatic in stating that neighborhood mothers strongly distrusted one another for any number of reasons. It was clear to insiders and outsiders alike that in order to develop a fictive kin network, the members would over time slowly need to grow the sense of mutual trust that is the basis of social capital.

After a year of weekly focus group sessions, insiders and outsiders agreed that the levels of trust they were starting to develop might be bolstered if each member moved to her own house close by other members within a cul-de-sac sited in their HUD development. Their physical proximity (similar to cohousing) would, we expected, make it easier over time to exchange physical help and provide emotional support, thus building the fundamental component of trust.[47] To that end, the HUD director agreed in principle to move the group's members into a selected cul-de-sac and also agreed to provide modest funding for renovations on the houses into which the members were moving—renovations that the mothers themselves came up with in consultation with Hasell and her graduate students.

Our ultimate objective was to increase each mother's sense of control over every facet of her life. She herself, in cooperation with others, would be taking charge of vital nonwork aspects (e.g., child care) of her life in order to increase her capability to pursue school and/or work, thus moving her further on the path toward self-sufficiency. Unfortunately, we discovered very late into the project that the HUD director did not share that same long-term objective. Before she would in fact allow the move and allocate the renovation moneys, she asked us to divulge any information we'd learned regarding the mothers' "deviant" behaviors, for example, drug use or having men hang around.

She also expressed concern that allowing the formerly dependent and passive mothers to develop the levels of control over their life that we had in view would make them harder to manage. That is, they might become more reluctant to conform without question to regulations she imposed on them and their children. Although we suggested that it might be a good thing for the mothers to participate in the framing of such regulations, she emphatically disagreed. In any case, because we could not and would not divulge any sensitive information to her, she terminated the project by revoking permission to operate on HUD's premises and by bringing its funding to a halt.

Besides imparting a feel for what AR is and how it might be carried out, this brief narrative accentuates the significance of the resistance, or adversarial, dimension identified in chapter 1 and alluded to repeatedly throughout the book. Biting the hand of one's feeder neither generates endearment nor does it increase the likelihood of more goodies. Marx, Henderson, Gouldner, Whyte, Flyvbjerg, and many others have argued that, in doing our research, it's essential for social scientists to anticipate and assess the dimension of resistance. That is especially the case when our goal is achieve a greater depth of understanding regarding efforts to bring about changes aimed at achieving a greater degree of social equity.

Recasting K–9–12

Recall that Bok, Boyer, and Duderstadt each believed that reforming K–12 exemplifies another long-term project in which universities are obliged to get involved.[48] Hence, let's assume that a certain module takes on K–12 reform as one of its empirical AR projects. Before it can devise a prescription, or social invention, it must arrive at the nature of what ails K–12. Dewey's diagnosis of what afflicts K–12, and his prescription for curing it, came to be known as "progressivism."[49]

During the course of the twentieth century, the progressive educational movement had several well-known leaders steering it through a turbulent history, and today it has numerous facets. Nonetheless, its wide range of advocates is unified by the simple idea of "starting with students' interests and letting students learn to do instead of making them listen."[50] One of progressivism's contemporary spokespersons is Theodore Sizer. Sizer diagnoses K–12's core ailment in a manner similar to Dewey and the University of Wisconsin's James Gee: "By high school, very often both good students and bad ones, rich and poor ones, don't much like school."[51]

Although K–12 students are compelled to memorize lower-order stuff for the test, they do not learn, says Sizer, to "think well," that is, to cultivate human capital skills.[52] Sizer describes human capital skills as certain *habits* that persons have and do, the foremost of which, he says, is the "habit of thoughtfulness, of bringing an informed, balanced, and responsibly skeptical approach to life. . . . School, simply, is about the habit of thoughtfulness."[53] Sizer's prescription for K–12's fatal flaw is that middle and high schools should make up their minds to explore the tortuous terrain from TP to some form of a learning paradigm.

Accordingly, let's say that the module elects to address the problem of structuring high school (grades 9–12) in the progressive tradition. They intend to do so from an AR perspective that, like Sizer's prescription, can also be traced back to the influence of John Dewey.[54] To that end, it cooperates with local officials to establish a unique high school. It's conceived of as a "magnet" school attracting students from the entire area interested in discovery-based learning. It aims, in effect, to cultivate their human capital skills by engaging them in social inventions—first hypothetical, and later on actual. University coaches, interns, and players are "outsiders," while local officials, teachers, and students are "insiders."[55] All stakeholders concur that the information age demands that, whether or not they ever attend college, all youth must be good problem solvers if they're to participate effectively both in the marketplace and in civic society, that is, the political and social circumstances that affect them, their community, and beyond.

Because youth from working-class and minority households are, in the new century, likely to suffer the greatest deprivation if they fail to cultivate human capital skills, the school's learning facilities should be located in a less advantaged section of the city, and it would be charged to attract and hold relatively disadvantaged students. Consequently, in this case, weaving the social fabric, or building a more just society, means inventing a 9–12 structure that, in some (but not all) respects, looks like the post-K–12 module.[56] One of 9–12's aims is to create the kinds of educational experiences that might inhibit disadvantaged youth from falling even further behind than they might already be. The hope is that the 9–12 invention would eventually become an established mechanism enabling disadvantaged persons to compete more effectively with advantaged persons in both the marketplace and in civic society.[57]

At the same time, advantaged 9–12 youth would be encouraged to participate in this magnet school for two prime reasons. One is self-interest: the chance for unique, high-quality educational experiences. A significant aspect of the self-interest dimension for 9–12 students from both advantaged and disadvantaged households is the promise (see below) of making imaginative learning technology integral to their team efforts. A sense of moral obligation is the second reason that advantaged youth are encouraged to participate in the magnet school. Because the 9–12 players would be organized into teams, most learning is peer-based, though facilitated by coach and intern. In those situations, advantaged youth would have much to offer as well as a whole lot to gain, even though the latter may erroneously assume they have little or nothing to get from their disadvantaged peers. Given that the 9–12 school is, like the post-K–12 module, committed to serving society, it seems perfectly reasonable to stress meaningful service, along with self-interest, in recruiting advantaged youth.

A particular team within the *post*-K–12 module could elect, as its yearlong hands-on experience, to participate in this ongoing social invention. In writing its mock-up during year II/1, the college players became aware of a serious concern voiced by a number of the insiders, that is, the students and teachers in 9–12. Their concern was over the conflicts generated by persons working so closely together in teams. The more advantaged 9–12 students tended, for instance, to construct the less advantaged to be free-riders, while the latter perceived the former as imperious and demeaning—especially when it came to mastering the innovative technology described below. Teachers and students alike were quite aware that this type of serious conflict tends to undermine the ultimate objective of cultivating team members' human capital skills.

In effect, one among several larger questions the college team would be addressing is how to make diversity genuinely happen at ground zero. Seeing to it that adolescents from differing economic and/or racial backgrounds are placed alongside each together in high school is, as we saw in chapter 1, the relatively easy part.[58] It's quite another, and much tougher, thing for both sides to begin to fashion anything close to what British social scientist Anthony Giddens called a "lifestyle pact between the affluent and the poor."[59] Hence, the college team has two objectives: One is to work with high school teachers and students in trying to redirect, that is, *change* the existing situation. By year's end, how much/little productive cooperation has the module's team been able to facilitate among 9–12 team members from differing backgrounds? Their second objective is to contribute to our *understanding* of the infinitely complex processes inherent in pursuing that type of vital social change.

To struggle toward both goals, the module's team wrestled (during II/1) with several bodies of literature, including research on conflict-management within task-oriented teams.[60] And now, during this hands-on year, they put their mock-up to an empirical test: to what extent, if at all, does their simulation help achieve productive cooperation within the high school teams? During the course of its yearlong, hands-on AR experiment, the college team would be consulting with its coach and interns and preparing a series of papers demonstrating two intrinsically linked matters. First, what is its level of success (or failure) in facilitating the complex processes of social change? Second, what is its level of success (or failure) in contributing to our understanding of those intricate processes?

Bear in mind that the character of an ongoing AR experiment is "much closer to the practices of . . . biological [life] sciences than any of the mainstream varieties of academic social research."[61] Davydd Greenwood and Morten Levin claim that AR generates findings that are more valid, that is, well founded, than basic social science research, mainly because AR, like the life sciences, aims to interrupt the course of the real world.[62] Schank and Cleary also observe that students must grasp the fundamental notion that the scientist typically seeks to "disturb the system under study from its natural state and observe the effects of the disturbance."[63]

Those disturbances of the real world supply a great deal of insight into it— vital understanding that could be gotten by no other means. Recall, for example, the life scientist described in chapter 1 studying HIV.[64] Her strategy is to use certain theoretical ideas to set up an empirical test attempting in some manner to thwart, that is, interrupt, the ongoing course of the deadly virus. The test either fails or succeeds in validating her theory (i.e., her comprehension of HIV) or, more likely, simply modifies it in some manner. Based on those findings, the life scientist then sets up another test, and so the story continues for an indefinite period. The biological conditions she faces are (like social conditions faced by the social scientist) generating an enormous amount of resistance to her attempts to disturb them.

Accordingly, the college team works with the high school team in order to experiment with a social invention—a strategy to disturb the real-world course of the 9–12 team's conflicts. The initial invention either succeeds or fails or, more likely, turns out to be a mixture of both. Based on those results, the module team and the high school team set up their next experiment, and so on, for the entire year. The module team hopes that by the time it departs it will leave in place some sort of invention that the 9–12 students and teachers can utilize, at least until they perceive the need to modify the invention that they and the college team previously constructed.

Hence, akin to the work of the life scientist, the series of papers prepared by the college team during year II/2 reflects their ongoing experiences at actually attempting to interrupt the real world and thereby to understand it in an in-depth manner—a degree of comprehension typically not attainable by the basic social science approach. Their final paper would bring together the sum total of their hands-on, year long, DBL, AR-based experiences. In what ways have their experiences helped to cultivate their own human capital capabilities? In what ways have their experiences enabled them, in some modest fashion, to weave the social fabric—to contribute to a more just society? In what ways have they failed? Added to the *extensive* range of simulations from the previous year, the in-depth and *intensive* experiences from their hands-on year should give each player an intimate feel for how wrenchingly difficult bottom-up empowerment actually is, and also how dissimilar it is from the typical top-down social policy approach that currently prevails.

Taken together, the sum total of three years of highly demanding experiences is, moreover, quite likely to lead the player to begin constructing her- or himself, at least in an embryonic sense, as a knowledge-producer, that is, a weaver/inventor of the social fabric. The player might begin to feel that *I possess a modicum of awareness of what that's all about. I'm at least a novice in the pursuit of the gargantuan and never-ending objective of inventing a more just society.* And, in any case, compared to what the prevailing post-K–12 system accomplishes for its degree holders, the module would likely show itself to be light-years ahead. Whether the comparison is the development of one's intellectual capabilities or the sense of one's obligation to something larger than oneself, the module promises a whole lot more, and is likely to be much more effective at making good on its promises, than most of today's post-K–12 situations.

TECHNOLOGY IN SERVICE TO DISCOVERY-BASED LEARNING—*NETGENERS AT WORK*

"Toward what ends" should we put computer technology? asks Larry Cuban.[65] My response is twofold: First, it should *symbolize* the makeover to a learning paradigm. Chapter 5 showed that, within the module, the technology is couched within the reconstructions of spaces and times. The module provides learning spaces and computer workstations at which teams may gather 24/7. Likewise, technology is integral to the creation of the roles of coach and players/teams.

Those new roles operating within that new situation maintain a distinctive fit with what the twenty-first century is all about. Any single element of that entire package is by itself insufficient. But the whole package taken together communicates a clear and unmistakable message—active learning is distinctive, and innovative technology is an essential part of it.

Second, it follows that the technology (in concert with spaces and times) facilitates the *substance* of the learning paradigm, that is, the ongoing struggles described above. Technology is not likely ever to replace the grueling face-to-face efforts of coaches, players, interns, and sometimes citizens struggling to resolve social issues. Nonetheless, at the same time, technology is virtually certain to be a vital and necessary means of making those struggles more productive.[66] Keep in mind that neither technology nor spatial and temporal redesign drives the module. Instead, the module's need to fulfill its DBL-based mission compels it to seek out innovations in spaces, times, and technologies. Indeed, it seems inconceivable to speak of reinventing the undergraduate experience in twenty-first-century terms and yet fall short of making cutting-edge learning technology integral to the DBL process.[67]

In the mid-1990s, Terry O'Banion argued that technology has yet to fulfill its promise to improve education or to improve instructional productivity, but there is mounting evidence, he said, that the promise will be kept.[68] O'Banion added that the principal reason why technology has not so far been more warmly received throughout post-K–12 and has not had more of a significant impact is that many academics construct it simply as one more device to "extend the old model of education."[69] By and large, technology continues to be seen as a discretionary add-on to the teaching paradigm, much as iron was added on to the hulls of nineteenth-century wooden warships. To solve their fundamental problem, naval officers were forced to abandon their add-on strategy and take a risky leap into uncharted territory. In the nineteenth century, it was the steel vessel. In the twenty-first, it is a learning paradigm.

Frank Newman and Jamie Scurry of the Futures Project: Policy for Higher Education in a Changing World take a similar tack. They argue that if computer technology is ever to deliver on its potential for upgrading post-K–12, there must first be a "shift [in] the faculty member's role from source of information to supervisor or coach of the learning process."[70] Recall from chapter 5 that the most disconcerting feature for professors working in the Math Emporium was being yanked suddenly out of their comfortable role of guru and then set down, without adequate preparation, into the unnerving role of coach. One could safely surmise, in short, that the demands of a learning paradigm (though different for coach and player) are just as taxing and scary for the coach as they are for the player.

And, in a similar vein, during their three-year research project (2001–2004), Robert Zemsky and William Massy explored the validity of several claims made by numerous technology promoters of the 1990s. One of the promoters' claims was that e-learning would "force a change in how we teach."[71] And what did the researchers find?

> Most faculty members today teach as they were taught—they stand in front of a classroom providing lectures to supply the basic knowledge students need. . . . Few processes have proved more resistant to change.[72]

They add that such ancient traditions persist in the face of the growing mass of data about student learning described in chapter 5. That such a paradox exists seemed incomprehensible to those investigators. Springing from the researcher side of their scholar role, academics pride themselves on risk-taking in pursuit of the new. But within the teacher side, they utterly disregard the significance of the new because, among other things, it is indeed taxing and scary. Regardless of how incongruous the current situation appears, the venerated teaching paradigm is alive and well: neither the recent mass of data about student learning nor computer technology has given it the decent burial it deserves.

An added twist to this bewildering saga is that failure to make technology integral to DBL tends to reinforce the already prevailing image that school at all levels is *so* non-real-world. Data collected in 2001 by the U.S. Department of Education revealed that "about 90 percent of people ages 5 to 17 use computers and 59 percent of them use the internet—rates that are, in both cases, higher than those of adults."[73] The headline of a full-page software ad in the *Chronicle of Higher Education* (with a fetching nine-year-old, pigtailed, smiling girl wearing oversized spectacles, seated primly with hands on her laptop and a miniature digital camera hanging round her neck) cautions us "Ready or not, here they come." Smaller print advises us, "If you think today's college students are tech-savvy, wait until you meet tomorrow's."

The inescapable conclusion is that being computer-*intimate* (not merely literate) is integral to the real world of proliferating numbers of twenty-first-century students. Sometimes called the NetGeners, they're oblivious to a time prior to the World Wide Web.[74] That their social and cultural worlds are presently being transformed by continually shifting computer technology is indisputable.[75] Furthermore, some academics go so far as to argue that the technology has also wrought certain types of physiological changes:

> Children raised in a media-rich, interactive environment tend to think and to learn differently because they are physiologically different from us. Their brains are wired in different ways.[76]

Not too long ago, I listened in to a group (a thirties adult, two adolescents, and an eight-year-old) talking about the video game they'd reluctantly interrupted in order to wolf down lunch so they could rush back to their game. Central to their discourse was how incredibly hard the game was, how much more difficult it was than any video games they'd ever played before (including the fact that it takes several weeks to complete), and their eager expectation that certain games they planned to buy would be harder still. Their obsession with seeking out greater levels of difficulty struck me as unbelievably strange (given the fact that students of all ages complain fiercely about how much work certain assignments entail, and how hard they are, and how much time they take) until I came across the investigations of Wisconsin's James Paul Gee.[77] He'd been baffled as to why an industry that produces video games (aimed at audiences aged preschool to 39) that require huge amounts of time to complete and that are becoming steadily more demanding "makes as much or more money each year than the film industry."[78] "Wouldn't it be great," he asked out loud, "if kids were willing to put in this much time on task on such challenging material in school and enjoy it so much?"[79]

Gee then launched an intensive research program to find out what overlap, if any, exists between the playing of *good* video games and the range of learning theories described in chapter 5. He discovered that they share a great deal of common ground, including the foundational principle of learning by doing. The doing is anchored in solving problems and occurs frequently in a group context. In effect, Gee found that good video games are governed by the two learning theory principles of interest and control. Players are absorbed by the games because, for one thing, they find them intriguing. And even more pivotal, players are absorbed due to the sense of gratification and accomplishment that the games impart as the players become ever more adept at mastering, that is, controlling, the challenging circumstances of the game.[80]

Many academics dismiss video games in principle, as I once did, on the grounds that at best they're trivial and no more than a passing fad. And, it's obvious that much of my colleagues' disdain is justified—especially their censure of the wanton violence of many games. But even if video games do eventually fade away from the real world of hundreds of thousands of high school and college students and young adults, clever entrepreneurs will quickly devise other means to capitalize on the simple reality that, whatever the games' negative features, the principles underlying them are hardly trivial. There is clearly a market for computer-based activities that are grounded in sound theories of learning though, as Gee surmises, today's game designers have, by and large, never studied those theories. They're instead too busy designing new ways to make more money based on the solid ideas that they grasp intuitively. And, among those sound ideas is the sense of well-being, and of fulfillment and gratification, that stem from enhancing one's awareness of greater control over external forces. Those feelings come about by facing and overcoming a very difficult set of conditions arrayed against one's attempts to achieve her or his goals.

Meanwhile, because K–12 remains locked into the non-real-world notions of TP, "by high school, very often both good students and bad ones, rich and poor ones, don't much like school."[81] Hence, it's no surprise that the growing numbers of NetGeners now wending their way to college bring with them that same sense of ennui.[82] Not because post-K–12 is too hard or because the bar is too high, but chiefly because it is, like K–12, it is *so* non-real-world. School at any level may mean a lot of things to students but, to borrow one of their favorite idioms, *cool* it definitely is not. One can feel the students' indifference (if not alienation) in their voices, see it in their eyes, and read it in their body language.[83] Both phases of the module aim to counter students' disaffection by implementing a real-world learning paradigm that's joined at the hip with creative learning technology (LT).

But how might inventive LT contribute to players' interest, control, fulfillment, and satisfaction? Recall that virtually all NetGeners now use computers, most employ the Web, and many play challenging and absorbing video games. If asked why they do those things, NetGeners would hardly respond, "It's because I'm forced to." Most would say simply, "It's fun." Why fun? Our own experience and common sense tell us that it's relatively enjoyable and satisfying (fun) to use a computer. A number of observers concur that the fun of doing something with a computer (manipulating its physical, that is, hardware aspects) can't be disentangled from the satisfaction of engaging the task facilitated by its software.[84] Whether word processing, surfing the Net, paying bills, ordering clothes or books, listening to NPR archives or classical music, or even playing video games, the satisfaction stems from influencing, that is, controlling, both features—software and hardware—simultaneously.

Searching for Next-Generation Learning Technology

Consequently, one long-term objective of both phases of the module is to search continually for the ways in which increasingly imaginative LT might facilitate the difficult work of coaches, players, and interns within the context of discovery-based learning.[85] There are at least three (and perhaps more) realms in which the module would create a demand for and, it is hoped, generate a supply of innovative software and hardware. The first of these is the matter of searches for significant and valid resources that teams can use for their deliberations in preparing their mock-up papers (phases I and II/1), as well as during their hands-on experience (II/2). The notorious unreliability of many items posted to the Internet is beyond any doubt.[86] Moreover, it's quite true that few of today's students possess either the will or the skill to winnow the wheat from the chaff that now chokes the Net. It is, however, unfair and unseemly to blame the victims for those shortcomings. Nor is the teacher-scholar necessarily to blame, because she or he has neither the time nor the incentive to train passive receptacles in the time-consuming task of distinguishing the meaningful from the suspect.

Despite the fact that undergraduates are not, by and large, being coached to winnow the stuff on the Internet, new facts, figures, and ideas are being posted there fast and furiously, and by no means is all of it rubbish. For example, increasing numbers of peer-reviewed journals (and some scholarly books) are now being placed online and, increasingly, effective search engines are being designed for students and citizens alike to access those and other reliable sources.[87] Unlike that type of trustworthy information, however, the validity of much of the material on the Internet remains uncertain at best. Schank observed that in the absence of being coached to winnow, many students retain the faulty impression that if it appears on the Web, the it's just as believable as what their professors tell them—ultimate truth.[88]

Recall that Sizer held that the habit of thoughtfulness embraces a "skeptical approach to life,"[89] including, I would add, to the Internet. Hence, because the coach's job is to cultivate a healthy skepticism (not cynicism) in her/his players, software designed to facilitate the task of winnowing would be most welcome. There seems little doubt that, in future, the means of searching for and finding resources on the Net will multiply at a breathtaking rate.[90] Indeed, those means are likely to race far ahead of the capabilities of most students and citizens to sort through the mountains of stuff and pull out the kernels of wheat scattered throughout the chaff. Accordingly, software that enhances the capabilities of its players to discriminate between what is useful and what is not and, importantly, to justify their decision, would be a strong asset to the module.

Simulation is the second realm in which the module might seek out innovative software/hardware. Simulation was used above (I/1, II/1) as synonymous with "mock-up" or "hypothetical." Although the team was not obliged to create an actual computer simulation of the issue it was trying to resolve, the team's option for doing so may, in future, become increasingly viable. Computer simulations have for many decades proved invaluable to the sciences, engineering, and the military, among others. A vital distinction, however, from past decades is that today's laptop has the capacity to simulate what once took "rooms of supercomputers."[91] Furthermore, the technology (software and hardware) is moving so rapidly that it's now "enabling scholars to address previously unsolvable problems."[92] After documenting how the sciences are simulating helpful solutions to some of their formerly intractable problems, a few observers then take a huge and uncertain leap of faith into the murky realm of the social sciences. They speculate that, analogous to the sciences, rapidly evolving technology might enable "interdisciplinary research teams to . . . tackle complex societal problems."[93]

Needless to say, social problems are by any stretch of the imagination incredibly multifaceted and unbelievably intricate. Striding atop the list of hurdles is the matter of resistance on the part of persons and groups feeling threatened by strategies purporting to resolve the issue. In many respects, social issues are at least as complex as the problems for which solutions are now being simulated within the emerging field, say, of "proteomics, the calculation of how proteins fold into the distinctive shapes key to biological function."[94] Furthermore, in terms of their implications for human betterment, the resolution of many social issues is clearly no less vital than resolving the problems of proteomics.

For the present at least, the social sciences are obviously unable to operate at the same level of technological sophistication as the sciences in pursuit of computer simulations aimed at addressing urgent problems.[95] One item now available to the social sciences is, by comparison, exceedingly primitive. A. W. Bates and Gary Poole call it "expert systems." Those are simply "computer programs that imitate an expert's decision process."[96] Bates and Poole report that the range of currently available expert-system software is quite limited, and its capacity to tackle complex questions is restricted. They add, however that, if there were sufficient demand, there's no compelling reason why both its quantity and its sophistication could not be increased. As one example, within the related field of clinical psychology some experts have recently been devising simulations to treat serious and persisting phobias.[97]

Within the module, coaches, players, and interns (and, in II/2, citizens) work together to devise inventions to try to resolve social issues. And, when feasible, they would surely utilize available expert-system software to assist them in their difficult and challenging work. When, however, they exceed the capabilities of existing software, they might then search for additional software that could be designed to address their simulation needs. In short, just as software that enhances the players' capabilities to winnow wheat from chaff would be welcomed, so would any type of software that facilitates the players' capabilities to imagine and create innovative solutions to their problems, that is, new social inventions.

The third class of software that the module would covet lies within the realm now called "groupware."[98] Ideally, the same software ought to be able to facilitate all three objectives—searches and winnowing, mock-ups, and collaboration among team members. Collaboration among members of a learning community lies at the very core of the module. Its advocates aim to build on and expand the growing body of research affirming Astin's conclusion that the student's peer group is the "single most potent source of influence" on the undergraduate's intellectual development.[99] Collaboration is not, however, intended solely for the benefit of the team members qua individuals:

> I promote team projects [using groupware] to accomplish ambitious goals, and I add the requirement that the projects be done for someone *outside the class-room.*[100]

The module's avowed intention is, in point of fact, to get each team to, as Schneiderman puts it, "Relate-Create-Donate."[101] To help achieve that ambitious, three-stage objective, advocates seek software that would enhance collaborative performance during each of the team's three interrelated stages. The most primitive way to organize the workstation is, say, to have the teammates at a pod—each with a computer linked to her/his mates. Although each player works at one's own computer, all speak repeatedly with one another, sharing what they're doing and offering suggestions to their mates. Unfortunately, their computer linkage allows, in addition to their oral exchanges, little more than instant file-transmission.

Somewhat less primitive software would allow, for instance, the same file to appear on all five screens simultaneously. The software would also permit any player at any time to enter data into that file and have the fresh data appear instantly on all five screens. Any of the other players could then respond to that data in any manner, such as deleting, modifying, or elaborating it. The beauty of this approach is that it helps to overcome a huge barrier that currently impedes the production of a genuinely group-based document. Today, each player tends to think in terms of *my* part vis-à-vis *his or her* section. The several sections are, in short, constructed as being greater than the sum of the whole. This distinctive type of software would, by contrast, assist in constructing the sense that the whole of *our* paper is in truth far greater than any one part.

In view of the fact that researchers now working the field characterize most of today's software and hardware as extremely primitive, it's impossible to visualize the looming advances in both spheres. Even our current reliance on the desktop and laptop could give way to something quite different. Already, competing hardware such as smartphones and handhelds are causing the "industry to try to figure out what role [if any] . . . the PC play[s] in the digital home [office, school] of the future."[102] Once a module is actually in place (whose goal is to get teams to relate, create, and donate) it would add to a demand for increasingly imaginative and innovative software/hardware. Hence, pertinent advances in both areas are almost certain to come about.

In that same vein of as yet unforeseen innovation, MIT's Hiroshi Ishii has, for some years, been experimenting with the next generation of ways to design the actual interface between the user and the computer.[103] His long-range goal is to "liberate society from the tyranny of computer keyboards, monitors, and mice by creating new ways for humans to view and manipulate data."[104] Ishii claims that he and his colleagues are "inventing a new medium. . . . In certain areas, like teaching or design . . . our interface is superior."[105] Among other inadequacies, the current interface is now conceived of largely in terms of the individual qua individual. The module would, by contrast, need and want an interface constructed in collaborative terms—an interface stimulating a sense of *our group qua group.*

Technology, Efficiency, and the Quality of Learning

Schank and Cleary observed that, during the twentieth century, progressive schools "are notable for the quality of students they produce. They are also notable for how much they cost to run."[106] In their view, a principal reason why the progressive movement faltered was because it lacked the practical means to make its grand vision a reality. But such means, they say, are now becoming a reality in the shape of learning technology. Michael Williams, the Virginia Tech administrator who oversaw the Math Emporium reported, "We have a governor who tells us . . . that we're spending too much money, and state schools are getting a free ride."[107] That "instructional-productivity pressure," added Williams, was one major reason for establishing the emporium. And, in fact, it turned out that the cost per student in its 1,600-person linear algebra course dropped from "$77 to $24, a labor savings of $97,000 a year."[108]

A big question is, of course, would the module—including its use of imaginative learning technology—be able to achieve any substantial degree of cost savings? And, if so, how great would those savings be per student when compared with a set of today's typical social science departments? Would coaches, players, and interns doing DBL turn out to be a more or less expensive proposition than the current system, even if the module builds in LT? Achieving the outcomes of higher quality at lower cost would demand comparisons with the currently prevailing system.[109] Unfortunately, previous attempts to assess value-added within that system have so far been futile.[110] Chapter 5 reminded us that we have no idea whether today's students possess more lower-order stuff coming out than they had going in.

Furthermore, value-for-dollar connotes some sort of ratio between the inputs and the worth, that is, the excellence or superiority of the outputs received.[111] Although one pays many more dollars for a BMW than, say, a Chevrolet Aveo, there's no doubt as to which car provides greater value— much more excellence in every sense. And, as far as post-K–12 is concerned, public officials worry increasingly that they're furnishing BMW-level dollars for an Aveo-type product.[112] In short, aside from its utility as a ticket for entry into one's first job, the issue of the merit and worth of today's college degree is very much an unsettled question.[113]

Complicating the matter still further is the growing realization that the continuing inflation of the college degree is tending to undermine its worth, even as a ticket.[114] In such an inflationary situation, the issue of educational quality takes on enormous significance. Observers believe that growing numbers of academics, officials, and citizens are likely to become increasingly dubious regarding the relevance of TP to meet students' needs in the new century.[115] Hence, as that unnerving prospect gets increasingly salient, those observers suggest that post-K–12 might become persuaded gradually to test various forms of a learning paradigm. One upshot of that trend, they reason, is that increasingly sophisticated software/hardware is likely to be developed in order to increase the productivity of entities governed by a learning paradigm, for example, the module described here.

In short, its advocates would suggest to officials that comparisons and contrasts with the current system are likely to reveal that the module would be far more successful on both dimensions—value-added as well as value-for-dollar. Furthermore, advocates would venture to add that the module could even turn out to be more cost-efficient. One reason for its potential efficiency is because learning technology is intrinsic to its operation. A second reason is what Florence Olsen, in her description of the Math Emporium, called "labor savings"—a matter to which I return in chapter 7.[116]

HOW HIGH SHOULD WE SET THE BAR?

Asking players to immerse themselves in DBL, and to do so via imaginative LT, is, say some critics, too difficult, out of reach, and economically unrealistic. It is, in their view, desirable yet dispensable. They protest that we can't expect undergraduates to scale such a bar—it's simply too high. Nor, they add, is it a very efficient proposition for the conventional research university. Most of those schools rely on "subsidies from low-cost, high profit-margin instruction . . . (e.g., large lecture courses) . . . to support graduate education and research."[117] Their need for those kinds of subsidies leads them to supply "mass higher education [that] centers on the transmission of knowledge."[118]

Although it was eminently aware of that grim reality, the 1998 Boyer Commission nonetheless audaciously charged every research university to "make research-based learning the standard." If DBL is in fact the benchmark, it should then evolve into becoming the common experience of almost every student. Three years after their report, the commission surveyed 123 research universities to ascertain the extent to which, if at all, its earlier recommendations were being followed.[119] The major change the commission detected was that by 2001 a number of the schools were indeed offering a greater number of optional research opportunities to specially selected undergraduates than they had in 1998.[120] Notwithstanding, even for those few students and faculty, as well as for the remaining masses of undergraduates and professors, college life in general had stayed pretty much business-as-usual. Discovery-based learning was hardly standard operating procedure.[121]

Reminiscent of Larry Cuban's conclusion that they are masters of the art of conjuring up cosmetic reform quite aside from genuine change, the universities' predominant reaction to the 1998 Boyer Report was to make much ado of the fact that they've finally agreed to encourage undergraduate research— but simply as a discretionary and distinctly peripheral activity. To be sure, it's no mystery why most schools ignored the Boyer Commission's directive to renovate their undergraduate experience away from the transmission of stuff and toward an experience that is in fact discovery based. The crescendo of the chorus pleading for money and time to enhance the reputation of both the school and its teacher-scholars more than drowns out the voices of advocates arguing that twenty-first-century students deserve and require a level of learning quality that they are not, by and large, receiving.

NOTES

1. Whyte 1982:1, italics in original.
2. Cited by Bulmer 1984:273–74.
3. Gouldner and Miller 1965:vii.
4. Carnegie Commission 1998.
5. Cohen 1998.
6. Other modules could, of course, elect to follow a different strategy on this and all other matters raised throughout these chapters.
7. Bollag 2004:A36.
8. Cameron 1978:67ff. See also Charles Anderson 1993:121ff and Gregorian 2004.
9. Duderstadt et al. 2002:97.
10. Duderstadt et al. 2002:97.
11. Duderstadt et al. 2002:96.
12. Bishop 2003. The quote is an excerpt from his book appearing in "Melange." *Chronicle of Higher Education*, August 8, 2003, B6.
13. Recall, however, that chapter 5 reported that the sciences are way ahead on issues of spatial designs to facilitate learning.
14. Bishop 2003.
15. Knoll 2003. The quote is an excerpt from his book appearing in "Melange." *Chronicle of Higher Education*, August 8, 2003, B6. See Handelsman et al. 2004 and also Schank 2000 for the same argument.

16. Haack, 2003. The quote is an excerpt from her book appearing in "Melange." *Chronicle of Higher Education*, October 17, 2003, B6.

17. See Brown 2003. His discussion of these and related issues may be found from excerpts of his book appearing in "Melange." *Chronicle of Higher Education*, October 17, 2003, B6.

18. Balch 2004.

19. Rossi 1969.

20. Wineburg 2003:B20. See Rabb 2004 for the same set of arguments.

21. Wineburg 2003:B20.

22. Showalter 2002.

23. Showalter 2003.

24. Wineburg 2003.

25. Newman et al. 2004.

26. Bartlett 2003a.

27. Bain 2004a, b.

28. Gottlieb 1969; O'Connor 2001.

29. Marinelli and Pausch 2004.

30. Whyte 1982.

31. Whyte 1982.

32. Lagemann 2000:50.

33. Whyte 1991a; Greenwood and Levin 1998; Reason and Bradbury 2001; Stringer 1999; Schon 1983; Levin and Greenwood 2001; Brulin 2001; Mora and Diaz 2004.

34. Vanecko 1969:610, italics added.

35. Giddens 1994; Coleman 1990.

36. Whyte 1982; Flyvbjerg 2001.

37. Postel 2002; and see Greenwood and Levin 1998:72–75.

38. Gouldner 1965; Flyvbjerg 2001; Greenwood and Levin 1998.

39. See Hays (2003) for a comparable participant observation strategy.

40. Greenwood and Levin 1998:4.

41. Greenwood and Levin 1998:53ff.

42. Whyte 1991b:97.

43. Hasell and Scanzoni 2000.

44. Fromm 1991.

45. Stack 1974; Jewell 1988; Rivers and Scanzoni 1997.

46. Coleman 1990.

47. Scanzoni 2004.

48. And see Newman et al. 2004.

49. Schank and Cleary 1995:65–67.

50. Schank and Cleary 1995:66; O'Banion 1997 passim; Nicholson 1971.

51. The quote is from Gee 2003a; and see Sizer 1992, 1996.

52. Sizer 1992:25; see Rabb 2004.

53. Sizer 1992:69; cf. Wineburg 2003.

54. Greenwood and Levin 1998.

55. Greenwood and Levin 1998:4.

56. Hebel 2003b.

57. Kahlenberg 2004.

58. Huget 2002.

59. Giddens, as cited by Robert S. Boynton, "The Two Tonys: Why Is the Prime Minister So Interested in What Anthony Giddens Thinks?" *New Yorker.* October 6, 1997, 67. See also Giddens 1994.

60. DeMatteo, Eby, and Sundstrom 1998; Bess and Associates 2000.

61. Greenwood and Levin 1998:53.

62. Greenwood and Levin 1998:54ff.

63. Schank and Cleary 1995:128.

64. Powell and Owen-Smith 2002.

65. Cuban 2001:193.

66. Lanham 2002.

67. Càrdenas 2000; Duderstadt 2000; Duderstadt et al. 2002; Brown and Duguid 2000; Schank 2000.

68. O'Banion 1997:69.

69. O'Banion 1997:69. Cuban (2001) makes the same point.

70. Newman and Scurry 2001:B7.

71. Zemsky and Massy 2004a:B7.

72. Zemsky and Massy 2004a:B7.

73. Associated Press 2003a.

74. A label coined, as far as I can tell, by Diane Oblinger, PhD, executive director of higher education, Microsoft Corp.

75. Cole 2004.

76. Duderstadt et al. 2002:62. The same point is made by Turkle 2004.

77. Gee 2003a, b.

78. Gee 2003a.

79. Gee 2003a.

80. See Carlson 2003c, 2003d.

81. Gee 2003a.

82. Cabin 2003; Rojstaczer 1999; Geller, as cited in Schank and Cleary 1995:74–75.

83. Perlmutter 2004a.

84. E.g., Gee 2003a, b; O'Banion 1997; Newman and Scurry 2001; Schank 2000; Schank and Cleary 1995.

85. Lanham 2002.

86. Brown and Duguid 2000.

87. Carlson 2003b; University of California 2003; Young 2004.

88. Schank 2000.

89. Sizer 1992:69.

90. Brown and Duguid 2000.

91. Duderstadt et al. 2002:69.

92. Duderstadt et al. 2002:69.

93. Duderstadt et al. 2002:71.

94. Duderstadt et al. 2002:28.

95. Carnevale 2003.

96. Bates and Poole 2003:63.

97. Monaghan 2004.

98. Hazemi et al. 1998:179ff; Hazemi and Hailes 2002.

99. Astin 1993:398, 402; Duderstadt et al. 2002:59; and see chapter 5 in this book, especially De Corte 1996.

100. Shneiderman 1998:xxii, italics added.
101. Shneiderman 1998:xxii.
102. Tim Bajarin, an analyst at the market research firm Creative Strategies, cited in Reuters 2003.
103. Ishii 1994.
104. Arner 2003:86.
105. Arner 2003:86.
106. Schank and Cleary 1995:66.
107. Olsen 1999:A31.
108. Olsen 1999:A31.
109. Lanham 2002; Newman et al. 2004.
110. Miller 2002.
111. Marchese 1995.
112. Olsen 1999:A31; Dziech 2002.
113. Boyer Commission 1998; Lawrence 1995; Astin 1993.
114. Collins 2002.
115. Newman et al. 2004.
116. Olsen 1999:A31.
117. Duderstadt et al. 2002:144.
118. Martin Trow as cited by Duderstadt et al. 2002:138.
119. Boyer Commission 2002.
120. Wilson 2002.
121. Kuh 2001.

Chapter Seven

A New Social Contract within a New American College— *From the Ivory Tower to the Commons*

Higher Education is in need of visions. We urge educators . . . to commit to a cherished value or a compelling vision and then to articulate a purpose that challenges the commitment of others. The callings, causes, and cries that make up the innermost commitments of people can become educational missions that chart new paths for higher education.[1]

PROBLEMS PAST, PRESENT, AND FUTURE

The behemoth called "higher education" has always been and continues to be moving—most often, however, about as fast as a glacier. Nonetheless, on rare occasions, post-K–12 creeps along at a somewhat more noticeable pace. And, that tends to occur when larger forces "out there" make it happen—forces, for instance, such as the "Renaissance, the Age of Discovery, and [especially] the Industrial Revolution."[2] Similarly, as we make our way into the twenty-first century, we find that a number of contemporary forces out there are indeed hard at work inducing certain noticeable shifts within post-K–12. One of those newer influences could turn out to be just as far-reaching as the cited historical forces above. This newer force is known variously as the postindustrial era or the information age. It has also been called the "third wave," that is, the successor to the "second wave" (the industrial era), which, in its turn, was the successor to the "first wave" of human history, the agricultural era.

The industrial revolution was, among many other things, a fundamental transformation in science and technology. That transformation wrought, over the course of many decades, a historic realignment within post-K–12 by requiring that the humanities give up their historic status as its sole regent. Although for a while simply coregent with the humanities, the sciences et al.

eventually replaced the humanities at the top of the university pecking order. The sciences achieved their remarkable coup because, among other things, they were the first segment of the university to form a strong and enduring financial partnership with government.

Mid-nineteenth-century national leaders wanted the United States to step up to what they saw as its rightful place alongside the great powers of Europe and to become a major player in the emerging industrial world order. Consequently, the 1862 Congress passed the Morrill Land Grant Act designed to help transform the United States from an agricultural into an industrial nation. That act handed over federal lands to the states that they could then sell for dollars to create new public colleges and universities. Those new schools would in turn provide educational opportunities for citizens (mostly white males) in the sciences, medicine, agriculture, engineering, mining, architecture, and so forth. The graduates of those institutions were, in their turn, expected to spearhead U.S. efforts to become a first-class industrial nation. In effect, a social contract was established between society and the sciences et al. Public officials agreed to provide money as well as intangible resources to professors in the sciences and to the universities in which they were located. And for their part of the bargain, the universities agreed to serve society through research, teaching, and public service.[3]

The importance of government largesse was not lost on the humanities and the social sciences and, toward the close of the nineteenth century they too began to portray themselves as worthy recipients of the public purse. Professors in those fields, like those in the sciences, went on to hone the twentieth-century role of teacher-scholar. Advocates for that role asserted that professors' research and scholarship informed their teaching. Professors working on the cutting edge of new discoveries in their field were believed to be the persons best suited to pass on their freshly minted knowledge to undergraduates. They were, at the same time, thought to be the persons most able to infect graduate students with the excitement of searching for and discovering new knowledge.

The imagery of a mutually beneficial partnership between professors and society became more firmly established than ever by a 1945 report, *Science: The Endless Frontier.*[4] The report, developed by a commission of academics and political leaders, declared that the nation's post–World War II prosperity and security rested on government support for research in the sciences. Furthermore, the report went on to state that "government had to preserve freedom of inquiry" and to "recognize that scientific progress results from the free play of intellects, working on subjects of their own choice, in the manner dictated by their curiosity for explanation of the unknown."[5] Those latter arguments were seen as, among other things, an acknowledgment of the importance of the social sciences, humanities, and other fields, alongside the sciences. "Progress," implied the 1945 report, comes not just from the sciences, but also from the research and scholarship of the social sciences and humanities, as well as from the several remaining spheres of higher learning.

That much heralded social contract became the basis for the golden age (1945–1975) of America's colleges and universities. The updated contract fueled the expansion and development of post-K–12 in a manner never before dreamed of. For their part, professors were left largely unattended to shape their teaching and their research in ways they alone deemed to be valuable for the public interest. Their remarkable autonomy was, however, accompanied by the tacit understanding that "even curiosity-driven research is expected to benefit society over the long term."[6]

So what happened to that munificent social contract? Why did the National Center for Public Policy and Higher Education feel compelled to issue an urgent January 2004 bulletin declaring that during recent decades state funding for post-K–12 has fallen off so precipitously that there now exists a "crisis in college opportunity?"[7] The center reiterated what many observers had been saying for some time, namely, that tuition costs have risen so far so fast that growing numbers of qualified students are either shut out of the college market altogether or are saddled with an overwhelming burden of debt to pay for it. As a result, governors and legislators have been thrust, according to the center, onto the "front line." Public officials should, says the center, take the initiative in addressing immediately the "emergency" or "short-term" needs of post-K–12, as well as the needs of the financially strapped undergraduates they're supposed to serve. To meet the crisis, public officials must come up at once, said the center, with the money necessary to "prevent further erosion of college opportunity." Once that emergency situation is alleviated, public officials and academics could then start talking, states the center, about the "long-term" issues in post-K–12. The two sides would sit down together to "begin a process to achieve major productivity increases in higher education—that is, maintain or decrease the costs of delivering high-quality education."[8]

The center is, in short, urging public officials to temporarily set aside their strongly held views that academics have not lived up to the terms of the existing bargain. Public officials must take the initiative, believes the center, for at least two reasons. First, it would once again make college affordable to the vast numbers of students (current and future) that are in danger of being denied access to its credential. Second, implies the center, such a good-faith effort by officials would ensure that academics would take the hint and finally do what officials have been after them to do for many decades, namely, respond by getting serious about accountability. Specifically, officials want academics to demonstrate that they are in fact good stewards of the public purse.

Officials would like academics to explain and defend what they actually *do* for students and the larger society, that is, aside from supplying credentials. In effect, how does their curiosity-driven work benefit society over the long term?

During the early years of the golden age, public officials adopted a laissez-faire, that is, hands-off, approach to how faculty interpreted their side of the social contract. Most officials and citizens believed that professors had a unique and lofty mission they fulfilled admirably. Gradually, however, faculty lost the high moral ground they once so proudly occupied. Legislators came, instead, to perceive academics as simply one more special interest group whose primary concern was to feather its own nest—and not to serve the public interest. A prime reason why legislators came to believe that professors pursued their own interests—at the expense of the interests of students and citizens—was faculty preoccupation with professional reputation via research and scholarship. Rightly or wrongly, officials came to the conclusion that professors were obsessed with what James Fairweather called the "mimicry of the elite," that is, personages of high status and prestige within each discipline.[9] Unable to get faculty to pay more serious attention to the interests of students and society, officials simply lost their historic concern with going to any special lengths to sponsor post-K–12. The upshot is that post-K–12 has squandered its most prized possession, that is, the respect and esteem it once held.[10]

ROLE SPECIALIZATION SLIPS IN THE BACK DOOR

That slow but steady withering away of the old social contract has not impacted all segments of post-K–12 equally. For well over a century, the sciences have been able to garner huge sums of research dollars from external sources including not just government and foundations but, increasingly, the private sector. Indeed, their successes at gaining external research dollars, coupled with the sharp declines in legislative funding, have resulted in the gradual emergence of what's been called the entrepreneurial university and, correspondingly, to the emergence of the role of entrepreneur/PI.[11] That label describes the professor capable of procuring so many external research dollars that he or she is a state employee in name only. In the sciences, the entrepreneur is expected to fund not only her or his own salary but also those of grad students and postdocs who work in his or her shop. And, in addition to paying for the shop's ongoing expenses, the entrepreneur is also expected to contribute dollars to the general overhead of the department, center, or college of which he or she is a part.[12] Plainly, the entrepreneur/PI is much closer to the notion of an independent contractor or freelance consultant than to the idea of a state employee, that is, a hired hand.

Furthermore, just as the entrepreneur is a state employee in name only, the university able to accumulate (quite apart from state dollars) huge sums of money to fund its activities is a state university in name only. For example, because of its successes in obtaining nonstate dollars, the University of Michigan was able to "restructure [its] finances so that [it] became, in effect, a privately supported public university."[13] Or, as the president of another similarly successful university succinctly put it, during his tenure "his university had changed from state-supported to state-assisted to state-located."[14]

At first glance, one might assume that public officials would be deeply distressed over the emergence of such circumstances. This state of affairs enables certain professors to pay so much attention to the enhancement of their own reputation that, if they possess star quality and marketability on the national and international scene, they may elect (at their own discretion) to avoid undergraduates altogether. Any distress is, however, eased partly by the officials' awareness that they're powerless to halt that seemingly inexorable trend. And, they're still more keenly tuned in to the fact that the more dollars the entrepreneur brings in, the less the legislature is obliged to kick in. If, for example, the star generates enough money to hire a proxy (graduate student, adjunct) to teach undergraduates, then officials feel less compelled to come up with those dollars.

By no means, however, does such a feeling imply that officials are unsympathetic to the kinds of issues raised by the public policy center—particularly the heavy burden that spiraling tuition costs impose on students and their families. One way that most legislatures exercise some degree of restraint on tuition increases is to refuse to allow the one thing that post-K–12 wants as much as anything else—unrestricted authority to set tuition and fees. Furthermore, officials are knowledgeable enough to know that the great majority of their professors are not marketplace stars. Compared to the sciences, there are many fewer entrepreneurs in the social sciences, and fewer still in the humanities. Rather than being an entrepreneur or independent contractor, most professors remain, in fact, state employees, that is, teacher-scholars. Also known as the superprofessor, he or she is said to be able to do it all (teaching, research, service)—and to do it very well, indeed. The superprofessor is analogous to the old-time doctor who, routinely making house calls with black leather bag in hand, was thought supremely qualified to cure any and all ills afflicting his or her patients. Indeed, it was not uncommon for that generalist MD to do surgery alongside everything else that he or she did.

As legislators see it, the commonsense way to provide degrees for the growing numbers of students clamoring to get into post-K–12, apart from driving up costs, is to have their employees teach more students.[15] Accordingly, if the policy center bemoans the lost opportunities suffered by the thousand students a school was forced to turn away because all its sections were overenrolled, why not, asks the legislator, have five superprofessors teach an additional section of two hundred persons each for the same salary they now receive? Wouldn't that, asks the official, make their employees more efficient and the school more productive? If an employee responds, however, that the additional workload is an unreasonable demand, growing numbers of officials are pointing to information technology as one strategy for increasing the superprofessor's efficiency and the university's productivity. The rub is, of course, that mining the full potential of technology is a task that in and of itself demands extraordinary amounts of time and creative energy. The teacher-scholar does not, unfortunately, have much time and energy left over after carrying out the demanding efforts necessary to mimic the elite of his/her discipline. New York University president John Sexton was no doubt well aware of the teacher-scholar's quandary when he proposed that his school "create or make new [nontenured] categories of faculty members. These include 'teaching professors' who are not judged by their research, *'cyberfaculty'* members who specialize in the use of the Internet."[16]

Just as the entrepreneur is a specialist who concentrates on a particular set of activities, the credentialer is just as much a specialist, though he or she focuses on quite a different set of activities. Furthermore, the description of a specialist as someone with distinctive and highly valued skills holds particular ramifications for the role of cybercredentialer or CC. Both the entrepreneur/PI and the CC have evolved out of and beyond the generalist known as the teacher-scholar. While it was quite feasible for the twentieth-century superprofessor to do everything reasonably well, that's no longer the case—any more than today's MD can do it all. Although there's a lot of fond sentiment attached to the old-time doctor, that is, the generalist, most citizens today much prefer the option of consulting a medical specialist whenever the need arises. That is not to minimize the anxiety that many teacher-scholars genuinely feel over the long-term prospects of being pressured (albeit gently) into either of these two new and unfamiliar roles. Their anxiety stems not only, and perhaps not even primarily, from concern for their own interests. Many are also persuaded that the evolution of the entrepreneurial university, alongside the corresponding development of the roles of entrepreneur and the CC, are not in the best interests either of students or of society.

Despite how teacher-scholars might feel about it, growing numbers of officials and administrators believe that if their employees cannot pay their own way in the style of an entrepreneur, then they're obliged to earn more of their keep by teaching many more students than is now typically the case. Randall Collins describes this long-term trend as the slow but steady emergence of a "teaching proletariat."[17] Faculty who are pushed into those proletarian circumstances will find it increasingly tough to play the twentieth-century role of superprofessor. Because public officials are unconvinced that such a role is worth the cost, they're becoming more and more reluctant to bear and sustain it. Instead, growing numbers of faculty unable and/or unwilling to become independent contractors will slowly be constrained to play the emerging role of credentialer. The credentialer is the state employee whose prime task is to provide degrees to the ever-increasing numbers of students seeking that credential. One proposed carrot that might induce professors to cooperate in becoming energetic credentialers is that their pay would be tied to the numbers of students they're able to graduate, that is, to credential.[18]

It turns out that complaints over the dearth of faculty accountability have badgered professors for a long time. Throughout much of the twentieth century, students, officials, and citizens repeatedly questioned them over their preoccupation with professional reputation. In response, faculty became exceedingly adept at conjuring up the illusion, but seldom the reality, of reform.[19] Professors established (though not with malicious intent) a "tradition of reform complete with symbols" such as student evaluation of faculty, peer-review of teaching, teacher-of-the-year bonuses, posttenure evaluations, teaching centers, and so forth.[20] But after the smoke cleared and all was said and done, superprofessors were able to "preserve their prerogatives, and maintain continuity in practice."[21]

And today? By way of example, in 2004 the State of Florida Board of Governors (BOG) imposed an "Academic Learning Compact" (ALC) on all the state's universities and colleges.[22] Each department was obliged to demonstrate student learning "above and beyond course grades." Alongside content, each unit must show how its students exhibit "communication skills" and "critical thinking skills." In a meeting I attended where the issue of how to respond to BOG/ALC was discussed, the administrator left no doubt that this is one more in a long series of burdensome chores forced on professors by public officials—chores that get in the way of faculty doing what they're "supposed" to be doing. Although the university wishes it would "go away," he said, we've no choice but to come up with "something we can live with, not something good." Translated, faculty must devise a schema that gives the appearance of conformity to the new ruling but in fact permits business as usual. In short, the highly effective twentieth-century strategy of taming reform by tweaking it to serve our own purposes seems to be alive and well in the new century. Throughout the last century, officials and citizens preferred to give academics the benefit of the doubt. Officials were quite willing to wait and see whether the academics' latest round of modifications would result in genuine changes or if, as occurred so often before, the facelift was no more than skin deep.

Contemporary officials seem, however, less tolerant of, and more impatient with, faculty insistence on their unique prerogatives. Added to that reality are the escalating demands on the public purse from worthy competitors to higher education: K–12, Medicare, Medicaid, prisons, courts, police, security, transportation, health and well-being of children/youth/families, and so forth. Alongside that competition is the stiffening resistance of citizens to pay higher taxes. Competing demands and limited tax revenues have joined to deliver a powerful rationale for trimming post-K–12 budgets to the bare bones. Hence, as far as anyone can tell, the upshot is that it's highly unlikely that many officials would respond favorably to the center's twin proposals (above), as meritorious as they might be. Officials are not, in the foreseeable future, expected to act by pumping huge numbers of dollars into higher education. For all intents and purposes, they've given up trying to get superprofessors to develop demonstrably authentic reforms, because time and again the hoped-for changes proved little more than cosmetic.

WHAT'S TO BE DONE?

We believe that the state of undergraduate education at research [and wannabe] universities is [in] . . . a crisis, an issue of such magnitude and volatility that universities must galvanize themselves to respond.[23]

If there actually is a crisis, the way out starts by asking ourselves what information age students require more than anything else.

Universities cannot call themselves successful unless they provide students with the fundamental skills that they require in the twenty-first century.[24]

Many observers both inside and outside the academy are convinced that the trials and tribulations facing post-K–12 in the new century demand twenty-first-century solutions. Today's complex circumstances are not amenable to warmed-over twentieth-century palliatives. So what to do? How can we begin to demonstrate that students are cultivating the kinds of capabilities that, in the new century, are fundamental to individual success as well as the public good? A good place to start is to consider the significance of a trend already in place—role diversity, or specialization, among professors. The inescapable reality is that growing numbers of professors are virtually certain to be attracted to the role of entrepreneur, especially in the sciences, and for obvious reasons. The potential rewards of such a role—both tangible and intangible—appear almost limitless. And, as far as other indicators of their successes are concerned, they can (in addition to attracting external moneys) point to the contributions they make to their field and/or to human betterment and also to the training in the fundamental skills of their field they provide to grad students.[25]

During the twentieth century, a younger person interested in serving as a college professor had but one predominant way of life to emulate. Today, that life pattern is in process of devolution, while two other models are in various stages of evolution. Furthermore, it's quite plausible that more and more younger persons interested in being professors may become increasingly attracted to the still amorphous role of *cyber*credentialer. Younger persons are, after all, NetGeners maturing in the presence of an ever-evolving computer technology, which is an integral element of their life. Accordingly, as Net-Geners come of age, they'll be in a position to comprehend both its possibilities and its limitations in a far more profound sense than persons coming to computer technology later in life. For most of us that are essentially outsiders, it's no more than a second language. In stark contrast, NetGeners are authentic insiders. Moreover, because they've grown up within the bosom of what many of us view as an alien culture, they could conceivably become quite adept at shaping what is now the rather murky role of cybercredentialer.

And, on the other side of the great divide between academics and officials, and perhaps helping to bridge it, is the fact that the ranks of public officials will include ever-increasing numbers of persons who likewise grew up as NetGeners. Hence, they might be amenable, in the interests of efficiency and productivity, to support innovative experiments with the CC role. They might be willing to provide, perhaps on a trial basis, the resources (salary, technical support, facilities) necessary for the CC to be successful, at least in the terms prescribed by the center, as well as by many politicians and some academics. Specifically, would the CC, using ever more sophisticated technology, be able to attract and to graduate the growing numbers of qualified undergrads—working-class, minority, and middle-class persons—that want and need the credential? If the answer is yes, then it's quite likely that the CC specialty shall evolve gradually but become increasingly common, at least in the near and intermediate future. At the same time, Collins sees a downside to growing numbers of persons getting credentialed. He worries about the inflation of the college degree, and thus its reduced value, if it becomes as commonplace as is the high school diploma today.[26]

ROBUST CREDENTIALS

J. S. Brown and P. Duguid take that disturbing matter to the next level by arguing that, in the new century, students shall require something more than the degree itself—they will need and demand *"robust* credentials."[27] During the last century, the credential was both necessary *and* sufficient for its holder to make it in the marketplace. But Brown and Duguid warn that, in the new century, although the credential will remain necessary, it is likely to be deemed *in*sufficient if it does not also carry with it some assurance of being robust, that is, high quality. That is so whether it is gotten in a cyber or in a more conventional setting. Collins observed that, so far at least, schools with higher national prestige rankings are perceived as offering a more robust degree. But, on a contrary note, the Boyer Commission, along with other critics, reminded us that schools accrue prestige not on the basis of what happens to their undergraduates' intellectual development, but principally because their professors distinguish themselves in the realms of research and scholarship. The grade of incomplete hangs over twentieth-century efforts to determine how much students actually "learn" during college and also over the question of whether learning does in fact vary by the school's research-based prestige.[28]

The issue of learning itself gets exceedingly complicated when we consider the fact that there at least two types of learning—lower- and higher-order learning. Stocking the student's mind with knowledge (lower-order learning) has been the mantra of higher education ever since Charlemagne.[29] And today, what's called the teaching paradigm still aims to pack the student's mind with stuff—facts, figures, dates, events, persons, and ideas. As long as lower-order learning remains the mark of an educated person and of a robust degree, the CC can perform at least as well as the superprofessor. Indeed, the CC could make a case to officials that he or she could perhaps do it better on two counts. First, the CC could conceivably provide degrees to more students at a lower cost per student than does the superprofessor. Second, the CC could argue that he or he is ready and able to remove the incomplete that presently hangs over higher education. The CC would pledge to officials to invest the time and energy necessary to find out how much or how little stuff students actually accumulated by the time of graduation. One essential step toward simplifying the task of the CC would be to cut back on the seemingly endless hodgepodge of courses from which students may now choose. Barry Schwartz compared those haphazard odds and ends of courses to the maze and disorientation of a "shopping mall."[30] Such a muddled potpourri serves the interests of the superprofessor quite well but makes it impossible to figure out what stuff is more important than other stuff for students to retain over the long term.

But, more to the point, should knowing lots of important stuff be in fact the most significant mark of an educated person in the information age? Or was that more properly a mark of the now fading industrial age? Can a college or university in truth call itself successful if that's the full extent of what it does? In order to truly call itself "successful" in the information age, should it not also be able to demonstrate that its students possess higher-order learning, that is, human capital skills or capabilities? In the new era, "not 'things,' but 'what we think about things'" becomes the ultimate issue.[31] How robust is its credential if a school fails to provide assurances that its holder is adept at cultivating those sorts of human capital capabilities? And that is, of course, the critical question that advocates for higher-order learning have posed ever since the days of John Dewey. For Dewey, an educated person must demonstrate an ability to solve problems via rigorous thinking characterized by thorough analysis, defensible evaluation, and a coherent and compelling synthesis.

At the same time, Dewey held that social science must attend to the massive social problems that plagued modern, urban society at the turn of the twentieth century. It was the task, he said, of educated persons to try to come up with ways to resolve those problems. Resolving those problems requires, first of all, thinking about them and, second, actually doing something about them, that is, putting one's ideas into action. And, it is from those actions (especially when they fail to solve anything) that one learns and incorporates that new information into one's thinking. That enhanced thinking becomes, in turn, the basis for additional actions, and so forth.

Admittedly, that scenario greatly oversimplifies the kind of pragmatic philosophy that Dewey spent the first half of the twentieth century writing about.[32] But it at least provides some initial sense of what he had in mind by his renowned phrase that almost everyone today is fond of reciting: "*We learn by thinking about what we're doing.*" No one disputes the profound wisdom of that commonplace aphorism. Not only is reflective thinking, followed by performing some activity, followed by carefully pondering the results of that activity the essence of the scientific method, it's also the strategy used by most human beings to manage a good deal of their everyday lives.[33] That is precisely and simply what Dewey meant when he asserted that "everyone is a scientist" and thus a "researcher" in the broadest sense of those terms.

Recently, that mode of learning has been labeled discovery-based learning (DBL). Because the researcher wants to know something, she or he takes certain actions designed to find out, or discover, what he or she wants to know. DBL has, obviously enough, been integral to human society ever since it began. It lies, furthermore, at the core of the model of the research university that came into being in Germany during the nineteenth century and was later imported to the United States. Subsequently, a learning paradigm shaped by DBL became the fundamental precept of *graduate* education.

Contrariwise, "Learning by Telling and Testing" (LTT), that is, lower-order learning, was the basis of *undergraduate* education long before the appearance of the research university. LTT was the mode of education holding sway within the ivory tower—the non-real world of post-K–12 cut off from everyday life. Moreover, its predominance continues to the present day:

> The experience of most undergraduates at most research [and wannabe] universities is that of receiving what is served out to them. In one course after another they listen, transcribe, absorb, and repeat, essentially as undergraduates have done for centuries. . . . The traditional lecturing and note-taking, certified by periodic examinations, was created for a time when books were scarce and costly. . . . The delivery system persisted into the present because it was familiar, easy, and required no imagination.[34]

Not only is the inert LTT thought to be cost-efficient, it's also believed to be *sufficient* for undergraduates. "It's good enough for them," a colleague remarked to me recently. A credential based principally on LTT is still today, for the most part, perceived as robust. But, on the other side, growing numbers of critics protest that it is not robust enough for the information age.[35] To assert that the information age is principally an era of *knowledge production* implies that in order to do well in both the marketplace and in civic society, the citizen must be an active producer or maker of knowledge (i.e., problem solver) in the Dewey sense.[36] Consequently, in order to call itself successful, the information age college or university is obliged to cultivate knowledge producers. Being able to demonstrate that students are problem solvers indicates that they have gotten reasonably comfortable with discovery-based learning. Only then may the school claim, without fear of contradiction, that its degree is indeed robust.

FORGING A NEW SOCIAL CONTRACT—*A LEARN GRANT ACT*

> Most colleges are not organized to help their students develop these kinds of [human capital] competencies. Indeed, no higher education system anywhere in the world is set up to do so.[37]

Recall that the National Center for Public Policy and Higher Education called for public officials to take their places in the front lines of managing the crisis in post-K–12. But Clara M. Lovett, president emerita of Northern Arizona University, took a rather different tack. Rather than anxiously waiting around in fond hopes that officials might one day take the lead in managing the crisis, she believes that academics should instead seize the initiative and start reaching out to officials. To overcome the prevailing adversarial and antagonistic relationship—the great divide—between the two sides, academics must take the first step, that is, make the initial move. Because Lovett deplored the "we-they mindset" and the "clash of cultures" isolating and insulating academics from officials, she contended that academics should

> Approach our elected representatives as potential partners in a common enterprise. . . . If the partnership is to work, we must all become advocates for a larger public good.[38]

If we professors are to recapture the high moral ground we once so proudly occupied, we must convince officials and citizens that our chief interest lies in serving the public good. We must persuade them that some professors are indeed willing to experiment with another type of role besides the entrepreneur/PI or the cybercredentialer—as full of intriguing possibilities as the latter may yet turn out to be. Earlier chapters described this pioneering role as the coach, or facilitator, of discovery-based learning. Cultivating DBL is the fundamental rationale for, and overarching objective of, the coach. To help achieve the ambitious objective of bringing a new academic role into being, some observers suggest that academics take the initiative by proposing to officials a *Learn* Grant Act for the twenty-first century.[39]

As its title implies, a Learn Grant Act would follow in the hallowed tradition established by both the nineteenth-century Land Grant Act and its mid-twentieth-century update. Those earlier agreements presumed that the professor's service for society would flow artlessly out of her/his research and scholarship. New discoveries might, for example, benefit human health, and at the same time any fresh knowledge would be passed on to students. A Learn Grant Act is strikingly different from those prior accords because it would significantly enlarge both the breadth and depth of professors' obligations to students.

The natural resources that the Land Grant Act meant to develop lay chiefly in the physical and biological world—energy, minerals, petroleum, soils, water, human health, and so forth. But today "we have come to realize that our most important natural resource for the future will be our people."[40] Consequently, "the national interest calls for an investment in human and intellectual capital."[41] In effect, continuing to stock the student's mind with stuff will no longer suffice to develop fully our most vital resource—citizens. Any credential—no matter how prestigious its source—based on that type of twentieth-century experience is liable to be called into question. Does the credential demonstrate convincingly that its robustness is framed in twenty-first-century terms? Consequently, under the provisions of a new social contract, some (but by no means all) social scientists, in league with some professors from other broad fields of inquiry, would commit themselves to address the issue of robustness by targeting students' human capital. And, for its part of the bargain, government (federal and state) could draw on the historic land grant concept as the rationale to support an innovative learn grant model for the new century. Such a model would be justified as a *"public good that merits support through public tax dollars."*[42]

Under the terms of some version of a learn grant, a cooperating university or college could voluntarily elect to establish a laboratory or module in which the twentieth-century concept of a student majoring in a relatively narrow field would give way to the twenty-first-century notion of the player becoming a part of the historic mission that once bound together the several social sciences.[43] Among professors electing to participate, the module would be a means to capture and experiment with some form of the New American College.[44] Boyer envisioned that such a pioneering school would, among other things, engage both students and professors in the struggle to try to resolve urgent social problems. Within the umbrella of this social science module, "creative students and faculty could join with colleagues [and citizens] from beyond the campus to develop and test new paradigms."[45] The laboratory would aim to be "student-centered," and thus a viable alternative to the typical "faculty-centered" university of today.[46]

Accordingly, the coaches would, alongside players and interested citizens, commit themselves, first, to cultivating students' human capital proficiencies and, second, to investigating and grappling with real life social issues. The module would aim to update the vision that President Harper and his colleagues held at the start of the twentieth century, namely, that the university should serve as the hub for human betterment within the social sphere just as it was and is the center for human betterment within, say, the health sphere. Consequently, public officials would understand that the module and its coaches would be serving society in both ways simultaneously. The social scientists would make the case that each feature (higher-order learning, grappling with social issues) represents a vital societal need. Advocates would add that as the new century wears on, each need is likely to morph further into a demand. Hence, in exchange for officials' support of the laboratory, the coaches would take on the two clearly stated and interrelated sets of obligations.

THE BOTTOM LINES

Bottom lines can be of all sorts, but whatever currency they deal in, they try to measure whether the enterprise is in good tone, in good form, as well as whether it has done what it proposed to do. Universities, public or private, do not operate this way. . . . Their . . . operating plan is to spend all the money they have—the faculty can always think up fresh ways to do this—and then ask for more. Complaining, all the while . . . about how society no longer values education.[47]

During discussions regarding the specific terms of a learn grant, officials shall, as they're obliged to do, raise two bottom-line issues. Compared to an existing array of social science departments, what would be the module's efficiency, that is, its cost per student? The other bottom line—in addition to, and just as vital as, the monetary dimension—is the element of quality. Humans invariably try to assess whether the money we give is worth what we get in return. Hence, the features of value-for-dollar and value-added are pivotal to the modular experiment. The first feature refers to the intrinsic and extrinsic worth of higher-order learning, the second to a demonstration that the players possess a greater level of human capital skills going out than they did coming in. The module would need to demonstrate that on both value scales it produces a much higher quality product than most of the current post-K–12. Hence, in making their case, its advocates would need to show that, when both bottom-line criteria—efficiency and quality—are weighed together, the module is a superior approach.

Chapter 6 reported that one of the highly touted outcomes of the Math Emporium was its greater efficiency compared to the old system. By lowering the cost per student, it produced a significant labor savings. Consequently, integrating innovative technology into the module would be constructed as one means for enhancing efficiency. Additionally, the module might save money by arranging to graduate its players in three calendar years instead of the four or more years that is now typically the case.[48] Furthermore, a significant source of labor-savings could arise from the size of the module's staff. In order to graduate, say, X number of students, the interdisciplinary module could conceivably require fewer coaches than the number of professors found today within the typical array of post-K–12 social science departments. The fundamental reason for this potential labor-savings is that the module would be student-centered rather than faculty-centered. Consequently, in considering whom to hire, the first question the module asks is, what do our players need? By way of contrast, the first question today's social science department asks is, what does our department need in order to enhance its national prestige rankings?

The module responds to its question by seeking professors that have the experience and/or potential to coach its players in DBL. Today's typical department, however, responds to its question by trying to hire as many professors as possible based on their actual and/or potential contributions to its national reputation. A department is said to have had a good year if it's hired a number of stars—actual or potential. The more stars it has, the greater the department's status and prestige. This virtually infinite proliferation of professors has nothing at all to do with the higher-order learning needs of undergraduates. That proliferation does, however, account for the escalating, and haphazard, odds and ends of courses censured by any number of critics.[49] In order to recruit the stars (actual or potential), the chair must guarantee that, on those indeterminate occasions when they elect to teach a course, they can do it within their research specialty. If the specialty is not in the current list of courses, it's added at once. The upshot is that the department's curriculum is professor-driven—the more professors it accumulates and the more specialized their research interests, the more stretched-out its menu.

The module, by contrast, bases its hiring agenda on matters other than the mimicry of the elite. Because its objective is enabling its players to become problem solvers, it is not obliged to keep on expanding its numbers indefinitely for reasons extraneous to its mission of serving players. Accordingly, while comparing and contrasting itself to conventional social science departments, the module may, in addition to the issues of value-for-dollar and value-added, be able to factor in the possibility of fewer total professors. It may, in short, be able to do a whole lot more for less.

Furthermore, when the floor is open to the question of efficiency in the form of labor savings, officials are certain to bring up the issue of tenure—a matter that has, for numerous decades, vexed many of them as well as certain influential citizens.[50] In recent years, it's even made some faculty uneasy. Harvard's Richard Chait, who has studied the issue of tenure for more than two decades, reports that "three extensive surveys between 1989 and 1999 consistently disclosed that more than one-third of all [U.S.] faculty members agreed that tenure was an 'outmoded concept.'"[51] A portent, perhaps, of tenure's future is that those same studies found that compared to while males, "women and faculty of color" were less satisfied with, and more critical of, the tenure system.[52]

In 1915, the newly established American Association of University Professors (Dewey was among its founders) began a lobbying effort to make tenure an essential feature of post-K–12.[53] Their fundamental rationale for tenure was that "academic freedom and job security were linked."[54] Moreover, at its 1925 national conference, AAUP established for the first time a set of formal guidelines regarding tenure that were later refined by, and widely disseminated in, its "1940 Statement of Principles on Academic Freedom and Tenure."[55] A more recent AAUP tenure update was released in 1995.[56]

It seems inconceivable that public officials would ever support any type of learn grant initiative apart from some modification of the notion that professors are entitled to a perk that, in the twenty-first century, virtually no other occupation retains. (Tenure in the UK was entirely abolished in the 1980s.)[57] Officials are certain to make much of the fact that a key element of the advocates' case for the module is the expected acceleration in job uncertainty within the shifting global marketplace of the new century. According to the module's advocates, one of the many reasons citizens must possess portable human capital skills is that whole categories of occupations could, owing to upgrades in technology and/or changes in marketplace demand, be severely downsized or perhaps even become obsolete, as discussed below in the case of computer programmers. Given that spreading uncertainty, it becomes entirely appropriate for officials to inquire how much sense it makes, and how fair-minded it is, for academics to insist that they should be allowed to retain a controversial perk that is slipping away from growing numbers of their fellow citizens. Why, in the face of such widespread diminishing job durability, should academics insist on lifetime employment security?

Although most officials endorse the principle of academic freedom, at the same time they concur with the blunt appraisal that "in reality the tenure system has evolved into a mechanism for lifetime employment security."[58] That unanticipated turn of events is something that Dewey never imagined and would never have endorsed.[59] Anyone that has ever sat through hundreds of endless hours of tenure deliberations knows full well that the question of protecting the candidate because she or he espouses unpopular ideas or causes seldom, if ever, crosses the radar screen. Even recent efforts to establish post-tenure reviews do not concern themselves with academic freedom.[60] Instead, the overriding and all-pervasive issue is whether or not he or she is *good enough* to become (or remain) a superprofessor on a permanent basis. If perchance the candidate is an entrepreneur with star quality, tenure is both undeniable and largely irrelevant.[61] Indeed, the growing awareness that tenure is peripheral for the star is strongly associated with the degree to which the entrepreneur constructs him or herself as an independent contractor. In any case, because of her or his track record, the university could hardly deny tenure to a star that sought it. But if for some peculiar reason tenure were denied, the entrepreneur/PI is so marketable that he or she could easily get another highly desirable job.[62]

Although recent research concludes that tenure has morphed into a mechanism for lifetime job security (despite lofty pronouncements about academic freedom), Chait's research has also uncovered one more feature. This third feature turns out, moreover, to be just as crucial as and inseparable from both job security and academic freedom. And that is the intangible but powerful element of social status, alongside its indivisible corollaries—prestige and self-esteem.[63] The significance of those highly salient dimensions is underscored by how the professor feels after he or she is denied tenure. A senior researcher that works with Chait at Harvard reports that its denial is a "stigma and a blow to one's self-esteem."[64] And, after interviewing a number of academics that actually experienced the denial of tenure, Fogg reported that its denial "amounts to being labeled a failure," that is, a loser.[65] On this intangible dimension, too, tenure has evolved into far more than what its AAUP inventors originally intended. Tenure is now indivisible from the professor's identity and self-concept.

At the same time, bear in mind that the percentage of tenured faculty in post-K–12 shrank from 70 percent in 1975 to less than half by the late 1990s.[66] If, in addition, the numbers of graduate students serving as credentialers were added to the base of all undergraduate teachers, the proportion of tenured faculty would drop even more dramatically. The chief reason for the continuing shrinkage in the proportion of tenured faculty has been a steady increase in the numbers of professors (both full- and part-time) serving as lecturers or adjuncts—largely as credentialers.[67] For the most part, such non-tenured persons do not have multiyear contracts, and are thus viewed as *temporary*. Another reason for the long-term trend away from tenured professors is that several U.S. universities and colleges do not provide tenure even to *permanent* full-time faculty. Instead, they offer their professors renewable contracts, ranging anywhere from three to ten years. Furthermore, many of those schools do not offer any inducements to forgo tenure in the shape, say, of a salary premium.[68]

The Boston University School of Management (BUSM) follows a somewhat different approach. It offers professors a "two-track system . . . that allows faculty to forgo or relinquish tenure."[69] Professors who give up tenure receive an 8–10 percent salary premium and a ten-year renewable contract. Newer faculty without tenure who elect the package that includes the salary premium and renewable contract must first pass through the same review process for tenure eligibility as faculty seeking tenure. BUSM dean Louis Lataif remarked that the principal rationale for establishing the tenure-free option is that their school's students will, in today's rapidly shifting labor market, be required to "prove themselves year-in and year-out. . . . Guaranteed lifetime employment . . . is not consistent with the competitive management environment."[70]

Despite salary premiums, multiyear contracts, and other inducements, available research suggests that, so far at least, no alternative has emerged which functions as a satisfactory "substitute for the status of tenure."[71] Furthermore, adds Chait, "without an alternative and equivalent source of status, tenure will remain the preferred choice of most faculty."[72] He suggests that an equivalent to tenure might perhaps be found in the standard though voluntary practice in medicine of becoming board certified in one of twenty-four specialties (e.g., internal medicine), many with subspecialties (e.g., nephrology). Although being board certified is not compulsory in order to practice, it is designed to provide the public with the assurance that the MD possesses the highest level possible of "knowledge, skills, and experience required to provide quality patient care in that specialty."[73] In effect, being board certified is the ultimate mark of professional status for today's MD, one without which she or he would hardly presume to practice. Constructing the coach as a specialist is essential to the module's negotiations with public officials regarding the terms of a new social contract. A medical specialist claims to possess particular skills that enable him or her to deliver a valued product that a generalist does not and/or cannot deliver. Having carved out a unique niche, the specialist (whether in medicine or in coaching players in DBL) argues that the niche should be recognized as a distinctive status. Furthermore, adds the specialist, successful delivery of the valued goods should get her or him both prestige and material rewards. That is, moreover, the precise reasoning that advocates for a module would use with officials. The coach ought to be recognized as a highly skilled specialist who, upon delivery of the promised goods, is rewarded in a distinctive manner.

But, officials would justly ask, on what grounds does the module presume to certify the coach as a specialist? Today's graduate schools train their students to focus on being an entrepreneur or, failing that, to settle for being the generalist known as teacher-scholar. But which schools now train their graduate students to be coaches? Where is the parallel with medicine in which the MD gets accredited as a board-certified specialist in, say, cardiology? What body of peers can award the imprimatur that he or she possesses the distinctive qualifications of a "coach" and is thus worthy of status, prestige, and a salary premium? In effect, asks the official, from what recognized source would the module recruit its coterie of specialists?

The response is, of course, that no graduate program in the social sciences (or in any other field) presently lists coach development as one of its specialties. However, by way of analogy, there were in the nineteenth century few, if any, specialties in medicine, at least as we know them today. Nor, compared to the situation now, were there many places for specialists to train. Eventually, over the course of many decades, certain generalists began to concentrate on particular parts (skeletal, circulatory, neural) of the body. And as they gradually developed a reputation for being experts within their specific realm, other generalists gravitated toward and learned from them. The result was that their distinctive specialty grew and became recognized by outsiders as important. Correspondingly, certain schools and teaching hospitals fashioned a reputation as the best places to train for particular specialties. Soon thereafter a board was created, that is, a group of specialists that certified, that is, officially declared, that the MD is now just like us, that is, *special*—a peer who is a recognized by a set of experts within that particular sphere.

Accordingly, advocates would convey to officials that the module ought to follow a long-term process comparable to that pursued over many decades by the medical specialties. The module would be a magnet for generalists (teacher-scholars) interested in figuring out how to become a very good specialist able to coach undergraduates in DBL. And within the social sciences, that means the cultivation of human capital skills blended with the weaving of the social fabric. Each module would, over time, aim to develop a reputation as the best place to become *board certified* to carry on that task. Such a board is, of course, made up of those professors who have developed into expert coaches. It is hoped that, in due course, a number of other modules will spring up around North America, Europe, and elsewhere, each seeking to outdo the other as the most prestigious place to carry on this high-status endeavor. Not only would its reputation attract professors, grad students, and postdocs, it would likely draw talented undergrads as well. Rather than being drawn to a school whose prestige stems from the scholarly reputation of its faculty—but whose capability at cultivating students' human capital is at best unknown—some undergrads might instead gravitate toward a place whose prestige stems from the skills of its specialists at meeting their players' information age needs.[74]

Chait asserts that if authentic tenure reform ever came about, it would never be driven solely by what he calls the "internal market," that is, professors working from within the ivory tower seeking to change it. That is the case even though an internal market for change currently exists among "some women and minority faculty with tenure."[75] One of the reasons those insiders are seeking to modify tenure is because they tend to agree with Stanford's former president who stated openly that the public perception "that tenure protects 'deadwood' is . . . 'alas, correct.'"[76] If tenure does indeed shield mediocrity, then women and minorities suffer the most because despite gains in recent years they remain underrepresented on university faculties. That issue is, moreover, joined at the hip with the fact that tenure was constructed during the past century by white males—virtually all of whom had stay-at-home wives. Hence, some academics pose an unsettling question—especially for social scientists: Have we not spent the last half century confronting and modifying an array of unjust social patterns created by and for white males with a full-time helper? Accordingly, why should tenure be exempt from similar scrutiny and potential modification? Why should we fail to construct a new reality that empowers, say, dual-professional couples, whether straight or gay/lesbian?

Chait believes that meaningful changes in tenure would come about only if the insiders (professors troubled about tenure) joined forces with "external stakeholders" who are equally interested in change.[77] Accordingly, the module's advocates would subscribe to Chait's strategy because they would, under the auspices of a learn grant, join forces with external stakeholders such as public officials and interested citizens. Both sets of advocates would labor together to create, over a long period of time, a new and recognized specialty whose professors are willing to negotiate "linking accountability with privilege on campuses."[78] Tenure merely as a mechanism to certify lifetime job security would not characterize the module.

It goes without saying that, at the same time, officials must agree explicitly to guarantee the right of every coach, intern, and student in the module to espouse unpopular notions and causes.[79] Once that nonnegotiable item is in place, a reasonable degree of permanence could be provided through, say, five- or ten-year renewable contracts based on demonstrable success in achieving the module's goals. It's just as much in the module's interest to hold on to a coach that's productive and successful as it is, say, in the shop's interest to hold on to a productive entrepreneur/PI. The module's flexibility in negotiating lifetime job security (but not freedom of expression) would give officials assurance that the module would not be saddled with the burdensome salary costs of mediocre, unproductive coaches.

At the same time, the pioneer professors who initiate the modular experiment and who already possess tenure would not be expected to give it up at once, though they may elect to do so later on. One obvious reason is that the trailblazers—those willing to transfer from their current department in order to participate in developing the module—are thereby risking their professional reputation. Setting aside the mimicry of their discipline's elite is by itself a built-in disincentive to take part in an untried experiment. If they are then also asked to relinquish tenure, that would be another weighty disincentive, because both the advocates and officials fully understand that the module must over time prove itself to be worthy of continued support.

Presently, any new entity created by post-K–12 assumes the mantle of immortality long after anyone can remember why it was created in the first place. By way of contrast, the module would deserve and receive support only as long as it's successful in achieving its stated goals. Unlike other parts of post-K–12, the module would exist only insofar as it's able to keep on demonstrating its worth via high-quality performance. Hence, the numbers of currently tenured professors willing to try to break new ground are likely to be unduly limited if doing so entails *both* risking one's professional reputation *and* trading lifetime job security for an arrangement that may not even be around in several years. Obviously, coaches that are not now tenured would be exposed to the risk of being out of a job if either the module folds or they turn out to be unsuccessful specialists.

In light of such deterrents, officials and advocates must engage in candid discussions over the need for incentives in the form of salary premiums high enough to attract and hold good coaches. The current long-term trend (apart from occasional blips) for the salaries of the typical teacher-scholar ranges between flat and downward.[80] The AAUP, for instance, reported that in 2003–2004, "average salaries of full-time faculty members rose by just 2.1 percent . . . the lowest percentage increase in three decades."[81] In sharp contrast, future prospects for the entrepreneur have never been brighter. For example, a consortium of eight universities recently obtained a $100 million foundation grant to help transform interested faculty into entrepreneurs.[82] The program targets professors outside the sciences, engineering, and business, and aims to develop within them both the frame of mind and the specific skills demanded by today's role of entrepreneur/PI. The existence of one such program designed to develop entrepreneurship among nonscientists is certain to spawn imitators, thus paving the way for growing numbers of professors to move in that direction and away from the conventional teacher-scholar role.

In any event, officials would need to be convinced that the degree of public good that the module supplies is sufficient to warrant a level of compensation commensurate with its accomplishments.[83] Because that salary level is likely to be higher than that available to the typical superprofessor, one obvious danger is that certain tenured faculty who are unsuited to the role of coach might nonetheless attempt to transfer to the module. The module's coordinators would, however, discourage their participation. But, if some tenured but unsuitable professors manage somehow to enter the module, they would be required and able to return to their home department once their incompatibility is determined. The point being that in pondering the matter of compensation for coaches, officials need not be concerned that they would end up supporting unsuccessful coaches on a permanent basis.

A BIG UMBRELLA OF BROAD SPHERES—
A NEW AMERICAN COLLEGE OF THE COMMONS

Issues of money, job security, and prestige take on added weight when we recall that phase I of the module is implemented by, alongside the social sciences, professors from several broad spheres of learning, for example, the sciences, humanities, history, the arts and design, and mathematics. Phase I professors plainly prefer something other than the roles of superprofessor, entrepreneur, or cybercredentialer. Although the role of coach intrigues them, they want to shape it in ways that make it entirely appropriate for their particular domain of learning. However, all the coaches in phase I aim to do two things. First, they seek to wean students from the milk of the teaching paradigm and get them comfortable chewing the solid food of the learning paradigm. Second, they intend to familiarize players with some of the core, significant, and problematic issues that characterize their distinctive sphere of learning. Within the sciences, for example, that would include the nature of the scientific method.

Advocates from the social sciences working together with public officials to hammer out a learn grant would hope that, from the start, persons from each of the five additional spheres would enlist as full and equal partners in conversations regarding the organization and operation of their module. Their long-term objective would be to establish not only a social science module, but also five additional and distinctive modules for each sphere of learning. All six modules would, of course, share phase I in common, including equal responsibilities to staff it. Phase II would, on the other hand, consist of six discrete modules. Despite the fact each is distinctive, the modules are bound together by their mutual allegiance to and accountability for DBL.[84]

The particular ways in which DBL is played out for the social sciences were described in prior chapters. Pivotal to those descriptions was their service to society in the shape of grappling with urgent social issues. The specific details of those efforts should be convincing to public officials and also to their fellow coaches from the other spheres. In a comparable manner, each of the other modules would also figure out how to accomplish DBL within its own distinctive domain. And that would, of necessity, include how it intends to synthesize DBL with important ways to serve society—ways to enhance the public good that flow naturally from its particular sphere of learning. Each of those modules is, like the social sciences module, accountable for those ways to their fellow coaches from the other spheres and also to public officials. The whole of the New American College is, in effect, an extraordinarily open, transparent, and mutually sustaining body. In sharp contrast to the aura of mystique and privacy that shrouds today's ivory tower, DBL occurs in a public arena.[85] Such an arena can be seen as a type of "commons," a place for dialogue and action among academics and between academics and citizens. A New American College of the Commons, struggling to invent itself in the sunlight and fresh air, is a far cry from the ivory tower and its musty confines.

Given the long-term objective of (at least) six independent, yet interdependent, spheres, it makes perfect sense to apply the same principles of job security, status, and compensation within each sphere. Academic freedom, explicitly including the right to espouse unpopular ideas and subversive causes of whatever type, would be guaranteed. But tenure simply as a mechanism to guarantee lifetime job security would be omitted from its list of basic principles. At the same time, each realm would have the long-term objective of developing the role of coach as a distinctive specialty within its sphere that possesses a high degree of status, prestige, and remuneration. An entity comparable to a board in medicine would officially declare that it has certified the coach as an expert, that is, someone who has demonstrated convincingly that she or he deserves status, prestige, and a salary premium. Finally, despite the demise of tenure, each coach from each domain would enjoy a benefit that few of our friends in other professions can, in the new century, reasonably expect—namely, multiyear contracts renewable on the basis of her/his continued performance as a successful coach.

GRADUATE STUDENTS AND POSTDOCS—
INTERNS AT WORK

Although we've focused primarily on the needs and interests of undergrads, graduate students and postdocs are in fact a major ingredient in the module and contribute both to its current and future successes. It's just as essential for them as it is for professors to have the option of pursuing the specialty of coach. Chapter 4 indicated that at least some grad students at certain high-prestige schools now possess misgivings over being channeled toward what they perceive to be a restricted set of future options.[86] The big problem currently hampering grads, postdocs, and undergrads aspiring to be a different kind of professor is that there's no place for them to learn in a hands-on manner how to become anything other than an entrepreneur or teacher-scholar. To be sure, many graduate schools try very hard to make the role of teacher-scholar more palatable to their students, mainly through special courses, workshops, programs, and teaching centers geared to help them become effective and stimulating teachers.[87]

The huge obstacle that those well-intentioned schools face in convincing their students to take such workshops and programs seriously is arguably more daunting today than what I faced in the late 1960s. Recall from the preface that I began my career believing I could indeed do it all. Although no one used the label back then, I assumed naively that I could follow a learning paradigm and, at the same time, try to contribute to the national prestige ranking of my department and university through developing my own national reputation. But wiser heads than mine prevailed—wiser, that is, if I expected to keep my job.

The dilemma facing graduate students and postdocs today is more vexing than the quandary confronting earlier generations. On the one side, the entrepreneurial role is much more salient, clearly visible, and insistent than ever before. Although I missed seeing it at first, it's impossible today *not* to see the role of entrepreneur/PI. Even broadcasts of the sports games of colleges and universities are replete with glowing reports over how much money its researchers have raked in—all in the interest, to be sure, of their students and the society at large. But, on the other side, today's grad student (prospective or actual) is becoming increasingly aware of what a 2002 *Chronicle of Higher Education* poll of U.S. citizens reported, namely, that at the same time that schools are growing more and more entrepreneurial, "the public says colleges should [instead] emphasize undergraduate education and preparing students for careers."[88]

Making the dilemma even more painful (at least among aspiring social scientists) is their belief that the marriage between the social sciences and human betterment described in chapter 1 should be as intimate as possible. For example, after working several years as a journalist, Paul Lachlier entered the graduate school of a prestigious state university. However, he says, "Now, eight years into my prolonged graduate education, I am thoroughly ambivalent as to whether sociologists' thoughts [or those of any social scientist] matter."[89] The context of his essay makes it quite clear that he entered graduate school with an image of achieving human betterment very much like the model posed by pioneering social scientist Robert Park during the early years of the twentieth century. Recall from chapter 1 that Park had likewise been a journalist who believed strongly that social science could "shape public opinion" by confronting citizens with incontrovertible social "facts."[90] But Lachlier complained that contemporary sociology (typical of the social sciences in general) fails to get engaged in the public arena. Social science is at fault for "privileging professionalism over populism."[91]

Recall, however, that Park's efforts at disseminating social facts (populism) in order to achieve social changes met either with bored yawns or stiff resistance. Moreover, recall too from chapter 1 that some of today's social scientists attempting to get policymakers to pay attention to their research are frustrated by their inability to influence public policy. Hence, what Lachlier takes to be the indifference of many professionals toward actively pursuing human betterment may instead be the sense that the implications of their research for social change are either ignored or are likely to stir up a great deal of resistance. Consequently, given that the chances for failure are great when trying to make a difference and that, in any case, social activism gets in the way of one's prestige and status in one's discipline, it's plain to see why the professionalism Lachlier criticizes trumps everything else.

Up to now, postdocs or grad students like Lachlier who found that style of professionalism unpalatable had no option but to turn to what chapter 1 called *applied* social science. J. M. Brooks writes, for instance, that his department is organized around "applied/clinical" work, and that he and his colleagues "do good social science."[92]

> My colleagues are here not because they are lesser intellects than one finds at flagship institutions but because they are committed to teaching and to one of the base roots of our discipline: making this world a better place in which to live by using our discipline to foster/guide positive social change.[93]

The gratifications that Brooks and his colleagues receive must necessarily exclude both the high salaries of marketplace stars as well as the prestige/status assigned to well-regarded *basic* social science research. Instead, they receive a lot of "satisfaction in seeing [their] research become a part of the positive change that is not publicized in national media or elsewhere."[94]

Although it might at first appear that Brooks and his colleagues seem quite content with their local source of essential gratifications, he makes it crystal clear that, at the same time, they would also like to receive an additional sort of intangible gratification—*respect* from their professional association. They would like to get national recognition for their brand of social science. Brooks closes his essay by appealing to the basic social science professionals that control their fields and asking them to start valuing applied social science by assigning esteem and worth to what it does.

Lachlier concludes his essay with a similar entreaty. He implies that after receiving his doctoral degree, he hopes to pursue a Park-like form of applied social science. Knowing full well, however, that such a route leads to zero recognition and esteem, he urges his discipline "to rethink its fundamental mission."[95] For Lachlier, rethinking the mission means popularizing the field, and for him that denotes, in essence, updating Park's agenda. Moreover, integral to the sort of rethinking Lachlier has in mind is the notion that the field should start assigning prestige, status, and esteem to the work of popularizing social science.

Whatever the merits of the case made by advocates such as Brooks and Lachlier for applied work, most basic social scientists pay them only polite lip service. There's little incentive or motivation to respond with anything else. But the module, on the other hand, would have an affinity for the grad student or postdoc seeking a closer union between the social sciences and human betterment. And such an affinity is *not* because the module does applied work. Instead, it does social science that, as economist James Spengler put it, "has two immediate outcomes."[96] First, scientific discovery helps us explain something—it enables the researcher to understand what's now going on in the realm she or he is studying. And the second step in scientific discovery, says Spengler, is to connect that current understanding with the "redirection of some course of events." In sharp contrast to that essential interplay between understanding and redirection, applied work accepts and maintains the longstanding disjuncture between its efforts and basic social science.

From a contrasting point of view, and in line with Spengler, action research (AR) demands the union of understanding with redirection. Needless to say, that union is very difficult to achieve for numerous reasons, including the certainty that, in the social sciences, understanding means something quite different than it does in the sciences.[97] Not only is our understanding much less precise, social science confronts a reality far removed from the sciences when it comes to the dimension of "resistance." Nevertheless, if the grad student or postdoc wants to participate in figuring out how to blend understanding with redirection from an AR perspective, then the module is the place for him or her. She or he would play the role, say, of assistant coach and labor very closely with coach and players alike in shared efforts to achieve the module's goals. Over time, the postdoc might become so proficient at coaching that the module would want to hire him or her on a permanent basis. Another live option is, of course, that she or he might go to another school that is either launching a module or has a module in place already.

Although the same options would be available to grad student and postdoc alike, there's an important contrast between them that must be considered. As such modules are launched, one could safely assume the postdoc got his/her degree within a particular social science field; thus she or he has a reasonable grasp of that field's core content. If that person either lost interest in the module or turned out to be unsuccessful in meeting its demands, he or she could then look for a job within his/her content field. Accordingly, and for similar reasons, some mechanism must be provided for the grad student to be qualified within a particular social science field.

Even though many additional vexing details of such an arrangement are not clear at this time, working them out would hardly be insurmountable. Because the module itself would be forever viewed as a work in progress, those kinds of matters, along with every other feature of the module, would always be open to negotiation.[98] Under the terms of a learn grant, the active involvement of public officials, coaches, assistant coaches, players, and citizens would be explicitly solicited. The several parties would be encouraged to contribute innovative approaches for doing things—new ways to achieve the module's DBL objectives in both higher-order learning and, within the social science module, enabling humankind to take possession of society in order to bring it under control.

LIFELONG LEARNING

From an AR perspective, taking possession of society requires that citizens participate in reshaping their life circumstances. Accordingly, citizens would become actively engaged in phase II/year 2 of the module. Citizen participation in II/2 would link the module intimately with the notion of "lifelong learning"—a trendy buzzword both in and outside the academy. Apart, however, from adults of all ages enrolling in classes online or on campus, or attending sessions at places like Chautauqua or Elderhostel, no one seems quite sure what to make of lifelong learning, except that it's a great idea. Observers concur that the information age explosion in new knowledge, and with it the obsolescence of the old, will require citizens to maintain some form of life-long learning.[99] They add, moreover, that post-K–12 must equip itself to meet this emerging public need—a need that is likely to morph into a demand.

The module would imprint its unique stamp on the issue of lifelong learn-ing. Importantly, citizen participation in the module would not be restricted to phase II/2. The module would invite citizens of all ages to become part of the active learning experiences of phase I and II/1. To be sure, it would in-vite them to participate on the same bases as it tries to attract typical under-graduates and graduates. Needless to say, the citizens would *not* repeat the deadly-dull passive mode they experienced in the conventional forms of ei-ther K–12 or post-K–12. They would not come to the module simply to be inert recipients of lower-order subject matter of any type. They would, in-stead, be there for the same reasons as the players, coaches, and interns. The citizens would participate principally to hone their human capital skills, and, in the process of doing so, they're likely to comprehend a lot of vital con-tent, some of which may or may not be applicable to their occupations. In ei-ther event, given the increasingly uncertain nature of many occupations in the new century, the foremost strength of the module would hardly lie with transmitting content. The fragility of counting on course content for job se-curity was highlighted recently by a report stating that after millions of dol-lars were spent training high school graduates for software-development jobs in the Seattle-Tacoma region, the jobs were then outsourced to India, an issue to which I return below.[100]

It's likely that, in the new century, all too many citizens (high school and college graduates alike) will, to their dismay, realize they possess credentials that are less than robust, as defined above. Hence, in order to cope most ef-fectively with built-in labor market ambiguities, they'll need to find a means to cultivate their human capital skills. And that need could conceivably attract them to the module. But, like the players, the citizens are not there simply to receive. They're obliged to give as well. The fact is that owing to their years of job experience, persons of all ages would have a lot to offer the module. In other words, their range of real-world encounters could have particular rele-vance for the module's efforts to create social inventions (both virtual and ac-tual) aimed at resolving social problems.

For example, working citizens (regardless of their years in school) may, among other things, possess a certain degree of insider insight into the core issue of resistance. A major impediment to making social science matter is the resistance of persons and groups feeling threatened by proposed changes.[101] The citizens participating in the module may have worked inside, say, of businesses, or nonprofits, or government agencies, and thus have firsthand knowledge about initiatives for change that were met by determined resistance. The changes might, among many other things, have pertained to issues of gender, race/ethnicity, economic equity, the environment, and so forth. But, because many social scientists may not have had firsthand experience of situations where personnel, owing to a perceived threat, are actively resisting change, they may tend to lack the insights and knowledge that accompany that type of real-life situation. But, on the flip side, citizens that have actually been there may have a lot to offer when it comes to shaping inventions aimed at resolving such issues.[102]

In any case, their insider's insight regarding resistance to change would be only one of a range of real-world experiences citizens might bring with them to the module. The module's inclusion of citizens beyond their early twenties would supply a distinctive facet of diversity (age, real-world know-how) that is largely missing from today's typical undergraduate experience. Keep in mind, however, that the module's approach to lifelong learning would contrast sharply with the prevailing image of older citizens relaxing in a flaccid manner while being served up tasty morsels of fascinating information. That outmoded image would be no more relevant for them than it is for the undergrads or grads.

A ROBUST DEGREE—*MARKET DRIVEN AND A MORAL OBLIGATION*

In the fall of 2001, a New York State Supreme Court justice ruled that every citizen has the "constitutional right to a sound, basic education."[103] She concluded that the state formula for K–12 financing was unconstitutional precisely because it deprived a large number of New York City students of that right. But what is a sound, basic education? *New York Times* journalist R. C. Archibold asked several persons of note to reflect on what that might mean. He reports that a "combination of basic factual knowledge along with some ability to think critically is emerging as a compromise of sorts among traditional educators and those who want to experiment with new ideas."[104] Those in the latter camp argued that a sound education develops the skills of "critical reasoning and the ability to form judgments and opinions independently." And one of those persons added that the student must "acquire some intellectual curiosity about learning more and exploring the possibilities of science and the understanding you get from literature and the arts." But regardless of how his respondents described a *sound* education (whether it targets lower-order or higher-order learning, or a mixture) "there is seemingly overwhelming agreement that many people are not getting one."

Consequently, New York advocates for a sound education are continuing to push their case in both the courts and the state legislature. They seek both the structural reforms and the funds necessary to achieve them. Furthermore, "all sides say they expect the debate over a sound, basic education to continue [for a long time to come]."[105]

Steady increases in public spending (though by no means large) for K—12 are, in part, an upshot of that live, real-time debate—officials and citizens holding all shades of opinion concur that something is dreadfully wrong and must be fixed. Further, that range of persons perceives that reforms of one sort or another are at least being tried out in K–12, even if most prove to be unsuccessful in the long run. But, by contrast, the debate over what makes for a sound education is markedly different for post-K–12 than it is for K–12. Throughout post-K–12, the majority opinion is by far that *we're doing just fine, thank you very much. All we need is more money to do more of it.*[106] That's the gist of the report from the National Center for Public Policy and Higher Education cited above: Colleges and universities must get more money *now* to do their necessary credentialing. Leave the issue of fixing things in post-K–12 for some unspecified future time. Alas, public officials don't quite see it that way, and more money is simply not forthcoming.[107]

The standoff between, on the one side, the academics agreeing with the center and, on the other, the officials who do not, should be a wake-up call to skeptics dismissing the notion of some sort of learn grant initiative as nothing more than a flight of fancy. Given the massive amounts of red ink overwhelming both state and federal budgets during the early years of the new century, skeptics claim that any proposed deal between public officials and advocates for some sort of experimental module in the shape of a new American college defies common sense. If, however, a learn grant initiative is not in the cards, neither is the sort of cash infusion urged by the center in order to do business as usual. What, then, are the detractors of a learn grant left with? Is the vision of an experimental module sustained in part by a Learn Grant Act so wild and woolly-headed after all? The Project for the Future of Higher Education doesn't seem to think so:

> Given what we know and likely future social, technological and economic realities, if we were creating a college or university today, what would it look like?[108]

Throughout this book, the point has been made repeatedly that in the new century, a college or university cannot claim to be successful unless and until its students demonstrate that they possess a robust degree.[109] The content that the student grapples with must get pressed into the service of a greater end. The hoped-for end is that the student achieves a certain level of human capital capabilities and cultivates those skills on a daily basis—he or she is a practicing, lifelong problem solver. *What was your major in college? Well, I studied in a context that targeted the social sciences, or the sciences, or the humanities, and so forth. But regardless of the domain, I majored in problem solving. I pride myself in having accomplished a great deal in college. Though I'm now but a novice, I've embarked on a lifelong pursuit. I'm in the earliest stages of becoming a disciplined thinker. I know how to work with peers in order to analyze, evaluate, and synthesize ideas, and thus create solutions to problems. I am, in those senses, a knowledge maker, and thus reasonably well fitted for both the economic and civic demands of the information age.* Such a response would be in close sync with what R. Crosby Kemper (head of a large financial services corporation and an appointed public education official) said that employers want from post-K–12:

> We don't want people who are trained for specific jobs coming out of the college system. We want people who can read and write, who are literate, who are numerate, who have some sense of engagement with the world.[110]

Alongside Kemper's observation, the highly practical significance of cultivating problem solvers becomes apparent by observing the unanticipated fate of U.S. computer programmers within the context of the information age/global economy. Their story was one part of the drama of the 2004 presidential campaign, during which both sides traded barbs about job losses and job creation. The matter of outsourcing jobs overseas was notably contentious. There has, of course, been a steady decline in the proportion of well-paying U.S. manufacturing (blue-collar) jobs at least since the 1970s. And many of them were sent overseas.

Historically, voter anger over the disappearance and/or export of entire categories of occupations can be traced back to the dawn of the industrial age and to the 1812 English Luddites.[111] The appearance of the Luddites signaled perhaps the first time that ordinary citizens began to realize that new technologies coupled with emerging international realities could, for some of them, hold devastating consequences. For three hundred years a guild of weavers located in central England had, inside their houses, produced high-quality lace and stockings that they sold both for British and export markets. That influential community of weavers consisted of socially and economically privileged craftsmen that kept their prices high, not in response to market forces, but according to tradition.

Nonetheless, steam power was, for the first time, being applied to spinning looms, and large factories were built able to mass-produce lace, stockings, and other textile products for both the domestic and export markets at a fraction of the prices set by the weavers. In response, some of the weavers, called Luddites, attacked the mills at night, smashing the equipment. Their impassioned uprising was eventually quelled by British troops, and the Luddite leaders were either executed or deported to Australia. Bear in mind that although the weavers despised and detested them, the mills created new jobs for many hundreds of desperately poor citizens. Furthermore, their numbers were far greater than the numbers of weavers they'd displaced. Nevertheless, the new jobs paid a whole lot less than what the weavers had earned. Significantly, that same general issue of the less privileged (foreigners) willing to do the same work for less pay than the privileged (U.S. citizens) was very much alive during the 2004 campaign.

The hot button word was outsourcing. The evaporation of middle-class, white-collar jobs has now become as much of a public issue as the historic disappearance of manufacturing, blue-collar jobs.[112] Growing numbers of U.S. companies are exporting white-collar, professional, and technical jobs overseas to countries such as India, where trained personnel can do the same quality of work for a whole lot less money than U.S. workers. Virtually all the fleeing jobs require a high level of specialized skills, and many demand a college degree for entry. One of the jobs much in the news was that of the "basic programmer," namely, the persons that "write the code for [computer] applications and update and test them."[113] Throughout recent decades, thousands of students attended college in order to major in computer science. For many working-class and lower-middle-class youth, it was perceived as a sure route to social mobility and job security, much as the job of K–12 teacher had been viewed by their parents' generation. *No matter what,* their parents were assured, *they'll always need programmers and I'll always have a job.* Regrettably,

> US software programmers' prospects, once dazzling, are now in doubt. . . . For many of America's software programmers, it's paradise lost. Just a few years back, they held the keys to the Information Age. . . . Now these veterans of Silicon Valley and Boston's Route 128 exchange heart-rending job-loss stories on Web sites such as yourjobisgoingtoindia.com. Suddenly, the programmers share the fate of millions of industrial workers, in textiles, autos, and steel, whose jobs have marched to Mexico and China.[114]

The vulnerability of any type of twentieth-century, content-based degree is poignantly illustrated by the story of a twenty-two-year-old man about to receive his master's degree in computer science from a prestigious private university.[115] At age seventeen, Stephen had placed second in a national programming competition sponsored by Microsoft. Starting with his senior year in high school and continuing throughout college, he earned a lot of money working as a freelancer for a New York software development company. Recently, however, that company informed Stephen that it could no longer afford his services. It had located a Romanian programmer who charged $250 for a project for which Americans typically charge $2,000. And, despite his forthcoming prestigious master's degree, he's had no offers for the type of high-paying programming job he'd fully expected to get. Thus far, Stephen's only job option is to do routine programming for financial services firms, but for far less money than he'd ever expected. Furthermore, it's anybody's guess as to how long it will take before those types of firms follow the trend of out-sourcing their routine programming work to India or Ireland, or to East European countries such as Romania and Bulgaria.

Hal has, on the other hand, fashioned a very different set of circumstances for himself. A thirty-four-year-old unemployed U.S. programmer, Hal finally landed a programming job for far fewer dollars than he'd earned prior to being laid off. However, after a short time on his new job, he demonstrated to his boss that he was "much more than a [mere] programmer," and his salary was nearly doubled.[116] The key to his success, said his boss, was that "he had great strategic thinking skills. . . . You can't outsource that."[117] Hal used his thinking skills to lead his team in coming up with innovative solutions to pressing problems. He'd evolved into a role called *software architect*—a person able to envision something that might possibly come about and, what is more, a person able to marshal the talents of his or her teammates in navigating the twists and turns of figuring out how to get there.[118]

Some universities have begun to realize that the old-time, content-based master's degree offered to students such as Stephen is gradually turning out to be inadequate; it is *not* robust. Accordingly, a few schools have already begun to "revamp their computer science programs" at the master's level.[119] Carnegie Mellon University (CMU) has, for instance, introduced the feature of having their students work in teams, struggling to invent solutions to resolve problems. Schools such as CMU are, in effect, doing DBL (in which the cultivation of strategic thinking skills is pivotal) because they sense that the market for their master's-level students now demands it. Hence, one might reasonably infer that the apparent reason for not also introducing DBL among their computer science *undergrads* is that, as far as their professors can divine, the market does not yet demand it.

Furthermore, most schools probably reason that there are still lots of conventional computer science majors willing to take the kinds of lower-paying jobs that earlier grads such as Stephen or Hal are unwilling to abide. Still, how much further can their pay drop before today's grads start to complain, too? And, even more disturbing, what happens if the role of the conventional, college-trained computer programmer finds itself being edged onto the path toward obsolescence? Bear in mind that the programmer's forebears—the mainframe computer operator and the keypuncher (the one who punched the cards that the operator fed into the mainframe)—passed into oblivion not too many years ago.[120] Given that some schools are already making changes at the master's level in order to meet the demands of a shifting marketplace, we could conceivably witness a comparable development at the undergrad level. That is, if computer science professors begin to sense that the market for their undergrads demands a shift toward developing the role of software architect (complete with strategic reasoning skills) there is, based on their current adaptations at the master's level, every reason to expect they would respond similarly at the undergraduate level. The marketplace could, in effect, drive them to develop a form of DBL for undergrads appropriate to their field.

That being the case, the detractors of a Learn Grant Act might reason that it should likewise be left to the marketplace to drive any potential changes within the university's remaining spheres of learning—including the six domains above. The market should, says the critic, be the prime influence on any changes deemed necessary by each sphere in order to make their undergraduate degree robust. If, for instance, social science undergrads begin to experience an ever-widening gap between their credentials and the information age marketplace, then let the teacher-scholar and the cybercredentialer within that sphere adapt accordingly. But do not, adds the skeptic, be so reckless and naïve as to try to form an alliance with public officials by offering a new social contract that claims to deserve tax dollars because the proposed changes would be in the public interest. Although such a skeptic would readily acknowledge that the Land Grant Act and its 1945 successor were in fact *both* market driven *and* a moral obligation, he or she might assert that the days of fretting about moral issues are now behind us. Our skeptic-turned-cynic might assert that within post-K–12 (as within every other segment of society), only money talks. Everything else is mute.

THE SMART THING AND THE RIGHT THING
TO DO—*THE GLION DECLARATION*

Although our skeptic's point of view might at first glance seem plausible, it is unacceptable for any number of reasons, not least being that it's wrong-headed. Marx to the contrary, human society has never been solely about economics. A number of European and North American scholars have, for decades, made it their life's work to show that Marx sometimes oversimplified social reality.[121] Those scholars held that society is always a complex amalgam of the *smart* thing to do (self-interest) and the *right* thing to do (moral obligations to ideas, people, God, and other entities beyond oneself and family). The Land Grant Act and its 1945 upgrade succeeded brilliantly because they were in fact about both things—they were both smart and right! In similar fashion, some type of twenty-first-century learn grant initiative is both the smart thing and the right thing to do. It is smart (for the self-interest of social scientists and professors from other domains) because it meets a need, that is, there is a market. It would prepare students (including the bourgeoning numbers of minority and working-class persons) more effectively than does the current post-K–12 for the indeterminate information age/global marketplace.[122] Furthermore, the notion of a learn grant is at the same time right because, within the social science sphere, its ultimate long-range objective is to enable humankind to try to create a more just and equitable society.

In May 1998, a group of ten Americans and ten West Europeans—each of whom had spent an entire lifetime in higher education—met for almost a week in Glion, Switzerland. Their purpose was to ponder the range of "Global Forces" unsettling their countries' colleges and universities. At the close of their gathering they issued the Glion Declaration, a comprehensive document about ideas and strategies for confronting those forces in the new century. The spirit of their declaration and a number of its core ideas are woven throughout the fabric of this book. Included in their declaration was, among many other entries, the following:

> Scholars have been slow to apply their skills to pressing social issues, partly, one supposes, because of their complexity and intransigence; partly, perhaps because of a lack of both means and incentives to address them, and partly because the issues are often controversial and the risks of failure are high.[123]

I've argued that it's both smart and right for colleges and universities to try to grapple with social issues within the context of a social science module whose aim is to enable humankind to try to take possession of society. A New American College of the Commons would be the latest in a series of century-long efforts seeking, in one way or another, to reconcile the troubled marriage of social science with human betterment. Needless to say, enabling humankind to take possession of society and bring it under control is a big job that will never entirely be finished. Consequently, the module would be akin to the shop of an entrepreneur in the sciences, where there are lots of failures but, from time to time, a few small successes in pursuit of a highly elusive quarry. Furthermore, those successes would inspire the module's participants (coaches, players, interns, citizens) alongside its partners (public officials) to carry on their pursuit.

NOTES

1. Cited by Kliewer 1999:xxx–xxxi from Townsend et al. 1992:69–70.
2. Duderstadt 2000:13.
3. Bok 1982:62.
4. Bush 1945.
5. Cited by Duderstadt and Womack 2003:53.
6. Duderstadt 2000:126.
7. "Responding to the Crisis in College Opportunity." January 2004. National Center for Public Policy and Higher Education. www.highereducation.org.
8. "Responding to the Crisis."
9. Fairweather 1996.
10. Dziech 2002.
11. Duderstadt 2000; Powell and Owen-Smith 2002; Collis 2002.
12. Duderstadt 2000.
13. Duderstadt 1999:51.
14. Rhodes 1999:169.
15. Carlin 1999.
16. Arenson 2003, italics added.
17. Collins 2002.
18. Burd 2003a.
19. Cuban 1999:88ff.
20. Cuban 1999:88.
21. Cuban 1999:88.
22. www.aa.ufl.edu/aa/alc/index.htm
23. Boyer Commission 1998:37.
24. Duderstadt et al. 2002:64.
25. See, however, Coppola 2002.
26. Collins 2002a; Uchitelle 2004.
27. Brown and Duguid 2000:234, italics added.
28. Ewell 2002.
29. Barbero 2004.
30. Schwartz 2004.
31. Lanham 2002:176.
32. Prawat 2000; Margolis 2002.
33. Rodgers 2002; Schon 1983.
34. Boyer Commission 1998:16.
35. Hirsch and Weber 1999b:179; Kuh 2001: Newman et al. 2004.
36. Powell and Owen-Smith 2002.
37. Kuh 2001:289.
38. Lovett 2001.
39. Duderstadt 1999, 2000.
40. Duderstadt 2000:128.
41. Duderstadt 2000:130.
42. Duderstadt 2000:320, italics added.
43. Lanham (2002:176) describes disciplinary structures as "fossils."
44. Boyer 1994.

45. Duderstadt 2000:286.
46. Duderstadt et al. 2002:106.
47. Lanham 2002:173.
48. Arenson 2004.
49. Schwartz 2004; Schank 2000; Gregorian 2004.
50. Carlin 1999; Mahoney 1997.
51. Chait 2002a:16.
52. Chait 2002a:17.
53. Balch 2004.
54. Cohen 1998:338.
55. Chait 2002b:313; Ward 2002.
56. Trower 2002:33.
57. Altbach 2002:165.
58. Duderstadt and Womack 2003:167.
59. Balch 2004.
60. Cohen 1998:344.
61. Duderstadt 2000.
62. Kirp 2003; Warwick 2004.
63. Chait 2002b:315.
64. Fogg 2004a:A8.
65. Fogg 2004a:A8.
66. Baldwin and Chronister 2002:127.
67. Fogg 2004b.
68. Baldwin and Chronister 2002:141.
69. Clotfelter 2002:230.
70. Cited by Chait 2002a:15.
71. Chait 2002b:315.
72. Chait 2002b:315.
73. Cited by Chait 2002b:317, from the Web site of the peer-governed American Board of Specialties (abms.org).
74. Evers 2004.
75. Chait 2002b:318.
76. Chait 2002a:11.
77. Chait 2002b:320.
78. Duderstadt and Womack 2003:201.
79. O'Neil 2004; Chemerinsky 1999.
80. Cahn 2003.
81. Wilson 2004.
82. Mangan 2004.
83. Schmidt 2004.
84. Gregorian 2004.
85. Shulman 2004.
86. Coppola 2002. See also Dutta 2001; Marino 2001; Arney 2003; Dee 2003a, b.
87. Wuff and Austin 2004; Bartlett 2003b.
88. Hebel 2003:A14. See also Selingo 2003b.
89. Lachlier 2003:11.
90. Bulmer 1984:70.

91. Lachlier 2003:11.
92. Brooks 2004:5.
93. Brooks 2004:5.
94. Brooks 2004:5.
95. Lachlier 2003:11.
96. Spengler 1969:454. See also Schank and Cleary 1995.
97. Balch 2004.
98. Among these would, for example, be the matter of accreditation and its link with the credit hour; see Wellman and Ehrlich 2003.
99. Duderstadt 2000.
100. Schmidt 2004.
101. Gouldner 1965; Flyvbjerg 2001.
102. Greenwood and Levin 1998.
103. Archibold 2001.
104. Archibold 2001.
105. Archibold 2001.
106. Marcy 2003.
107. Conklin and Reindl 2004.
108. Project for the Future of Higher Education (home page), Antioch University, www.pfhe.org.
109. Duderstadt et al. 2002:64.
110. Cited by Schmidt 2004. See Newman et al. 2004 for the same point.
111. Durvall 1969; Reid 1986.
112. Uchitelle 2004.
113. Baker and Kripalani 2004:86.
114. Baker and Kripalani 2004:87.
115. Baker and Kripalani 2004.
116. Baker and Kripalani 2004:88.
117. Baker and Kripalani 2004:88
118. It turns out that even the software architect cannot be certain of continued employment. Lohr (2004) reports that Microsoft has in response to competitive pressures recently outsourced to India some of its work done by the "software architect."
119. Baker and Kripalani 2004:88.
120. Try asking today's students what either of those roles was, or what a mainframe computer was.
121. Dahrendorf 1959.
122. Wilgoren 2000; Steinberg 2000; Schmidt 2003; Madrid 2003:B8; Olivas 2003:B9.
123. "The Glion Declaration" 1999:180.

References

Agger, Ben. 2000. *Public Sociology—From Social Facts to Literary Acts.* Lanham, MD: Rowman & Littlefield.

Allen, Mike. 2002. "Bush, Dole, Push Volunteerism." *The Washington Post.* July 31. A17.

Altbach, Philip G., 2002. "How Are Faculty Faring in Other Countries?" In *The Questions of Tenure*, ed. R. P. Chait, 160–81. Cambridge, MA: Harvard University Press.

Altschuler, Glenn C. 2001. "Battling the Cheats." *The New York Times.* January 7.

Anderson, Charles. 1993. *Prescribing the Life of the Mind: An Essay on the Purpose of the University, the Aims of Liberal Education, the Competence of Citizens, and the Cultivation of Practical Reason.* Madison: University of Wisconsin Press.

Anderson, Martin. 1996. *Impostors in the Temple—A Blueprint for Improving Higher Education in America.* Stanford, CA: Hoover Institution Press.

Archibald, E. H. H. 1968. *Wooden Fighting Ships in the Royal Navy—897–1860.* London: Blandford.

Archibald, Kathleen. 1965. "Social Sciences Approaches to Peace." In *Applied Sociology: Opportunities and Problems*, ed. A. W. Gouldner and S. M. Miller, 266–84. New York: Free Press.

Archibold, Randal C. 2001. "What Kind of Education Is Adequate? It Depends." *The New York Times.* September 14. Sec. 1, 33.

Arenson, Karen W. 2003. "N.Y.U. President Says Teaching Isn't Such a Novel Idea." *The New York Times.* September 3.

Arenson, Karen W. 2004. "Many Collegians Do Not Graduate in 6 Years." *The New York Times.* May 26.

Argetsinger, Amy. 2001. "When Tenure Turns Over." *The Washington Post.* May 8. B01.

Arner, Faith. 2003. "It Only Looks Like Child's Play." *BusinessWeek.* November 3. 86–89.

Arney, Katharine. 2003. "Ten Telltale Signs that Scaling the Ivory Tower Is Not For You." *Science—Next Wave.* February 14, viewed online.

Arnone, Michael. 2003. "The Wannabes." *The Chronicle of Higher Education.* January 3. A18–A20.

Aronowitz, Stanley. 2000. *The Knowledge Factory—Dismantling the Corporate University and Creating True Higher Learning.* Boston: Beacon Press.

Associated Press. 2003a. "Studies: 90 Percent of Kids Use Computers." *The New York Times.* October 30.

Associated Press. 2003b. "Texas Religious Groups Fight Biology Texts." *The New York Times.* November 6.

Astin, Alexander W. 1993. *What Matters in College? Four Critical Years Revisited.* San Francisco: Jossey-Bass.

——. 2000. "The American College Student." In *Higher Education in Transition: The Challenges of the New Millennium,* ed. Joseph Losco and Brian L. Fife, 7–28. Westport, CT: Bergin & Garvey.

Bain, Ken. 2004a. "What Makes Great Teachers Great?" *The Chronicle of Higher Education.* April 9. B7.

——. 2004b. *What the Best College Teachers Do.* Cambridge, MA: Harvard University Press.

Baker, Stephen and Manjeet Kripalani. 2004. "Software—Will Outsourcing Hurt America's Supremacy?" *BusinessWeek.* March 1. 84–94.

Balch, Stephen H. 2004. "The Antidote to Academic Orthodoxy." *The Chronicle of Higher Education.* April 23. B7–B9.

Baldwin, Roger G. and Jay L. Chronister. 2002. "What Happened to the Tenure Track?" In *The Questions of Tenure,* ed. R. P. Chait, 125–59. Cambridge, MA: Harvard University Press.

Barbero, Allessandro. 2004. *Charlemagne: Father of a Continent,* trans. Allan Cameron. Berkeley: University of California Press.

Barr, Robert B. and John Tagg. 1995. "From Teaching to Learning: A New Paradigm for Undergraduate Education." *Change.* 13–25.

Bartlett, Thomas. 2003a. "Why Johnny Can't Write, Even Though He Went to Princeton." *The Chronicle of Higher Education.* January 3. A39–A40.

——. 2003b. "The First Thing about Teaching—Colleges Try Harder to Prepare Graduate Assistants for the Classroom." *The Chronicle of Higher Education.* September 26.10–12.

——. 2003c. "What Makes a Teacher Great?" *The Chronicle of Higher Education.* December 12. A8–A10.

Basinger, Julianne. 2001. "Power-Building President Seeks Stature for Florida International." *The Chronicle of Higher Education.* October 12. A36.

Bates, A. W., Tony Bates, and Gary Poole. 2003. *Effective Teaching with Technology in Higher Education.* San Francisco: Jossey-Bass.

Bell, Daniel. 1990. "Resolving the Contradictions of Modernity and Modernism, Part II." *Society* 27:66–75.

Berman, Morris. 2000. Review of Murray Sperber, *Beer and Circus: How Big-Time College Sports Is Crippling Higher Education. The New York Times* Book Review. September 17, viewed online.

Berube, Michael and Cary Nelson (eds.). 1995. *Higher Education Under Fire: Politics, Economics, and the Crisis of the Humanities.* New York: Routledge.

Bess, James L. and Associates. 2000. *Teaching Alone, Teaching Together—Transforming the Structure of Teams for Teaching.* San Francisco: Jossey-Bass.

Bishop, J. Michael. 2003. *How to Win the Nobel Prize: An Unexpected Life in Science.* Cambridge, MA: Harvard University Press.

Bloom, Allan, 1987. *The Closing of the American Mind: How Higher Education Has Failed Democracy and Impoverished the Souls of Today's Students.* New York: Simon & Schuster.

Bok, Derek. 1982. *Beyond the Ivory Tower: Social Responsibilities of the Modern University.* Cambridge, MA: Harvard University Press.

——. 1990. *Universities and the Future of America.* Durham, NC: Duke University Press.

——. 2003a. *Universities in the Marketplace—The Commercialization of Higher Education.* Princeton, NJ: Princeton University Press.

——. 2003b. "Closing the Nagging Gap in Minority Achievement." *The Chronicle of Higher Education.* October 24. B20.

Bollag, Burton. 2004. "Degrees of Separation." *The Chronicle of Higher Education.* October 15. A36–A37.

Bowers, Raymond V. 1967. "The Military Establishment." In *The Uses of Sociology,* ed. Paul F. Lazarsfeld, William H. Sewell, and Harold L. Wilensky, 234–74. New York: Basic Books.

Boyer, Ernest L. 1990. *Scholarship Reconsidered : Priorities of the Professoriate.* Princeton, NJ: Carnegie Foundation for the Advancement of Teaching.

——. 1994. "Creating the New American College." *The Chronicle of Higher Education.* March 9. A5.

Boyer Commission Report on Reinventing Undergraduate Education—A Blueprint for America's Universities. 1998. New York: The Carnegie Foundation for the Advancement of Teaching.

Boyer Commission on Educating Undergraduates in the Research University—Reinventing Undergraduate Education. 2002. *Three Years After the Boyer Report.* New York: The Carnegie Foundation for the Advancement of Teaching.

Brainard, Jeffrey. 2004. "Stem-Cell Research Moves Forward." *The Chronicle of Higher Education.* October 1. A22.

Brint, Steven (ed). 2002a. *The Future of the City of the Intellect—The Changing American University.* Stanford, CA: Stanford University Press.

Brint, Steven. 2002b. "The Rise of the 'Practical Arts.'" In *The Future of The City of the Intellect—The Changing American University,* ed. S. Brint, 231–59. Stanford, CA: Stanford University Press.

Brooks, J. Michael. 2004. "Public Sociology . . . It's What Teaching-Oriented Departments Do . . . " *ASA Footnotes.* January. 5.

Brown, John Seely and Paul Duguid. 2000. *The Social Life of Information.* Boston: Harvard Business School Press.

Brown, Lester R. 2003. *Plan B: Rescuing a Planet Under Stress and a Civilization in Trouble.* New York: W. W. Norton.

Brulin, Goran. 2001. "The Third Task of Universities, Or How to Get Universities to Serve Their Communities." In *Handbook of Action Research: Participative Inquiry & Practice,* ed. Peter Reason and Hilary Bradbury, 440–46. Thousand Oaks, CA: Sage.

Brydon-Miller, Mary, Davydd Greenwood, Patricia Maguire. 2003. "Why Action Research?" *Action Research* 1:9–29.

Bulmer, Martin. 1984. *The Chicago School of Sociology: Institutionalization, Diversity, and the Rise of Sociological Research.* Chicago: University of Chicago Press.

Burd, Stephen. 2002a. "Colleges Catch a Glimpse of Bush Policy on Higher Education, and Aren't Pleased." *The Chronicle of Higher Education.* March 8. A25.

——. 2002b. "Lack of Aid Keeps 170,000 from College, Report Says." *The Chronicle of Higher Education.* July 5. A12.

———. 2003a. "Education Department Wants to Create Grant Program Linked to Graduation Rates." *The Chronicle of Higher Education.* January 3. A31.

———. 2003b. "Republican Leaders Want to Stress Accountability and Cost Issues in Hearing on Higher Education Act." *The Chronicle of Higher Education.* May 14. A8.

———. 2004. "Graduation Rates Called a Poor Measure of College." *The Chronicle of Higher Education.* April 2. A1.

Burke, Dolores L. 1988. *A New Academic Marketplace.* New York: Greenwood.

Bush, Vannevar. 1945. *Science, the Endless Frontier,* a Report to the President on a Program for Postwar Scientific Research. Office of Scientific Research and Development, July, Washington DC: National Science Foundation, 1990.

Cabin, Robert. 2003. "Why College Can Wait." *The Chronicle of Higher Education.* October 17. B5.

Cahn, Peter S. 2003. "Number Crunching." *The Chronicle of Higher Education.* December 12. C1.

Cameron, J. M. 1978. *On the Idea of a University.* Toronto: University of Toronto Press.

Cárdenas, Karen Hardy. 2000. "Technology in Higher Education: Issues for the New Millennium." In *Higher Education in Transition: The Challenges of the New Millennium,* ed. Joseph Losco and Brian L. Fife, 189–211. Westport, CT: Bergin & Garvey.

Cardozier, V. Ray (ed.). 1993. *Important Lessons from Innovative Colleges and Universities.* San Francisco: Jossey-Bass.

Carnevale, Dan. 2003. "The Virtual Lab Experiment—Some Colleges Use Computer Simulations to Expand Science Offerings Online." *The Chronicle of Higher Education.* January 31. A30.

Carlin, James F. 1999. "Restoring Sanity to an Academic World Gone Mad." *The Chronicle of Higher Education.* November 5. A76.

Carlson, Scott. 2002. "Wired to the Hilt." *The Chronicle of Higher Education.* March 29. A34.

———. 2003a. "A $20 Million Carrot." *The Chronicle of Higher Education.* April 18. A39–A40.

———. 2003b. "New Allies in the Fight against Googling." *The Chronicle of Higher Education.* March 21. A33.

———. 2003c. "Video Games Can Be Helpful to College Students, a Study Concludes." *The Chronicle of Higher Education.* August 15. A32.

———. 2003d. "Can Grand Theft Auto Inspire Professors? Educators Say the Virtual World of Video Games Help Students Think More Broadly." *The Chronicle of Higher Education.* August 15. A31.

———. 2004a. "The Next-Generation Classroom." *The Chronicle of Higher Education.* February 27. A26.

———. 2004b. "With This Enrollment, a Toy Surprise." *The Chronicle of Higher Education.* September 17. A29.

Castaldi, Basil. 1994. *Educational Facilities: Planning, Modernization and Management.* Boston: Allyn & Bacon.

Chait, Richard P. 2002a. "Why Tenure? Why Now?" In *The Questions of Tenure,* ed. R. P. Chait, 6–31. Cambridge, MA: Harvard University Press.

———. 2002b. "Gleanings." In *The Questions of Tenure,* ed. R. P. Chait, 309–21. Cambridge: Harvard University Press.

Chemirinsky, Erwin. 1999. "Is Tenure Necessary to Protect Academic Freedom?" In *The Social Worlds of Higher Education: Handbook for Teaching in a New Century,* ed. Bernice A. Pescosolido and Ronald Aminzade, 340–51. Thousand Oaks, CA: Pine Forge.

Chenoweth, Karin. 2003. "Our Education Obligations Extend Far beyond Affirmative Action." *The Washington Post*. April 24. GZ05.

Ciotola, Kathy. 2002. "The University of Florida Will Lead NASA's Shuttle-Replacement Program." *The Gainesville Sun*. June 18.

Clark, Burton. 1970. *The Distinctive College: Antioch, Reed, and Swarthmore*. Chicago: Aldine.

———. 2002. "University Transformation: Primary Pathways to University Autonomy and Achievement." In *The Future of The City of the Intellect—The Changing American University*, ed. S. Brint, 322–44. Stanford, CA: Stanford University Press.

Clawson, Don. 1997. "War on the Poor." *Contemporary Sociology* 26:vii.

Clotfelter, Charles T. 2002. "Can Faculty Be Induced to Relinquish Tenure?" In *The Questions of Tenure*, ed. R. P. Chait, 221–45. Cambridge, MA: Harvard University Press.

Cohen, Arthur M. 1998. *The Shaping of American Higher Education—Emergence and Growth of the Contemporary System*. San Francisco: Jossey-Bass.

Cohn, D'Vera. 2002. "Census Report Says Education Pays, Even More So Now." *The Washington Post*. July 18. A20.

Cole, Jeffrey. 2004. "Now Is the Time to Start Studying the Internet Age." *The Chronicle of Higher Education*. April 2. B18.

Coleman, James S. 1990. *Foundations of Social Theory*. Cambridge, MA: Harvard University Press.

Collins, Randall. 2002a. "The Dirty Little Secret of Credential Inflation." *The Chronicle of Higher Education*. September 27. B20.

———. 2002b. "Credential Inflation and the Future of Universities." In *The Future of The City of the Intellect—The Changing American University*, ed. S. Brint, 24–46. Stanford, CA: Stanford University Press.

Collis, David J. 2002. "New Business Models for Higher Education." In *The Future of The City of the Intellect—The Changing American University*, ed. S. Brint, 181–204. Stanford, CA: Stanford University Press.

Conklin, Kristin and Travis Reindl. 2004. "To Keep America Competitive, States and Colleges Must Work Together." *The Chronicle of Higher Education*. February 13. B20.

Coppola, Brian P. 2002. "Treating Graduate Students with Dignity." *The Chronicle of Higher Education*. August 9. B16–B18.

Cornell, P. 2002. "The Impact of Changes in Teaching and Learning on Furniture and the Learning Environment." *New Directions in Teaching and Learning* 10:1–9.

Crimmel, H. H. 1984. "The Myth of the Teacher-Scholar." *Liberal Education* 70:183–98.

Cuban, Larry. 1999. *How Scholars Trumped Teachers: Change without Reform in University Curriculum, Teaching, and Research, 1890–1990*. New York: Teachers College Press.

———. 2001. *Oversold and Underused: Computers in Classrooms*. Cambridge, MA: Harvard University Press.

Dahrendorf, Ralf. 1959. *Class and Class Conflict in Industrial Society*. Stanford, CA: Stanford University Press.

Dash. Eric. 2004. "Top Colleges, Rated by Those Who Chose Them." *The New York Times*. October 20.

De Corte, Erik. 1996. "New Perspectives on Learning and Teaching in Higher Education." In G*oals and Purposes of Higher Education in the 21st Century*, ed. Arnold Burgen, 112–32. London: Jessica Kingsley Publishers.

Dee, Phil. 2003a. "Are You PI Material? Assess Yourself." *Science—Next Wave*. January 17, viewed online.

———. 2003b. "Score Your Own PI Potential." *Science—Next Wave*. February 21, viewed online.

DeMatteo, Jacquelyn, Lillian T. Eby, and Eric Sundstrom. 1998. "Team-Based Rewards: Current Empirical Evidence and Directions for Future Research." *Research in Organizational Behavior* 20, ed. L. L. Cummings and Barry M. Straw. New York: JAI Press.

Dennis, Brian M., Carl S. Smith, and Jonathan A. Smith. 2004. "Team Teaching, Team Learning." *The Chronicle of Higher Education.* April 16. B9.

Denzin, Norman K. 1970. "Who Leads: Sociology or Society?" *The American Sociologist* 5:125–27.

Detweiler, Richard. 2004. "At Last, We Can Replace Lectures." *The Chronicle of Higher Education.* July 9. B8.

Deutscher, Irwin. 2002. "Gazing at the Disciplinary Bellybutton—A Review Essay on *Liberation Sociology.*" *Contemporary Sociology* 31:379–85.

DeZure, Deborah (ed.). 2000. *Learning from Change—Landmarks in Teaching and Learning in Higher Education from Change Magazine, 1969–1999.* Sterling, VA: Stylus Publishing.

Dippold, Christine. 2002. "Ohio State U Faculty Fed Up with Low Salaries." *The New York Times.* May 24.

Donovan, M., J. Bransford, and J. Pelligrino (eds). 1999. *How People Learn: Bridging Research and Practice.* Washington DC: National Research Council, U.S. Department of Education.

Duderstadt, James J. 1999. "The Twenty-First Century University—A Tale of Two Futures." In *Challenges Facing Higher Education at the Millennium,* ed. Werner Z. Hirsch and Luc E. Weber, 37–55. Phoenix: Oryx Press.

———. 1999–2000. "New Roles for the 21st Century University." *Issues in Science & Technology* 16:37–44.

———. 2000. *A University for the 21st Century.* Ann Arbor: University of Michigan Press.

Duderstadt, James J., Daniel E. Atkins, and Douglas Van Houweling. 2002. *Higher Education in the Digital Age: Technology Issues and Strategies for American Colleges and Universities.* Westport, CT: Praeger.

Duderstadt, James J. and Farris W. Womack. 2003. *The Future of the Public University in America: Beyond the Crossroads.* Baltimore: Johns Hopkins University Press.

Durvall, Frank Ongley. 1969. *Popular Disturbances and Public Order in Regency England.* London: Oxford University Press.

Dutta, Irene. 2001. "First Post-PhD Job: From Bacteria to Balance Sheets." *Science—Next Wave.* December 21, viewed online.

Dziech, Billie Wright. 2002. "Why Academe Gets No Respect." *The Chronicle of Higher Education.* November 22. B7–B9.

Eggers, Dave. 2003. "Muting the Call to Service." *The New York Times.* August 3.

Evers, Marco. 2004. "The Battle for Brains—How Elite Universities in the U.S. Compete for the Best Students." *New York Times.* January 12. (Translated by Christopher Sultan from *Der Spiegel.*)

Ewell, Peter R. 2002. "Grading Student Learning: You Have to Start Somewhere." http://measuringup.highereducation.org/2002/articles/peterewell.htm

Fairweather, James S. 1996. *Faculty Work and Public Trust: Restoring the Value of Teaching and Public Service in American Academic Life.* Boston: Allyn & Bacon.

Fay, Brian. 1987. *Critical Social Science: Liberation and Its Limits.* Ithaca, NY: Cornell University Press.

Finkelstein, Martin J. 2001. "Understanding the American Academic Profession." In *In Defense of American Higher Education,* ed. Philip G. Altbach, Patricia J. Gumport, and D. Bruce Johnson, 323–52. Baltimore: John Hopkins University Press.

Fish, Stanley. 2003. "The War on Higher Education." *The Chronicle of Higher Education.* November 28. C2.

Flaherty, Julie. 2002. "What Should You Get out of College?" *New York Times.* August 4.

Florida, Richard. 2002. *The Rise of the Creative Class—And How It's Transforming Work, Leisure, Community, and Everyday Life.* New York: Basic Books.

Flyvbjerg, Bent. 2001. *Making Social Science Matter—Why Social Inquiry Fails and How It Can Succeed Again.* Cambridge, UK: Cambridge University Press.

Fogg, Piper. 2004a. "Tenure Denied. Now What?" *The Chronicle of Higher Education.* February 20. A8–A10.

———. 2004b. "For These Professors, 'Practice Is Perfect.'" *The Chronicle of Higher Education.* April 16. A12–A14.

Fogg, Piper, Jennifer Jacobson, Robin Wilson, and Sharon Walsh, 2003. "As Good As It Gets—Faculty Perks that Are Widely Envied." *The Chronicle of Higher Education.* August 15. A10–A14.

Fromm, Dorit. 1991. *Collaborative Communities: Cohousing, Central Living, and Other New Forms of Housing with Shared Facilities.* New York: Van Nostrand Reinhold.

Furner, Mary O. 1975. *Advocacy and Objectivity: A Crisis in the Professionalization of American Social Science, 1865–1905.* Lexington: University of Kentucky Press.

Gaff, Jerry G. 1970. "The Cluster College Concept." In *The Cluster College,* ed. J. G. Gaff and Associates, 3–32. San Francisco: Jossey-Bass.

Gamson, William A. 1999. "Beyond the Science-versus-Advocacy Distinction." *Contemporary Sociology* 28:23–26.

Gee, James Paul. 2003a. "From Video Games, Learning about Learning." *The Chronicle of Higher Education.* June 20.

———. 2003b. *What Video Games Have to Teach Us about Learning and Literacy.* New York: Palgrave/Macmillan.

Giamatti, A. Bartlett. 1988. *A Free and Ordered Space: The Real World of the University.* New York: W. W. Norton.

Giddens, Anthony. 1994. *Beyond Left and Right: The Future of Radical Politics.* Stanford, CA: Stanford University Press.

Gitlin, Todd. 1987. *The Sixties: Years of Hope, Days of Rage.* New York: Bantam Books.

"The Glion Declaration: The University at the Millennium." In *Challenges Facing Higher Education at the Millennium,* ed. Werner Z. Hirsch and Luc E. Weber, 177–182. Phoenix, AZ: Oryx Press.

Goode, Erica. 2003. "New Method Aids Evaluation of Alzheimer's Drugs." *New York Times.* February 6.

Gose, Ben. 2002. "The Fall of the Flagships—Do the Best State Universities Need to Privatize to Survive?" *The Chronicle of Higher Education.* July 5.

Gottlieb, David. 1969. "Social Science and Social Policy: An Introduction to a Symposium." *Social Science Quarterly* 50:443–48.

Gouldner, Alvin W. 1965. "Explorations in Applied Social Science." In *Applied Sociology: Opportunities and Problems,* ed. A. W. Gouldner and S. M. Miller, 5–22. New York: Free Press.

———. 1970. *The Coming Crisis of Western Sociology.* New York: Basic Books.

——. 1973. *For Sociology: Renewal and Critique in Sociology Today.* New York: Basic Books.

Gouldner, Alvin W. and S. M. Miller. 1965. "Preface." In *Applied Sociology: Opportunities and Problems*, ed. A. W. Gouldner and S. M. Miller, vii–viii. New York: Free Press.

Grant, Gerald and David Riesman. 1978. *The Perpetual Dream: Reform and Experiment in the American College.* Chicago: University of Chicago Press.

Greenwood, Davydd and Morten Levin. 1998. *Introduction to Action Research—Social Research for Social Change.* Thousand Oaks, CA: Sage.

Gregorian, Vartan. 2004. "Colleges Must Reconstruct the Unity of Knowledge." *The Chronicle of Higher Education.* June 4. B12–B14.

Haack, Susan. 2003. *Defending Science—Within Reason: Between Scientism and Cynicism.* New York: Prometheus Books.

Handelsman, Jo, et al. 2004. "Scientific Teaching." *Science.* April 23. 521–22.

Hanford, George H. 2003. "We Should Speak the 'Awful Truth' about College Sports." *The Chronicle of Higher Education.* May 30. B10–B11.

Hannan, Andrew and Harold Silver. 2000. *Innovating in Higher Education: Teaching, Learning and Institutional Cultures.* Philadelphia: Society for Research into Higher Education & Open University Press.

Hannan, Michael, Nancy Tuma, and Lyle P. Groeneveld. 1977 (February). *A Model of the Effect of Income Maintenance on Rates of Marital Dissolution: Evidence from the Seattle and Denver Income Maintenance Experiments.* Stanford, CA: Stanford Research Institute. Research Memorandum 44.

Harmon, Amy. 2002. "New Premise in Science: Get the Word Out Quickly, Online." *New York Times.* December 17.

Harris, Judith Rich. 1998. *The Nurture Assumption—Why Children Turn Out the Way They Do.* New York: Free Press.

Hartocollis, Anemona. 2002. "Harvard Committee Works to Restore Honor of the B Plus." *New York Times.* April 21.

Hasell, Mary Joyce and John Scanzoni. 2000 "Cohousing in HUD Housing—Prospects and Problems." *Journal of Architectural and Planning Research.* Summer: 133–45.

Hays, Sharon. 2003. *Flat Broke with Children: Women in the Age of Welfare Reform.* New York: Oxford University Press.

Hazemi, Reza and Stephen Hailes (eds.). 2002. *The Digital University: Building a Learning Community.* London: Springer-Verlag.

Hazemi, Reza, Stephen Hailes, and Steve Wilbur (eds.). 1998. *The Digital University: Reinventing the Academy.* London: Springer-Verlag.

Hebel, Sara. 2003a. "Public Colleges Emphasize Research, but the Public Wants a Focus on Students." *The Chronicle of Higher Education* 49. May 2. A14–A16.

Hebel, Sara. 2003b. "VA Governor Wants to Inject College into the Senior Year of High School." *The Chronicle of Higher Education.* October 31. A22.

Hedges, Chris. 2004. "An A for Effort to Restore Meaning to the Grade." *The New York Times.* May 6.

Henderson, Charles. 1984. *The Chicago School of Sociology: Institutionalization, Diversity, and the Rise of Sociological Research.* Chicago: University of Chicago Press.

Henriksson, Anders. 2001. *Non Campus Mentis: World History According to College Students.* New York: Workman.

Hirsch, E. D. 1987. *Cultural Literacy: What Every American Needs to Know.* Boston: Houghton Mifflin.

Hirsch, Werner Z. 1999. "Financing Universities through Nontraditional Revenue Sources." In *Challenges Facing Higher Education at the Millennium*, ed. Werner Z. Hirsch and Luc E. Weber, 75–84. Phoenix, AZ: Oryx Press.

Hirsch, Werner Z. and Luc E. Weber (eds.). 1999. *Challenges Facing Higher Education at the Millennium.* Phoenix, AZ: Oryx Press.

Honan, William H. 2002. "The College Lecture, Long Derided, May Be Fading." *New York Times.* August 14.

Hough, Richard. 1969. *Fighting Ships.* London: Michael Joseph.

Huber, Mary Taylor and Sherwyn P. Morreale (eds.). 2002. *Disciplinary Styles in the Scholarship of Teaching and Learning.* Washington, DC: American Association for Higher Education.

Huber, Richard M. 1992. *How Professors Play the Cat Guarding the Cream—Why We're Paying More and Getting Less in Higher Education.* Fairfax, VA: George Mason Press.

Huget, Jennifer. 2002. "Promoting Cross-Racial Friendships in Schools." *The Washington Post.* June 11. HE03.

Huitt, Ralph. K. 1969. "Rationalizing the Policy Process." *Social Science Quarterly* 50:480–86.

Hutchings, Pat. 1999. "Behind Outcomes: Contexts and Questions for Assessment." In *The Social Worlds of Higher Education: Handbook for Teaching in a New Century,* ed. Bernice A. Pescosolido and Ronald Aminzade, 206–19. Thousand Oaks, CA: Pine Forge.

Hutchins, Robert M. 1947. *The Education We Need.* Chicago: H. Regnery.

Ikenberry, Stanley O. 1999. "The University and the Information Age." In *Challenges Facing Higher Education at the Millennium,* ed. Werner Z. Hirsch and Luc E. Weber, 56–64. Phoenix, AZ: Oryx Press.

Ishii, Hiroshi. 1994. "Groupware Design." Information Frontier Series 3, Information Processing Society of Japan, February. Tokyo: Kyoritsu Shuppan.

Iutcovich, Stephen F. and Joyce M. Iutcovich (eds.). 1997. *Directions in Applied Sociology, 1985–1995.* Arnold, MD: Society for Applied Sociology.

James, William. 1955. *Pragmatism.* New York: Meridian Books.

Janofsky, Michael. 2002. "Deficits Looming, Governors Worry about Antiterror Costs." *New York Times.* December 7.

Janowitz, Morris. 1974. Foreword to Albert Hunter, *Symbolic Communities: The Persistence and Change of Chicago's Local Communities.* Chicago: University of Chicago Press.

Jewell, K. Sue. 1988. *Survival of the Black Family: The Institutional Impact of U.S. Social Policy.* New York: Praeger.

Johnson Valen. 2003. *Grade Inflation: A Crisis in College Education.* New York: Springer-Verlag.

Kahlenberg, Richard D. 2004. "Toward Affirmative Action for Economic Diversity." *The Chronicle of Higher Education.* March 19. B11.

Katz, Stanley N. 2001. "In Information Technology, Don't Mistake a Tool for a Goal." *The Chronicle of Higher Education.* June 15. B7.

Kennedy, Donald. 1994. "Making Choices in the Research University." In *The Research University in a Time of Discontent,* ed. J. Cole, E. Barber, and S. Graubard. Baltimore: Johns Hopkins University Press.

Kerr, Clark. 1963. *The Uses of the University.* Cambridge, MA: Harvard University Press.

Kirp, David. 2003. "How Much for That Professor?" *New York Times.* October 27.

Kliewer, Joy Rosenzweig. 1999. *The Innovative Campus: Nurturing the Distinctive Learning Environment.* Phoenix, AZ: Oryx Press.

Kluge, P. F. 2003. "Our Coddled Students—Kamp Kenyon's Legacy: Death by Tinkering." *The Chronicle of Higher Education.* February 21. B9.

Knoll, Andrew H. 2003. *Life on a Young Planet: The First Three Billion Years of Life on Earth.* Princeton, NJ: Princeton University Press.

Kohn, Alfie. 2002. "The Dangerous Myth of Grade Inflation." *The Chronicle of Higher Education.* November 8. B7.

Kuh, George D. 2001. "College Students Today: Why We Can't Leave Serendipity to Chance." In *In Defense of American Higher Education,* ed. Philip G. Altbach, Patricia J. Gumport, and D. Bruce Johnson, 323–52. Baltimore: Johns Hopkins University Press.

Lachlier, Paul. 2003. "A More Public Sociology." *ASA Footnotes.* December. 11.

Lagemann, Ellen Condliffe. 2000. *An Elusive Science—The Troubling History of Education Research.* Chicago: University of Chicago Press.

Lagemann, Ellen Condliffe and Lee S. Shulman (eds.). 1999. *Issues in Education Research—Problems and Possibilities.* San Francisco: Jossey-Bass.

Lanham, Richard A. 1993. *The Electronic Word: Democracy, Technology, and the Arts.* Chicago: University of Chicago Press.

Lanham, Richard A. 2002. "The Audit of Virtuality: Universities in the Attention Economy." In *The Future of The City of the Intellect—The Changing American University,* ed. S. Brint, 159–80. Stanford, CA: Stanford University Press.

Lauber, Michael C. 2003. "Science Teaching and Research Facilities." In *Building Type Basics for College and University Facilities,* ed. David J. Neuman, 121–60. New York: John Wiley & Sons.

Lawrence, Francis L. 1995. "Preface—Quality in Higher Education." In *Quality in Higher Education,* ed. Brent D. Ruben, vii–xiv. New Brunswick, NJ: Transaction Publishers.

Lazarsfeld, Paul F. 1962/1993. "Sociology of Social Research." In *On Social Research and Its Language,* ed. Raymond Boudon, 257–74. Chicago: University of Chicago Press.

Lazarsfeld, Paul F., William H. Sewell, and Harold L. Wilensky. 1967. "Introduction." In *The Uses of Sociology,* ed. Paul F. Lazarsfeld, William H. Sewell, and Harold L. Wilensky, ix–xxxiii. New York: Basic Books.

Lee, Alfred McClung Lee. 1986 (2nd ed.) *Sociology for Whom?* Syracuse, NY: Syracuse University Press.

Levin, Morten and Davydd Greenwood. 2001. "Pragmatic Action Research and the Struggle to Transform Universities into Learning Communities." In *Handbook of Action Research: Participative Inquiry & Practice,* ed. Peter Reason and Hilary Bradbury, 103–13. Thousand Oaks, CA: Sage.

Levine, Arthur. 1980. *Why Innovation Fails.* Albany: State University of New York Press.

Levine, Donald N., Ellwood B. Carter, and Eleanor Miller Gorman. 1975. "Simmel's Influence on American Sociology I." *American Journal of Sociology* 81:813–29.

Liberal Education and the New Economy. 2004. *Occasional Papers Series.* Loudonville New York: Sienna College.

Lohr, Steve. 2004. "High-End Technology Work Not Immune to Outsourcing." *New York Times.* June 16.

Lovell, Cheryl D. 2000. In *Higher Education in Transition: The Challenges of the New Millennium*, ed. Joseph Losco and Brian L. Fife, 109–32. Westport, CT: Bergin & Garvey.

Lovett, Clara M. 2001. "State Government and Colleges: A Clash of Cultures." *The Chronicle of Higher Education*. April 27. B20.

Lynd, Robert S. and Helen Merrell Lynd. 1929. *Middletown: A Case Study in American Culture*. New York: Harcourt Brace.

Madrid, Arturo. 2003. "Educating the Largest Minority Group." *The Chronicle of Higher Education*. November 28. B6–B9.

Mahoney, Richard J. 1997. "'Reinventing' the University: Object Lessons from Big Business." *The Chronicle of Higher Education*. November 17. B4–B5.

Mangan, Katherine S. 2003. "Physician, Teach Thyself." *The Chronicle of Higher Education*. November 28. A18.

———. 2004. "Entrepreneurs in Every Department." *The Chronicle of Higher Education*. May 28. A10.

Mannheim, Karl. 1932. *The Chicago School of Sociology: Institutionalization, Diversity, and the Rise of Sociological Research*. Chicago: University of Chicago Press.

Mansfield, Harvey C. 2001. "Grade Inflation: It's Time to Face the Facts." *The Chronicle of Higher Education*. April 6. B24.

———. 2003. "Our Coddled Students—How Harvard Compromised Its Virtue." *The Chronicle of Higher Education*. February 21. B7.

Marchese, Ted. 1995. "TQM: A Time for Ideas." In *Quality in Higher Education*, ed. Brent D. Ruben, 137–44. New Brunswick, NJ: Transaction Publishers.

Marcy, Mary B. 2003. "Why Foundations Have Cut Back in Higher Education." *The Chronicle of Higher Education*. July 25. B16.

Margolis, Joseph. 2002. *Reinventing Pragmatism—American Philosophy at the End of the Twentieth Century*. Ithaca, NY: Cornell University Press.

Marinelli, Don and Randy Pausch. 2004. "Edutainment for the College Classroom." *The Chronicle of Higher Education*. March 19. B16.

Marino, Melissa. 2001. "A Misfit Goes to Washington." *Science—Next Wave*. November 2, viewed online.

Martin, Jay. 2003. *The Education of John Dewey*. New York: Columbia University Press.

Massy, William F. 2003. "Auditing Higher Education to Improve Quality." *The Chronicle of Higher Education*. June 20. B16.

Mathews, Jay. 2001. "Better than Famous." *The Washington Post*. April 8. W24.

———. 2002. "A New Assessment of Student Life." *The Washington Post*. November 22. A13.

———. 2003. "Testing the Limits of Late-Night Cramming—Review Blitzes Are Helpful for Rote Information, but Not for Long-Term Retention, Experts Say." *The Washington Post*. May 27. A09.

McHenry, Dean, 1993. "University of California, Santa Cruz." In *Important Lessons from Innovative Colleges and Universities*, ed. V. Ray Cardozier, 37–54. San Francisco: Jossey-Bass.

Melton, R. H. 1998. "Gilmore Takes Colleges to Task on Spending." *The Washington Post*. August 22. D01.

Merton, Robert K. 1973. "The Normative Structure of Science." In *The Sociology of Science*, ed. R. K. Merton, 267–78. Chicago: The University of Chicago Press.

Miller, Margaret A. 2002. "Measuring Up and Student Learning." http://measuringup .highereducation.org/2002/articles/margaretmiller.htm

Monaghan, Peter. 2004. "Real Fear, Virtually Overcome." *The Chronicle of Higher Education.* October 15. A12–A13.

Mora, Juana and David R. Diaz (eds.). 2004. *Latino Social Policy—A Participatory Research Model.* New York: Haworth.

Moyers, Bill. 2003. "Acceptance of America's Future." *Alternet.* June 10.

Moynihan, Daniel P. 1969. *Maximum Feasible Misunderstanding.* New York: Free Press.

"National Science Foundation Study: Science Literacy Poor in U.S." 2002. *New York Times.* April 30.

Nemko, Marty. 2003. "Take My Advice . . . " *The Chronicle of Higher Education.* July 4. B16.

Newman, Frank and Jamie Scurry. 2001. "Online Technology Pushes Pedagogy to the Forefront." *The Chronicle of Higher Education.* July 13. B7.

Newman, Frank, Lara Couturier, and Jamie Scurry. 2004. "Higher Education Isn't Meeting the Public's Needs." *The Chronicle of Higher Education.* October 15. B6–B8.

Nicholson, Simon. 1971. "How Not to Cheat Children—The Theory of Loose Parts." *Journal of Landscape Architecture* 62:30–34.

Norman, David A. 2001. "In Defense of Cheating." http://www.jnd.org/dn.mss/In DefenseOfCheating.html

O'Banion, Terry. 1997. *A Learning College for the 21st Century.* Phoenix, AZ: Oryx Press.

O'Connor, Alice. 2001. *Poverty Knowledge: Social Science, Social Policy, and the Poor in Twentieth-Century U.S. History.* Princeton, NJ: Princeton University Press.

Olivas, Michael A. 2003. "Educating the Largest Minority Group." *The Chronicle of Higher Education.* November 28. B6–B9.

Olsen, Florence. 1999. "The Promise and Problems of a New Way of Teaching Math." *The Chronicle of Higher Education.* October 8. A31.

Olsen, Marvin E. 1981. "Epilogue: The Future of Applied Sociology." In *Handbook of Applied Sociology—Frontiers of Contemporary Research*, ed. M. E. Olsen and Michael Micklin, 561–581. New York: Praeger.

O'Neil, Robert. 2004. "Controversial Weblogs and Academic Freedom." *The Chronicle of Higher Education.* January 16. B16.

O'Neill, William L. 1967. *Divorce in the Progressive Era.* New Haven, CT: Yale University Press.

Ostby, Kristin. 2003. "U. Michigan Professor's Book Links Grade Inflation, Evaluations." *New York Times.* September 4.

Owen, Whitney L. 2004. "In Defense of the Least Publishable Unit." *The Chronicle of Higher Education.* February 13. C1–C4.

Parker, Ian. 2001. "Absolute PowerPoint: Can a Software Edit Our Thoughts?" *New Yorker.* May 28. 76–87.

Patel, C. Kumar N. 1995. "Introductory Remarks." In *Reinventing The Research University*, ed. C. Kumar N. Patel, 7–24. Los Angeles: Regents of the University of California Press.

Petrides, Lisa Ann (ed.). 2000. *Case Studies on Information Technology in Higher Education: Implications for Policy and Practice.* Hershey, PA: Idea Group Publishing.

Perlmutter, David D. 2004a. "Thwarting Misbehavior in the Classroom." *The Chronicle of Higher Education.* April 2. B14.

———. 2004b. "Teaching the 101." *The Chronicle of Higher Education.* September 10. C1.

Pescosolido, Bernice A. and Ronald Aminzade (eds.). 1999. *The Social Worlds of Higher Education: Handbook for Teaching in a New Century.* Thousand Oaks, CA: Pine Forge/Sage.

Pollack, Andrew. 2002. "'Politically Correct' Stem Cell Research Is Licensed to Biotech Concern." *New York Times.* December 11.

Pollack, Andrew and Lawrence K. Altman. 2003. "Large Trial Finds AIDS Vaccine Fails to Stop Infection." *New York Times.* February 24.

Postel, Danny. 2002. "Sidney Hook, an Intellectual Street Fighter, Reconsidered." *The Chronicle of Higher Education.* November 8. A18.

Powell, Walter W. and Jason Owen-Smith. 2002. "The New World of Knowledge Production in the Life Sciences." In *The Future of The City of the Intellect—The Changing American University*, ed. S. Brint, 107–30. Stanford, CA: Stanford University Press.

Prawat, Richard S. 2000. "The Two Faces of Deweyan Pragmatism: Inductionism versus Social Constructivism." *Teacher's College Record* 102:805–40.

President's Research Committee on Social Trends. 1933. *Recent Social Trends in the United States.* New York: McGraw-Hill.

Putnam, Robert D. 2000. *Bowling Alone—The Collapse and Revival of American Community.* New York: Simon & Schuster.

Rabb, Theodore K. 2004. "What Has Happened to Historical Literacy?" *The Chronicle of Higher Education.* June 4. B24.

Reason, Peter and Hilary Bradbury, (eds.). 2001. *Handbook of Action Research: Participative Inquiry & Practice.* Thousand Oaks, CA: Sage.

Reid, Robert. 1986. *Land of Lost Content: The Luddite Revolt, 1812.* London: Heinemann.

Resnick, Lauren B. 1987. *Education and Learning to Think.* Washington, DC: National Academy Press.

Reuters Press. 2003. "Plugged In: SmartPhones, Handhelds May Someday Threaten Laptops." *New York Times.* December 6.

Revkin, Andrew C. 2004. "Bush vs. the Laureates: How Science Became a Partisan Issue." *New York Times.* October 19.

Rhodes, Frank H. T. 1998. "The University and Its Critics." In *Universities and Their Leadership*, ed. William G. Bowen and Harold T. Shapiro, 3–14. Princeton, NJ: Princeton University Press.

———. 1999. "The New University." In *Challenges Facing Higher Education at the Millennium*, ed. Werner Z. Hirsch and Luc E. Weber, 167–74. Phoenix, AZ: Oryx Press.

Rimer, Sara. 2003. "Justifying a Liberal Arts Education in Hard Times." *The New York Times.* February 19.

Rivers, Rose Merry and John Scanzoni. 1997. "Social Families among African-Americans: Policy Implications for Children." In *Black Families*, ed. Harriette Pipes McAdoo, 333–48. Newbury Park, CA: Sage.

Robson, Colin. 1993. *Real World Research: A Resource for Social Scientists and Practitioner-Researchers.* Oxford: Blackwell.

Rodgers, Carol. 2002. "Defining Reflection: Another Look at John Dewey and Reflective Thinking." *Teachers College Record* 104:842–66.

Rogoff, Barbara. 2001. "Why a Nonconventional College Decided to Add Grades." *The Chronicle of Higher Education.* September 14. B17.

Rojstaczer, Stuart. 1999. *Gone for Good—Tales of University Life after the Golden Age.* New York: Oxford University Press.

———. 2001. "When Intellectual Life Is Optional for Students." *The Chronicle of Higher Education.* April 20. B5.

Rooney, Megan. 2002. "A Surge of Students." *The Chronicle of Higher Education.* November 1. A33–A34.

Ross, Edward A. 1907/1973. *Sin and Society—An Analysis of Latter-Day Iniquity.* New York: Harper & Row.

Rossi, Peter H. 1969. "'No Good Idea Goes Unpunished: Moynihan's Misunderstandings and the Proper Role of Social Science in Policy Making." *Social Science Quarterly* 50:469–79.

Ruben, Brent D. 1995. "The Quality Approach in Higher Education: Context and Concepts for Change." In *Quality in Higher Education*, ed. Brent D. Ruben, 1–34. New Brunswick, NJ: Transaction Publishers.

Sacks, Peter. 1999. *Standardized Minds—The High Price of America's Testing Culture and What We Can Do to Change It.* New York: Perseus Publishing.

———. 2003. "Class Rules: The Fiction of Egalitarian Higher Education." *The Chronicle of Higher Education.* July 25. B7.

Scanzoni, John. 2000. *Designing Families: The Search for Self and Community in the Information Age.* Thousand Oaks, CA: Pine Forge/Sage.

———. 2004. "Household Diversity—The Starting Point for Healthy Families in the New Century." In *Handbook of Contemporary Families—Considering the Past, Contemplating the Future,* ed. Marilyn Coleman and Larry Ganong, 1–22. Thousand Oaks, CA: Sage.

Schank, Roger C. 1994. "What We Learn When We Learn by Doing." Technical Report 60 of the Institute for Learning Sciences, Northwestern University, Evanston, IL.

———. 2000. "The Disrespected Student—Or—The Need for the Virtual University." Technical Report of the Institute for Learning Sciences, Northwestern University, Evanston, IL.

Schank, Roger C. and Chip Cleary. 1995. *Engines for Education.* Hillsdale, NJ: Lawrence Erlbaum Publishers.

Schmidt, Peter. 2003. "Academe's Hispanic Future." *The Chronicle of Higher Education.* November 28. A9–A12.

———. 2004. "A Public Vision for Public Colleges." *The Chronicle of Higher Education.* June 11. A16–A18.

Schon, Donald A. 1983. *The Reflective Practitioner: How Professionals Think in Action.* New York: Basic Books.

Schwartz, Barry. 2004. "The Tyranny of Choice." *The Chronicle of Higher Education.* January 23.

Seldin, Peter. 1997. *The Teaching Portfolio—A Practical Guide to Improved Performance and Promotion/Tenure Decisions.* Boston: Anker.

Selingo, Jeffrey. 2003a. "The Disappearing State in Public Higher Education." *The Chronicle of Higher Education.* February 28. A22–A24.

———. 2003b. "What Americans Think about Higher Education." *The Chronicle of Higher Education.* May 2. A10–A16.

Shneiderman, Ben. 1998. "Foreword." In *The Digital University: Reinventing the Academy,* ed. Reza Hazemi, Stephen Hailes, and Steve Wilbur, xxi–xxii. London: Springer-Verlag.

Shoichet, Catherine E. 2002. "Reports of Grade Inflation May Be Inflated, Study Finds." *The Chronicle of Higher Education.* July 12. A37.

Showalter, Elaine. 2002. *Teaching Literature.* Cambridge, MA: Blackwell Publishing.

Showalter, Elaine. 2003. "What Teaching Literature Should Really Mean." *The Chronicle of Higher Education.* January 17. B7.

Shulman, Lee S. 2004. *Teaching as Community Property—Essays on Higher Education.* San Francisco: Jossey-Bass.

Sikes, Janine Young. 2004. "State Seeks 46% More Bachelor's Degrees." *Gainesville Sun.* May 19, viewed online.

Sinnott, Jan and Lynn Johnson. 1996. *Reinventing the University: A Radical Proposal for Problem-Focused University.* Norwood, NJ: Ablex Publishing.

Sizer, Theodore R. 1992. *Horace's School—Redesigning the American High School.* Boston: Houghton Mifflin.

———. 1996. *Horace's Hope—What Works for the American High School.* Boston: Houghton Mifflin.

Slosson, Edwin A. 1910/1977. *Great American Universities.* New York: Arno Press.

Spengler, Joseph E. 1969. "Is Social Science Ready?" *Social Science Quarterly* 50:449–68.

Sperber, Murray. 2000. *Beer and Circus: How Big-Time College Sports Is Crippling Higher Education.* New York: Henry Holt.

Stack, Carol. 1974. *All Our Kin—Strategies for Survival in a Black Community.* New York: Harper & Row.

Steele, Stephen F., AnneMarie Scarisbrick-Hauser, and William J. Hauser. 1999. *Solution-Centered Sociology: Addressing Problems through Applied Sociology.* Thousand Oaks, CA: Sage.

Steinberg, Jacques. 2000. "U.S. Projects School Growth throughout the 21st Century." *The New York Times.* August 22.

Steinberg, Jacques. 2002. "Princeton Embraces Scholar of Black Studies." *The New York Times.* January 27.

Stouffer Samuel A. 1962. *Social Research to Test Ideas.* New York: Free Press.

Strange, C. Carney and James H. Banning. 2001. *Educating by Design: Creating Campus Learning Environments that Work.* San Francisco: Jossey-Bass.

Straus, Anselm (ed.). 1964. *George Herbert Mead on Social Psychology.* Chicago: University of Chicago Press.

Stringer, Ernest T. 1999. *Action Research* (2nd ed.) Thousand Oaks, CA: Sage.

Suggs, Welch. 2003. "Sports as the University's 'Front Porch'? The Public Is Skeptical." *The Chronicle of Higher Education.* May 2. A17.

Sykes, Charles J. 1988. *Profscam: Professors and the Demise of Higher Education.* Washington, DC: Regnery Gateway.

Theall, Michael, Philip C. Abrami, and Lisa A. Mets. 2001. *The Student Ratings Debate: Are They Valid? How Can We Best Use Them?* San Francisco: Jossey-Bass.

Tierney, John. 2002. "Beware the Yikes of March." *The New York Times.* January 29.

Tomlinson-Keasey, Carol. 2002. "Becoming Digital: The Challenges of Weaving Technology throughout Higher Education." In *The Future of The City of the Intellect—The Changing American University,* ed. S. Brint, 133–58. Stanford, CA: Stanford University Press.

Toner, Robin. 2002. "Welfare in the Post-Welfare Era." *New York Times.* March 3.

Townsend, B. K., L. J. Newell, and M. D. Wiese. 1992. *Creating Distinctiveness: Lessons from Uncommon Colleges and Universities.* ASHE-ERIC Higher Education Report No.

6. Washington, DC: George Washington University, School of Education and Human Development.

Troop, Don. 2003. "Who's No. 1?" *The Chronicle of Higher Education.* September 26. A8.

Trow, Martin. 1996. "Continuities and Change in American Higher Education." In *Goals and Purposes of Higher Education in the 21st Century*, ed. Arnold Burgen, 24–36. London: Jessica Kingsley Publishers.

Trower, Cathy A. 2002. "What Is Current Policy?" In *The Questions of Tenure*, ed. R. P. Chait, 33–68. Cambridge, MA: Harvard University Press.

Tsichritzis, Dennis. 1999. "Research and Education." In *Challenges Facing Higher Education at the Millennium*, ed. Werner Z. Hirsch and Luc E. Weber, 99–110. Phoenix, AZ: Oryx Press.

Turkle, Sherry. 2004. "How Computers Change the Way We Think." *The Chronicle of Higher Education.* January 30. B26.

Uchitelle, Louis. 2004. "In This Recovery, a College Education Backfires." *The New York Times.* March 14.

"University of California International-Studies Program Offers Free Peer-Reviewed Articles Online." 2003. *The Chronicle of Higher Education.* March 21. A33.

Vanecko, James J. 1969. "Community Mobilization and Institutional Change: The Influence of the Community Action Program in Large Cities." *Social Science Quarterly* 50:609–30.

Wade, Nicholas. 2002. "Gains in Understanding Human Cells." *The New York Times.* October 25.

———. 2003. "Scientists Say Human Genome Is Complete." *The New York Times.* April 14.

Wallerstein, Immanuel. 1999. "Social Sciences in the Twenty-First Century." [Viewed online—UNESCO, *World Social Science Report.*]

———. 2000. "Where Should Sociologists Be Heading?" *Contemporary Sociology* 29:304–08.

Ward, Lester. 1883. *Dynamic Sociology or Applied Social Science, as Based upon Statistical Sociology and the Less Complex Sciences.* New York: Appleton.

Ward, Nathaniel. 2002. "History of Tenure Shows Rise in Popularity in '60s, '70s, Followed by Disparate Challenges in '80s." *The New York Times.* April 3.

Warwick, Regina. 2004. "To Spurn a Star." *The Chronicle of Higher Education.* January 16. C2.

Washington Post. 2003. "Nancy Reagan Backs Cloning for Research." February 7. A10.

Weaver, R. Kent. 2000. *Ending Welfare as We Know It.* Washington, DC: The Brookings Institution Press.

Weinstein, Jay. 2000. "A (Further) Comment on the Differences between Applied and Academic Sociology." *Contemporary Sociology* 29:344–47.

Wellman, Jane and Thomas Ehrlich (eds.). 2003. *How the Student Credit Hour Shapes Higher Education: The Tie that Binds.* San Francisco: Jossey-Bass.

Whyte, William Foote. 1982. "Social Inventions for Solving Human Problems." *American Sociological Review* 47:1–13.

———(ed.). 1991a. *Participatory Action Research.* Newbury Park, CA: Sage.

———. 1991b. "Comparing PAR and Action Science." In *Participatory Action Research*, ed. W. F. Whyte, 97–98. Newbury Park, CA: Sage.

Wilgoren, Jodi. 2000. "Swell of Minority Students Is Expected at Colleges." *The New York Times.* May 24.

Williams, Harold M. 1999. "The Economics of Higher Education in the United States—What Can Other Developed Countries Learn from It?" In *Challenges Facing Higher Education at the Millennium*, ed. Werner Z. Hirsch and Luc E. Weber, 65–72. Phoenix, AZ: Oryx Press.

Wilshire, Bruce. 1990. *The Moral Collapse of the University—Professionalism, Purity, and Alienation.* Albany: State University of New York Press.

Wilson, Robin. 2001. "Ohio State 'Taxes' Departments to Make a Select Few Top-Notch." *The Chronicle of Higher Education.* A8–A12.

———. 2002. "Report Says Undergraduate Education Has Improved in Recent Years." *The Chronicle of Higher Education.* March 22. A12.

———. 2004. "Faculty Salaries Rise 2.1%, the Lowest Increase in 30 Years." *The Chronicle of Higher Education.* April 23. A12.

Wineburg, Sam. 2001. *Historical Thinking and Other Unnatural Acts—Charting the Future of Teaching the Past.* Philadelphia: Temple University Press.

———. 2003. "Teaching the Mind Good Habits." *The Chronicle of Higher Education.* April 11. B20.

Winerip, Michael. 2003. "In 'No Child Left Behind,' a Problem with the Math." *The New York Times.* October 1.

Winter, Greg. 2004. "Public University Tuition Is Up Sharply for 2004." *The New York Times.* October 20.

Wyatt, Graham S. 2003. "Academic Buildings and Professional Schools." In *Building Type Basics for College and University Facilities*, ed. David J. Neuman, 93–120. New York: John Wiley & Sons.

Wuff, Donald H. and Ann E. Austin. 2004. *Paths to the Professoriate—Strategies for Enriching the Preparation of Future Faculty.* San Francisco: Jossey-Bass.

Young, Jeffrey R. 1998. "Students Dislike Va. Tech Math Classes in which Computers Do Much of the Teaching." *The Chronicle of Higher Education.* February 20.

———. 2004. "Libraries Aim to Widen Google's Eyes—Search Engines Want to Make Scholarly Work More Visible on the Web." *The Chronicle of Higher Education.* May 21. A1.

Yudoff, Mark G. 2002. "Is the Public Research University Dead?" *The Chronicle of Higher Education.* January 11. B24.

Zalk, Sue Rosenberg and Janice Gordon-Kelter (eds.). 1992. *Revolutions in Knowledge—Feminism in the Social Sciences.* Boulder, CO: Westview Press.

Zemsky, Robert. 2003. "Have We Lost the 'Public' in Higher Education?" *The Chronicle of Higher Education.* May 30. B7.

Zemsky, Robert and William F. Massy. 2004a. "Why the E-Learning Boom Went Bust." *The Chronicle of Higher Education.* July 9. B6.

———. 2004b. "Thwarted Innovation—What Happened to E-Learning and Why." A final report for the Weatherspoon Project of The Learning Alliance at the University of Pennsylvania, in cooperation with the Thompson Corporation.

Zernike, Kate. 2002. "Tests Are Not Just for Kids." *The New York Times.* August 4.

Index

About the Author

John Scanzoni is professor of sociology at the University of Florida. He is the author of more than a dozen books, including *Contemporary Families and Relationships*.

DATE DUE

MAY 1 6 2005			
NOV 0 6 RECD NOV 0 8 2005			

GAYLORD   PRINTED IN U.S.A.

WEBER STATE UNIVERSITY
STEWART LIBRARY
DISCARDED

LA 227.4 .S32 2005

Scanzoni, John H., 1935-

Universities as if students mattered